Investigating the Ordinary

Florida Museum of Natural History: Ripley P. Bullen Series

FLORIDA MUSEUM.®

Investigating the Ordinary

Everyday Matters in Southeast Archaeology

Edited by Sarah E. Price and Philip J. Carr

UNIVERSITY OF FLORIDA PRESS

Gainesville

First cloth printing, 2018
First paperback printing, 2024

29 28 27 26 25 24   6 5 4 3 2 1

Library of Congress Cataloging-in-Publication Data
Names: Price, Sarah E., author. | Carr, Philip J., 1966– author.
Title: Investigating the ordinary : everyday matters in southeast archaeology
     / Sarah E. Price and Philip J. Carr.
Other titles: Ripley P. Bullen series.
Description: Gainesville : University of Florida Press, 2017. | Series:
     Florida Museum of Natural History: Ripley P. Bullen series | Includes
     bibliographical references and index.
Identifiers: LCCN 2017030444 | ISBN 9781683400219 (cloth) | ISBN 9781683404439 (pbk.)
Subjects: LCSH: Indians of North America—Southern States—Antiquities. |
     Excavations (Archaeology)—Southern States. | Southern States—Antiquities.
Classification: LCC E78.S65 P75 2017 | DDC 975/.01—dc23
LC record available at https://lccn.loc.gov/2017030444

University of Florida Press
2046 NE Waldo Road
Suite 2100
Gainesville, FL 32609
http://upress.ufl.edu

UF PRESS

UNIVERSITY
OF FLORIDA

Contents

Figures

Tables

1

Why the Archaeology of Everyday Matters?

SARAH E. PRICE AND PHILIP J. CARR

Indeed, it seems a common assumption that everyday life in prehistory is simple to understand, essentially unchanging, and merely a backdrop against which the more important action was played out. Where everyday life is discussed or portrayed, it is usually in popular accounts, museum displays, and reconstruction drawings. The picture painted contains little which is not immediately familiar to our own lived experience, or at least to our recent rural forebearers.

Hill (2001:432)

The foundation of this volume was doing something different, outside of the norm. We asked a group of archaeologists to discuss everyday matters, a scale not often utilized or made explicit in the archaeology of a particular period or topic. Our proposal was met with some resistance, both from participants and from conference attendees; it was even interpreted as a postprocessual symposium, as if one paradigm owned a concept or scale of investigation. It is difficult, at first consideration, to think seriously about single events, thoughts, or actions of people that are represented in the pieces and parts of an imperfect archaeological record, which is why that is not what we asked the contributors to do. As Carr and Bradbury (Chapter 10) and Miller and Tune (Chapter 2) discuss, the archaeological record as we excavate and document it is a palimpsest of everyday events. It is too coarse-grained (and our methods are not developed in such a way) to tease apart singular aspects (sensu Kuhn 2013). However, considering everyday life, even if it is unseen with current archaeological methods, is not without utility. Archaeologists generally want to investigate the how and why of variation and change in past human cultures, and change is the result of many small, individually unimportant actions. Thus the culmination of everyday actions of people in the past is where cultural change occurs (sensu Gladwell 2000).

This volume is not meant to be a guidebook to doing a particular type of research, on a particular topic; nor is it intended to be a jargon-laden theoretical treatise for a particular brand of archaeology. Case studies and data-dense papers were discouraged from the outset. We did not specify a theoretical approach; rather, we encouraged looking outside archaeology for inspiration and indeed found ourselves at odds over theory during the course of writing and editing this volume. Our intent was, and is, to spur researchers to think about the archaeological record in new ways and about how the scale of everyday life for people in the past and our everyday archaeologies as professionals affect the perception and consumption of our field by both other archaeologists and nonprofessionals.

Defining "Everyday"

"Everyday matters" is a phrase with more than one meaning and can be seen as simple or very complex. It can refer to daily concerns or events that are common and ordinary. Or it connotes that actions occurring daily or "every day" are of significance, that such actions matter. From an archaeological perspective, we think that common concerns reveal something about the lives of the people in the past that we investigate. Additionally, it is clear that the archaeological record is formed on a daily basis, so the events of a day are significant regarding the evidence that archaeologists have or lack. For example, getting food is an everyday, and every day, matter for any human being on earth. However, on some occasions, people fast and choose to ignore this biological imperative for a time, and this time of fasting informs the everyday. Basket weaving, while probably not an activity that took place every single day, produced an item of material culture that once manufactured was part of some everyday activity. What mattered every day to an Early Archaic female child (Hollenbach and Carmody, Chapter 5) is probably not what mattered to a nineteenth-century Cherokee man (Greene, Chapter 4). Likewise, the authors in this volume chose their approach to everyday matters based on how they envisioned their particular topic articulating with an everyday concern in the past.

So why did the everyday appeal as a way of examining what we think we know about the prehistoric Southeast? We see archaeology in the Southeast at a similar point in development as the field of physics in the 1970s. James Gleick (1987:5) states: "Science was heading for a crisis of increasing specialization," as all of the major questions within grasp of physicists at the end of the twentieth century had been answered. Out of their crisis rose chaos theory, which was essentially a return to the most basic, and often complex, phenomena (e.g., weather prediction, the behaviors of smoke, waves, and turbulence), in essence a return to questions of everyday matters. These seemingly simple problems are actually the most complex processes and the most difficult to predict and formulate and had been ignored because they were considered too mundane by researchers. Although these topics are everyday processes, they are very complex and nonlinear systems (meaning that we cannot predict the output from known input). Chaos theory deals with these nonlinear phenomena and accepts that they are effectively impossible to predict or control (e.g., human behavior?). But chaos theory posits that the connections can be understood and predicted by understanding how our social, economic, and ecosystems are interconnected (see Rodning et al., Chapter 3).

These everyday matters in physics would be something akin to excavating a "lithic scatter" versus Moundville. Scientists in general, and archaeologists specifically, are not enamored with everyday matters when it comes to research topics. For example, medical researchers were quick to figure out sickle cell anemia, a disease that affects many people, because it has a single gene root; but to this day they have not distinguished the genes that determine skin color or hair texture or inner ear balance, as these "everyday" questions do not have devastating health consequences and are genetically very complex. Likewise, a site such as Moundville is so readily observable that its significance is taken for granted by archaeologists and the public alike. A lithic scatter is a site type commonly identified by archaeologists during Phase I survey but invisible to most of the public, who would view arguments for the significance of a site without impressive features or diverse and exotic material culture as forced. In short, everyday matters can be seemingly mundane but in actuality are incredibly complex, as demonstrated by the medical example above and the varied contributions to this volume.

Conversely, in archaeology, the kinds of questions asked about sites like Moundville are easier to answer due to preservation, context, and range of available data and thus more satisfying to answer. These same questions and methods do not work with "lithic scatters." This pejorative site type persists in archaeology today. There is only one Moundville for every thousand lithic scatters, so perhaps we should take a cue from physics and turn our archaeological powers to understanding the activities and behaviors that produced these sites, rather than the object-centric view that has dominated and continues to pervade southeastern archaeology. Looking at lithic scatters as everyday expressions of Moundville might cause us to rethink our everyday archaeology in terms of how we interpret and preserve this site type.

The Everyday in the History of Archaeology

Americanist archaeology, with its strong ties to anthropology, has a deep interest in people in the past. Therefore, it is not hard to imagine that major theoreticians over the course of Americanist archaeological history did not on occasion envision the daily life of the people that they investigated. Looking back over Americanist archaeological literature, it is possible to see the study of everyday matters, in various forms and guises; but, for the most part, everyday life is not an explicit matter to archaeologists. We provide a brief overview of how the everyday is, or is not, present in archaeological theory.

The earliest practitioners certainly filled their writings about prehistoric monuments and artifacts with annotations of how they envisioned prehistoric peoples engaging with the artifacts. George Sternberg (1876:286) provides just such an example when discussing hollow-head effigies from the Bear Point mound: "It is hollow and contains fragments of something which rattle when it is shaken. I imagine that the absence of the ears, and the generally dilapidated condition of this specimen, are due to its having been mouthed by some drooling Indian baby while teething." He also interprets the pottery of less "fine quality" as that which was "made for every day [sic] use" (Sternberg 1876:286). Our early bias toward the extraordinary is also rooted in these earliest writings. Warren Moorehead (1910:365) discusses "ceremonial swords" and states that "we must seek their explanation and purposes along other lines that [sic] those suggested by common every-day usage, to which the smaller and more easily made object were put." These earliest archaeologists certainly considered the everyday, but only as annotated thoughts or as a base from which to contrast the burial goods that they sought.

The more thoroughly developed paradigm of culture-history provides another avenue to consider how everyday life in the past was or was not envisioned. Gary Webster (2008:11) cleverly defined culture history in a cultural historical fashion, as "one among several archaeological traditions to which archaeologists contributed, mainly during the first half of the twentieth century." This nontextbook definition could be said to leave out as much as it contributes, but Webster goes on to discuss normative theory, cultural typologies, and historical explanations (namely diffusion), in an attempt to characterize culture-history. The everyday was not a concern to the practicing culture historians. They were consumed with ordering massive amounts of data generated by large-scale excavations. Gordon Willey (1949), Philip Phillips et al. (1951), and other titans of the Southeast were innovative and influential in producing methods and chronologies for southeastern archaeology, but they were not concerned with the everyday matters of pottery. A culture historian would probably be reluctant to engage with the concept of the everyday or a single day. Phases, horizons, and traditions do not have room for how everyday events and processes shaped and changed them.

In order to understand how cultural historians viewed daily life, we might investigate the dioramas and illustrations of past peoples produced in consultation with archaeologists who worked in the first half of the twentieth century. Diane Gifford-Gonzalez (1993:29, 38) accomplished something akin to this for dioramas dating from the 1960s to 1980s of "Cro Magnon people from Europe during the last Ice Age" using a feminist approach and found patterning indicating that "visual narratives embodied in many representations are rooted in didactic missions of 19th and early 20th century middle class social theory." We suggest that additional patterns would emerge if we more finely examined an expanded sample produced during the heyday of cultural-historical archaeology, processual archaeology, and postprocessual archaeology.

Processual archaeology developed out of the post-Works Progress Administration excavations (and generation of massive datasets) in the wake of new scientific tools (e.g., radiocarbon dating). With better control over time, the focus could be shifted to culture change. As a primary architect, Lewis Binford (1962) offered the technomic/socio-technomic/ideotechnic framework as an attempt at a more holistic and anthropological archaeology. This processual archaeology was a break from the focus on culture history and on elaborate mounds and ritualized sites. Importantly, processual archaeology added investigation of cultural lifeways as well as explanation of culture change as a significant goal: hence the term "cultural process." By focusing on lifeways, archaeologists broadened their investigation to include systematic consideration of the full range of site types, in addition to mounds and sites with rich archaeological records. In emphasizing the mundane over the exemplary, Binford and other processualists unknowingly sparked what has become a fractured field of archaeological research. In order to get at the various facets of any particular class of artifacts, we have to become specialized. Additionally, there is the ever-growing burden of who and what have come before in each field of specialty. It is why almost every Cultural Research Management (CRM) report contains segregated discussions of lithics, ceramics, paleobotanicals, and so forth, with little meaningful synthesis (sensu Nassaney and Sassaman 1995:xxiii).

Everyday people and everyday life, while not explicitly investigated by processualists, were implicated in the stated goals. In the wake of World War II efficiency and conservation, coupled with formalization of federal laws (e.g., National Historic Preservation Act, National Environmental Policy Act), and development of federal funding sources, archaeology became "science." And feasibly that is where the everyday, and people, became lost in the push to make the study of past peoples a science, especially with positivist science as the focus. This brand of scientific archaeological theory and methods worked to develop clearly defined categories (e.g., hunter/gatherer/forager/collector, extraction camp/village) for human behavior. Although archaeologists were examining more "everyday" sites, they were not embracing the scale of everyday life.

Postprocessual archaeology, as the name implies, came after processualism and is a direct reaction to the perceived deficiencies of processual approaches: that humans were absent from archaeology. Although postprocessual approaches strive to identify and understand humans as agents in the archaeological record, or how the practice of everyday life codifies ideologies and ritual, they are often so bogged down in jargon that discussion of the everyday tends to exist only in theoretical discourse. Also, there is a tendency to emphasize an abstract symbolism of humans "at the expense of the practical" (Brück 2007:291). However, Marcia-Anne Dobres and John Hoffman (1994) offer an insightful discussion of technology, social agency, and day-to-day artifact manufacture, use, repair, and discard. The limitation of practice theory (and related paradigms) in archaeology is that it is difficult if not impossible to articulate material culture with the agency that produced them (Dobres and Robb 2005). In other words, agency is the wrong scale for investigating human practices if viewed as a "fundamental quality of human existence," as the "archaeology of agency" is akin to examining the "archaeology of breathing" (Dobres and Robb 2005:160).

It appears to us that the lens of everyday life in relation to this volume is not one in use in existing theories regularly employed by southeastern archaeologists individually or in an eclectic fashion (sensu Knight 2014) that address everyday matters in a direct manner. Culture history and its practitioners do not see the relevance of everyday life in examining the diversity of material culture across time and space. Processualist paradigms, while recognizing the importance of secular context and the range of everyday material culture in understanding the past, in reconstructing cultural lifeways tend to have cultural adaptation on a seasonal or annual basis as the focus or adaptation during a site's occupation. Varied postprocessualist approaches, especially as employed in the Southeast, have tended to focus on the individual and the symbolic, but not the everyday.

One important exception is the work by Kenneth Sassaman (2010) in his examination of the Eastern Woodlands Archaic in *The Eastern Archaic, Historicized*. He offers a potential entry to the everyday following what would best be referred to as an outgrowth of the postprocessual paradigm. Indeed, as many have characterized this paradigm as a critique of processual archaeology, this work heavily criticizes those who dehumanize hunter-gatherers with strict ecological models. Sassaman (2010:5, 144), drawing inspiration from "theorists of practice, agency, memory and tradition," discusses three realms of "everyday" living (fishing, shellfishing, and storing mast) "to consider how some of the more mundane aspects of Eastern Archaic life were structured culturally by experience and how the larger context of interconnectedness . . . motivated people to live beyond the 'everyday' and, in so doing, recursively structure everyday life." His goal is to demonstrate that ecological models fail to account for the data. He offers a "historical" way of thinking defined as "*the ongoing process of making culture through social interactions*" (Sassaman 2010:5; emphasis in original) as an alternative. In examining "cultures of daily practice," Sassaman (2010:143–181), demonstrating an impressive understanding of the archaeological record across the region, finds variation in material culture and features that he suggests cannot be explained by environmental constraints. For Sassaman (2010:180), this diversification across the Eastern Archaic in everyday matters raises questions of labor arrangements, sharing, and so on. His historical approach holds promise for including the investigation of the everyday. While contributors here do not necessarily draw inspiration from the same theorists or follow the same manner of archaeological investigation, the focus on the everyday does often lend the "humanistic voice" (Sassaman 2010:231) for which he strives.

The Everyday and Holism

We see potential in an everyday framework for specialists to remain specialized but to bring a degree of holism back to archaeology. Paralleling the trajectory of physics, we see a return to the basic questions of human life as a way to get at the interconnectedness of lithic scatters and sites like Moundville. Instead of painting broad swaths of history, we can revel in the details while still moving the discipline forward.

Continuing with the example of Moundville and extraordinary sites, and as discussed by Kidder and Sherwood (Chapter 12), Barrier and Kassabaum (Chapter 13), Pluckhahn et al. (Chapter 9), and Randall and Gilmore (Chapter 8), the everyday refers not only to the mundane but to how things that are seemingly spectacular or unique have roots in, and potentially an impact on, the everyday lives of people. The planning, construction, and maintenance of some mounds may have been a daily concern. Plazas, or more generally gathering spaces, serve to reinforce bonds within communities through shared experiences and in some cases were the places where the everyday reinforcement of various activities, social bonds, and networks took place. Dumas (Chapter 6) and Pluckhahn et al. (Chapter 9) discuss how everyday skills and activities could be transformed or develop into alternative applications, which often are proscribed as extraordinary by archaeologists, such as salt pan production or quartz crystal plummet manufacture. Pluckhahn et al. point to specific neural firing for domestic production transferring to craft production and use the example of archaeological skills transferring to everyday domestic life when plumbing a drain line and the like. Growing up as obsessive collectors of books, comics, coins, and stamps, we suggest that typing and classification of these items in various ways made for budding cultural historians.

The chapters concerning Late Archaic ritual vessels and Middle Woodland crafting further this idea by suggesting that items we often view in a specialized or ritualized context have an everyday foundation that we do not communicate to ourselves, to other archaeologists, or to the general public. Was the acquisition of materials part of everyday activities, did the items follow the owner/user daily or was the manufacture incorporated into everyday activities using skill sets developed in more secular pursuits? By not making these connections explicit, we maintain a distance between the people in the past and people today, which is a disservice to all of us. Without establishing common ground, how can we expect to understand ourselves or expect archaeology to contribute to the here and now?

How Southeastern Archaeologists Address the Everyday

As this volume demonstrates in a myriad of ways, thinking about the everyday in various ways can broaden perspectives, posit new questions, present testable hypotheses, and perhaps (because it is a shared scale) bring some level of consilience to southeastern archaeology. Most simply defined, "consilience" is evidence from independent or unrelated sources converging into strong conclusions. The *process* of reaching consilience is perhaps more meaningful for southeastern archaeology. The "I believe" essay series (Knight 2014) indicates that there is little consilience among southeastern archaeologists, reflected in the variety of theoretical orientations of many of its practitioners. Edward Wilson (1998) posits that the issue with modern studies of the natural and cultural world is overspecialization, which has fragmented fields of knowledge.

So even though we are all doing archaeology, we have developed terminology, jargon, and outlets of dissemination that prevent constructive dialogue and building consilience. Modern businesses recognize that overspecialization inhibits creativity and problem solving (Heffernan 2015). Successful and innovative companies encourage creative conflict (which southeastern archaeologists avoid), building social capital (something that we should be doing outside of archaeology), physical thinking, collective problem solving, and dissolution of hierarchies. Archaeology could perhaps gain much from looking beyond simply borrowing methods and technology from other fields and more thoroughly incorporating nonarchaeologists into doing archaeology. If all the public does is assist with excavations and wash artifacts, no wonder the prevailing view is that archaeologists are essentially antiquarians who want to dig everything up, give objects names, and isolate people from their heritage.

The authors in this volume examine the everyday in unique ways. We did not dictate how authors should approach their subject matter but rather asked that they write about their area of expertise in relation to everyday matters. From our editorial vantage point, we see commonalities across the chapters, which is encouraging given the broad and ambiguous task assigned to the contributors. The volume chapters fall into four broad groups: novel thinking, data-based narratives, entanglements/itineraries/biographies/lifeways, and reconsidering archaeological rarities as everyday things. Many alternative groupings are possible, and the original symposium was organized by more traditional groups of time and materials. But in light of more fully developed papers this heuristic does not reflect our intent or the effectiveness of an everyday approach well.

The Everyday in a Different Way

Chapters 2 (by Miller and Tune) and 3 (by Rodning et al.) are focused not so much on the everyday lives of people during the Paleoindian and Contact periods but on how everyday life plays out in landscapes that are vastly different from those of today. Both draw inspiration from nonarchaeological research to provide a different viewpoint or perspective on everyday life and rhythms at very disparate points in time. Their approaches (complexity and chaos respectively) are well outside the constraint of traditional archaeological thinking. These approaches to the everyday are perhaps equivalent to the "aha" moments when seemingly unrelated questions and answers are found to coincide. The everyday framework caused them to look outside of archaeology and to explore potential applications and provide paths forward for future research.

Narrating the Everyday

Our second grouping (represented in chapters by Greene, Hollenbach and Carmody, and Dumas) is the data-based narrative. These authors chose to write
fictional accounts that are firmly grounded in their respective archaeological
datasets. In other words, these are not narratives inspired by a single object
and seeking to highlight the agency of an individual (sensu Spector 1993) but
accounts that intertwine the archaeological record (recovered assemblages, contexts), ethnohistorical or ethnographic information, and the authors' imaginations to flesh out the parts of the story that are not recovered in the dirt. As
both Dumas and Green point out, this process of thinking through the range of
possibilities for even a single day at a single site is overwhelming, but it forced
them explicitly to consider people and behaviors, to accept and reject previously
held assumptions, and to work back and forth between the archaeology and the
narrative. Hollenbach and Carmody discuss the utility in thinking about the archaeological record, not only for the archaeologist but for communicating with
nonarchaeologists. Greene furthered his commitment to the approach, stating
that he will incorporate the method earlier on in upcoming Shawnee research
as a way of testing his knowledge and understanding of the archaeology. Dumas
as well as Hollenbach and Carmody extend the impact of their existing data to
themselves, other archaeologists, and the general public. This impact was immediately seen when Walker was inspired after the conference to think about
her topic from a narrative perspective.

Detangling the Everyday

The chapters in the third group (represented by Moore and Jefferies, Randall
and Gilmore, Pluckhahn et al., and Carr and Bradbury) are clearly linked by
the idea that specific pieces of the archaeological record, which are traditionally treated as separate, are entangled not only with the rest of the archaeological past but in ways that we do not see in the dirt. Quantum entanglement (in
physics) is a phenomenon that occurs when particles interact in such a way that
they cannot be described independently; the system can only be described as
a whole. The authors break down the layers of incorporation of classes of artifacts (deer bone, shell cups, Middle Woodland craft specialization, and lithics) against the backdrop of their presence in everyday life. In other words, they
move from objects to activities and thus people. These chapters demonstrate the
vagaries of the various approaches through their use of specific terminology but

also indicate the potential for beginning to form consilience among researchers concentrating on Archaic and Woodland periods, faunal remains and lithic artifacts, and other topics. In physics the paradox of entanglements is that individual measurements cannot be taken on individual particles: measurements of one particle determine measurements of the second. While the entire archaeological record would not collapse like an entangled particle system, this does make us rethink the data that we collect on separate artifact classes that are part of an entangled system.

Reconsidering the Rare as Rote

The last set of chapters (contributed by Walker, Kidder and Sherwood, and Barrier and Kassabaum) are probably most akin to what was originally envisioned for the symposium. These authors approached their topics as somewhat of a free-for-all or "mound building every day," as Kidder and Sherwood state. Each chapter summarizes the known archaeological record as the jumping off point but brings humans and behaviors into the discussion by considering the everyday. This is where archaeology should be, developing a behavioral perspective on the past, asking: "What is the behavior that resulted in this?" These chapters consider how each of the contributors' respective topics was active or present in the everyday lives of people. Archaeologically speaking, mounds, plazas, and dog remains are not something that we consider mundane, but the perspective on the everyday forces us to reconsider our etic perspectives on the extraordinary and ordinary. Whether it is consideration of dogs' presence and participation in everyday life, viewing sediments as artifacts, or seeing the everyday in "monumental" landscapes, these chapters certainly influence us to see the everyday presence of the archaeologically rare.

The last two chapters are meant to provide alternative perspectives and perhaps more mundane solutions to our perceived crisis. Beth Conklin (Chapter 14), as a cultural anthropologist, can speak to the experience of the everyday in other cultures. Her work in the Amazon is a tantalizing, and frustrating, reminder of exactly what we will never see in the archaeological record: the smell of rotting human flesh being roasted, the keening of mourners. It is also a reminder that we do not have an excuse not to think about archaeology and the lived experience of the past beyond the objects we recover just because we cannot recover those specific experiences. The last chapter is a reminder that our everyday archaeology is how we can make what we do relevant in the present. Reconstructing and restoring past environments are valuable contributions. But we should be challenging ourselves to make archaeology accessible, understandable, and relative to the everyday person today in order to bring archaeology into the forefront of creating positive change and learning from the past to improve the here and now. It is perhaps not entirely on our shoulders to make archaeology relevant to everyday life in the here and now, but we must make it accessible enough for others to carry the task to fruition.

Conclusion

We see a connection to everyday archaeology in these chapters in three additional ways. First, some of these chapters serve as an inspiration to other archaeologists, on how to think about, interpret, and challenge existing archaeological knowledge. The Moore and Jefferies chapter is an example of how to think more holistically about the past and the archaeological record, while remaining specialized and knowledgeable. Second, some chapters should serve as inspiration for how to articulate with the public about archaeology and perhaps bring our own implicit assumptions and biases to the forefront, where they can be adjusted or dispelled. Whether through data-driven narratives (Dumas, Greene, Hollenbach and Carmody) or making the exemplary relatable and understandable (Barrier and Kassabaum), the everyday approach brings us to this essential part of archaeology. Third, the everyday can inspire archaeologists to look beyond the confines of our discipline. Greene takes inspiration from fictional accounts concerning the past of the people that he excavates. Beyond looking to published work outside of books and journals in our discipline, we suggest that archaeologists seek out and collaborate with nonarchaeological professionals to further our field and the impact that it has on the everyday lives of people.

We hope that the following chapters inspire readers to think about the everyday lives in the past and their own everyday practice of archaeology in a different way. Whether thinking in terms of itineraries, biographies, use-lives, narratives, or chaos theory, forcing ourselves to consider different scales and beyond the field and lab methods and technical reports affects the hypotheses/narratives that we produce in our head and on paper and how these hypotheses/narratives can expand your horizons of possibilities regarding the past and the archaeological record. We cannot continue to employ the view of the archaeological record as too coarse grained to limit our theory and method; we must force ourselves to consider and seek what we currently cannot find. We are not advocating a particular approach to the everyday and think that disagreeing with all of the approaches presented here might even be as productive as thinking about the everyday—gaining inspiration by disagreement!

Acknowledgments

We would like to thank the contributors to this volume, and to the original symposium, for being game to take up our task of everyday matters. We are grateful to the two anonymous reviewers for pointing out how to focus the volume and improve our discussion and presentation of everyday matters. We take full responsibility for any omissions, errors, or egregiously faulty logic.

2

When the Levee Breaks

Small Decisions and Big Floods at the End of the Last Ice Age

D. SHANE MILLER AND JESSE TUNE

At face value, the archaeological record of North America at the end of the last Ice Age appears to be a strange place to discuss human behavior at the scale of a single day. We cannot, for example, discuss "the Last Thursday of the Clovis Culture" for many reasons, the most obvious of which is that the archaeological data are much too coarse. In this chapter we argue that in order to shift the scale of Paleoindian period archaeology to examine "everyday matters" archaeologists have to grapple with the well-known "palimpsest problem" (Binford 1981) and reorient their theoretical positioning to include more "bottom up" models from complexity theory. Using three examples from the southeastern United States, we first discuss how Anderson et al. (2016) used a refit analysis at the Topper site to illuminate how people may have learned to make stone tools, which yields insights into how the learning networks that we can detect with archaeological data may have developed. Next we discuss how the everyday decisions regarding stone tool maintenance and discard can help us determine how people may have altered where they lived and what they ate in relation to climate change. Finally, we discuss how these decisions might have led hunter-gatherers during the Younger Dryas to target deer and other animals during spring floods so that taking advantage of short-term abundance led to increasing scarcity over the long term.

The Paleoindian Palimpsest Problem

Discussing Paleoindian "everyday matters" using the archaeological record is difficult and stems from the types of questions that are most often pursued by people studying this period. For one thing, Paleoindian period archaeologists remain obsessed with determining when the first people arrived in North

America and, as a legacy of evaluating the Clovis-First model, are preoccupied with residential mobility and subsistence (Meltzer 2009; Smallwood 2014). It is precisely because of this that archaeologists studying this period have gravitated to human behavioral ecology (e.g., Borgerhoff Mulder and Schacht 2005; Smith et al. 2001:128; Winterhalder and Smith 2000). At face value, the foundation for behavioral ecology is meant to model snapshot decisions with well-defined parameters as an analytical baseline to compare against the decisions that people actually make (Kelly 2013; Kennett and Winterhalder 2006:18–19).

However, archaeologists taking this theoretical perspective must grapple with the fact that archaeological datasets are averages of many decisions made over long periods by many people: the classic "palimpsest problem" (Binford 1981). Furthermore, in the case of the Clovis culture, the minimum estimate for its duration is approximately 200 calendar years (Waters and Stafford 2007). If the average generation span for ethnographic hunter-gathers is 28.6 years (Fenner 2005), then there are at least seven generations of individuals represented by the distribution of Clovis points across North America. In other words, drilling down from the archaeological record to the scale of a single day is impossible. Regarding everyday matters, we only can observe those averages of decisions for the most part.

Paul Martin's (1984) classic "Pleistocene Overkill" model best illustrates the disjunction in scale between the instantaneous decisions modeled by behavioral ecology versus the palimpsests of material accumulated over multiple centuries. One key component of the model is the assumption of high rates of mobility in order to move people across a continent in a few centuries. It is as if we must assume that Clovis people had a "plan" to colonize a continent quickly and that it is the job of the archaeologist to work backward from the data to envision the plan. That is like analyzing the movements of football players to determine the structure of the play called in the huddle. This is obviously problematic, as it is highly unlikely that the Pleistocene colonists of North America huddled up at the mouth of the Ice-Free Corridor and called a "Hail Mary" to scatter people to the far reaches of the continent as quickly as possible. Granted, subsequent attempts to model the colonization of North America, and in particular birth rates and residential mobility, are much more nuanced than our anecdote (e.g., Anderson and Gillam 2000; Barton et al. 2004; Hamilton and Buchanan 2007; Surovell 2000, 2003). Yet we contend that there is likely significant variability in the everyday decisions made by the earliest colonizers of North America versus subsequent generations that are masked by the coarse-grained nature of the Pleistocene archaeological record.

Complexity Theory, Archaeology, and Ant Hills

As a way to bridge the scalar gap between everyday matters and the archaeological record, archaeologists have increasingly drawn from complexity theory (e.g., Holland 1995; Kauffman and Johnsen 1991; Langton 1991; Lansing 2003; Wolfram 1984). As an example, J. Stephen Lansing (2003) studied how small local interactions could lead to much larger emergent patterns. He frequently used his research from Bali to show how small local meetings between rice farmers at Water Temples resulted in broad coordination in planting cycles and water distribution—all without a master plan. In fact, when a master plan was instituted as part of the Green Revolution, it undermined local coordination at the Water Temples and led to a brief increase in agricultural productivity, followed by a rapid collapse.

As a nonhuman example of "emergent complexity," we recommend a documentary on the careers of Bert Hölldobler and Edward O. Wilson and in particular the segment showing the interior of a large ant colony. An ant nest was filled with concrete and then excavated, exposing intricate networks of tunnels and rooms that, if human-made, would suggest a small army of architects, engineers, and city planners involved in its creation (Thaler 2012). Instead, this structure was built by ants responding locally to pheromones produced by the queen in much the same way that rice farmers on Bali were adjusting to locally changing environmental conditions and the activities of their neighbors.

These examples provide case studies for how to reconcile the scalar disjunction between the extant Paleoindian archaeological record and considering everyday matters. In other words, rather than evaluating whether a plan like the Overkill Model (Martin 1984) matches the archaeological record, archaeologists should be looking for the types of small, everyday decisions that, when made in the same way over long periods, could generate patterns that are detectable with our coarse-grained archaeological data (Bentley and Maschner 2008; Kohler 2011). While most proponents of applying complexity theory to archaeology are heavily reliant on agent-based models (White 2015), we provide three heuristic examples to illustrate how archaeologists have worked backward from big patterns in archaeological datasets to the everyday matters that likely caused them.

Projectile Points and Learning Networks

Projectile points are the most ubiquitous and temporally diagnostic artifacts for the Pleistocene archaeological record (Meltzer 2009). This is especially the case in the southeastern United States, where surface finds are abundant and buried sites dating to the Late Pleistocene are rare (Anderson et al. 2015; Dunnell 1990; Goodyear 1999; Miller and Gingerich 2013). Instead, archaeologists in the southeastern United States heavily rely on sites associated with stone outcrops that have yielded information on how these, and other artifacts, are produced (Anderson et al. 2015; Smallwood 2012).

At the Topper site in South Carolina, Derek Anderson et al. (2016) found evidence for what this process may have looked like by reconstructing the production of a stone tool through a refit analysis. Anderson et al. argue that, based on the distribution of burnt flakes, it appears as if several people were sitting around a fire and the tool was passed among them with more difficult expert removals happening over and over in the same spot. In other words, less experienced knappers would work on the tool until they reached a point where they could not proceed any further then would hand it to the more experienced knapper. Today we would call this scaffolded learning (Wood et al. 1976). These kinds of everyday interactions made repeatedly over time are precisely those that allow us to detect social networks at larger regional scales (Eren et al. 2015; Thulman 2006). For example, Ashley Smallwood (2012) studied the way in which Clovis bifaces were produced in areas that David Anderson (1995) identified as staging areas and could identify subtle differences. Smallwood concluded that emerging divisions in learning networks were well underway during Clovis times and are more consistent with a stepped model of colonization (e.g., Anderson 1995; Meltzer 2004) rather than with a rapid pulse of people moving across the landscape (e.g., Kelly and Todd 1988).

Projectile Points, Hunting, and Landscape Use

With the onset of the Younger Dryas (ca. 12,800 cal B.P.), Clovis bifaces give way to full-fluted Cumberland bifaces in the Mid-South and fishtailed Suwannee points in Florida and the South Atlantic Coastal Plain (Anderson et al. 2015). The appearance of regionalized point styles is often cited as evidence of cultural reorganization spurred by environmental change, especially given the decrease in the frequency of these post-Clovis types (Anderson 2001; Anderson et al. 2011; Meeks and Anderson 2012). How does a consideration of everyday matters and daily microeconomic decisions inform us regarding sweeping changes that result in cultural reorganization?

These point types remain poorly dated at best (and in the case of the Cumberland not at all) (Tune 2015). Given a weak chronology plus the "cliff" in the radiocarbon calibration curve at the onset of the Younger Dryas, it may be nearly impossible to determine whether those people would have noticed the onset of the Younger Dryas, an event that may have spanned only a few decades, while projectile point types spanned at least several centuries (Fiedel 2015; Meltzer and Holliday 2010). Moreover, does a reduction in post-Clovis points mean fewer people or less time (Smallwood et al. 2015:26–27)? Again, the lack of chronological resolution makes it difficult to assess.

Rather than tracking the frequency of projectile points to make inferences about demography, D. Shane Miller (2014) and Jesse Tune (2015) examined the economic decisions that people made in regard to resharpening their projectile points and where on the landscape they discarded them. In other words, by analyzing patterns in projectile point resharpening and discard, archaeologists have at their disposal a time-averaged reflection of many everyday decisions made, presumably, when hunting. For example, Steven Kuhn and Miller (2015) examined how Clovis and Cumberland bifaces varied in terms of resharpening in the Tennessee Fluted Point Survey (e.g., Broster et al. 2013), where both types were discarded, on average, with very strong correlations between length and width. This pattern is indicative of very little resharpening, which would differentially affect the length relative to the width. On the other hand, Beaver Lake and Dalton types that occur during the latter half of the Younger Dryas are extensively resharpened, as indicated by the lack of correlation between length and width. Miller (2014) was able to replicate this pattern with a sample of projectile points from Benton and Humphreys Counties on the Tennessee River, and Tune (2015) found the same pattern with a larger regional sample from Kentucky, Tennessee, and Alabama.

Moreover, when Miller (2014) examined the distribution of archaeological sites across physiographic sections along the Duck River using data from the Tennessee Division of Archaeology and the Tennessee Fluted Point Survey, Clovis and Cumberland sites were distributed along the confluence with the Tennessee River, whereas over the course of the Younger Dryas points were discarded in increasing numbers at higher elevations. Leon Lane and Anderson (2001) have also replicated these findings in the Appalachian Highlands, as have Greg Maggard and Kacy Stackelbeck (2008) on the Cumberland Plateau in Kentucky. Miller and Stephen Carmody (2016) argue that the lag in the sustained presence of people at higher elevations likely coincides with the lag in the replacement of boreal with deciduous forests at higher elevations and that boreal forests would have been a deterrent to hunter-gatherers due to their lower biodiversity.

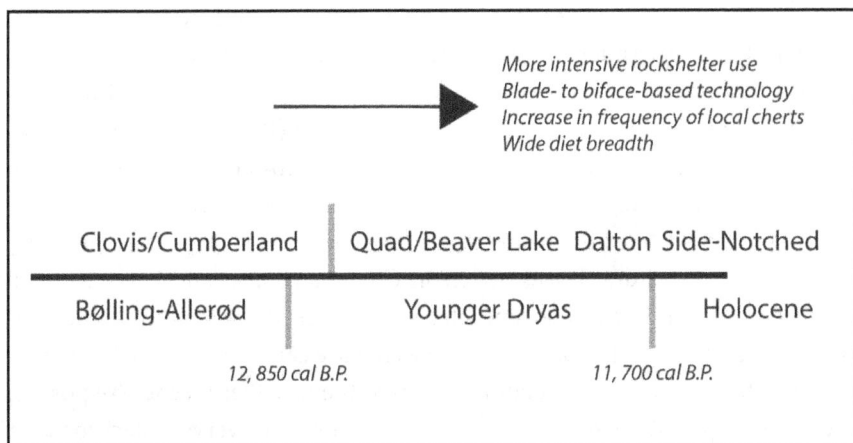

Figure 2.1. Major cultural trends during the Late Pleistocene in the Mid-South.

Consequently, rather than a break in the archaeological record between Clovis and Cumberland that we would expect with a dramatic depopulation or reorganization at the onset of the Younger Dryas, we would put the break between the early and later parts of the Younger Dryas (Figure 2.1). More broadly, this break coincides with the increase in the use of rock shelters (Walthall 1998), a shift from blade to biface-based technological organization (Sherwood et al. 2004:541), an increased focus on local stone resources (Jones et al. 2010; Koldehoff and Loebel 2009; White 2014), and a surprisingly wide diet-breadth, as exhibited at Dust Cave and other Late Younger Dryas sites in the region (Carmody 2009; Hollenbach 2007; Styles and Klippel 1996; Walker 2007). Although making comparisons with Clovis and Cumberland is hampered by a complete lack of sites with preserved flora and fauna in the Mid-South (Anderson et al. 2015; Miller and Gingerich 2013). While these are all broad trends that span several centuries, they are ultimately a reflection of daily microeconomic decisions about everyday matters: what to eat, where to live, and how to make stone tools accomplish those goals.

When the Levees Break

What stays constant? Archaeologists and artifact collectors have long recognized that the natural levees along the Cumberland River, and particularly the lower and central Tennessee River, have historically produced an enormous number of bifaces (Anderson 1995; Anderson et al. 2015). Famous sites such as Quad (Cambron and Hulse 1960; Soday 1954), Nuckolls (Lewis and Kneberg 1958; Norton and Broster 1992), Carson-Conn-Short (Broster and Norton 1993, 1996), Kirk Point (McNutt et al. 2008), Widimeier (Broster et al. 2006), Johnson (Barker and Broster 1996), Puckett (Norton and Broster 1992:), and the recently published Parris Collection from the Lower Tennessee River (Tune et al. 2015) are all found on natural levees. Jefferson Chapman (1985) and Larry Kimball (1996) argued that Early Holocene sites in the river bottoms in the Little Tennessee River drainage in East Tennessee were base camps, and there has been a tendency to push this interpretation back into the Late Pleistocene. We pose an alternative explanation, rooted in complexity theory and everyday decisions, for why there were so many points found on the levees of these rivers.

Based on paleoethnobotanical data, Kandace Hollenbach (2007; Hollenbach and Carmody, Chapter 5) argues that Late Pleistocene and Early Holocene hunter-gatherers followed a seasonal cycle that was largely dictated by the availability of gathered resources. People would leave the uplands during the late winter/early spring once mast resources were tapped out and gravitate toward river bottoms to take advantage of early ripening plants. However, if this is indeed the time when people were using levees, there is a big problem with situating a base camp on a levee—spring floods.

Our own everyday experiences with rivers in the Mid-South are shaped by the Army Corps of Engineers and the Tennessee Valley Authority, which have preemptively flooded bottomlands in rural areas to prevent catastrophes in more populated ones, like Chattanooga (Lewis et al. 1995). Floods obviously still happen today, but they only really affect areas along rivers that are not flood controlled, like the Doe River flood in upper east Tennessee, where snowmelt coupled with heavy rains caused an estimated $20 million in damage in 1998 (Gorey 2013). We also only notice incidences where precipitation and runoff overwhelm dams and other infrastructure, like the May 2010 flood that affected the Cumberland and Duck Rivers, which resulted in 30 counties in Tennessee being declared disaster areas by the federal government (National Weather Service 2010).

Based on limited geomorphological data, some evidence supports the hypothesis that flooding could have been much more prevalent prehistorically, especially during the Late Pleistocene and Early Holocene. In the Duck River, G. Robert Brackenridge (1984) observed that sedimentation occurred faster than soil formation after a Late Pleistocene down-cutting event throughout much of the Early Holocene. Along the Middle Tennessee River, this same general pattern is seen in the stratigraphy at Dust Cave, where a major down-cutting event on the Tennessee River dropped the base level of the river, which helped flush sediments from Coffee Slough and the cave entrance (Sherwood et al. 2004). Then, over the course of the Younger Dryas and early Holocene, overbank flooding in conjunction with slopewash and anthropogenic sediments began filling the cave once more. In the Little Tennessee River, classic Early Holocene sites like Ice House Bottom and Rose Island are buried under meters of sediment (Chapman 1985). While the episodes of flooding would have been more random in headwaters, the main channels of the Tennessee and Cumberland Rivers would have averaged the flooding for a region, which may have included greater amounts of spring snow melt during the Late Pleistocene and Early Holocene. However, data for the region are admittedly sparse, with Eric Grimm et al. (2006) arguing that the lower southeastern United States became warmer and wetter and David Leigh (2008) demonstrating that Late Pleistocene rivers of the region displayed much larger meanders as a result of larger flood discharge. At a human scale, the shift from snow to rain and warming temperatures served as a seasonal cue that flooding was likely on the way.

Why would people be drawn to river bottoms that were prone to flood in the winter and spring? A clue may come from an unlikely place and a remarkable photo. In May 2011 holes were blown in the New Madrid levee to alleviate flooding along the Mississippi River and in the process inundated the area around the platform mound at the Towosaghy site, where deer, turkey, and coyotes took refuge (see photographs at https://footprintmag.wordpress.com/2011/05/23/animals-cling-to-dry-spots-during-mississippi-river-flood/). More broadly, modern floods appear to prompt white-tailed deer to leave low-lying areas for high ground via established migration routes. Floods also appear to cause an increase in mortality and lower body weights the following year, especially among fawns (Jacobson et al. 2011; MacDonald-Beyers and Labisky 2005). Following a flood, deer have a tendency to return to the same home area. Perhaps one of the consequences when levees adjacent to rivers break during late winter and early spring floods is that they leave animals, particularly white-tailed deer, stranded and clustered on areas that are high and dry (Figure 2.2).

Humans taking advantage of such a situation could have had a devastating effect on deer, the most abundant large mammal targeted as prey by humans (Moore and Jefferies, Chapter 7), who were also likely moving to rivers once upland mast resources diminished. If stranded by spring floods, their primary defensive strategy—running—would be limited and hunters could corner entire

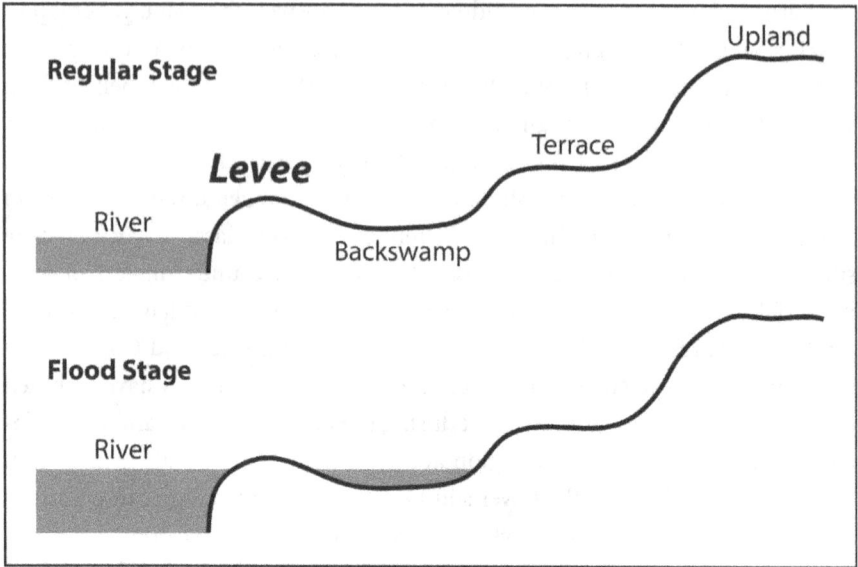

Figure 2.2. A schematic of a levee system at regular and flood stage.

groups of does and fawns—the very reason why it is illegal to hunt during the spring now (McShea et al. 1997). However, we argue that hunters in the Mid-South likely employed the same strategy that other Paleoindian groups have been inferred to have used: ambushing large animals in clusters, as at Blackwater Draw (Boldurian and Cotter 1999), Fin del Mundo (Sanchez et al. 2014), Lehner Ranch (Haury et al. 1959), Wally's Beach (Kooyman et al. 2006; Waters et al. 2015), Vail (Gramly 1982), and Folsom bison kills in the western United States like Casper (Frison 1974) and Folsom (Meltzer 2009). The effect of competing with deer for limited mast resources and then ambushing them (with their young) in the early spring might not have been noticeable at a human scale, but employing this strategy over many centuries could go a long way toward explaining why 84 percent of the deer at Dust Cave were juveniles—a pattern that Renee Walker (1998) argues could be indicative of overhunting. Even if people did notice a change in the availability of hunted resources, the response seems to have been a broadening of diet, adjusting toolkits to hunt smaller, faster prey, and to lay claim to resources within sections of the drainage—a Pleistocene example of everyday decisions leading people down the path that Garret Hardin (1968) described in "The Tragedy of the Commons," where short-term decisions lead to long-term consequences over the duration of the Younger Dryas.

Conclusion

Discussing everyday matters during the Paleoindian period is not exactly a straightforward task. However, at second glance, despite a record that encompasses many centuries and millennia, archaeologists do it quite regularly. More specifically, by employing complexity theory, we attempt to make sense of big patterns by trying to discern what kinds of small everyday decisions could have lasting effects if repeated with sufficient frequency. As examples, several studies have argued that variation in how people learn to knap at quarry sites could lead to regionalization of projectile point styles and that everyday microeconomic decisions about what to eat, where to live, and what tools to use generated macro-scale patterns that give us insights about people adapted to climate change and in particular the Younger Dryas. Finally, we argue that decisions made by hunters to take advantage of species clustered and stranded by floods could have altered their long-term availability during the Younger Dryas. To echo the theme of this volume, everyday matters *really matter*, and the Pleistocene archaeological record is no different.

Acknowledgments

We would like to thank Phil Carr and Sarah Price for providing us with the opportunity to think out loud about everyday matters in the Pleistocene. Part of the research discussed here was funded by the SRI Foundation and facilitated by the Tennessee Division of Archaeology and the McClung Museum at the University of Tennessee. We would like to thank David Anderson, Steve Kuhn, Mary Stiner, John Broster, Derek Anderson, Stephen Carmody, Thad Bissett, and Aaron Deter-Wolf for all of the conversations about hunter-gatherers and archaeology.

3

Chaos Theory and the Contact Period in the Southeast

CHRISTOPHER B. RODNING, JAYUR MADHUSUDAN MEHTA,
BRYAN S. HALEY, AND DAVID J. WATT

European contact sparked dramatic culture change in the Native American Southeast. Mississippian chiefdoms were already experiencing cyclical episodes of emergence and collapse during late prehistory. The focal points of Mississippian political geography periodically shifted across the landscape. These patterns continued through the post-Contact period and perhaps were even accelerated in the aftermath of mid-sixteenth-century Spanish entradas in the Southeast. New forms of warfare and the slave trade altered the relationships among and relative statuses of Mississippian polities. Meanwhile, new networks of trade and exchange altered the domestic economy and political economy of Mississippian communities and led to changes in settlement concentrations and patterns. Missions, trading posts, and related colonial outposts introduced new forms of religious thought and practice and made some Native American groups more susceptible to colonial rule, more vulnerable to attacks, and more dependent on colonial enterprise and economy. Eventually, disease epidemics decimated Native American populations in terms of public health and demography and probably in terms of spirituality and community vitality as well. Through it all, Native American groups resisted these forces of culture change, pursued strategic initiatives and agendas of their own, and formed new kinds of communities and identity than those that were present before European contact and colonialism in the Americas. How did these broad-scale patterns of change affect the lives of people at particular places across the Southeast, and how can archaeologists relate explanatory models about these developments to evidence of and interpretations about everyday life at specific sites? How did long-term patterns of cultural continuity and change in the Native American Southeast affect the course of colonial history and, particularly, responses by Native American peoples to colonial encounters and entanglements?

Our approach to these topics is grounded in chaos theory, the field of study in mathematics and mechanics that concentrates on how initial conditions in dynamic systems shape the outcomes of changes to those systems. We review some basic tenets of chaos theory as a step toward developing an interpretive framework for studying the Contact period in the Americas and consider the "shatter zone" model of the fractured and fragmented cultural system of the protohistoric Southeast, in which actions and developments at particular points had unpredictable but nonrandom impacts on people and places elsewhere. We then consider how broad trends related to European contact and colonialism affected everyday life for Native American groups, with an emphasis on how developments that affected the Southeast as a whole would have impacted the lives of people and groups at specific locales within this landscape (or, from the perspective of chaos theory, at specific *points* within the larger cultural *system* of the protohistoric Southeast).

The four cases that we consider in most detail here include the Yazoo Basin in northwestern Mississippi, the Apalachee province of northern Florida, Cherokee town areas of the southern Appalachians, and areas of Natchez and Taensa settlement in southwestern Mississippi and northeastern Louisiana. Despite ethnic and linguistic differences between groups in these areas, they were all part of the broader Mississippian cultural tradition. Native American groups in these areas cultivated maize, beans, and squash and hunted game such as deer, bear, and turkey. People lived in towns and farmsteads, and the focal points of towns were sites where large public structures, temples, plazas, and in some cases monumental earthen mounds were present. There are some examples in the Southeast of mound stages that postdate European contact, such as the Jordan site in Louisiana (Kidder 1992) and the Haynes Bluff site in Mississippi (Brain 1988). But large-scale mound-building was largely a practice of the past, even though earthworks were both a backdrop to everyday life and an enduring aspect of the cultural landscape (see Kidder and Sherwood, Chapter 12). Tasks related to processing, storing, preparing, and consuming food took place in and around domestic structures, as did activities like making pottery, chipping and grinding stone tools, weaving baskets, and carving wooden implements. It is not clear where the production of shell beads and gorgets, copper ornaments, clay and stone smoking pipes, and other items related to political economy and ideology took place, but perhaps such activities occurred on or near mounds (Mehta et al. 2016). During a day, people might traverse distances by land or water to visit neighboring communities, to participate in trade and exchange, to acquire resources and raw materials, and to tend fields. On some days throughout the year, people would gather at community centers to participate in religious ceremonies, dances, feasts, town council deliberations, and community renewal events such as those associated with the Busk. Everyday life in the protohistoric Native American Southeast was guided by tradition and was also affected in seemingly unpredictable ways by colonial exploration, trade, missionization, and settlement. None of those forms of interaction between Native Americans and newcomers can be fully considered in this chapter, but we seek here to begin developing an interpretive framework for the archaeology of the protohistoric Southeast grounded in chaos theory.

Chaos Theory

Archaeologists have applied chaos theory toward studying how Ancestral Pueblo groups responded to periods of environmental and social instability in late prehistoric southwestern North America (Cordell 2000; Stone 1999), considerations of the effects of climatic changes on Iroquoian settlements and societies in the Northeast during the period just before European contact (Kapches 1995), and the study of encounters between Spanish colonists and Native American chiefdoms of the Caribbean (Keegan 2007). Chaos theory offers an interpretive framework to relate the conditions and macroscale processes affecting large areas and cultural systems to the dynamics and developments at points within those systems. This property of chaos theory makes it relevant to studying the effects of European contact on people and peoples of the Mississippian Southeast. Each site offers its own vantage point on the cultural system of the Mississippian Southeast and the effects of developments at those points on the broader nonlinear system of which they were part. Following the points of early encounters and entanglements with European explorers and colonists, everyday life for Native American groups in the Southeast was shaped by the larger colonial world, even as everyday life shaped the development of that larger colonial world system.

According to chaos theory, small differences in the initial conditions of dynamic systems can lead to large differences in the outcomes of changes to those systems (Smith 1998). This phenomenon of sensitivity to initial conditions is known as the butterfly effect (Lorenz 1996). Within systems that demonstrate chaos, changes are unpredictable, especially from particular vantage points within those systems, but changes are not random (Kellert 1993).

These concepts are applicable to the archaeology of everyday life during the Contact period in the Southeast in the following ways. First, during encounters and interactions among people from very different cultural backgrounds—including diverse Native American groups and newcomers from distant lands— events probably often did not make sense, given that different people acted according to their own cultural logics and perspectives. From the perspective of chaos theory, events were unpredictable, but they were not random. Second, there was diversity in Mississippian societies across the Southeast or, put another way, variation in the initial conditions of the Mississippian cultural system, broadly speaking (Anderson 1990a, 1994a, 1994b, 1996a, 1996b; Butler and Cobb 2002; Cobb and King 2005; King 2001, 2002, 2003a, 2003b; Knight 2010; Milner 1996; Muller 1986, 1997, 1998; Pauketat 2004; Rogers 1995, 1996; Scarry 1994a, 1996a, 1996b; Schroedl 1998; Smith 1986; Steponaitis 1986, 1991, 2009; Williams 1994; Williams and Shapiro 1996). Third, those initial conditions of the Mississippian landscape shaped the outcomes of European contact. Fourth, there was no single point of equilibrium within the cultural systems of the Mississippian or protohistoric Southeast but, instead, many points of potential equilibrium and stability. While the cultural systems of the Native American Southeast periodically approached these points of equilibrium and stability, they never fully reached them: some sources of instability were always present. Fifth, chaotic systems never return to preceding states and conditions; similarly, after European contact, the normal dynamics and cycling of Mississippian chiefdoms were irrevocably altered (Hally 2006; King 2006). Finally, broad patterns of change in the geopolitical landscape and colonial world system impacted the entire Southeast but probably were, and are, imperfectly understood from any particular vantage point, given the global scale of networks of interaction that developed in the aftermath of European contact in the Americas.

Shatter Zone

Ethnohistorians and archaeologists have recently begun to refer to the protohistoric Southeast as a "shatter zone," referring to the fractured geopolitical relationships that developed after European contact and the aftershocks of changing trade relations, patterns of warfare, shifting alliances, and changing fortunes of Native American groups and colonial newcomers alike (Ethridge 2006; Marcoux 2010). These developments led to the coalescence of multiethnic groups such as the Catawbas, the Chickasaws, the Choctaws, and the Creek confederacy (Braund 2008; Ethridge 2003, 2010; Galloway 1994, 2002; Johnson 2000; Knight 1994a; Merrell 1989, 2006; Wesson 2008). They led to entanglements of many groups in cycles of warfare in which the focus shifted away from status rivalry between Mississippian chiefdoms to raids aimed at capturing slaves. Alliances with colonial groups affected the outcomes of this kind of warfare, as in the case of English traders encouraging and sponsoring Cherokee warriors in an attack on the Yuchi town of Chestowee (Riggs 2012) and English traders arming

Native American warriors to attack Apalachee settlements, contributing to the beginning of an Apalachee diaspora (Hann and McEwan 1998).

Given the rearrangements of people and towns in the Southeast, and periodic realignments of diplomatic relations and alliances for trade and warfare among Native Americans and newcomers alike, some areas and towns came to have new forms of cultural and ethnic diversity. The Creek confederacy encompassed towns in Georgia, northwestern Florida, and Alabama that included speakers of several languages and people of diverse cultural and geographic origins. This diversity is reflected in pottery found at relevant archaeological sites (Hally 1994a, 1994b; Knight 1994a, 1994b; Smith 2000, 2006; Waselkov and Smith 2000; Worth 2000). The Choctaw confederacy formed as an amalgam of different groups in Mississippi, with towns situated in areas that were not focal points for settlement during the period just before European contact in the Southeast (Galloway 1995). Similarly, multiethnic Catawba towns formed in areas of the Carolinas that were adjacent to, but distinct from, the provinces of major sixteenth-century chiefdoms such as Joara and Cofitachequi and concentrations of Siouan villages in the North Carolina and Virginia Piedmont (Beck 2013; Davis 2002; DePratter 1994; Ward and Davis 1993, 1999, 2001). Before the Contact period, the different groups that were brought together within these coalescent societies would have known of each other and would have interacted with each other, but the stresses of warfare, the new opportunities for trade and diplomacy, and longer-term cycles of chiefdom development and collapse created more diversity within at least some if not most communities in the Native American Southeast (Ethridge 2006).

The establishment of European settlements and trading posts contributed to cultural diversity within selected locales in the Southeast as well. For example, several Spanish mission settlements in coastal Georgia and northeastern Florida drew in people from Timucuan, Guale, and other groups (Hann 1996; Milanich 2000; Saunders 2000a, 2000b; Stojanowski 2005, 2008). As another example, the establishment of Macon Trading House by English colonists in 1685 prompted some Creek towns to move from the Chattahoochee Valley to the Ocmulgee River, although many of those towns moved back to the Chattahoochee and other areas within the Creek confederacy several years later (Mason 2005; Waselkov 1994). The trading post at Macon led to an unsuccessful attempt by Spanish colonists and Apalachee settlers to establish an outpost along the Chattahoochee, in an effort to stem the spread of English hegemony in the northern borderlands of La Florida (Hann and McEwan 1998). Very soon after Macon Trading House was founded, the Chickasaws in northern Mississippi became actively involved in this trade network (Johnson et al. 2008), contributing to the militarization of Chickasaw society (Ethridge 2010), broadly speaking, and to the devastating impacts that Chickasaw slave raids had on Native American groups across much of the Southeast during the seventeenth century and perhaps before that.

Outbreaks of both violence and disease probably created periodic crises, especially in cases in which large numbers of people within communities were affected. Such episodes would have challenged community leaders and structures of community leadership, including leadership in politics, religion, and spirituality, and other domains. Outcomes of violence and disease also impacted the capacities of households and communities to devote labor and other resources to farming, foraging, hunting, and other economic pursuits necessary to sustain and to reproduce themselves. Several disease epidemics are known to have had devastating demographic impacts during the 1700s and 1800s. Written accounts of Spanish and French expeditions and explorations contain hints of apparent epidemics dating to the 1500s and 1600s (Hutchinson 1990, 2006; Hutchinson and Mitchem 2001; Kelton 2002, 2004, 2007). Such epidemics probably had more pronounced effects in large towns; areas of dense Mississippian settlement such as the Lower Mississippi Valley (Kidder 2002) and the Central Mississippi Valley (Mainfort 2001; D. F. Morse 1990; Morse and Morse 1983, 1990; P. A. Morse 1990); and areas with direct and sustained contact between Native American and colonial groups, as in the case of Spanish mission settlements along the Atlantic coast (Saunders 2002; Stojanowski 2008).

Areas of particularly dense Mississippian settlement in the Southeast were probably major targets for slave raids as well, including, perhaps, the province of Joara (Beck 2013), the province of Coosa (Smith 1987, 2000, 2001, 2002), and other similar areas. Traditional forms of Mississippian warfare focused largely on status rivalry and tributary relationships (Dye 1990, 2004, 2009). But European contact and the development of the slave trade brought new incentives to generate large numbers of war captives, leading to new forms of warfare that decimated some groups (Dye 2002) and generated new forms of geopolitical instability across the Southeast. Given these developments, provinces with some of the most powerful and prosperous chiefdoms at the point of early Spanish contact were probably the most greatly disrupted and destabilized by encounters with Spanish entradas, including those in the Central and Lower Mississippi Valley.

The Yazoo Basin and Chiefdom Collapse

The Yazoo Basin in northwest Mississippi was home to the powerful and prosperous mid-sixteenth-century chiefdoms of Quizquiz and Quigualtam (Brain

1978; Hudson 1997) and home to tribal groups such as the Tunicas, Koroas, Yazoos, Ibitoupas, Ofos, and Tious during the late 1600s and early 1700s (I. W. Brown 1990; Ethridge 2010; Williams 1990, 2001). Most of these groups spoke Tunican languages, although some were Siouan and Muskogean speakers (Swanton 1911). During the Late Woodland period, groups associated with the Coles Creek culture built many earthen mounds at many sites in the Yazoo Basin (Kidder 2002; see also Kassabaum et al. 2014). During the Mississippi period, more mounds were built, including some very large earthworks (Kidder 1998; Mehta et al. 2012). If late prehistoric mound sites are indicative of the power and status of chiefs and chiefdoms, then there was probably some rigidity in social hierarchy and political centralization in the Yazoo Basin, political competition among closely spaced rival polities (Brain 1978:354), and some variability in the power and prosperity of different polities.

Archaeological evidence demonstrates a pattern of nucleated settlement in the northern Yazoo Basin but more spatially dispersed settlement in areas of Mississippi farther to the south, and, similarly, dispersed settlement patterns in northeastern Louisiana (Kidder 1998:147). Chiefdoms in the Yazoo Basin included some of the most powerful in the Mississippian Southeast at the point of Spanish contact in the 1500s. But those kingdoms collapsed when French explorers arrived from points upstream in the late 1600s, and the Yazoo Basin was home to more segmented, more scattered, and more decentralized tribal societies (Brown 2008). At the point of French contact, six or seven generations had elapsed since the Hernándo de Soto expedition had traversed the fields and villages of the province of Quizquiz and encountered large numbers of warriors at the principal town of this powerful chiefdom, and since large numbers of Quigualtam warriors in dugout canoes had chased Luis de Moscoso and surviving members of the Soto entrada downstream and out of the Southeast. Written descriptions of the provinces of Quizquiz and Quigualtam indicate that farming generated large surpluses within those chiefdoms and that the chief of Quigualtam was a dominant leader within the Lower Mississippi Valley as a whole. Considerable effort was probably invested in managing the landscape of farmland and floodplain settlements, necessitating mobilization and management of labor and surplus resources and probably related forms of hierarchy. The demographic and geopolitical collapse of these chiefdoms led to the more fragmented cultural landscape of the 1600s and early 1700s.

As Jay Johnson (personal communication, 2012) has noted, Native American groups of the Yazoo Basin may have been decimated by slave raiding during the seventeenth century. Given the numbers of people and the density of settlement in some areas, disease epidemics probably had more dramatic impacts in the Yazoo Basin than they did elsewhere in the Southeast. Those developments probably diminished the power and status of chiefs and chiefdoms who were associated with earthworks and mound building and who mobilized fleets of warriors to harass the fleet of Spanish brigantines. Challenges to chiefly power, and decreasing numbers of people, probably contributed to declines in the workforce necessary to maintain the highly productive agricultural landscapes of Quizquiz and Quigualtam. Native American groups in the Yazoo Basin lived amid overgrown fields, mazes of waterways formerly traveled by canoes laden with people and food and other cargo, and ruins of an ancestral civilization that was of course their own but that in other ways was very different from the culture and landscape of the Mississippian chiefdoms encountered by Soto and Moscoso. The preexisting conditions of a highly competitive geopolitical landscape made Native American groups in the Yazoo Basin resistant to early encounters with Spanish conquistadors but vulnerable to the aftermath of contact in the longer run. These impacts unfolded over several generations after the Soto and Moscoso expeditions, and these lasting impacts were far greater than the relatively ephemeral and intermittent presence of Spanish conquistadors in only some areas of the Yazoo Basin itself.

The Apalachee Province and Mission Settlements in La Florida

The case of the Yazoo Basin demonstrates the long-term impacts on Native American chiefdoms of relatively short-term contact with Spanish conquistadors. Northern Florida was a setting both for recurrent and relatively prolonged encounters between Apalachee and Spanish conquistadors in the 1500s and for more sustained interactions between the Apalachee and Spanish mission communities in the 1600s. During the 1400s and 1500s, one of the major Mississippian mound centers in northern Florida was the Lake Jackson site, an important conduit for circulation of marine shell from the Gulf Coast and copper from the southern Appalachians (Blitz and Lorenz 2006:133–134; Scarry 1994b, 1996b). Mississippian populations in the Tallahassee Hills region were quite high, with evidence for large-scale surpluses generated through the cultivation of maize and other crops and pronounced status differentiation in mortuary practices. The regional settlement hierarchy includes small farmsteads, larger rural hamlets, sites with single platform mounds, and the major multimound center at the Lake Jackson site (Scarry 1990:238). The productivity and prosperity of this region drew in sixteenth-century Spanish conquistadors and supported the development of Apalachee chiefdoms that mounted stiff resistance to those entradas.

The agricultural potential of the Apalachee province encouraged seventeenth-century Spanish mission settlements (Hann and McEwan 1998).

The Apalachee played decisive roles in shaping the course of Spanish colonial history in the Southeast (Hann 1988, 1994). Apalachee warriors battled the Pánfilo de Narváez expedition in 1528 and drove the expedition to the Gulf Coast, from which point Álvar Nuñez Cabeza de Vaca launched his epic journey. Apalachee warriors met the Soto expedition with stiff resistance in the winter of 1539 and 1540 and periodically harassed the Soto winter encampment at Anhaica (Hudson 1997; Milanich 1990). Spanish colonists did not revisit the Apalachee province in great numbers again for four to five generations, when the first of several Catholic missions were established beginning in 1633, first at Anhaica, and then, in 1656, at San Luis (Ewen 1990, 1996). Not surprisingly, all of these sites were located close to each other and close to the Lake Jackson mound site, the dominant geopolitical center within the Apalachee province during late prehistory (Scarry 1994b, 1996b). Thousands of Apalachees converted to Catholicism, motivated in part by disease epidemics that challenged traditional Native American ceremonialism and perhaps motivated as well by the perceived benefits of alliances with Spanish conquistadors and colonists. The numbers of and diversity of Spanish goods in the house of the Apalachee chief at San Luis, and the absence of such items in the adjacent Apalachee council house, demonstrate the interests of the Apalachee chief in acquiring Spanish goods and the cultural conservatism that persisted in some aspects of public life in the Apalachee community. The presence of a Catholic church and Christian crosses beside an Apalachee plaza, ball pole, and council house collectively form a blend of Apalachee and Spanish architecture and built environment and a setting in which cultural differences were visibly emphasized.

Cherokee Towns and Indirect Contact

Whereas the Apalachee province was a setting for direct contact and sustained interaction between Spanish colonists and Native Americans in La Florida in the 1500s and 1600s, some groups were situated at points more removed from early European exploration routes and colonial outpost, including Cherokee towns in the relatively remote and rugged mountain ranges of the southern Appalachians, situated along the headwaters of the Savannah and Tennessee Rivers. In 1567 leaders of Cherokee towns visited the Spanish conquistador Juan Pardo at the town of Joara, which was the location of the Spanish colonial outpost of Cuenca and Fort San Juan, in the upper Catawba Valley of western North Carolina (Beck and Moore 2002; Beck et al. 2006, 2010, 2016; Booker et al. 1992;

Hudson 2005; Moore 2002). In 1693 leaders of Cherokee towns visited Charles Town to complain about slave raids on Cherokee towns; by 1698 there were trade relations between many Cherokee towns and English traders from South Carolina and Virginia; by 1711 the South Carolina colony had established formal trading posts in Cherokee town areas (Boulware 2011; Duncan and Riggs 2003; Goodwin 1977; Hatley 1993; Hill 1997; Schroedl 2000; Smith 1979). During the eighteenth century, some Cherokee towns favored alliances and trade relations with the British and others with the French, comparable to factionalism and strategies of diplomatic pluralism within Chickasaw, Choctaw, and Creek towns and within the Natchez chiefdom.

Given this timeline, direct and sustained interaction with Europeans began later in Cherokee towns than it did in other areas, but early stages of European colonialism in the Southeast did have an impact on life in Cherokee towns at an early date. Spanish conquistadors did not travel directly through core areas of Cherokee towns, which did not experience the same upheavals as the provinces and polities of Coosa and Cofitachequi during the sixteenth century. Warriors from Northern Iroquoian villages raided Cherokee towns during the 1600s and 1700s, and there were cycles of warfare and diplomacy between Cherokee and Creek towns during the eighteenth century.

These and other forces acted upon life in Cherokee towns from afar. One such impact was change in the supply of marine shell. During late prehistory, marine shell circulated north and inland from the Gulf Coast toward the Etowah mound center, and copper from the southern Appalachians moved south, toward the Lake Jackson mounds in the Apalachee province (King 2003a, 2003b; Scarry 1990, 1994b, 1996a). Marine shell was transported to areas along the headwaters of the Tennessee and Savannah Rivers as raw material to produce shell beads and gorgets, in the form of finished beads and gorgets, or both (Hally 2007; Smith and Smith 1989; Sullivan 2007). Some of the most recent archaeological examples of burials with such items are found at the Coweeta Creek site, in southwestern North Carolina, where shell mask gorgets were buried with some young adults and children, shell ear pins were buried with several adults, and an engraved rattlesnake gorget was buried with a male elder, whose burial was the setting for a hearth at a later date (Rodning 2009a, 2009b, 2010a, 2011, 2015). Such items became less and less common during the 1600s and 1700s, perhaps because of disruption and destabilization in and around the sources of marine shell itself, including the Gulf Coast, and the emergent role of European items as status goods within the Native American Southeast (Worth 2002).

As Gregory Waselkov (1989) and Marvin Smith (1987) have noted, metal items circulated through networks of interaction and exchange in the Southeast that were formerly conduits for the movement of copper and shell. People living in Cherokee town areas had already had access to marine shell before European contact. During the seventeenth century, however, both shell and metal were less accessible. Developments at distant points in the Southeast impacted ceremonial life at this Cherokee town and probably at other towns as well.

In many respects, people in the Cherokee town at Coweeta Creek lived everyday life much as ancestral Cherokee generations did (Dickens 1976, 1978, 1979; Keel 1976; Rodning 2015). They cultivated maize, beans, and squash; hunted deer, bear, and turkey; made pottery and stone tools similar to those that are typical throughout the greater southern Appalachians during late prehistory; conducted public events in a townhouse and plaza; and had household dwellings and domestic activity areas situated around the edges of the plaza. The plaza itself was a setting for casual social gatherings and interaction within the community on most days and periodically a more formal setting for important dances and other rituals. The sequence of building and rebuilding the townhouse at Coweeta Creek created a mound, and this architectural history of the townhouse probably represents a typical pattern at Cherokee town sites. Houses and households were spatial and social domains closely associated with women, given the matrilineal kinship system and matrilocal residence patterns typical of Cherokee towns. Some men became prominent as town leaders, and some male elders probably spent a great deal of time in and around the townhouse, tending the townhouse fire and participating in other events important to Cherokee public life. Concentrations of burials in and around houses and townhouses connected household and community members to preceding generations. The past was always present in the built environment of the Cherokee town at Coweeta Creek.

In other respects, life in the town at Coweeta Creek was different than it had been before. People had access to new items like glass beads, kaolin clay pipes, and some metal implements, although such items probably had greater ceremonial than utilitarian significance (Rodning 2010b). The presence of a redstone calumet pipe fragment at Coweeta Creek demonstrates that life in the local community was affected by broader networks of interaction and exchange connecting this town to others across a large swath of eastern North America (Rodning 2014).

The Natchez, Taensa, and French Contact in La Louisiane

An important source of calumet ceremonialism for Native American groups in eastern North America was the Mississippi Valley (Brown 2006; Hall 1997), home to diverse communities and speakers of several languages, including the Natchez in southwestern Mississippi and the Taensas in northeastern Louisiana (Barnett 2007; Brown 1989; Ethridge 2010; Lorenz 2000). During the early eighteenth century, shortly after early episodes of French contact and six to seven generations after Spanish contact, the Natchez and Taensas lived in spatially dispersed settlements, with mounds constructed as community centers. Written accounts demonstrate pronounced status differences between chiefs and commoners in these communities (Kidder 1998). The Natchez may have been descendants of the powerful chiefdom of Quigualtam, and Natchez chiefs may have ascended to power in part because of the instability generated by mid-sixteenth-century Spanish entradas (Mehta 2013). The most powerful Natchez town during the early 1700s was the Grand Village of the Natchez, located at the Fatherland site; but, interestingly, the sizes of the mounds at Fatherland and the scale of the site as a whole are considerably smaller than nearby earthworks such as those at the Anna and Emerald sites (Brain 1978; I. W. Brown 1990; J. A. Brown 1990; Lorenz 1997; Steponaitis 1986). Large mound centers such as Raffman, Routh, Fitzhugh, and Transylvania dominated the landscape of northeastern Louisiana during late prehistory, although the chronology of components at these sites that may date to the Contact period is currently not well known (Kidder 1998:143–148).

Following early encounters and interactions with French explorers and traders, settlement in Natchez towns by Catholic missionaries, and the spread of English trade networks across the Southeast in the late seventeenth century, factionalism developed within and between Natchez towns in support of alliances with French or English colonists. This factionalism pervaded life within Natchez towns from the late seventeenth century through the Natchez Revolt of 1729, the movement of the Natchez from the Grand Village to the Natchez Fort site on the west side of the river, and decisive retaliatory raids by the French in 1731, which prompted Natchez survivors to seek refuge among Chickasaw, Choctaw, and Cherokee towns.

Neither the Natchez nor Taensa chiefdoms persisted past the early eighteenth century, but perhaps the dispersed settlement patterns in northeastern Louisiana and southwestern Mississippi conferred some resilience on groups in these areas during the period between Spanish and French contact. Large and dense settlements in the northern Yazoo Basin were largely abandoned by the 1600s and perhaps as early as the late 1500s (Brain 1978; Brown 2008). More spatially dispersed communities—perhaps with less rigidity in political centralization and social hierarchy than those in areas further upstream—may have favored greater stability in Mississippian societies of southwestern Mississippi and northeastern Louisiana in the immediate aftermath of Spanish contact.

Conclusions

One of the challenges in studying the Contact period in the Southeast and other areas is that everyday life for particular people at particular places was shaped both by local history and local forces as well as the increasingly global forces of change that affected both Native American peoples and European colonists. For the Contact period, everyday life was affected by microscale and macroscale trends and by both long-term history and shorter-term occurrences and events. The effects of entanglements with European colonists and European goods were diverse, especially when comparing cases of direct and indirect contact (Smith 1987, 2002), although networks of trade and exchange connected Native American groups across the Southeast and created conduits for the effects of European exploration and colonialism to spread widely and rapidly (Waselkov 1989, 2006). Different kinds of contact, and the localized manifestations and effects of distant developments within the cultural landscape of the Southeast, probably often seemed unpredictable and even random from any given vantage point. From the perspective of the broader cultural system of the colonial Southeast as a whole, and the global system of which it was a part, developments during the Contact period may often have been locally unpredictable, but they were not random and were guided in part by the "initial conditions" of the Mississippian world. These characteristics of the post-Contact Southeast are analogous to the properties of chaotic systems. Chaos theory thus offers an interpretive framework that merits further consideration in the study of colonial encounters and entanglements in the American South and elsewhere. This approach is compatible with recent characterizations of the protohistoric Southeast as a "shatter zone," in reference to a fractured geopolitical landscape in which the "ripple effects" of widespread political destabilization emanated across large areas (Ethridge 2006, 2010; Marcoux 2010:30; Worth 2007:xiii), affecting politics and the economy as well as domestic life. European contact led to rapid changes in the geopolitical landscape and political economy of the Southeast. Domestic life and the domestic economy also changed, as trade networks were established, new forms of warfare and diplomacy were developed, and new crops and livestock were introduced. At first, however, many aspects of everyday life—farming, hunting, gathering, food preparation, tool production, craft production—probably were similar to those from before European contact.

During the sixteenth century, the Mississippian cultural system in the Native American Southeast encompassed different communities and polities, but that entire system was altered by the introduction of Europeans and European goods. Variation in the "initial conditions" of that system shaped the course of culture change in the Southeast and the development of the "shatter zone" in the aftermath of European contact. The ability of powerful chiefs and chiefdoms in the Lower Mississippi to mobilize large numbers of warriors and large resource surpluses made them resistant to early Spanish contacts but vulnerable to collapse in the longer run. By contrast, there was less direct contact between European colonists during the 1500s and 1600s in Cherokee town areas of the southern Appalachians, which stayed more intact through the early eighteenth century. For the Apalachee and the Natchez, different episodes of contact with Spanish and French colonists presented both challenges and opportunities. Pronounced differences in power and status within Apalachee and Natchez chiefdoms shaped cycles of alliance and rivalry between Native American chiefs and Spanish colonists in these and other areas of the American South.

The study of Native American culture change after European contact is sometimes framed as a study of how Native American groups responded to both the challenges and opportunities posed by colonial entanglements and access to European goods. Indeed, they did respond and pursued their own interests and agendas through relations with European colonists. However, variation in the initial conditions of life in the Mississippian Southeast—that is, outcomes of long-term cultural and historical developments that predate European contact—also significantly shaped the shorter-term changes that took place after European contact. Applying chaos theory to the study of the protohistoric Native American Southeast foregrounds the importance of Native American prehistory as a force of change in the post-Contact period. Chaos theory also challenges us to consider how developments at many different loci throughout the Southeast affected the everyday lives of people at other sites and in other areas, in ways that probably seemed unpredictable and periodically random when considered from local scales but were not random from the perspective of an increasingly global colonial system.

One of the challenges in exploring the applicability of chaos theory to culture change in the Native American Southeast is connecting broad-scale system-wide patterns to practices of everyday life at particular places. We think these efforts can enrich our understanding of how people navigated the "chaos" (in the sense of disorder and confusion) that was unleashed by European contact. We encourage further consideration of these issues through the study of individual sites and comparative analyses of datasets from sites in different areas of the Southeast.

Acknowledgments

Thanks to Philip Carr and Sarah Price for the invitation to participate in the "Everyday Matters" symposium at the Southeastern Archaeological Conference (SEAC) in 2015 and to contribute to this volume. We appreciate comments and contributions from Carr, Price, Ken Sassaman, Charlie Cobb, Robbie Ethridge, Rob Beck, David Moore, Victor Thompson, Jen Birch, and anonymous reviewers. We are grateful for support from the Department of Anthropology, the Center for Archaeology, the New Orleans Center for the Gulf South, the Middle American Research Institute, the Committee on Research, and the School of Liberal Arts at Tulane University; the Louisiana Division of Archaeology; the Mississippi Department of Archives and History; the Center for Archaeological Studies at the University of Mississippi; the Department of Anthropology at the University of Alabama; and the Department of Anthropology, Research Laboratories of Anthropology, and Center for the Study of the American South at the University of North Carolina at Chapel Hill. The lead author takes responsibility for any problems or shortcomings with this chapter.

4

Community Practice in a Post-Removal Cherokee Town

LANCE GREENE

During the last 50 years, archaeologists have spilled a considerable amount of ink theorizing about artifacts, decoding their functional, political, and symbolic meanings. As Pluckhahn et al. (Chapter 9) state in their chapter on prehistoric craft production, however, most activity was "rooted in the everyday rhythms of domestic life." It is ironic that a field of study largely devoted to the remnants of everyday life in the past rarely explicitly investigates the actual people who created those remnants. For me, this is a major part of the problem that Price and Carr (Chapter 15) see as a "crisis of relevance" in archaeology. I see this crisis as involving two closely associated issues: the lack of discussion about those actual people and the narrow audiences that we try to reach. The vast majority of archaeological writing is academic, written for specialists, and published in journals and books with limited exposure. While public archaeology has become much more widespread over the past decade, it is largely limited to on-site education. This has proved a meaningful change in educating the public and creating more interest in archaeology. But very little education is provided in written form. This problem has become even more profound with the rise of popular "digging" shows and related productions on pseudoscientific topics such as aliens, which garner public interest. The relative silence of professional archaeologists is detrimental both to the archaeological record and to our profession. We need to convince the public that the archaeological record is worth protecting and that the lives of past people are valuable and interesting. One way to do this is to discuss the lives of those people, to make them relatable to the reader, to create a narrative that engages the nonspecialist.

Alternative forms of writing, such as historical fiction, can help address these shortcomings. In this volume Hollenbach and Carmody, Dumas, and Walker successfully use the genre to personalize people and animals that lived in the past and to create new questions about how they lived their lives. In this chapter I use historical fiction, based on archaeological and historical data, to describe a single event in the lives of a Cherokee family in the wake of Removal and to elicit new research questions not considered through traditional forms of research. In addition to helping solve some of the issues of archaeology's crisis of relevance, I argue, historical fiction can also serve as a method of research, helping to identify new questions and therefore enabling us to create a richer and more detailed account of past lives. Writing fiction forces an author to create an unbroken narrative, to dwell on details of characters, behaviors, and materials.

Archaeologists (and others) pose several potential uses for fictional writing, for both academic and popular audiences. These include "bringing historical characters to life," giving agency to individuals and communities in the past, and humanizing historical events or periods. Some archaeologists have also argued that fiction has another potential use that applies to archaeological research. Fiction potentially raises questions that archaeologists have not considered, by requiring us to describe events, tasks, and interactions in detail.

Many critics argue that fiction can never provide historical fact or truth. In response, proponents have argued that more standard approaches to archaeological research cannot provide fact either and that fiction, when written with the same rigor, can provide significant insight. As Teresita Majewski (2000:19) stated: "Archaeologists rarely, if ever, know with certainty that their reconstructions of past lifeways are accurate, even if 'scientific' methods are used to construct them . . . we are all storytellers to some degree." Proponents of the genre see it as an accompaniment to more traditional forms of research, not as a replacement.

Archaeologists have employed interpretive historical fiction for decades. James Deetz (1977) presented a series of brief vignettes in his book *In Small Things Forgotten: The Archaeology of Early American Life*. These glimpses into past lives, as well as Deetz's readable prose, have made this one of the most popular archaeology books on the market. Janet Spector (1993) published *What This Awl Means: Feminist Archaeology at a Wahpeton Dakota Village*, which describes excavations at the mid-nineteenth century Dakota village site of Little Rapids in Minnesota. Spector spent considerable time pursuing methods of research and writing not commonly used in archaeological research. Spector (1993:1) noted that, while writing the book, "I was reminded of my original reasons for wanting to be an archaeologist. These motives are empathetic—a longing to discover essences, images, and feelings of the past—not detached, distanced, objective."

During her work at the site, Spector's crew discovered an intricately carved bone-awl handle. During her subsequent review of the archaeological literature, she found these kinds of artifacts summarily dismissed, placed under headings such as "Maintenance and Repair" (Stone 1974 in Spector 1993). She also found that European items, such as brass awl tips, were given much more discussion than the carved bone handles, thereby valuing items of European over Native American production. This led her to write a fictional narrative focusing on a Dakota girl and the events that led up to her losing her cherished bone awl. In the account she describes the significance of these items, which served as ways in which girls and women could document the things that they had accomplished and the skills that they had acquired. By delving into the primary historical literature, she found that the women were often quite competitive with skills such as sewing. This competitiveness is expressed in her narrative, questioning common assumptions about the role of women in that society.

Spector (1993:34) also discusses the tendency of archaeological publications to be dry and boring and criticizes archaeologists for not paying close attention to what she terms the "political implications of their writing styles." In particular, she argues that detached, descriptive styles of writing can dehumanize the people we study and that we should not see these as the only legitimate form of writing. Spector argues that we should create a space for other forms of rhetoric.

In 1997 Mary Praetzellis and Adrian Praetzellis organized a symposium on storytelling at the Society for Historical Archaeology (SHA) conference, the contents of which were published a year later in the SHA journal, *Historical Archaeology*. One of the participants, Daniel Mouer (1998), wrote a fictional piece about a late-seventeenth-century backcountry Virginia plantation. His fictional petition from William Harris to the governor was written using the language of the period and was based on primary documents and on his own archaeological excavations at the Curles Plantation in Henrico County. After writing the piece, Mouer (1998:9) found that it revealed "how little we know of language, costume, gesture, or other aspects of daily social life on late seventeenth-century Virginia's frontier." What Mouer found is potentially one of the most exciting strengths regarding fictional writing: the ability to enhance our knowledge and interpretations of past lives.

Fictional narratives provide other potential benefits. As Spector found, they can help place emphasis on Native American peoples or other groups or segments of past populations that have suffered a loss of history or incorrect histories based on western concepts of race or gender. Fiction can stimulate curiosity and provide a more intimate sense of a culture.

The Welch Family and Welch's Town History

To investigate the use of fictional writing, I use the Welch house site as a case study. The Welch family lived in southwestern North Carolina, in the mountainous northeastern corner of the Cherokee Nation (Figure 4.1). John Welch was a

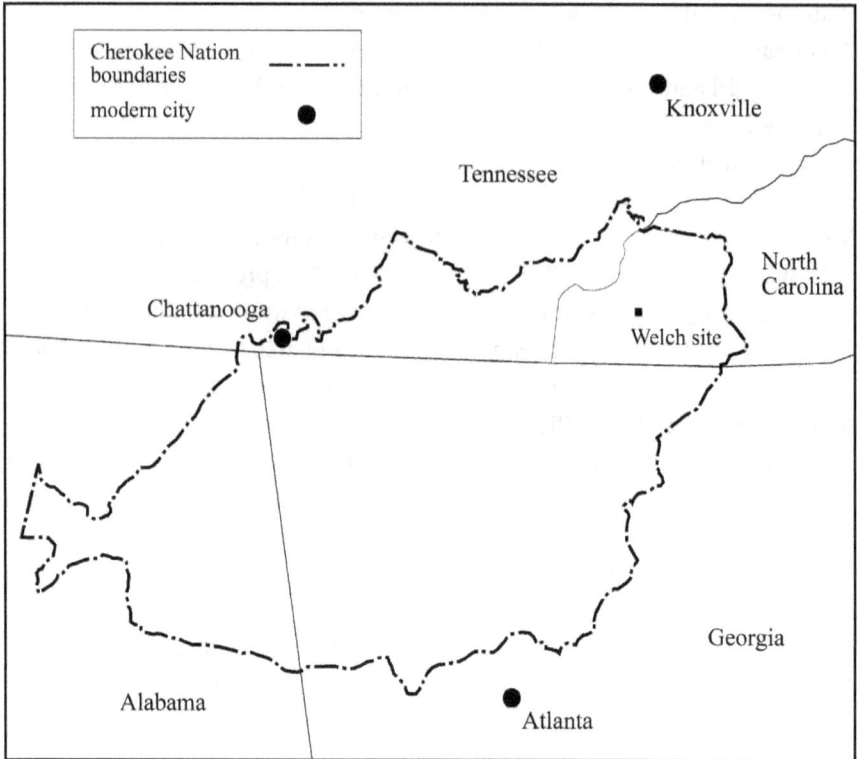

Figure 4.1. Location of the Welch site.

Cherokee man and his wife, Betty, a white woman. They owned a large plantation in the 1830s. Because of their wealth and the presence of a white person
in the family, the Welches could have survived the Removal in 1838 relatively
unaffected. But they risked everything by providing aid to the Cherokees hiding
in the mountains.

By the spring of 1838 over 7,000 federal and state troops were stationed in the
Cherokee Nation to prepare for the forced removal of the Cherokees west of the
Mississippi River. The mountainous section of southwestern North Carolina was
the home of the most traditional and, from the army's perspective, most dangerous communities in the Cherokee Nation (Finger 1984). While most Cherokees
in the region did not contemplate armed resistance, they did envision avoiding
Removal. Many Cherokee families had decided to remain in the area and had
made their plans. Roughly four hundred Cherokees in the region hid out in the
steep mountains during the summer and fall of 1838. Many died from starvation
and disease, but these groups successfully waited out the army.

In response to the Welch's assistance to "fugitive" Cherokees, the army placed John Welch in solitary confinement for four months, pilfered the Welch farm, and imprisoned their nine enslaved African Americans in a prisoner of war camp. Three of them died there, including a young woman named Nelly and her newborn baby. She left behind a young daughter, Jane. John Welch survived his imprisonment but never fully recovered; he was permanently blind and physically disabled. After the Removal, the Cherokees who remained in the mountains found themselves in a marginalized space. They were unsure of their status regarding citizenship and land tenure, and many local whites were unhappy with a continued Cherokee presence (Finger 1984).

Most of the Cherokees who remained in North Carolina after Removal settled in one of several discrete communities, most of which had a wealthy patron who owned enough land for them to live on. The Welch family served in this role. For years John had served as a headman for the small traditional communities along the Valley River, although the Welches operated a large plantation there. As I mentioned earlier, however, they risked everything by providing aid to the Cherokees hiding in the mountains.

The Welches served as patrons for around one hundred of these Cherokees. They were forced to repurchase their land at a state auction. By doing so, however, they created a safe haven not only for themselves but for over a dozen Cherokee families. From 1839 until 1855 they supported a traditional Cherokee community, known as Welch's Town, on their land. While the Welches operated an upland South plantation along the Valley River, hidden from view in the uplands was a traditional Cherokee town, which included a townhouse, stickball field, and dance grounds (Barnard 1840; Thomas 1840).

Archaeology of the Welch Plantation

I use theories of hybridity to investigate the Welch family and their actions (Card 2013). Betty and John moved to the property in the early 1820s, and Betty lived there until her death in the 1880s. During this sixty-year period, the family interacted with people from a variety of racial, ethnic, and class backgrounds. I argue that they were able to maintain their plantation during this period because of their ability to adapt a hybrid culture that drew from traditional Cherokee culture and embraced a capitalist ethic.

The Welch house site was located on a prominent knoll overlooking the Valley River. In 2004 I excavated a small block area and exposed three aligned cellar pits that were subjacent to an external kitchen described by the army in 1837 as part of the Welch plantation complex (Figure 4.2; also see Greene 2009). Each pit feature contained three or four well-defined strata. The material assemblage from all feature contexts included 981 identifiable artifacts (as well as unidentified fragments of iron). The majority of these artifacts (n = 642, 65 percent) were associated with food production and serving. A total of 563 (57 percent) were ceramic sherds, including whitewares, yellowwares, and alkaline-glazed stonewares. Vessel forms include plates, cups, saucers, bowls, platters, mugs, and several other forms. Decorative styles include shell-edged, hand-painted, transfer-printed, sponge-decorated, and dipped. The minimum number of vessels (MNV) was 108, and several ceramic refits were found in the various strata and pits. Numerous pieces of flatware were recovered, including two- and three-tined forks, table knives, and spoons. Glasswares include bottle, vial, and tumbler fragments.

Floral and faunal remains were numerous and well preserved. The faunal assemblage has a number of identified specimens (NISP) of 1,099. The variety of food remains includes wild and domesticated species: cow, pig, chicken,

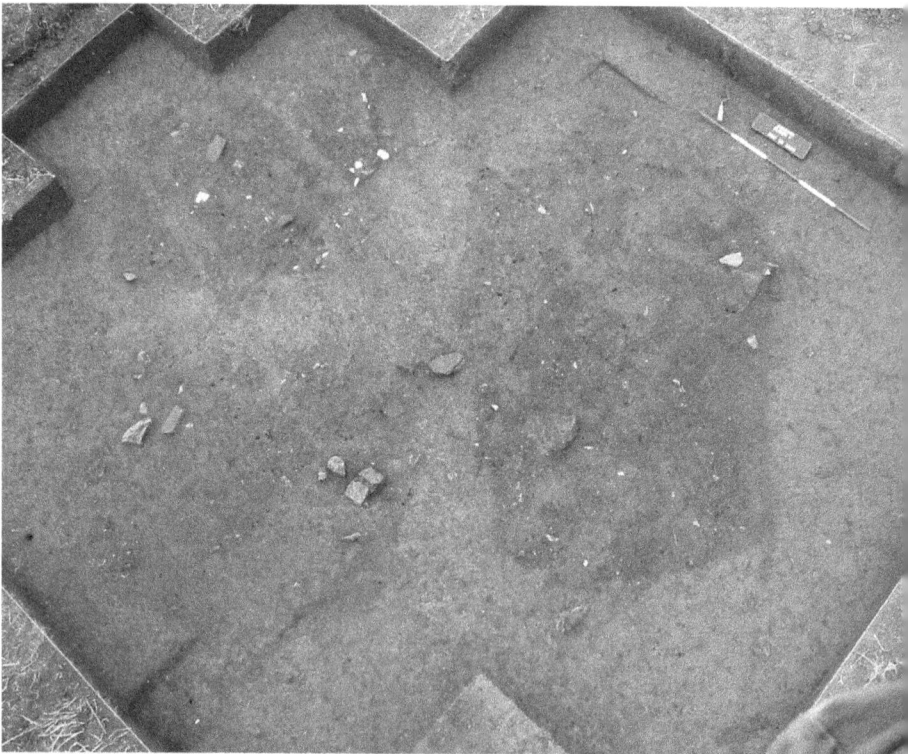

Figure 4.2. Three cellar pits adjacent to the external kitchen at the Welch site.

white-tailed deer, black bear, squirrel, raccoon, rabbit, turkey, and largemouth bass as well as wheat, rye, corn, beans, squash, chestnuts, hazelnuts, blueberries, mulberries, and grapes. The Welch family supplied the domesticated foods from their plantation, while the members of Welch's Town brought with them the wild foods that they had gathered from the mountains.

The food remains provide additional information about the activities that resulted in their accumulation. Seasonality data place the backfilling of the features in November or December. Roughly two dozen fragments of long bones, from cow and other large mammals, were crushed and chopped with an ax and boiled. This was a traditional Cherokee practice, used to get marrow as well as meat from the bone. Each soil zone contained a unique assemblage of organic remains. For example, Zone 3 of Feature 1 contained the remains of several largemouth basses and a brass pin that had been converted into a fishhook. Zone 2 of Feature 1 contained the remains of several wild rabbits and seven pieces of lead shot. Although the faunal material was well preserved, only five fragments showed evidence of gnawing by dogs or rodents.

Several aspects of the material assemblage suggest that it represents a single short-term communal event. There was a small percentage of nonkitchen or dining artifacts; large, diverse assemblages of floral and faunal remains and ceramics and utensils; discrete assemblages of artifacts and food remains in each soil stratum; numerous ceramic refits from different strata; and a small number of gnaw marks in the faunal assemblage. I argue that the artifacts and organic remains represent a communal event that included a labor project—tearing down the old kitchen and constructing a new kitchen ell—and a feast. These kinds of events were part of traditional Cherokee culture in the mountains, predating European contact. Formal community organizations included the *gadugi* or communal work party. These events included feasting and labor and sometimes late-night traditional dances (Fogelson and Kutsche 1961).

Such events are well documented in Cherokee history, including from the Valley River area. Two decades after the three cellar pits were filled, William Holland Thomas, a leader of the Qualla Town Cherokees nearby, asked Cherokees to bring food and work tools to a council meeting. Thomas wrote:

> Such of you people as wish to do so are requested to meet your brethren of Qualla Town and me in council in the Fork of Nantahala and Tennessee [Rivers] on the 2[?]d of this month. Please bring with you three days rations of Cawosatih or Parched meal, venison, broadswords composed of beans and meal. I would take it as a favor if you would bring me some bear meat & deer meat, turkies, squirels for myself and wife and such lawyers

as may come with me. Also come prepared with arms of the following description. Matocks, axes, hoes, shovels, etc. to aid in opening the road so that the carriages can pass. On the day of the council a beef will be barbecued to eat with the bear meat and venison, and at night it is designed to have an old fashioned dance with Tarapin [*sic*] shells. (Thomas 1871)

Here we see that these kinds of communal events continued well into the nineteenth century. The foods that Cherokees brought to the meeting were very similar to what we see in the Welch faunal assemblage.

The army described the Welch residence as a one-and-a-half story log house with an older, smaller external kitchen nearby (Welch and Jarrett 1837). A map of the area made in 1860 to record possible gold deposits along the valley shows the Welch house (Blake 1860). Here there is a kitchen ell attached. Sometime between 1838 and 1860 the old kitchen was dismantled and a kitchen ell was built onto the house. The terminal date of ceramics and other artifacts is roughly 1850, placing the backfilling episode between these two dates. I argue that the communal event was tied to a project that involved dismantling the old kitchen and constructing a new kitchen ell on the back of the house. John Welch died in June 1852, about the time the cellars were backfilled (Welch 1855). The communal event occurred in November or December. It might have occurred near the end of his life or just after he died.

In my fictional account he is still alive, although blind and barely able to walk. The segment of the account that I present begins with the Cherokees of Welch's Town walking to the plantation to begin the task of dismantling the kitchen, largely performed by the men, and preparing a variety of foods in the yard, largely performed by women. The entire population of those living on Welch land (the Welches, the members of Welch's Town, and the enslaved African Americans) are participants in the narrative.

Fictional Account

On the chosen day, most of Welch's Town came to the farmhouse. Chinoque and Liddy Owl led the largest group from the small cluster of cabins on Townhouse Branch. The Axe and Aqualla walked with their children—Salkana, Nelly, Ihuhy, Eteganah, and George—and their families, some of whom lived close by, on Welch's Mill Creek. In all, there were over 50 people, young and old, from the scattered cabins of Welch's Town. They had lived here for just over a decade on Welch land, and the small community was growing. They brought with them food collected in the mountains.

Betty had prepared for their arrival. The area behind the old kitchen was set up for cooking on a large scale—massive cast iron pots and kettles were hanging over cooking fires. Piles of firewood bordered the area, and tools had been set out around the kitchen. Stacks of colorful dishes brought from the kitchen had been put on a long table near the back of the house. Betty had her slaves working on that. She depended on Phillis, whom they had owned almost as long as Isaac. Phillis had been preparing nonstop, cleaning out every item from the old kitchen and bringing up plenty of food from the large new cellar under the main house. Phillis's baby was not a year old and required more care than most her age. Phillis had Jane helping her, mostly by keeping the baby while she cleaned or hauled food. Phillis loved Jane as she loved her own daughters; she was the only thing left to remind Phillis of Nelly. Jane couldn't remember her mother, and Phillis often described Nelly's funny ways, which had always made her laugh.

Just cleaning out the old kitchen had taken most of the previous day. Most numerous were the items used in cooking for the three dozen or so people on the plantation. The dishes—blue-rimmed plates, delicate red, green, and blue hand-painted bowls and cups, and sponge-patterned saucers—were stacked and moved carefully to the main house. The heavy stoneware crocks used to store fruit through the winter and the stoneware butter churns were carried to the barn or into the house. Women had spent untold hours there, churning the fresh buttermilk into cream and butter; they made good money selling butter in Murphy, although not nearly as much as they made selling homemade clothing. Countless other items for cooking and serving food, the glassware and utensils, tinware cups and bowls, and a large tin coffeepot were all moved to the main house until the new kitchen could be stocked. Several rough chairs scattered around the dark kitchen provided a space for women to sit and sew. The fireplace and a candle in a brass candlestand that sat on a small table didn't provide much light. They talked as they worked, and the small items they were working with in the dark and smoky room often slipped from their fingers. Brass pins, bone buttons for rough work clothes and brass buttons for jackets, and tiny brass hooks for clasping handmade dresses all fell onto the uneven puncheon floor. The split-log floorboards were old and sagging, and gaps had opened up between them. Hooks and pins that fell through the large cracks could not be recovered and were forgotten. In this old kitchen, all of the women living on the plantation worked at tasks as long as there was daylight. Mostly they talked in English. Neither Phillis nor the younger slaves spoke Cherokee very well, and the Welch women spoke English as easily as they spoke Cherokee. After dinner, the Welches would return to the main house. Phillis and her daughters would continue working into the evening. At one time Nelly had kept her company, but that was before the army marched them all across the mountains to the prison camp.

Early the next morning, the women built and maintained the fires in the yard and began preparing an astonishing variety of foods. Betty was in charge of organizing the food preparation, but she, like everyone else, deferred to Aqualla, who gave orders to the younger women. They would keep the fires burning and the pots cooking for the next two days.

People huddled around the smoky fires, thinking about the work ahead of them. They roasted and boiled several kinds of meat: beef, pork, chicken, turkey, and domesticated rabbit. During the fall, the people in Welch's Town had been tending the Welch cattle and hogs in the mountains, where they fattened on mast, thick beds of acorns and chestnuts. A cow had been butchered for the occasion, and the beef was boiled. Chinoque chopped the limbs into pieces with an ax and crushed the dense long bones with a hammer. He then chopped the limbs into even smaller pieces. The women dumped these into the large cast-iron kettle with the other pieces where they simmered all day. Chinoque had learned this method from his parents and grandparents. They had done it with deer, cooking the broken limbs for hours in handmade pots. This way they got all of the marrow. Its fat was needed to survive harsh winters. Chinoque, like others his age, had found that it worked just as well with cows and pigs, although whites who saw the practice refused to try it.

Betty had selected several chickens and turkeys from their fowl yard and rabbits from the hutch. She preferred the domesticated European rabbits, which grew larger, to the wild cottontail rabbits that were native to the area. She had Phillis bring out corn from the crib and beans, apples, and peaches from the cellars. Betty had bought rice from Thomas's store; it couldn't be grown in the mountains but was a regular import from the Lowcountry. She also bought coffee beans, and a large tin coffeepot was kept full all day. The women of Welch's Town prepared fires to cook other kinds of foods. They had brought white-tailed deer, wild rabbit, raccoon and squirrel, wild greens, and nuts.

As the wind carried the heavy smell of wood smoke mixed with the scents of numerous dishes, the men faced the most difficult part of their job: dismantling and moving the large hewn logs that made up the walls of the structure. The logs had been set in place 30 years before and had settled and been sealed together with years of chinking—clay used to fill the gaps between the logs, hardened by long exposure to sunlight. Many of the logs were still in good shape and would be reused. John and Isaac had originally hewn and notched them by hand to fit one on top of the other, and Ned carefully marked them with a thick pencil carved out of talc. The old puncheon floor, which was worn and rotted in places, was discarded. A plank floor would be built in the new kitchen.

The new kitchen would be a single room, with the same dimensions as the old one, built onto the back of the main house. Although it was not far from the site of the old kitchen, John Cobb and Chinoque harnessed two horses to drag the logs to the back of the house. New logs that had already been cut were placed on flat pier stones collected from the banks of the Valley River, raising the entire structure off the ground. In this way, the addition would last longer.

If it had been warmer, there might have been a stickball game and dancing. The evening chill was already setting in, though, and people mingled around various fires and in the house. Several men gathered around one of the fires, which had been stoked high with old wooden shingles to provide warmth against the cold. Each took out a small bluish-green stone pipe. Many had carved their own from small cobbles gathered at outcroppings of pipestone along nearby creek banks. Others had purchased theirs from Thomas's store for a quarter. They talked as they smoked, first discussing the progress of the work so far. Cherokee was the first language for all in the group and the only language that all the older men spoke. John would normally have been inside already on such a cold night, but he would not miss the chance to visit with so many old friends and hear news and maybe some of the old stories.

Like John, Eteganah loved the old stories. He was a good storyteller. His favorites were the "wonder stories" that told of monsters and spirits. He began to recite the story of Tlanusiyi and the Great Leech. They all had heard it before but loved the story when told by a good teller. John loved this one especially, because it had all happened so close by. Tlanusiyi, the "Leech place," was only about ten miles downstream, at the mouth of Valley River. There was a deep hole where the river emptied into the Hiwassee, with a large rock ledge running beside it, across the riverbed. No one walked across that ledge. Too many had been carried off by the Great Leech, red and white striped and as big as a house, diving down into the hole in the rock and sending up such a plume of water that people were knocked into the hole. Their mutilated bodies were found later along the riverbank.

By the time Eteganah had finished his story, John noticed the cold seeping through his frail, stiffened body. He tried to stand but lost his footing and dropped his pipe. It fell with a sharp clink, as it landed on a large cobble laid against the fire. John slowly crouched and picked up the small object. He looked at it and saw the large chip knocked out of the polished bowl. Muttering quietly, he hesitated and then tossed the pipe into the fire.

The work continued for three days. After the old kitchen was dismantled and the new kitchen ell complete, the last thing to do was fill in the three open cellars that had been beneath the old kitchen, now a hazard. The clutter of the last three days, ashes, food remains, broken pottery and glass, and bent nails were dumped in, load by load. People shoveled the waste into large handmade baskets, made by the women of Welch's Town and traded to the Welches. Thick beds of ashes still smoldered in some baskets. At the same time, children swept the entire yard. The ground around the pits, which had been under the old structure for 30 years, was thick with debris; lost pins and buttons, broken pieces of pottery and utensils, and discarded pieces of tin were swept in. Later the holes were capped with fresh dirt. The area of the old kitchen was transformed into part of the swept yard of the main house, with the fill and trash in the old cellars eventually becoming hard-packed, invisible, and forgotten.

Conclusions

I wrote the fictional account after several years of historical and archaeological research on the Welch family. In some ways I used it as a method to test my knowledge of the Welch farm. How much detail could I write about the Welch family's interactions with other Cherokees, with whites, and with blacks? How well did I understand mid-nineteenth century Southern Appalachia? Given the abundant faunal remains, did I understand what their meals were actually like? I found that writing a narrative of a single episode on the plantation challenged my knowledge regarding all of these important issues. Just as importantly, it also made me realize what I had never even considered asking during several years of research. For example, I did not fully realize until writing the narrative that the kitchen was probably almost entirely occupied and used by women. The kitchen was likely a space where women of different ages, races, and ethnicities spent time together. Were there similar spaces for the men on the farm? Writing the account also prompted questions about more material aspects of life: did all of the artifacts from the assemblage relate to the Welches or were some artifacts associated with Welch's Town or other communities? It also raised questions regarding depositional events. I had interpreted the backfilling of the cellar pits as a single short-term event. But how long did the entire dismantling of the kitchen actually take?

Most archaeologists consider themselves anthropologists and therefore show an interest in discussing the lives of the people they study. We distance ourselves from antiquarian or collector viewpoints, in which the artifact is the endgame. We should therefore strive to write something akin to ethnography: detailed narratives of quotidian existence. Where is the thick description for archaeological cultures? While archaeologists obviously cannot be participants in the cultures that we study, we can give more attention to the meanings of behaviors. Historical fiction can steer us away from seeing the people that we study as "faceless blobs" (Tringham 1991) and force us to consider them as individuals.

While researching Cherokee history and archaeology, I read several novels written by Robert Conley, a prolific Cherokee author. Conley wrote about different periods of Cherokee history and prehistory. His accounts of the eighteenth and nineteenth centuries caught my attention. In *Mountain Windsong: A Novel of the Trail of Tears*, he wrote about the cultural differences, often stark, between Cherokees who were more "traditional" and others who embraced more aspects of Western culture (Conley 1992). Conley describes the material implications of different political stances. He discusses clothing, hairstyles, tattoos, architecture, and foodways. The variety in the daily material aspects of life that archaeologists try to define are all there. Conley thoroughly researched his narratives. The story contains characters who were real, such as Chief John Ross and Junaluska, who interact with Conley's fictional characters. He also includes primary documents, such as the Treaty of New Echota, in the text.

Interpretive historical fiction can serve both broad audiences and academic research. Learning more about everyday life and the "essences" of people in the past humanizes those that we study. Historical fiction, when used as a part of a broader research project, can potentially pose new questions and directions of research. Hollenbach and Carmody (Chapter 5) reveal the everyday life of a family in their fictional account told through the eyes of a young girl. She illuminates daily and seasonal patterns during the Early Archaic period, revealing details on foodways, kinship, and subsistence that standard archaeological texts do not investigate. For example, how much time did men and women within a family spend apart? How did people within a group decide to share resources, such as deerskins? Hollenbach and Carmody answer these questions. Although their answers might not be the "truth," they are as close to a "real" answer as we can have right now.

Fiction will play a more important role in future research than it did when I was researching the Cherokee Removal. I am currently beginning a project on eighteenth- and early-nineteenth-century Shawnee towns in western Ohio. My research has included investigating key primary and secondary sources such as collections within the Draper Manuscript and documentary research by anthropologist Erminie Wheeler-Voegelin. In addition, I am reading *That Dark and Bloody River: Chronicles of the Ohio River Valley* by novelist Allan Eckert. Eckert (1995:xiv) describes his writing as narrative history incorporating "reconstituted dialogue that lies hidden in abundance in historical material." The book is an account of the warfare between Native American groups in the Ohio Valley and white settlers moving into the region. It provides a vivid backdrop for the region and era and is spurring questions about the interactions between these groups, the material culture, and the choices that people made.

I shall also write fictional accounts as my research proceeds, prior to major excavations. The locations and history of several Shawnee towns in western Ohio are well known, and fictional narratives will be used in the preparation of hypotheses and predictive models. If Shawnees from the town of Piqua on the Mad River were allied with the British during the Revolutionary War and were fighting against settlers on the Kentucky frontier, a fictional account of the village might describe expectations regarding material culture supplied by the British versus what the Shawnees were producing for themselves. After excavations, I plan to edit those narratives to tie archaeological and historical data together, to test my understanding of what happened at a site, and to generate more questions and interest in the subject.

Fictional writing can serve these purposes, whether the subject is deep prehistory or the nineteenth century. The racialized politics of the antebellum South was the backdrop for my account of the Welch communal labor and feast. Using this method helped me investigate the social and racial complexities of a Cherokee slave-owning family after Removal. I hope that these approaches can help solve the problem of our crisis of relevance. I agree with Moore and Jefferies (Chapter 7) that descriptions of everyday life "provide more humanizing and dynamic accounts of the past" and "can be a valuable means of hypothesis building." Both are worthy goals.

5

The Daily Lives of Early Archaic Foragers in the Mid-South

KANDACE D. HOLLENBACH AND STEPHEN B. CARMODY

It is somewhat rare for archaeologists researching the Early Archaic period to have an opportunity to consider the "everyday," which in our view is incredibly complex. Everyday actions are the building blocks of the archaeological record: what archaeologists collect from sites are the results of these actions. Everyday interactions are important for understanding gender roles, interpersonal relations, politics at both large and small scales, economics, and social interactions. Everyday actions form the basis for socially embedded behaviors, the foundation for social learning/memory, the rhythms of daily rituals. One hickory nutshell reflects one cracking event but also encapsulates (or entangles) a set of knowledge about hickory trees and landscapes and masting cycles, nutting stones, hickory soup recipes, and storage pits as well as the transmission of that knowledge from one generation to the next (e.g., Hodder 2011; Hollenbach 2007; Moore and Jefferies, Chapter 7).

The trick is figuring out how to go from the archaeological record, which is often meager, to re-creating everyday lives, especially as we look farther back in time. In our attempt we first present the characteristics that archaeologists have generally agreed upon for Early Archaic groups living in the Southeast. Second, we list our assumptions about Early Archaic peoples that are less widely shared among archaeologists: in particular, those assumptions that inform day-to-day activities. Finally, we venture a guess about what several days in several seasons of a young girl living in the middle Tennessee Valley about 10,000 years ago might have been like. We approach our fictional interpretation of the past from the framework of human behavioral ecology, which we have found particularly useful in our everyday research because it focuses on the decisions of individuals that result in the everyday actions from which the archaeological record is constructed. By imagining the daily seasonal activities through the eyes of a young girl, we can give those individuals identities and begin to think about the social relationships among earlier Archaic peoples and the landscape that are rooted in these economic relationships.

Background

The Early Archaic period in the southeastern United States falls between 11,500 and 8,900 cal B.P. Archaeologists understand Early Archaic peoples to have been mobile bands of hunter-gatherer-fisher peoples, with the mix of resources varying depending on geographic location as well as the season of the year (Anderson and Sassaman 1996, 2012). The type of mobility (whether logistical or residential) and degree of mobility (whether a group stayed at a particular spot for several hours, days, weeks, or months) also would have depended at least in part on the local resource base (Kelly 2013), which varies seasonally in the temperate forests of the Southeast.

In addition to the physical landscape, Early Archaic peoples would have traversed a social landscape. They would have negotiated with neighboring groups; met up with sister bands to exchange stories, information, ideas, goods, mates; tended to internal group relationships; dealt with internal divisions that caused bands to split up, particularly when they got too large; and in all likelihood engaged, petitioned, and appeased a realm of spirits and supernatural beings— including ones that embody the landscape (Ingold 1996; Kelly 2013). These various relationships also had their own seasonal and annual rhythms. For example, researchers generally assume that smaller groups aggregated at regular intervals to form macrobands, most likely in autumn, when food resources like hickory nuts were most plentiful in the Eastern Woodlands (e.g., Anderson and Hanson 1988; Anderson and Sassaman 2012).

Various researchers have linked the mobility of early foragers in the Southeast to the physical landscape. Dan and Phyllis Morse (Morse 1973, 1975; Morse and Morse 1983, 1997) posited movements of Dalton peoples across river drainages in Arkansas. David Anderson and Glen Hanson (1988) situated Early Archaic groups within river drainages in South Carolina. I. Randolph Daniel (1998, 2001) tethered their movements to lithic quarries in the Carolinas. Jefferson Chapman (1985) suggested that early foragers in eastern Tennessee used major sites adjacent to abundant resources along the rivers, such as Icehouse Bottom, as residential base camps and moved into the uplands for specific tasks, such as gathering nuts in autumn. We have argued that in northern Alabama, where high-quality tool stone was easy to come by, mobility would have been organized around the availability of highly predictable food resources like fish, nuts, and berries, which are also seasonally and annually variable (Carmody 2014; Hollenbach 2005, 2009). More recently, J. Christopher Gillam (2015) has modeled primary habitation/foraging zones for Early Archaic peoples along the lower terraces and adjacent to tributary streams in the Central Savannah River Valley, similarly noting the rich diversity of plant and animal resources in these habitats.

As groups grew too large in size for effective communication and collective decision-making, members voted with their feet and split off, expanding into new territories, as available, to form new bands. They likely would have chosen new territories based on familiarity, proximity, and productivity (perhaps not in that order) in order to fill the most productive areas of land first (Kelly 2013). Early Archaic groups appear to be more locally oriented than their Paleoindian predecessors, as seen by an increase in the variation of diagnostic hafted bifaces and greater use of locally available stone for the manufacture of tools (Anderson and Sassaman 2012).

To this general characterization of Early Archaic peoples—with which few archaeologists would argue—we would add a gendered division of labor. We posit that, as in the case of other historic and modern foraging groups (while there is plenty of crossover in activities), men performed much of the hunting, while women, children, and the elderly did most of the gathering (Kelly 2013; Panter-Brick 2002). Gathering includes not just plant resources but also animal resources such as fish, shellfish, and trapped animals, which are highly predictable in time and space.

Human behavioral ecologists explain the gendered division of labor in terms of differing strategies for reproductive success between males and females: females benefit most from ensuring that their offspring survive to reproductive age, while males benefit most from increasing their mating opportunities. Women thus have a greater incentive to make sure that their infants and children obtain adequate and consistent nutrition—neither young children nor pregnant or lactating mothers can go without food for long without incurring negative health consequences (Bird 1999; Hawkes 1993, 1996; Kelly 2013). So, while there are a number of issues in using modern foragers as analogs for Archaic hunter-gatherers, we feel comfortable extending a gendered division of labor into the Early Archaic period.

Archaeological Subsistence Data

This set of understandings and assumptions serves as a backdrop for our data. We focus on plant and animal remains from several rockshelter sites in northern Alabama (Hollenbach 2005, 2009) and southern Tennessee (Carmody 2014)

(Tables 5.1 and 5.2). Our discussion of use of animal resources rests almost entirely on the materials analyzed by Renee Walker (1998; Walker and Parmalee 2004) from Dust Cave. The faunal assemblage from this site is incredibly rich due to the remarkable preservation of bone. We also include the plant remains from several open-air sites along the Little Tennessee River analyzed by Jefferson Chapman and Andrea Shea (1981; see also Chapman 1973, 1975, 1977, 1978; Schroedl 1978).

These data are critical for moving researchers past the generalities of a "hunting and gathering lifestyle." Rather than simply stating that various groups gathered wild nuts, berries, and seeds, we can use our understanding of the decisions and activities involved in order to flesh out some of these details. For example, we can state the following about an assemblage characterized by many times more hickory nutshell fragments than black walnut shells. First, the site occupants likely targeted the collection of nuts during the three weeks in the fall when the hickory nuts are at their peak availability on the forest floor, with tough competition from wildlife, molds, and mildew (Gardner 1997; Scarry and

Table 5.1. Plant Remains from Early Archaic Sites

	Rockshelter Sites							Riverine Sites			
NUTS:	Dust Cave[a]	Stanfield-Worley[a,b]	LaGrange[a]	Rollins[a]	Michaels[c]	Uzzelles[c]	Patrick[d]	Icehouse Bottom[e]	Bacon Farm[e]	Rose Island[e]	Calloway Island[e]
Acorn	x	x	x	x	x	x	x	x	x	x	x
Beechnut								x			
Black walnut	x	x	x	x				x	x		
Chestnut								x	x		
Hazelnut	x	x	x					x			
Hickory	x	x	x	x	x	x	x	x	x	x	x
Beech family	x										
Walnut family	x	x						x	x		

	Rockshelter Sites							Riverine Sites			
	Dust Cave[a]	Stanfield-Worley[a,b]	LaGrange[a]	Rollins[a]	Michaels[c]	Uzzelles[c]	Patrick[d]	Icehouse Bottom[e]	Bacon Farm[e]	Rose Island[e]	Calloway Island[e]
FRUITS:											
Bramble								x			
Grape	x	x	x	x	x		x	x			x
Hackberry	x										
Honey locust										x	
Honey locust cf.		x									
Mulberry			x								
Peppervine								x			
Persimmon	x	x	x	x				x	x		
Sumac	x	x	x		x			x			x
GREENS/EDIBLE SEEDS:											
Amaranth								x			
Aster family											x
Bedstraw	x		x		x						x
Chenopod	x		x			x		x			x
Cheno-am	x										
Composite family											x
Composite family cf.			x								
Copperleaf								x			
Knotweed									x		
Maygrass											
Pokeweed	x						x	x			x
Pokeweed cf.	x										
Weedy legume	x		x	x							

[a] Hollenbach 2005.
[b] Stanfield-Worley includes a mixed Dalton/Early Archaic zone.
[c] Carmody 2014.
[d] Schroedl 1978.
[e] Chapman 1973, 1975, 1977, 1978; Chapman and Shea 1981.

Table 5.2. Seasonality of Plants Recovered from Early Archaic Contexts

Category														
Common Name	Taxonomic Name	Jan	Feb	Mar	Apr	May	Jun	Jul	Aug	Sep	Oct	Nov	Dec
NUTS:													
Acorn	Quercus spp.									x	x	x	
Beechnut	Fagus grandifolia									x	x	x	
Black walnut	Juglans nigra										x	x	
Chestnut	Castanea dentata								x	x	x		
Hazelnut	Corylus sp.							x	x	x			
Hickory	Carya spp.									x	x	x	
FRUITS:													
Bramble	Rubus sp.						x	x	x	x			
Grape	Vitis sp.							x	x	x	x		
Hackberry	Celtis sp.	(x)	(x)						x	x	x	x	(x)
Honey locust	Gleditsia triacanthos	(x)	(x)					x	x	x	x	x	(x)
Mulberry	Morus sp.					x	x	x	x				
Peppervine	Ampelopsis cordata								x	x	x		
Persimmon	Diospyros virginiana								x	x	x	x	
Sumac	Rhus sp.						x		x	x	x		

EDIBLE SEEDS:

Common name	Taxon	1	2	3	4	5	6	7
Amaranth	*Amaranthus* sp.	x	x	x	x			
Chenopod	*Chenopodium* sp.		x	x	x	x		
Knotweed	*Polygonum* sp.		x	x	x	x		
Maygrass	*Phalaris caroliniana*						x	x
Weedy legume	Fabaceae		x	x	x	x		

LEAFY GREENS:

Common name	Taxon	1	2	3	4	5	6	7
Amaranth	*Amaranthus* sp.					x	x	x
Bedstraw	*Galium* sp.					x	x	x
Bramble	*Rubus* sp.					x	x	x
Chenopod	*Chenopodium* sp.				x	x	x	x
Knotweed	*Polygonum* sp.					x	x	x
Pokeweed	*Phytolacca americana*					x	x	x
Purslane	*Portulaca* sp.				x	x	x	x
Smartweed	*Polygonum* cf. *pensylvanicum*					x	x	x
Sumac	*Rhus* sp.					x	x	x

Hollenbach 2012; Talalay et al. 1984). Second, once they brought the hickory nuts back to their home camps, they likely processed them in bulk using a crush-and-boil technique similar to what the Cherokees use today to make *ke-nu-che* (Fritz 2001). They would have lined a small pit with skins, filled it with water, dropped in hot rocks to heat the water not quite to boiling, and then added quantities of crushed hickory nutshell and meats, with the result that the nutshells would sink to the bottom and the nutmeats could be skimmed from the top. This technique vastly improves the return on hickory nuts—picking the nutmeats by hand from the convoluted shell requires more energy than is gained from eventually eating the nutmeats (Gardner 1997; Talalay et al. 1984). In contrast, black walnuts cannot be processed in the same manner: the hull, which is full of tannins, sticks between the ridges of the walnut shell and would be released into the liquid, making the water/nutmeat soup inedible. Thus black walnuts must be processed by the cracking-and-picking method, which may account for its more limited recovery and presumably more limited use by prehistoric peoples (Scarry 2003; Talalay et al. 1984). We have identified thousands of fragments of hickory nutshell from all sites—including a greasy midden laden with hickory nutshell in the Early Archaic deposits at the base of Michaels Shelter (Carmody 2014), which suggests significant use of these nuts that cannot be explained by cracking and picking alone.

We could march through each of the plant taxa recovered from the various sites, detailing the decisions, activities, and cooking methods associated with each. But rather than going through each of these resources one by one, we use the available archaeological dataset as a backdrop to paint a picture of daily life and seasonal rounds from the perspective of the "diary," if you will, of a young girl living in the middle Tennessee Valley approximately 10,000 years ago. Throughout the fictional piece, we weave in strands of data and understandings about the activities and decisions made by foragers, drawing from foraging theory (e.g., Elston and Zeanah 2002; Hollenbach 2009; Reidhead 1981; Zeanah 2000) as well as more generalized hunter-gatherer studies (e.g., Kelly 2013; Panter-Brick et al. 2001). By assigning social and familial roles, however flawed, to these individual foragers, we can explore the relationships among them and with the landscape and begin to think about how their individual and group identities, histories, and social memories would have been embedded in these landscapes and seasonal rhythms as well as how information about the cultural landscape was passed from parents, grandparents, aunts, and uncles—both fictive and true kin—to children during the course of these daily and seasonal activities (Cattell and Climo 2002; Crumley 2002; Ingold 2000; Lowenthal 1975).[1]

Second Day of the Strawberry Moon

We just set up camp at the Wide Shoals at the Big River today. Father and Uncles returned from their hunting trip ten nights ago with a deer, but it was so lean, Mother laughed that hickory nut soup would make a richer meal. She helped Aunties dress the hide—she kept enough to make me a new pair of moccasins, but most went to Auntie G so she could make a carrier for when her new baby comes. This morning we rolled up our blankets and mats and packed them on the travois, along with the baskets of nuts, persimmon cakes, and dried venison. Father whistled up several of the dogs so they could pull the travois—I was glad that I only had one almost-empty basket of dried berries to carry.

Older Brother checked the traps on the way down to the Fish Camp at the Shoals. He came back with three skinny rabbits—they were pitiful. He rejoined us as we came down the slope and into the flat lands of the valley. Grandmother began telling me and Little Sister and our cousins the stories about Goosefoot and Box Turtle and pulled off the leaves of a new goosefoot plant and handed them to us to chew on as we walked along. I heard Mother tell Auntie G that we would come back tomorrow to the large patch of goosefoot where Mulberry Creek meets the Big River. I know Father and Uncles and Older Brother will catch many fish tomorrow—the fish have just begun their run, and they know the best places along the shoals to drop their nets. They have been checking the nets the last three days and mending them with twine that Mother made from the stems of sedges. We are all anxious to eat fish and goosefoot after so much lean deer and hickory nut soup. Uncle B says that the geese will fly through the valley in the next few days too. In bed tonight, under our thick, warm hide blankets, Little Sister and I listed all the ways Mother and Aunties and Grandmother would cook fish and goose and duck and turtle and goosefoot and amaranth and poke greens and grape shoots until the next full moon . . .

Fourteenth Day of the Blackberry Moon

We spent all day picking blackberries—me, my little sisters and brothers, our little cousins, and of course Mother, Aunties, and Grandmother.[2] It was a slow walk to the blackberry patch, but Auntie L sang about Raccoon and Possum and the Berry Patch and made us all laugh. Because we were walking so slowly, with all those young children along, Auntie G took me off the path several times to collect shoots and leaves, like bedstraw, poke, and sassafras, for our medicine pouches. She was carrying her baby—almost one moon old—so she asked me to carry the basket. Mother laughs that he is a fat and hungry baby, nursing all the time. But Auntie G just sings to him, songs about the Sun and Moon and Wind and River, low and sweet. I love to hear her sing and listen to her stories about the medicine plants, so I was glad that she chose me to help her.

We spent most of the day at the blackberry patch. I think that the young children ate more than they put in the baskets. The youngest slept in the shade under the trees when their bellies were full; a couple of the young boys fed berries to the dogs that had followed us. I like gathering mulberries better—they're easier—we knock them off the trees, they fall to the mats, and we pull them into the sun to dry. Blackberries—those you have to pick, and there are thorns involved! But the thorns help keep the birds away: we have to be sure to get to the mulberries before the birds do. We left the blackberry patch with four full baskets. Mother cooked the berries with fish when we got back to camp. Father and Uncle B returned later with a turkey. Uncle kept the wings special, to make blowing tubes for smoke medicine.[3]

Eighteenth Day of the Big Chestnut Moon

We have been at the Cliff Base Camp for five days now and have filled a dozen baskets with chestnuts and hickory nuts and acorns. Father and Uncles are with us to help collect nuts, but they spend the early morning hunting, since the deer and turkeys are also in the hills, eating the same nuts that we are collecting. In six days we will head to the Big River, along the Wide Shoals, for the big meeting with the Great-Aunts and Uncles. There must be about four hundred of us, total. Mother and Aunties and Grandmother will bring the hides they have tanned as well as the fresh hides and join the other women to prepare hides and sew and mend clothing, as they chat and share gossip and compare the numbers of baskets that they have filled with food stores. I am hoping this year that they will let me join in with the sewing work, I have had to watch the younger ones the past three years. They are fun, but I want to listen to the women's chatter and hear the stories and the gossip that they are telling.

Second Day of the Bear Moon

We spent nearly half a moon at the Big River camp before heading to the Rock-shelter Camp. It seems so quiet compared to the meeting at the Big River—not so many people, not so many dogs. I traded the braided fiber belts that I had made over the summer with Cousin P for a woven bag—she uses black walnut bark to stain patterns into the weft. Father traded tool stone with Great-Uncle J—he always brings stone with light gray bands. Father made several spear tips with it, with our family's notched corner markings. He gave me some of the large pieces that he first knocked off as he started shaping the points—I will make quick knives from them. It will make cutting goosefoot leaves next spring more fun—the banded stone will make me think of Father and Great-Uncle J and the Big River meeting.

It is quieter at Rockshelter Camp, but I like the slower days and the warmth of the shelter. During the day, I go with Mother to collect seeds and berries that the birds and squirrels have not gotten to yet, like the goosefoot seeds and the hackberries and persimmons that have dried on the branches. We also check on the traps. Two days ago, we found a fat possum in the trap closest to the creek. Younger Brother was excited for roasted possum.

When the Sun heads low in the sky, Mother and I return to the rockshelter and join the other women, and we all sit to crack nuts. This is my favorite rockshelter; the nutting cups are pecked right into the big base rocks.[4] Grandmother tells me that her Great-Aunties wore down these holes right here in this rockshelter. She shows me and Little Sister how to hit a black walnut just so, so that the nut pops right open. And then Grandmother, Mother, and Aunties start singing songs and telling us stories about the animals and the spirits and talking about what they heard at the Big River meeting. This is my favorite time of year, listening to their stories and songs as we all work together in the warm rockshelter. They keep talking after we go to sleep—I listen as long as I can, watching the fire shadows on the shelter walls to stay awake. Tomorrow Grandmother and Mother and Aunties will mend clothes and blankets and start making new ones.

I am grateful for our bear fur blanket at night to keep us warm. Little Sister and I sleep right next to each other—during the night, she finds her way over and cozies up next to me. She warms me up, so I don't complain. We stay under the bear blanket in the morning as long as we can until Mother pulls me out to go looking for berries and seeds and check the traps again. Tomorrow Mother will show me the bark of the different trees, with their bare branches, and tell me again how to make medicine from each. I hope Father and Uncles will return from their hunting trip tomorrow too. They have been gone four nights now—they should come home soon, I hope with a deer or turkey. The meat will taste good after so much hickory nut soup and persimmon cakes.

Seventh Day of the Deer Moon

Grandmother has begun singing in spring. She showed us the buds on the tree branches and the shrubs as we walked to the Upland Camp. She is always pinching off buds and branches, telling us that for each branch removed, two more will show up. I am not sure if she is right—I will have to remember to look closely at the branches as we travel through again during the warmer months. Auntie L pointed out the tiny goosefoot plants, just up from the warming soil, as we wound along the trail. We had been digging tubers in the sandier soils near the river. I like the roasted tubers—they are a change of pace from chestnut bread and hickory nut soup with a little meat added—mostly skinny rabbits now that spring is almost here. Father and Uncles will leave camp in two days for a hunting trip. The deer are lean this moon, but Mother needs the hide to make new moccasins and new skins for lining the wet cooking pits. When Father returns, we will start preparing to head back to Fish Camp. Then it will really feel and taste like spring to me.

Conclusion

Fictionalizations drawn from the archaeological record serve several purposes. First and foremost, they help us envision the peoples who obtained and used the artifacts and ecofacts that we recover. When we can give faces to these peoples, and therefore identities (genders, ages, roles within families, roles within the larger group), we can begin to see the various relationships among them. The plant and animal remains that we find represent food, but they also underscore the relationships embedded in those food-related activities: the relationships between people and the natural world, between men and women and children, and between groups on the landscapes.

While the identities and roles imagined here are relatively simplistic, this engendering exercise is particularly important for research on early foragers. Far too often, gathering activities of Paleoindian and Archaic peoples are summed up in several sentences. This short treatment implies an underlying notion that gatherers simply collected the resources that they came across in their day-to-day happenings and ignores the rich relationships among gatherers, plants, animals, landscapes, and seasons. It also neglects the roles that these played in the sociopolitical decisions of the larger group and in shaping the histories and social memories of the group.

Fictionalizations like ours, then, can bring these relationships hazily into view and push us to ask more of the data we do have. How did gatherers' and hunters' decisions and activities feed into the increasing regionalization of the Archaic Southeast? How did the activities of early gatherers, as they manipulated plant resources through harvesting, coppicing, pruning, burning, and transplanting, create the anthropogenic landscapes upon which trails, base camps, foraging camps, and eventually mounds were constructed and situated? How did the seasonal rounds of foragers shape the social, historical landscapes in which they lived and remembered their dead? If gathering and hunting were indeed tasks assigned by gender and age, then what can these social, historical landscapes tell us about the relationships of males and females, the young and the old, within Archaic groups? And how would these relationships shift if there was not a gendered/age division of labor? In these ways, fictionalizations can help us to think more creatively about the data at hand and fill in where the data are scanty at best.

Just as importantly, these fictionalizations help us to communicate our findings with the general public and students of all ages. The fourth-grade students that the senior author recently visited found it difficult to imagine that someone who used a stone tool 10,000 years ago would have been just as smart as themselves and their gadget-wielding friends. But if we can show them that ten-year-old Early Archaic children living in the Mid-South knew their way around the rivers, creeks, forests, and hills, knew the best places to catch fish and pick berries, could trap and skin and cook small animals, could chip a knife out of a rock in a matter of minutes, then we can give those fourth-graders a greater appreciation of human diversity and capability in both time and space.

Thus we recommend that, as archaeologists mull over their data, they take some time to sketch out what the data tell them about the daily, seasonal, yearly tasks performed by the peoples that they are studying. We have found it to be a fruitful exercise for better understanding the relationships between and among ancient peoples, landscapes, and biotic communities; for presenting additional questions that might be asked of current and new data; and for sharing our findings with those who do not speak archaeological jargon but who share our interest in the stories of the past.

We hope this fictionalization of a slice of everyday life of a young forager helps enliven future interpretations of the archaeological record associated with the Early Archaic, considering activities and individuals beyond those associated with the stone tools that archaeologists encounter on every site. The everyday matters conducted by Early Archaic individuals dramatically changed the cultural, social, and political landscape as well as the biogeography of the region.

As decisions made by Paleoindians shaped the landscape and informed the decisions made by Early Archaic foragers, the everyday decisions of Early Archaic foragers set up social, economic, and ecological relationships that significantly shaped those that followed. These seasonal and yearly rhythms of plentiful harvest and want, of congregation and dispersal, of learning and teaching, laid the foundations for the Middle Archaic trade networks and Late Archaic domestication. Embedded in these seasonal and yearly rhythms are the social identities, histories, and memories that connect these groups across time and space. By exploring the relationships represented by each nutshell, seed, bird, fish, or shellfish recovered, facilitated by fictional histories such as the one presented here, we can attempt to animate the life histories of these early foragers.

Acknowledgments

We would like to thank Phil Carr and Sarah Price for inviting us to participate in the "Everyday Matters" symposium and to think more broadly about how we might present our interpretations of the archaeological record.

Notes

1. Rather than using the Gregorian calendar, we have chosen to use named moons drawn from descriptions of calendars used by historic southeastern American Indian tribes by John Swanton (1946). We hope that you forgive us this bit of artistic license.

2. Among modern foraging groups, mothers face tradeoffs between childcare and foraging efficiency. Children often contribute significantly to the procurement of their own diets, particularly foodstuffs like fruits with low handling costs (Hawkes 1996; Tucker and Young 2005).

3. Renee Walker and Paul Parmalee (2004) speculated that 23 paired goose humeri recovered from a cache in the Early Archaic deposits at Dust Cave were held aside as blanks for a hollow tool or ornament.

4. The bedrock at Stanfield-Worley, which would have been exposed during the earliest occupations (Dalton and perhaps Early Archaic), is covered with "cupules" that were ground into the stone and presumably used to hold nuts steady while cracking them open (Hollenbach 2005).

6

An Ethnoarchaeological Interpretation
of the Salt Life, A.D. 1200

ASHLEY A. DUMAS

Papers on archaeological methods do not often discuss the role of imagination. They present the theoretical orientation of the author, the methods of excavation, and the application of appropriate statistical tests but rarely examine the creative process driving the implementation of these methods. Perhaps it is not considered part of rigorous science and, as some may say, has no place in the practice of archaeology, only in the interpretation of it to the general public. A large body of literature within the history of science and evolutionary psychology deals with the creative process, and some of the greatest scientists in the world have spoken about the importance of imagination for the production of new knowledge (Simonton 1999). Archaeologists, certainly, have sometimes felt obligated to identify their profession as either science or humanity, or both, and perhaps have drawn distinctions that do not exist or are not useful, in an attempt to legitimize their work. In this atmosphere, abductive reasoning, where hypotheses are generated from incomplete datasets, is generally considered to be less scientific and something to be avoided. Embracing our innate creativity, our imaginations, guided by data and tempered with rote method and theory, can be a pragmatic acknowledgment of how our brains work.

Another issue seems to be a tendency to equate imagination with personal bias, as if the two cannot be mutually exclusive. If bias is a concern, discussing the process of interpretation is a means to acknowledge and, if not reduce, then at least honestly display our bias in the same way that we are obligated to reveal our theoretical frameworks. Yet another concern with the direct implementation of imagination in archaeology, particularly when attempting to imagine "what it was like" in the past, may be the fear of being accused of cultural appropriation. While we should be sensitive to the rights of any cultural or ethnic group to the emic view of their history and culture, if some understanding or profitable theory-building cannot be achieved by anyone but a member of the group being studied, then anthropology is a fruitless endeavor.

Creating a fictional narrative of the past using archaeological evidence is nothing new, and it is a popular method for sharing and teaching (e.g., Jean M. Auel's classic Earth's Children series; the dozens of novels by archaeologists Kathleen O'Neal Gear and W. Michael Gear; Eubanks 2015; Hudson 2003, 2009, 2014; Kneberg 1951a, 1951b, 1952a, 1952b; Searcy 1981 [1971], 1991, 1995, 2009 [1974]). Narratives, exhibits, and films are increasingly being studied as effective tools for communicating complicated principles of science (e.g., Baron 2010; Bell et al. 2009; Chittenden et al. 2004; Olson 2015). In this tradition, creating descriptions of fully developed, everyday moments seem to be an interesting method for stimulating new discovery. Thinking about the past in terms of the literal quotidian—as much the space of a typical day as the common, everyday activities—requires the most imaginative yet careful and precise hypothesis-building. When we are led out of the safety of broad models, well-established patterns, and 2-sigma probabilities, we are required to read into things at a microscale level of time and place, simultaneously arranging many pots and post molds and then filling in the gaps around all the missing pieces presumptively.

Museum professionals, whose job is to manifest two- and three-dimensional narratives from incomplete evidence, are familiar with the interpretive process. They have learned to eliminate the noise of extraneous data and distill a clear picture, literally, of what is being proposed, whether it is the Big Bang, a *Spinosaurus* catching a fish, or a prehistoric wedding procession at Moundville. The creative process for this chapter began with an invitation to contribute to an international exhibit on salt production, for which I was asked to provide an illustration of prehistoric salt-making in the southeastern United States. Having little artistic talent, I asked my archaeologist husband to work with me to create a drawing. We were to illustrate the process of prehistoric salt-making at a salt spring in southwest Alabama, where I surveyed or excavated and analyzed artifacts from four saline sites. The results of that work are found in my dissertation (Dumas 2007), wherein I present the results of an analysis of thousands of potsherds in an attempt to understand the process of salt production, what cultures were involved, and changes in production intensity as they occurred between 1,000 and 500 years ago. With a large assemblage of artifacts, few features, and 500 years to synthesize, I concluded my dissertation with a set of lengthy hypotheses and possibilities but no definitive answers about the salt-making process itself or the people involved.

The requested exhibit drawing, however, forced me to think differently about what the archaeological and ethnographic records provide on the production of salt and its importance to prehistoric people. In thinking about the "end product" or solution, I had to make decisions about specific artifacts to represent, to reconsider features, and to integrate ethnographic evidence into a single imagined moment in the lives of salt-makers. Each part of the drawing is an explicit hypothesis into which I organized a great amount of data. As the drawing took shape, I had to make concrete decisions about whether the human figures were to be male or female, whether they were working together or apart, and whether they were dressed for warm or cold weather. I had to decide not only what types of pottery would be represented but exactly how they were employed and if they would even be near one another on the site. Would everyone have been busy making salt or were other everyday activities occurring too? Were the salt-makers local or had they traveled far? The illustration required reconsideration of the details for multiple simultaneous activities, both specialized and domestic. It required the reduction of 500 years of possibilities and change to one day. As if constructing an exhibit, I had to curate the information necessary to elucidate a technical process but also situate it genuinely within the context of peoples' everyday needs and relationships.

The invisibility of salt itself in the archaeological record increases the difficulty of examining its daily production, use, or distribution. Production sites in the eastern United States demonstrate that acquisition of this valued resource involved the application, and sometimes alteration, of everyday skills and knowledge such as making pots or weaving to a specialized seasonal activity (see also Pluckhahn et al., Chapter 9). However, we possess almost no knowledge of the gender or age of prehistoric salt-makers or of how they organized production. There are also large gaps in our understanding of salt's importance in health and ritual practices. By placing existing archaeological evidence in the context of worldwide ethnohistoric and ethnographic records on salt manufacturing and use, we can narrow our hypotheses and reduce idiosyncratic interpretations.

I do want to make clear that the ethnoarchaeological approach does not involve unequivocal cross-cultural comparisons or cherry-picking of cultural elements to suit our purposes without an acknowledgment of the necessary archaeological evidence to support them. In the case of salt, there are limited means of extracting crystallized salt from solution, so the same basic methods are found across widely different environments and cultures (Gouletquer and Weller 2015:24–25; Harding 2013). This reduces the amount of inference required to hypothesize how certain artifacts from salt-processing sites might have been used. In this chapter I present a sample of the vast ethnographic literature for how salt was obtained and its roles in society and then summarize the archaeological evidence for salt-making from four sites in Alabama. Finally, I distill this information into an afternoon in the life of Mississippian salt-makers and salt-users in the lower Tombigbee River valley, circa A.D. 1200, in order to demonstrate the value of the fictional narrative as a hypothesis-building tool.

Salt in Prehistory

I propose that salt was an everyday sort of substance for many prehistoric southeastern peoples. This is grounded in biological, archaeological, ethnohistoric, and ethnographic evidence from cultures around the world that salt was important to many ancient peoples for their physical, spiritual, and social well-being. Salt resources were not evenly distributed in the Southeast, and it was not necessarily bountiful. Inland peoples without access to salt springs or lakes are known to have collected plants that are used as a salt substitute when burned (Dyson 2006; Gilbert 1978:184; Hamel and Chiltoskey 1975:56). During the Mississippian period, areas with many salt springs may have been controlled or monitored by elite lineages, who would have overseen its distribution and trade. European colonists and archaeologists (Brown 1981; Meyers 2002; Muller 1997; Smith 2015; Waselkov and Gums 2000) have recorded salt trading networks among southeastern Indians, making salt an important if sometimes overlooked part of Native American political economies during late prehistory. Salt has probably been valued in this region for thousands of years, as it has been around the world, as a dietary additive, as a commodity, as a ritual and healing substance, and for compensatory payments and other integrative social functions.

Salt is a common additive among people who obtain a large portion of their calories from plants. Once tasted, salt has an addictive quality much like sugar. Thus communities with a nearby source of salt—crystalline, brine springs, salt marshes, salt lakes, salty earth, or others—developed methods of extracting and purifying salt for consumption, distribution, and trade. The amount of salt needed is still a mystery, even to modern biologists, who have discovered that people in the world today, regardless of their subsistence traditions (and with the exception of Amazonian hunter-gatherers), all seem to consume around

3,500 mg of salt per day, far more than the body's minimum requirements for health (Beauchamp 1993; Bertino et al. 1982; Denton 1982; Dethier 1977; Intersalt Cooperative Research Group 1988).

The anthropology of salt includes scholarship on ancient and modern applications of salt for health and healing. The use of salt for medicinal purposes in the Southeast is not well known, but we can postulate that southeastern Indians possessed the same awareness of salt's medicinal benefits as other peoples in the world. Written records reveal deep stores of cultural knowledge regarding medicinal plants and other healing provisions found in nature. It is plausible that sources of salt, and perhaps specific sources of salt with particular mineral concentrations, were sought after and valued for their healing and purifying effects on the body. Salt sources are usually not pure sodium chloride, especially salt springs and salty earth, which include minerals that affect not only taste and color but medicinal properties, physiological or psychosomatic. Samples taken from six salines in south Alabama document the presence of calcium, magnesium, potassium, bicarbonate, and sulfate, in addition to sodium and chloride ions (Dumas 2007). Magnesium sulfate, commonly known today as Epsom salt, is used widely as an anti-inflammatory, for relief of muscle cramps, healing open wounds, and even reducing stress by countering the effects of adrenaline. It is also an effective laxative. Sodium sulfate or Glauber's salt is a known laxative and may soothe heartburn. It has been suggested that spring water with various sodium ions may have been used as a purgative by Mississippian peoples (Beahm and Smith 2006), perhaps in a manner similar to the ritual and healing purposes of holly leaf teas.

Health and healing, as dimensions of traditional culture, are often entwined with religious belief. Salt did figure prominently in the spiritual lives of many premodern peoples, as it may have for southeastern Indians. It is a substance derived directly from the earth or the sea, and this association with the underworld or a vast, little-known expanse probably contributed to the way in which it was perceived and placed within ancient cosmologies. The worth of salt to humans is perhaps best signified by how it is embedded in the rituals and mythologies of so many cultures. Ritual objects of wood, bone, and ceramic have been found at salt production workshops and are believed to be offerings, charms, or used to evoke blessings for the salt-makers and their work (Andrews 1983:85–86; Flad 2004; McKillop 2002). Some salt sources are considered to be sacred because they produce salt of a particular taste or color or because of long-forgotten tradition, and the salt is designated for religious purposes. Salt springs are commonly associated with the female body. Among some Papuan tribes, salt springs emanate from the blood of a wounded woman or even from her mucus (Pétrequin et al. 2001:49). A female salt deity was known to the Postclassic Aztecs in the Basin of Mexico. Huixtocihuatl—the Goddess of Salt—is the older sister of the rain god Tlaloc and closely related to the god of stone and the goddess of earth. Huixtocihuatl protected those who were engaged in extracting and trading salt (Andrews 1983:113; Flores 2015).

Among the agricultural tribes of southwestern North America, annual pilgrimages to gather salt are closely interwoven with and an expression of social organization and mythology. Accounts of salt-gathering expeditions exist for the Hopi, Zuni, Papago, Pueblo, and Navajo tribes (Harrington 1927; Hill 1940; Hunter 1940:11–20; Titiev 1937). Common to their mythology are descriptions of the origin of salt sources, which center on a reverence for the Salt Woman, Salt Mother, or Salt Grandmother (Grinnell 1940; Titiev 1937:255; Woods 1953). This mythological figure lives at the source of salt in the area, most often a shallow lake (Hill 1940:5–6). Although the methods of collecting salt and the rituals for handling it vary by tribe, the members of each society have a particular role in the annual expedition based on gender, kinship, age, and status divisions, resulting in a general integration of society (Hunter 1940:14, 16). The remarkable place of salt in southwestern cultures is reinforced by their observance of salt taboos during at least one or more of the following occasions: pregnancy and birth; girls' puberty rites; menstruation; boys' puberty/initiation rites and vision quests; and mourning (Kroeber 1942:5).

Southeastern salt-makers also may have had mythologies of salt entwined in their cultures, but accounts have been lost to time. We do know that salt was often associated with taboos against its use before, during, or after the Green Corn Ceremony, a time of purification through fasting. Many Creek towns had a taboo against the consumption of salt during the Busk until after ball play. Swanton (1928:572–573) reports: "On the fourth day the meat is prepared with salt and eaten for breakfast. After breakfast the women dance in the square, the men merely looking on. Until this day those who have eaten salt are not allowed to touch the ones engaged in the ceremony, who do not, until the fourth day, touch salt themselves." Historical records also describe prohibitions against salt during the Busk of the Chickasaws, Yuchis, and Cherokees, who, like the Creeks, would reincorporate salt, certain foods, and sexual intercourse after a specific number of days (Adair 2005 [1775]:143; Hawkins 2003:765, 785; Neumann 1977:294–295; Speck 2004:45, 114, 118; Swanton 1928:573, 577–578, 604). Taboos against salt are also documented in conditions relating to the birth of a child and preparing a body for burial (Speck 2004:92), though some nineteenth-century Cherokees placed a small vessel of salt on the chest of the body (Mooney and Olbrechts 1932:121), perhaps as an offering of purification for the deceased or as a folk tradition adopted from Europeans.

Applying humoral theory to an examination of salt as part of an entire complex of Native American nutritional practices helps to explain particular food proscriptions and taboos. The humoral theory of illness supposes that all foods, drugs, and climatic conditions have hot and cold properties and that illness results from an imbalance of the hot and cold elements of the body (Logan 1973:385). James Mooney (1982:610) recorded the Cherokee practice of treating illness by forbidding "lye, salt, and hot food . . . when there is any prohibition at all." The denial of salt and meat during menstruation and pregnancy may be explained not by a physiological instinct for avoidance of both but rather by the perception of these foods as "hot" and therefore out of balance with conditions that require treatment with "cold" foods instead. During her first menstruation, for example, a Zuni girl is prohibited from eating salt and meat and is kept in the shade. As part of the Zuni scalp ceremony, salt, meat, hot food, and women became taboo for four nights (Elsie Clews Parsons in Hunter 1940:43–44). Each of these items has been recorded among Mesoamerican and South American groups as "hot" (Andrews 1983:12; Currier 1966:255; Logan 1973:386; McCullough 1973:33; Redfield and Redfield 1940:64; Worrle 1997:295). A more direct implication of the "hot" or dangerous nature of salt is found among some West African groups, who believe that salt and fire have the same ability to cause illness and misfortune if used inappropriately (Gray 1945:474). Among several tribes in Papua New Guinea, the "hot" nature of salt has curative properties (Pétrequin et al. 2001:49).

Throughout the world, salt has exceeded its value as a dietary supplement to become a key ingredient in technological processes. In *Salt: A World History*, Mark Kurlansky (2002) explores the Old World use of salt for curing meat and fish and how its value as such affected the economic and political affairs of the world for centuries. Its functions in hide-tanning, dyeing textiles, working precious metals, mummification, cheese-making, and glazing pottery are well documented (Adhead 1992; Eskew 1948; Kurlansky 2002; Laszlo 2001; Mollat 1968; Multhauf 1978; Nenquin 1961; Parsons 2001). Native inhabitants of the New World had other traditions. There are no ethnographic accounts of southeastern Indians using salt as a precolonial tradition of meat preservation, which was done through smoking and drying, or to tan hides, which was accomplished through other processes. Salt appears to have been employed as a preservative in the European manner only after a marked increase in demand for meat and skins for trade to Europeans (e.g., Eubanks 2015, 2016 on the Caddos; Knight and Adams 1981 on the Tomés; Perdue 1995 on the Cherokees). Salt is widely used as a fixative or mordant for plant-based dyes. The dyes might have been used for textiles, mats, and baskets, so it is conceivable that salt's value in the prehistoric Southeast was due to its necessity in the process of creating commonly used materials. A modern Cherokee basketmaker reports adding salt to pots of yellow root or bloodroot dyes "to keep the splints from fading after they are dyed" (French et al. 1981:177). There is little indirect archaeological evidence, such as dye pots, with which to study the use of dyes in clothing or other textiles, but it may be that we have not yet recognized them in the archaeological record.

The process of making salt would have structured many days in the lives of salt-makers. Documentation of nonindustrial salt production, from Mesoamerica (e.g., Andrews 1983; Parsons 2001; Reina and Monaghen 1981; Williams 2015), to Africa (e.g., Connah 1996; Gray 1945; Lovejoy 1986), to New Guinea (e.g., Hooley and Terit 1972; Pétrequin et al. 2001) demonstrates that the process is not technologically complex. It is determined by the source of the salt—whether in solution, saturated in soils, as rock salt, or in sodium-rich plants—and the available fuel—solar or fire. Filtering brine is performed to separate it from salt-laden soils, to concentrate it, and to remove impurities. Anthropologists have recorded a wide variety of filtering mechanisms, including baskets, perforated wooden troughs or canoes, ceramic pots, animal skins, and masses of thorns (Brown 1980, 2010; Gouletquer and Weller 2015). Making a saturated salt solution increases the efficiency of evaporation and reduces the necessary quantity of fuel and time. If filtering does not complete this process, solar evaporation may be employed in places with long days and little rain. When wood fuel is scarce, it makes sense to use filtering and solar evaporation to create as strong a brine as possible before cooking it over a fire to obtain salt crystals. Figure 6.1 is the result of a comprehensive survey of archaeological and ethnographic salt-making across the world (Gouletquer and Weller 2015).

Guided by these principles of salt production, I can briefly describe the range of possibilities available to salt-makers at the salines of southwest Alabama based on my excavations and analyses of four salt production sites. We know that by A.D. 1200 people associated with the Moundville chiefdom had been using the salt springs on the lower Tombigbee River for around two generations. Along with a few jars typical in form and decoration of their home in the Black Warrior River Valley, they left behind thick middens containing primarily large, shallow plain bowls and fabric impressed saltpans. These

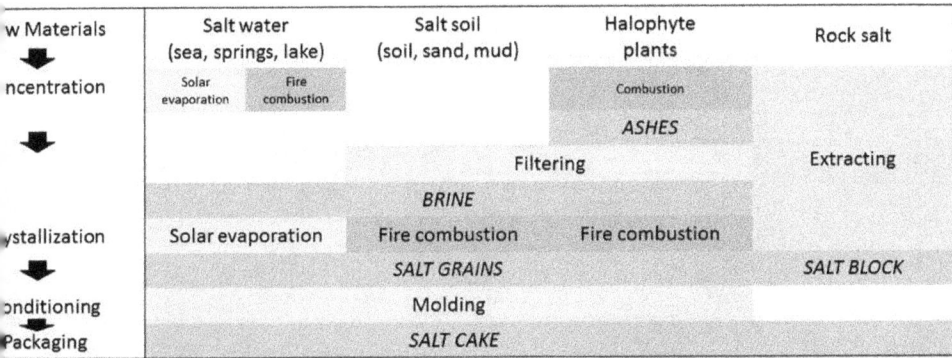

w Materials	Salt water (sea, springs, lake)	Salt soil (soil, sand, mud)	Halophyte plants	Rock salt
ncentration	Solar evaporation / Fire combustion		Combustion	
			ASHES	
		Filtering		Extracting
		BRINE		
ystallization	Solar evaporation	Fire combustion	Fire combustion	
		SALT GRAINS		SALT BLOCK
onditioning		Molding		
Packaging		SALT CAKE		

Figure 6.1. General principles of salt production (modified from Gouletquer and Weller 2015:Figure 1).

are the known tools that were used to extract crystallized salt from the saline springs and the expanses of surrounding salt-impregnated soil. Descriptions of baskets, mats, wooden ladles, or shell scrapers and other perishable items we must borrow from ethnographic accounts. Based on the presence of scraping, fire-clouding, and sooting, and lack thereof, I propose that plain and fabric-impressed vessels, used simultaneously, served different purposes in the production process and that both solar and fire methods were used. Plain pans perhaps were used to concentrate the brine by solar evaporation. Fabric-impressed pans, with a larger average diameter, thicker bodies, and increased surface areas from the impressions on their exteriors, were made for efficient direct heating of the concentrated brine, as the last step to crystallization. We have almost no data on how the salt was packaged, how much was made, and for whom (Dumas 2007).

In 1702 a Frenchman reported that the Tomés and Naniabas maintained "salt lakes" near the lower Tombigbee River for trade to the Choctaws (Charles Levasseur in Waselkov and Gums 2000:17–18). Nearly 50 years later, Choctaws were reportedly making salt at a Tomé salt spring (Waselkov and Gums 2000:20). By the late eighteenth century, however, salt manufacture and trade by many Native American peoples had ceased due to colonial disruptions to the salt trade and the importation of cheap salt from Europe. In 1796 United States Indian agent Benjamin Hawkins (2003:21) described two Creek women who were desperate to trade for salt in order to preserve meat. Similar tales are told of the Cherokees, whose health declined in the late eighteenth century due partly to a lack of salt (Hatley 1989:231). The apparent reliance on European methods of preservation

Figure 6.2. Salt-making at the Lower Salt Works (1CK28), ca. A.D. 1200 (drawing by Steven M. Meredith).

and European salt sources in the eighteenth century marks a shift in foodways and the end of Native American salt production.

The following short narrative attempts to weave together the ethnographic, historical, and archaeological evidence outlined above in order to create a visual model for what life might have been like one summer day in A.D. 1200 at the Lower Salt Works (1CK28) near the Tombigbee River. It was inspired by the drawing in Figure 6.2.

A Day at the Salt Springs

The young girl twitched when she felt the yellow fly land on her arm. She knew that the sting was coming, but she could not risk dropping the jars of saltwater to slap it. Since she had come of age last winter, her mother decided that she was ready to help make salt on their family's annual trip to the salt springs. The girl was eager to prove her worth. In years past, she had spent many weeks here running through the forest with her cousins and siblings, collecting limbs, competing to see who could reach the dead ones not yet fallen, and stacking them into neat piles to be hauled to the fires by the family's dog. But this time was different, because she was treading across the salt flats, back and forth to the dark bubbling pool of saltwater to fill the jars from its depths. She took the water to the low knoll where her older sister stood on an old poplar stump and slowly poured the brine into baskets full of soil. The conical baskets, which the girls had helped weave during the spring, were mounted on a wooden frame and were all full of soil dug from the salt flats. Her older cousins were there now, scraping up the salty earth with hoes and deer scapulas into baskets. One of them yelped when her basket's tumpline became entangled with her hair as she swung it around on her back. The digging was the hardest work, thought the girl. She didn't mind so much toting the water, remembering how her mother had told her that it was special to be so close to the Salt Mother, from whose body the briny water flowed.

A harsh word from her sister brought the girl back to her task, and she bent over to adjust the jars that were placed under the baskets. Into each jar dripped a rivulet of concentrated brine. When the jars were poured into one of the big bowls set up on the exposed salt flat, the sun's heat would quickly change the solution into a thick paste of wet salt. There her mother and her aunt worked in unspoken rhythm to move wet salt to the large pans in the fire. They seemed to know almost instinctively when to add more wood, when to adjust the embers, when to shift a pan or wedge in a clump of clay, ensuring that the salt crystallized evenly and that the pans didn't crack. Still, the area was littered with broken pans, in places so densely that the sand was not visible. It would be several years before the girl was apprenticed to the fire work, and she had not yet perfected making baskets or pots. She was expected up the hill in her grandmother's hut that evening to repair baskets and mats. Another aunt was already there busily stripping apart palmetto fronds, occasionally stirring a pot of hominy stew. These were her only responsibilities this year, as she was pregnant and could not set foot on the salt flats.

Distant thunder signaled a threat to the day's work. The girl's mother made a few quick motions with her shell scraper, removing the last warm, dry grains from a pan onto a growing pile of pale gray salt. This she poured into a skin bag. As she stood to take it up to her hut for protection from the coming rain, she called to her daughters to cover the pans with the poles and mats that were stacked nearby. It was a short rain, as they usually were this time of year, but it was enough to bring brothers and uncle up from the river, where they had been fishing all morning. She could just see them as they skirted the edge of the salt flat headed toward the men's shelter. The women gathered under their shelter and set about dividing the salt into smaller and smaller piles, each one to be wrapped tightly in palmetto leaves for the trip home. As she tied up each bundle with pieces of cordage, the girl wondered if the Salt Mother would always spring forth from this piece of earth and if one day she would bring her own daughters to make salt. She thought about how proud they always were to arrive home with their canoes laden with the little green packages, ready for trade, for distribution to friends and relatives, and for gifts to the shaman and elders. The rain ended, the buzzing of the yellow flies returned, and the girl returned to her jars, looking forward to the weeks of salt-making ahead and then returning home, where the ripening corn awaited.

Conclusion

The visual narrative method of interpreting data about the everyday will not appeal to everyone. Imagination, however, is germane to good science and necessary for discovery. Regardless of differences in methodology or theoretical approach, imagination drives a question for which all of us seek an answer: *what was it like?* If we could use a time machine to witness one day in the prehistoric past, I doubt that we would turn down the opportunity just because it was not necessarily representative of the larger phase, period, or theory. Whatever we might see, hear, and smell, such as how salt was being made and by whom, would give us details of salt production, inform theories of culture change, and permanently alter our relationship to pottery typologies and feature cross-sections. Without a time machine, the combination of the ethnoarchaeology of salt and narratives is as close as we can get, rendering it less idiosyncratic and materializing its presence in the daily lives of prehistoric southeastern peoples.

Working with visual narratives does have limited explanatory value—much like a museum exhibit, it can show what we think a religious procession might have looked like, how artifacts were used, and where symbolic icons were placed. In looking at this moment in time, however, little is revealed or explained about historical processes or culture change. We are left with a two-dimensional, synchronic keyhole picture. Our question becomes: is this anthropology? I have proposed that the answer is "yes." Limited explanatory value does not mean zero explanatory value. The narrative approach, like any useful interpretive tool, is based on data from excavations and analysis of artifacts, but it unites cultural ideals about family, religion, housing, subsistence, reproduction, and other elements of daily life that are embedded within salt production and consumption and many other practices. These interrelationships may be obfuscated if interpreted from a theoretical approach that emphasizes one aspect of macroculture as manifested over multiple generations, such as political economy, craft specialization, or even agency. My initial studies of the salt works, for example, centered on analyzing pottery to look for evidence of standardization for big-picture economic interpretations of human behavior. This is useful, but the daily life experiences of the people who made the pots were lost. If I were to excavate there again, my research design would include a survey and excavation of the areas where the salt-makers slept, ate, weaved, made pots, and performed other tasks structured by and around salt production in a day. From this perspective, approaching an understanding of the everyday through the creation of data-based texts is an extension of postprocessual and interpretive archaeologies. Indeed, it is simply another perspective, no less valid than hypotheses hung on broader theories; it is a matter of resolution. If it helps some of us to structure our questions better, organize our thoughts, prepare for further work, or teach others about the past, then it might be an approach worth applying across the discipline, perhaps every day.

Acknowledgments

Steven Meredith's thoughtful drawing of a salt-making scene is a product of our many years of archaeological collaboration. Conversations with Sarah Price, Phil Carr, Steven Meredith, James Lamb, Mary Spanos, Paul Eubanks, Elizabeth Horton, and Ian Brown influenced this work for the better. I extend much gratitude to Sarah and Phil for their encouragement and to two dubious but game reviewers, reserving for myself the ownership of any oversights and errors.

7

Maintaining Relations with Deer

A Day in the Life in the Middle Archaic

CHRISTOPHER R. MOORE AND RICHARD W. JEFFERIES

Subsistence, extraction, reduction, organization of production: the language of Archaic period studies is attractively multisyllabic and has served archaeologists well in elucidating what Archaic peoples ate and how they obtained and used stone tools. If we take a moment to reflect critically on this language, we will find that it is largely, and unintentionally, a language of extraction. Someone unfamiliar with archaeological values (or jargon) might read up on Archaic lifeways and conclude that we think of our hunter-gatherer subjects as unidimensional, focused on exploitation of their environments. One goal of this volume is to nuance the general nature of our data, thereby providing empathetic and relevant accounts of indigenous North American lifeways that broaden the perspective of those traditional approaches that are more firmly grounded in the hard materiality of the archaeological record (Price and Carr, Chapter 15). It is our task to contribute to this goal by developing a plausible account of human-animal relations in the Middle Archaic (see also Moore 2015; Moore and Dekle 2010; Moore and Thompson 2012). Anticipating our critics, we readily admit that the account of Middle Archaic lifeways we provide is something of a just-so story in that we develop a narrative of Archaic life that elaborates beyond the simple cause and effect conclusions that can be reliably drawn from our data. In this sense, ours is an "interpretive" account of Archaic lifeways whose validity (or lack thereof) rests on the extent to which we can convincingly infer to the best explanation (e.g., Fogelin 2007). It is not our goal to provide the final account of some universally applicable Middle Archaic history of animal-human relations. Rather, we hope our just-so story can contribute to a broader, expanded approach to Archaic research in general. We need to think of Archaic peoples as individuals, as humans, as ancestors and forebearers rather than as subjects. In sum, we hope this account will help us both to do better archaeology and to provide more humanizing and dynamic accounts of the past.

To set up our narrative we are going to provide two sources of that information we consider relevant to understanding Middle Archaic human-animal relations. First, we are going to delve into hunter-gatherer ethnography, principally from northern hunting societies and argue that hunting cultures are rarely extractive at their core. Rather, human-animal relations in hunting societies are better conceived as a meshwork of entanglements and mutual obligations. Relations between humans and the animals that they hunt in these cultures are more social than purely economic. This elaborates on an understanding of hunter-gatherer social relations termed a "dwelling perspective" by Tim Ingold (2000:189).

The concept "everyday" fits naturally within a dwelling perspective in that the social relations that permeate an individual's lifeworld are actively maintained through daily practices (e.g., Moore 2015). In this chapter we apply this familiar (to us) framework to social relationships that we argue were essential to Middle Archaic hunter-gatherers—the relationships that they maintained with deer. This approach proved highly productive in that it caused us to think about the ways in which deer as social beings articulated with (and were entangled among) other aspects of Middle Archaic lifeways. It also caused us to consider ways in which a study of the everyday practices of Middle Archaic peoples could be operationalized in the field and in the lab.

Second, we draw on the Middle Archaic archaeological record, focusing on the Black Earth site in southern Illinois and several Green River Archaic sites in west central Kentucky, to argue that white-tailed deer were extremely important to Middle Archaic hunters not only as sources of food but also as social and spiritual creatures. We describe the ubiquity of deer remains on Middle Archaic sites and provide a sample of some of the contexts in which deer are present in the Middle Archaic archaeological record. Finally, we weave the ethnological and the archaeological records into our plausible account of a day in the life in the Middle Archaic.

Ethnography

The crux of our ethnological argument is that hunting societies perceive of "hunting" as a complex assortment of actions directed at maintaining good relations with the animals that they hunted (Ingold 2000) or, at the very least, with an overriding "Animal Spirit" (Knight 2012). Ingold (2000) frames this relational understanding of human-animal relations in his book *The Perception of the Environment*. According to him, hunter-gatherers perceive animals or other organism-persons not as separate and distinct entities "out there" but as potential social partners. Interacting with those potential partners involves entering into relations with them, which can be as significant as the relations among kin—so much so that kin relations and other social relations are inevitably linked. Treating kin poorly can result in a failed hunt; treating prey inappropriately can result in trouble among kin (Ingold 2000; Ridington 1982).

This is the case among the Athapaskan Dunne-za, a northern hunting society located in northeastern British Columbia. The Dunne-za traditionally lived in bands of 25 to 35 people and were seasonally mobile with an annual range up to 400 km (Ridington 1982:472). They relied heavily on mountain sheep, moose, deer, caribou, and black bears for food and a variety of other fur-bearing animals for clothing (Ridington 1982). For the Dunne-za knowledge is a person's most important possession, and the world is formed through myths, dreams, and visions that act as sources of knowledge. Ritual leaders are people who "know something"—powerful shamans called Dreamers who heal the sick, conduct soul flights, help the dead follow the Trail to Heaven, and aid hunters by following animal trails revealed to them in dreams (Ridington 1988).

For the Dunne-za, the act of dreaming is both a ritual and a social act, and the outcome of the hunt is dependent upon it. Hunters and their prey enter into and maintain social relations through dreams, and an animal must have given itself to a hunter in a dream before it can be taken. Failure to get this permission (failure to maintain good social relations) would result in a failed hunt. Human-animal interactions are not simply predator-prey relations; humans seek to understand animals to be able to predict their behavior—follow their trails—and animals seek to understand how humans have fulfilled their obligations to them (Ridington 1982:473).

The Khanty of Siberia hold similar beliefs regarding animal spirits. For them, hunting is not so much a predator-prey relationship as a relationship among the hunters and the spirits. Animals, primarily elk, are considered gifts of the spirits, given to those who maintain proper social relations through appropriate disposal of the gifted animal's remains (Jordan 2001). Bones and other animal parts are deposited at holy sites, and certain elements are consumed in specific ways as necessitated by the spirit gifters. Peter Jordan (2003) provides consumption of elk heads at holy sites and placement of bear bones in deep pools as examples. Returning these objects to their rightful places creates an encultured, ritualized landscape. The consumption of elk heads in a special way and deposition of bear bones in a particular place are forms of ritual exchanges—the animal parts acting as means of communication for the creation and maintenance of human-animal-spirit social relations.

John Knight (2012) further elaborates on this distinction between human-animal and human-spirit relationships. He argues that hunters do not develop social relations with the individual animals that they hunt in the same way that they create and maintain relations with human persons. Rather, he contends that human-animal sharing "pertains to animals as members of a class" (Knight 2012:337). Hunters (and shamans) develop asymmetrical personal relationships with Animal Spirits. It is this Spirit who controls access to the class of hunted animal; personal relations are created and maintained with the Animal Spirit via interactions during the hunt.

Knight's (2012) discussion of the Animal Spirit is intended as a critique of Ingold's dwelling perspective on human-animal sociality. As David Anderson (2012a) points out in his comments on Knight (2012), however, human-animal relations are developed in myriad contexts outside the hunt (for example, in dreams), providing ample time for significant social engagement. Furthermore, the Animal Spirit conceived by Knight is not always an individualized spirit being as we might understand it through the lens of Western culture. Rather, the Animal Spirit often is literally in the person of the individual animals hunted (Anderson 2012a). The ontological distinction between animal and Animal Spirit, body and soul, found in Western culture cannot be uncritically extended to Amerindian worldviews (Ingold 2000; Viveiros de Castro 1998).

Animal Effects

We have already mentioned patterned behavior (ritual deposition) of animal remains as a means of creating and maintaining social relations with animals and other spirits. One other interaction with animal remains is relevant to this discussion—animal effects. The literature on shamanism is rife with examples of shamans using animal remains or representations of animals to control, interact with, transform into, and/or adopt the perspectives of animal-persons. Often shamans do this by donning animal "clothing" such as furs or masks or wearing costumes that include representations of mythical animals and cosmological features like the sun and the earth (Eliade 1964; Viveiros de Castro 2004). According to Anne-Christine Hornborg (2006), shamans learn about being a bear by becoming a bear, wearing a bear's fur or mask, or walking like a bear. Cross-culturally, Mircea Eliade (1964) identified the three most common animal forms adopted by shamans as birds, deer, and bears.

The animal furs, masks, and other objects used to adopt animal perspectives should not be mistaken as mere ritual tools, however, for in a relational world these objects have spirits and are agents (VanPool and Newsome 2012). Donning a mask and adopting an animal perspective is a transformative process that creates a new personhood; the objects are not passive catalysts but actively contribute to the creation of the social relations necessary for the success of this transformation. Objects do not merely represent the world (any more than shamans in costumes are "representing" animal-persons). Rather, they construct the world through interactions and, like other organism-persons, contribute to the construction of the web of relations that is the lifeworld (Ingold 2006, 2007; Olsen 2003; VanPool and Newsome 2012).

Chantal Conneller (2004) refers to this generative and transformative quality of some kinds of objects as "animal effects." For her, the act of donning an animal's skull, fur, or antlers was a means of extending the human body and adopting that animal's perspective. She interprets modified red deer frontlets and antler points at Star Carr as evidence that these objects had been used in ritual headgear as animal effects employed by Mesolithic shamans to connect themselves to deer and re-create themselves as a new deer-human-person.

Deer in the Middle Archaic

Deer were likely the most important source of meat and protein among indigenous peoples in eastern North America from initial colonization until venison was replaced by pork and beef in the eighteenth and nineteenth centuries. For instance, Miller and Tune (this volume) point out the importance of understanding deer behaviors during floods for our interpretations of Paleoindian biface distributions along natural levees in the Mid-South. Narrative references to "lean deer" and the "Deer Moon" during the Early Archaic by Hollenbach and Carmody (Chapter 5) aptly illustrate the significance of "thinking about deer" in hunting societies.

Unfortunately, preservation conditions at Paleoindian and Early Archaic sites often obscure the significance of deer and other animals for these early peoples. The improved preservation conditions of shell-bearing sites and increased visibility of large middens during the Middle to Late Archaic, in contrast, result in a much more abundant zooarchaeological record. While deer and other animal remains are common at Middle and Late Archaic sites in the midcontinent, however, we rarely discuss the potential importance of those remains for understanding human-animal interactions beyond basic subsistence. Unfortunately, the nature of reported data is such that it is often difficult to compile a detailed comparative database of animal uses by species, since the species of individual bones or elements are rarely reported, particularly in older works. With these caveats in mind, we now briefly describe the archaeological evidence for the importance of one particular species to Middle Archaic hunter-gatherers in southern Illinois and western Kentucky: white-tailed deer.

Subsistence

The importance of deer in Middle Archaic diets is so well understood that it is almost common knowledge. In their important comparative study of Mid-Holocene faunal exploitation in the southeastern and midcontinental Archaic, Bonnie Styles and Walter Klippel (1996:133) found that deer was a major component of prehistoric diets throughout all periods but that deer consumption increased throughout the Early Archaic to peak during the Middle Archaic.

Looking specifically at the Black Earth and Green River sites, white-tailed deer is the most abundant mammalian taxon at Black Earth, constituting more than 80 percent of the documented meat yield and more than 70 percent of the identified bone specimens from the late Middle to Late Archaic midden (Breitburg 1982:865–874; Styles and Klippel 1996) (Table 7.1). The presence of both cranial and postcranial remains at Black Earth indicates that entire deer carcasses were returned to, butchered, and processed at the site (Jefferies 1982:1477).

Middle to Late Archaic faunal assemblages from Green River Archaic sites are consistent with others in the Southeast and Midcontinent, with white-tailed

Table 7.1. Animal Remains from Late Middle to Late Archaic Midden Contexts (Zone 3) at Black Earth

Species	Black Earth Site Area A, Zone 3	
	NISP[a]	Percentage
White-Tailed Deer	7749	72
Raccoon	88	0.8
Dog	51	0.5
Turkey	161	1.5
Duck	102	0.9
Painted/Map Turtle	178	1.7
Eastern Box Turtle	154	1.4
Stinkpot	574	5.3
Eastern Snapping Turtle	128	1.2
Bowfin	84	0.8

[a] Only animals represented by an NISP of 50 or more are listed here. The total NISP of identified specimens is 10,767.

Table 7.2. Animal Remains from Waterscreen and Flotation Samples from DeWeese, Haynes, and Carlston Annis

	DeWeese		Haynes		Carlston Annis	
Species	NISP[a]	Percentage	NISP	Percentage	NISP	Percentage
White-Tailed Deer	314	10.2	260	12.4	520	9.4
Unidentified Large Mammal	1142	37.2	518	24.8	3734	67.3
Fish	122	3.4	244	11.7	224	4
Unidentified Turtle	611	19.9	478	22.9	247	4.5
Box Turtle	141	4.6	70	3.3	78	1.4
Birds	345	11.2	205	9.8	281	5.1
Fox/Gray Squirrel	65	2.1	82	3.9	70	1.3

[a] Only animals represented by an NISP of 50 or more are listed here. The total NISP, not including bones classified as "unidentified vertebrate," is 3,072 for DeWeese, 2,090 for Haynes, and 5,546 for Carlston Annis.

deer dominating and riverine resources like fish, turtles, and freshwater mussels acting as important secondary resources. Deer is the most abundant mammalian taxon represented at DeWeese, Haynes, and Carlston Annis, ranging between 9.4 and 12.4 percent of all bones identified at least to class (Table 7.2). If we assume that most of the "unidentified large mammal" bones from these sites are white-tailed deer, these frequencies increase to 37.2 to 76.7 percent (Crothers 1999:220–225, 2005; Glore 2005). As Michael Glore (2005:327) succinctly states, "Terrestrial subsistence pursuits at Carlston Annis were conspicuously centered around the hunting of white-tailed deer." George Crothers (2005:312) found that representation of deer remains at Carlston Annis suggests that the feet and head were selectively carried back to the site, leaving the trunk (possibly with the prime cuts of meat removed) at the kill site.

Tool Manufacture

While the data are sparse, at least at Carlston Annis and Black Earth, we can begin to see some variation in the treatment of deer carcasses. Certain elements were transported to base camps and habitation sites and others were not. Likewise, once the carcass was processed, certain elements were selected for use as tools, ornaments, and so forth. At sites with good bone preservation, modified bone and antler objects are well represented in tool assemblages, often equaling chipped-stone tools by counts and percentages. Typically, these bone tools were most commonly manufactured from deer and unidentified large mammal (likely deer) longbone elements (Moore 2011).

Emanuel Breitburg's (1982) detailed study of the bone and antler tool assemblages from Black Earth illustrates the importance of deer in the manufacture of Middle to Late Archaic organic tools. He found that 680 of the modified bone and antler implements from Black Earth were manufactured from deer remains (60 percent of antler) and another 1,071 were made from unidentified large mammal bones that were likely deer (Breitburg 1982:918) (Figure 7.1). Antler was used to manufacture chipped-stone tools (percussors, punches, and drifts); antler tines were used as projectile points, awls, and flaking tools; and three antler beads were recovered (Breitburg 1982:920). Bone tools manufactured from deer remains include deer mandible awls, deer scapula awls and hide-scraping tools, a variety of longbone and metapodial pointed and spatulate implements, bone fishhooks, and carved and decorated bone pins (Breitburg 1982:920–929).

Karli White's (1990, 2005) analysis of bone tools from the Carlston Annis site indicates a similar focus on use of deer remains as tools in the Green River

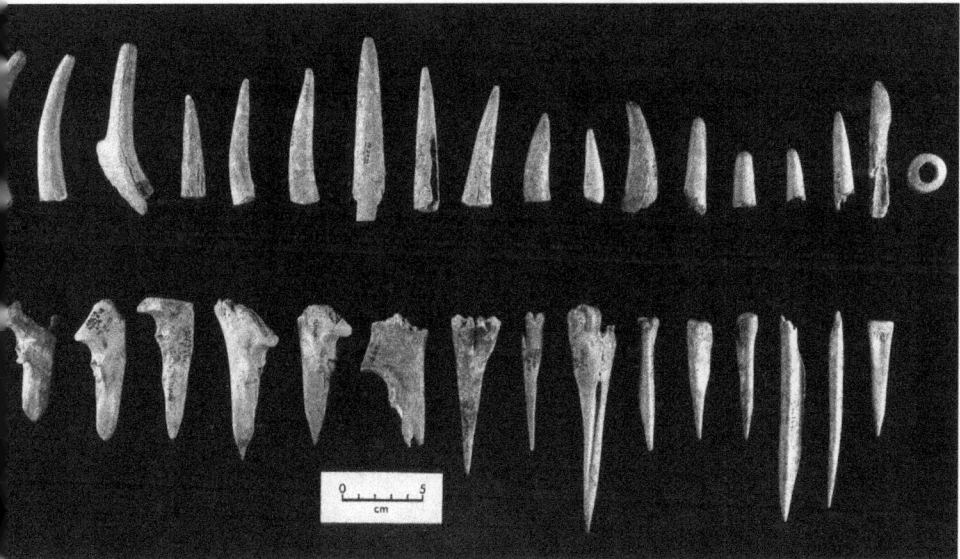

Figure 7.1. Modified bone implements from the Black Earth site, Area A (image courtesy of the Center for Archaeological Investigations, Southern Illinois University at Carbondale).

region. Her analysis included modified bone implements recovered by Shell Mound Archaeological Project (SMAP) investigations and a limited sample of implements recovered by the Works Progress Administration (WPA). While most modified bone implements were too small for taxonomic identification, most that could be identified were manufactured from deer remains. These objects included a variety of shaped and modified antler and bone pointed implements, fishhooks and fishhook production debitage, and antler handles or hafts (White 2005).

Ritual and Mortuary Uses

Not surprisingly, these same deer bone and antler artifacts occur with human burials at both Black Earth and the Green River sites. Bone awls, worked antler tines and drifts, a bone pin, and a deer scapula scraper all were found with human burials at Black Earth. Interestingly, an antler cup was discovered with Burial No. 86, although this may be made from elk antler. A second antler cup was discovered with a burial placed on a ridge adjacent to the Black Earth site. Also recovered with human burials at Black Earth were examples of unmodified deer bones (e.g., with Burial No. 111) that may indicate the ritual disposal of deer remains in special contexts (Lynch 1982).

Unfortunately, comparable data pertaining to unmodified deer remains found with human burials are not available for the Green River sites; however, numerous examples of modified bone and antler objects are included among the mortuary assemblages from these sites. While precise zooarchaeological identifications of most of these objects have not been made, burial objects that are likely manufactured from white-tailed deer remains include bone and antler awls; pins and other pointed implements; antler projectile points; antler tool production debitage and other modified antler tines; antler drifts and other flaking tools; and bone and antler spatulas, gouges, and chisels. Most interestingly, bone and antler atlatl hooks, weights, and handles are most commonly recovered from mortuary contexts at Green River sites, suggesting that these objects were special tools requiring ritual deposition (Figure 7.2). They often incorporated deer bone and antler remains into their construction, which may indicate that some form of hunting magic was being invoked in their production and use. Finally, the only possible evidence for the use of deer remains to invoke animal effects that we have identified so far is the presence of two deer jaws with Burial Nos. 487 and 698 at Indian Knoll (Webb 1950a, 1950b, 1951, 1974; Webb and Haag 1939, 1947).

With the possible exception of the ritual deposition of unmodified deer bones with human burials at Black Earth and the ritual implications of deer

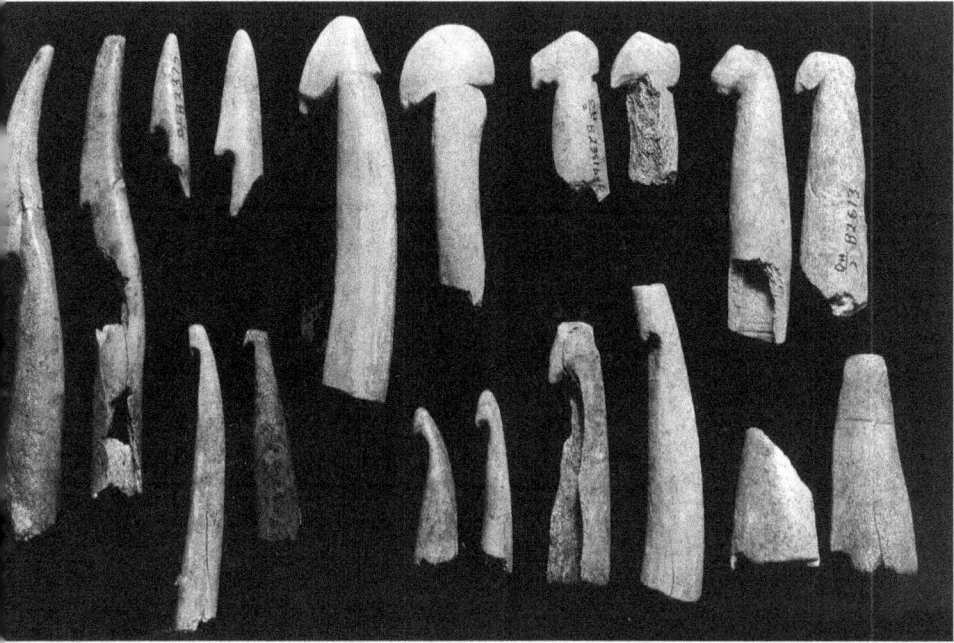

Figure 7.2. Deer antler atlatl hooks from the Indian Knoll site (image courtesy of the William S. Webb Museum of Anthropology, University of Kentucky).

bone and antler atlatls at the Green River sites, evidence for the ritualized uses of deer bone and antler in the Middle Archaic is sparse. Human burials are only one potential source of ritual data, however, and it is likely (based again on hunter-gatherer ethnography) that we are either missing or misinterpreting many thousands of other ritualized contexts where deer and other animal remains were treated in special ways and invoked in ritual practices. Equating animal remains with subsistence (and only with subsistence) while failing to fully explain the rich contextual data associated with those remains has likely led us to miss hundreds of ritual features in our excavations, ritual features that we hope will be identified and fully evaluated by future archaeologists.

A Day in the Life in the Middle Archaic

Integrating the ethnological and the archaeological, every day in the life of a person living in the greater Ohio River valley region during the Middle Archaic would have been spent immersed in white-tailed deer (Figure 7.3). From the moment of awakening in the morning, people were surrounded by deer.

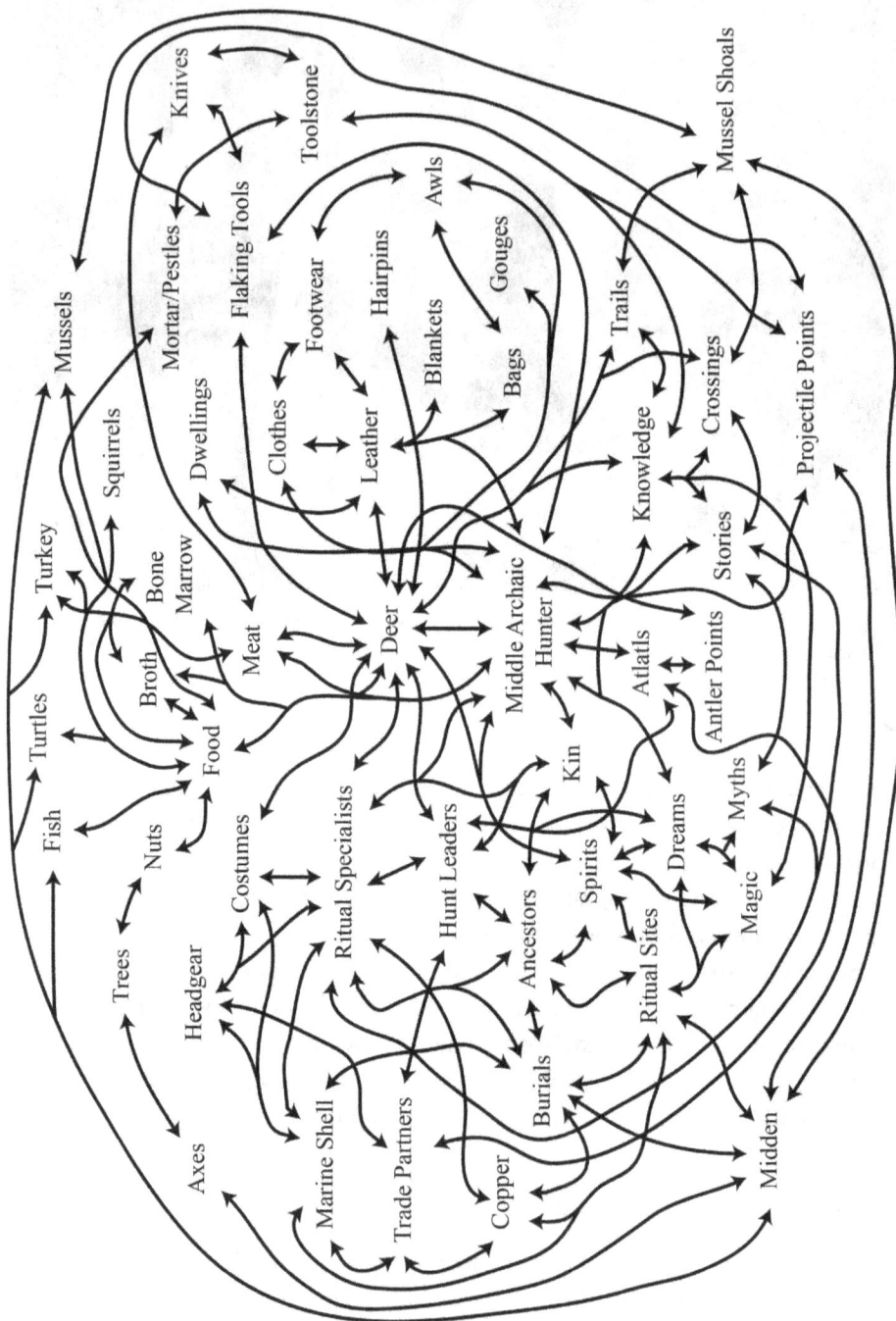

Figure 7.3. Tanglegram depicting the integration of deer in the Middle Archaic lifeworld.

Clothes, blankets, and tools were often manufactured from deer elements. Hair pieces and personal ornaments were made from deer bone or antler. Deer hides were likely used as clothing and shelter. Leather manufactured from deer hides was used as thongs to tie bags, lace clothing and footwear, and hang objects. Antler and larger bones were used for handles for a variety of tools, and the tips of awls and flaking tools often were manufactured from deer bones and antler. Everywhere people looked upon waking in the morning they would have seen the evidence of the importance of white-tailed deer in their life.

When it came time to eat, deer became even more important. Deer meats were cooked and roasted, probably in a variety of ways and using a variety of seasonings. On long journeys deer pemmican was likely the predominant source of protein. Fats rendered from deer meats and bone marrow were likely used in a variety of soups and stews. Every member of the group would have had a clear understanding that deer were the givers of life, the most important subsistence resource, guardians of every individual's health and well-being.

This was equally clear to the hunters, whose task it was to obtain these deer products for the group. For the hunters, and potentially also the shamans or other ritual specialists who guided the hunters in their task, deer were an ever-present occupation. To hunt deer successfully, the hunters had to be ever wary of their movements, their behaviors, their health, and their life cycles. A hunter walking through the woods would always have been vigilant, looking for the most recent signs of deer activity—a scraping on a tree here, a fresh pile of scat there. Signs of deer, the paths of deer, and stories and myths of deer likely occupied hunters' days. It is even possible that dreams of deer and Deer Spirits occupied their nights.

If we accept the premise that Archaic hunter-gatherers, like so many other Amerindian peoples, held a relational worldview, then Middle Archaic hunters and shamans would have invested energy in developing and maintaining social relations with deer or Deer Spirits. They likely practiced forms of hunting magic, told myths and stories of deer, and performed rituals to maintain their social standing with deer. They may have butchered deer carcasses in particular ways, sharing many cuts of meat but saving select cuts for special ritual occasions, or consuming certain elements immediately to placate the spirit of the deer. It is possible that certain parts of the carcass had to be disposed of at ritual sites or returned to the Deer Spirit. Other elements, however, were collected for use as bags, hides, and bone and antler tools. In either case, there likely was no ontological distinction between the ritual and the utilitarian. All actions involving deer were highly meaningful and served as evidence for the good relations between the hunters and the deer.

Venturing further into the speculative we can postulate that some of the most important rituals involved in securing a successful hunt were restricted to ritual specialists, hunters, or perhaps just hunt leaders. Given that atlatls bearing deer bone and antler handles, hooks, and elaborate stone, bone, or shell atlatl weights were most commonly disposed of with burials, it is highly likely that these were special objects, not just routine weapons of the hunt. Most utilitarian atlatls probably were made entirely of wood or were minimally adorned with simple handles and hooks. While it seems probable that the special atlatls held multiple meanings, perhaps as important symbols of leadership or emblems of trade alliances, it also seems likely that they were invoked in hunting rituals.

Whether atlatls functioned literally as hunting weapons to harvest deer or ritually as tools of hunting magic (or both), the act of reducing deer bone and antler into atlatl components likely had great symbolic meaning. In a society where good relations with deer meant the difference between life and death, health and hunger, the act of invoking deer in the manufacture of the tools of the trade takes on special significance. Perhaps the shaping of deer remains into an atlatl was a means of "giving back" to the Deer Spirit or was deemed pleasing to deer. Perhaps it was a means of magically invoking the essence of deer, thereby providing the hunters with access to special knowledge that would aid them during the hunt. Perhaps these atlatls (their shapes and sizes) came to hunters in their dreams or in visions or their manufacture was a materialization of the hunters' good relations with deer.

If special atlatls did have magical properties associated with the hunt, they likely were not the only objects that did so. Unfortunately, identifying ritual objects in the archaeological record is incredibly difficult and almost always based on circumstantial evidence. The deer jaws found with Burial Nos. 487 and 698 at Indian Knoll are one contender for a second deer-related class of ritual objects. We have not yet examined these objects for use-related wear, so it is possible that the jaws are simply unmodified bones or cutting tools. In other contexts where mandibles are found with burials in the Green River, however, they are often associated with clusters of artifacts that were likely contents of medicine bundles or are modified in such a way as to suggest that they were worn (Marquardt and Watson 2005; Webb 1950a, 1974). If they were worn, then it is possible that the deer jaws were part of headgear, perhaps shamanic paraphernalia, and that they served to evoke animal effects, like the deer tines and frontlets at Star Carr described by Conneller (2004). The hunters or ritual specialists donning these objects or the costumes that included them as components may have done so in an effort to "become deer" and adopt a deer perspective. Among northern hunting societies, such ritual transformations were a dangerous means of communing with animals and with spirits to gain their unique perspectives (VanPool 2009; Viveiros de Castro 1998).

Conclusion

Archaeological evidence from sites that have intensive Middle Archaic occupations like Black Earth, Indian Knoll, and Carlson Annis clearly indicates that white-tailed deer played an extremely important role in Archaic lifeways. Subsistence data indicate that most meat consumed during the Middle Archaic came from deer. Where organic preservation is good, it appears that many of the tools used by Middle Archaic peoples were made from deer bones and antlers. Given the unique importance of deer in the lives of Archaic peoples, then, it is not too much of a stretch of the imagination to posit that deer also played a significant role in their ritual lives or at least in the ritual lives of the hunters, whose task it was to provision the group with this life-sustaining staple food source. Unfortunately, what those rituals were and how they manifest themselves in the archaeological record is currently a matter of speculation.

Fortunately, though social relations are not material, the practices of creating and maintaining those social relations are inherently material. They require hunting tools, offerings, masks, and ritual paraphernalia and the purposeful and meaningful disposal of animal carcasses. Unfortunately, the kinds of rich contextual data needed to test hypotheses about the everyday or the degree to which humans and animals entered into social relations with one another are often lacking outside of burial excavations. A more detailed assessment of the importance of deer in the social lives of Middle Archaic peoples requires detailed reporting and recording of the contexts of deposition of deer remains at archaeological sites. Detailed field zooarchaeology, particularly at special context sites in secluded locations like caves and rockshelters, is necessary to identify patterns that could be tested against ethnoarchaeological data from Siberia, South America, and other regions. In the lab, zooarchaeological reporting should include detailed inventories of the elements recovered, the ages of the animals represented, and the presence of any modifications like butchery marks and burning that might provide evidence for ritualistic treatment. Reporting where, how, and in what manner deer (and other animal) remains were utilized and discarded is essential for understanding the everyday significance of deer in the social lives of Middle Archaic peoples. Zooarchaeology must be a central component of research designs at hunter-gatherer sites if we ever hope to elevate narratives such as this one beyond the realm of an informed just-so story.

In this chapter, we have made it our purpose to highlight the obvious (deer were important) as a prelude to our speculation. We do not insist that our just-so story of Middle Archaic relations with deer is a correct and true history of Middle Archaic peoples in general or even of those who lived at Black Earth or along the Green River in particular. We do feel that the narrative that we have spun here is reasonable and consistent with both the archaeological record and the comparative ethnological record of hunting societies and hope that it can spark some interest in further pursuing the richness and texture of the lives of those we study through more detailed reporting of the depositional contexts of animal remains and consideration of their social significance.

We need to do a better job of humanizing the Archaic. Thinking about the everyday and using our imaginations to speculate on the meanings assigned to the objects we encounter in the archaeological record can be a valuable means of hypothesis building (see also Dumas, Chapter 6). It can lead to more intensive investigations of special use contexts. Twenty years ago, Patricia Galloway (1998) asked why there are no menstrual huts in the Late Prehistoric Southeast. The answer was that no one was asking the right questions or looking for them. Likewise, we need to start asking better questions about the ritualized actions of daily practice that infuse the lives of peoples living in hunting societies if we truly seek to understand the past—if we truly seek an anthropological archaeology.

8

The Itineraries of Late Archaic Shell and Ceramic Cooking Vessels

ASA R. RANDALL AND ZACKARY I. GILMORE

The archaeology of Archaic period hunter-gatherers has often been regarded as a material account of the mundane, a record of the "everyday" par excellence. The apparent longue durée through which many practices persisted has led some to see Archaic lifeways as "monotonous sameness" (Fogelson 1989:139), characterized more by concerns over nourishment and tool acquisition than by social relations (see also Moore and Jefferies, this volume). Quite to the contrary, in the past two decades archaeologists have revealed seemingly extraordinary Archaic practices, including widespread exchange networks, monumental construction, and ritualized interactions (Sassaman 2010). These discoveries certainly task us with rethinking the Archaic generally and the nature of what constituted the nonmundane and the everyday. In this chapter, we argue that any account of everyday must wrestle with the ways in which perhaps more socially poignant moments were embedded within, and at times likely even impinged upon, the ongoing flow of daily life (see also Pluckhahn et al., Chapter 9). Specifically, we highlight how neither of these broadly construed social contexts (everyday and extraordinary) is meaningful without the other and show that they perhaps were not easily separable into different spheres.

Our contribution focuses on containers made from clay or marine shell, whose use is often presumed to reflect the processing of consumables for everyday fare. In the southeastern United States, one of the most widely noted transformations during the Late Archaic (ca. 5700–3200 cal B.P.) was the emergence of portable and durable container technologies, the so-called container revolution. In our study area, the St. Johns River valley and associated coasts of northern Florida, this process is evident first in the use of cooking and serving vessels manufactured out of marine gastropod shells (which goes back to at least 7,000 years ago) and their replacement after 4,600 years ago by fiber-tempered ceramics of the Orange tradition. The container revolution in the Southeast has been understood by some to reflect the need for efficient technologies to generate or store food resources for increasing populations (Saunders and Hays 2004; Smith 1986). We find little support for such an interpretation in our study area, where the subsistence economy was virtually unchanged (Blessing 2011; Russo et al. 1992). This may have to do with the fact that containers, generally speaking, were nothing new in Florida or elsewhere. Containers of various sorts were used by virtually all ancient southeastern communities. Aside from the numerous pits used for storage and/or processing that have been recorded, the occasional impression of textiles or fragments of textiles from saturated locations attests to the importance of things that contain in the daily lives of past southeasterners.

Our method in this contribution is to trace how Late Archaic cooking vessels moved through the lives of inhabitants of the St. Johns River, from their production to their ultimate deposition. These so-called itineraries follow the wanderings of vessels and persons as they came together in various social contexts. In brief, we find that vessels were implicated in the daily happenings of many persons, affording both the opportunities to transform substances into consumed foods and the occasions for individuals to interact. Yet they were also central to people's commemorative or ceremonial lives, as the vessels both contained and sustained memories and meanings (see also Pluckhahn et al., Chapter 9). The earlier marine shell vessels were rare and were unlikely to be used frequently but were nonetheless found in many different social contexts. These vessels disappear with the advent of pottery production in the St. Johns valley during the Orange period. Ceramic containers were likely widely available and were produced by a variety of persons. Yet some vessels were more likely than others to be used in social gatherings, with evidence for some coming from as far away as southwest Florida. A subset of early pottery may have even been surrogates for the earlier marine shell vessels. Despite the lack of coherence between a shift in cooking technologies and subsistence pursuits on the St. Johns River, change can nonetheless be seen in the organization of domestic practice, the relations between local inhabitants and regional communities, and the structure of commemorative practice involving feasting and mound construction. In the next section we briefly discuss object itineraries and explore how they can be used to illuminate matters in the lives of past persons.

Object Itineraries of the Everyday and Extraordinary

Human lives are saturated with objects. Things inform our everyday experiences as we go about making do in the world. They allow us to transform substances, to sustain ourselves, to communicate with others, to commemorate specific events or persons, and to transform and experience places. Thus things not only "function" but generate networks among different experiences and meanings. For example, as noted by Pluckhahn et al. (Chapter 9), it is not necessarily the case that objects crafted for a specific destination, such as incorporation in ritual contexts, were crafted on certain occasions. Instead these objects could be crafted amid everyday experiences. Yet the destination of the objects and the timing of the event no doubt influenced the tempo and situatedness of everyday practice.

While Late Archaic durable containers were not revolutionary in their impact on the subsistence economy, we argue that they were transformative in their role in generating social relations through daily and extraordinary practice. We suggest that one way to expose the daily experiences of past persons, and articulate how the apparently mundane articulated with the extraordinary, is through a consideration of objects and their various biographies and itineraries. Generally speaking, the concepts of biography and itinerary regard the life history of an object through its inception, production, use, and final disposition. Objects attain biographies as they intersect particular life events and can be revalued according to how they are embedded socially (Carr and Bradbury, Chapter 10; Gosden and Marshall 1999; Hahn and Weiss 2013). A modern example would follow the history of a watch. Acquired for its functionality, style, or as evidence of status, the watch may evoke memories that were experienced during its use. When given as a gift to a younger person, that same object not only may provoke the memory of the exchange but may become inalienable as an heirloom, may be associated with wider social memories, and may have to be cared for or disposed of in certain ways. Containers (our example) facilitate these sorts of memories through bundling the social contexts of their production, technological knowledge embedded in tradition, the collection of consumables and their preparation of meals, via serving and consumption, and even during their deposition (Gilmore 2016).

A related concept is the itinerary, which involves the wanderings of objects in time, space, or historical consciousness (Joyce and Gillespie 2015). Objects move through space; thus their value or relevance may become associated with their place of origin, the history of exchanges, or their relations between persons, materials processed in them, and the transpiring of such events. Yet objects also move through time and traditions. Along their wanderings, they may be revalued or rebundled with other associations. So, too, objects may come to rest, perhaps through deposition or forgetting, only to be reanimated through their rediscovery or renewal (Knappett 2013). In some cases, it may not be any specific object but the memories or associations of past practice.

Taken together, then, object biographies and itineraries may help reveal how ancient persons interacted throughout their natural and social landscapes. While this is perhaps abstract in the discussion, from a methodological perspective, a focus on biographies and itineraries is actually something that archaeologists are well equipped to address (consider Nelson 1991; Schiffer 1972). As our case study shows, techniques are available for determining the use of vessels, including experimental studies, technological approaches, and even residue analysis. Similarly, provenance studies provide the basis for inferring where objects have been. Traditions of object production, decoration, and even food consumption can help us infer the wanderings of containers through the daily lives of persons. Of equal importance is attention to the social contexts of objects, where they were produced, used, and deposited. In the following sections we trace the itineraries of Late Archaic containers by first providing a brief outline of their social contexts of use and then illustrating as best we can how they moved, were used and deposited, and potentially were revalued as they moved between daily and extraordinary settings.

Shell Vessel Itineraries of the Preceramic

On the St. Johns River, the start of the Late Archaic is coincident with the Thornhill Lake phase of the Mount Taylor period (Endonino 2008; Randall 2013). The Mount Taylor period has its origins during the Middle Archaic, beginning at least 7,400 years ago. Many of the patterns that persisted throughout the late Archaic were established at this time. Broadly speaking the Mount Taylor period is a time of intensive land use and aquatic exploitation, registered in the generation of scores of shell mounds and smaller shell-bearing and nonshell-bearing places (Randall 2015) (Figure 8.1). The relation of any of these particular places to daily practices, such as residence or resource processing, has been called into question by our research. Shell mounds typically experienced complicated histories of abandonment and reuse, such that a location that was once a residential camp or village may be monumentalized through mortuary practice or mound surface renewal (Randall 2013).

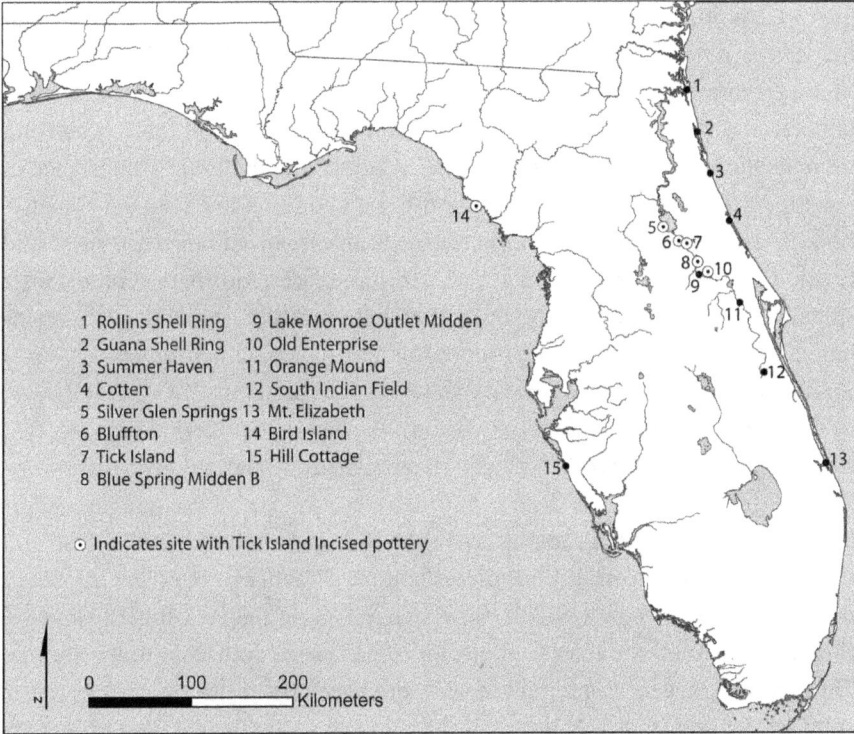

Figure 8.1. Late Archaic archaeological sites mentioned in the text.

Daily Life

For our purposes, we can delimit a few aspects of Thornhill Lake phase life-ways. We see the emergence of a regional system that is represented in at least three kinds of localities (Randall 2013). The most obvious are some of the larg-est shell sites on record. Those sites best known to us include the mounds at Silver Glen Springs, Bluffton, Hontoon Island North, and Lake Monroe Outlet Midden. These mound complexes often contain evidence for the structured use of space. For example, Silver Glen Springs and Lake Monroe Outlet Midden contained areas for lithic tool production sited away from the areas of shell midden (Archaeological Consultants and Janus Research 2001; Randall et al. 2011). Several nonmounded localities have been identified throughout the ba-sin. These include sites with variable evidence for shell deposition. The non-mounded localities show a diversity in intensity and use. Some were likely short-term camps, perhaps for fishing or plant collection. Others, such as Locus B at

Silver Glen Springs or the Thursby Mound, were more structured affairs and may better reflect daily practices away from the more collective happenings at the larger mound complexes (Gilmore 2011). These sites often contain a diversity of objects, while the presence of cooking hearths and other pit features attest to more extended stays. Zooarchaeological analysis highlights the importance of aquatic resources, particularly smaller fishes, in addition to terrestrial exploitation (Blessing 2011). A final layer of the landscape involved mortuary ritual and feasting (Endonino 2010; Randall 2015). In some cases, mortuary mounds were situated on top of old shell mounds; elsewhere mortuary mounds were maintained adjacent to places of apparent residence.

The daily lives of Late Archaic inhabitants of the St. Johns River valley cannot be divorced from their regional extensions. We have good reason to suspect that some, if not all, Late Archaic individuals circulated throughout peninsular Florida and that in this regard their own itineraries were cosmopolitan. Sites affiliated with the Thornhill Lake phase have been found on the Atlantic Coast, and there may be earlier connections there. Isotopic evidence from earlier mortuary mounds illustrates how some persons interred along the St. Johns River spent their childhood on the coasts, while others may have come from south Florida. Throughout the year some individuals were traveling to the coasts during the summer (Tucker 2009). Numerous objects have spatially extensive itineraries (Wheeler and McGee 1994). The presence of marine shell objects provides evidence for contact with coastal areas. In addition to serving as vessels, these objects were used for woodworking, personal adornment, fishing, and other tasks. Sourcing of chipped-stone tools and debris also indicates that materials were coming from as far away as Tampa Bay (Randall et al. 2011). That is, the very material of making do in daily life was extraregional in origin.

Marine Shell Vessels

The preceding discussion highlights the regional extension of Late Archaic northeast Floridians. Cross-cutting all these experiences are what we refer to as marine shell vessels (Figure 8.2). These objects are preferentially manufactured from shells of the lightning whelk (*Busycon perversum*). This species is notable for its unusual spiral: this species is left-opening, unlike many of the larger marine gastropods. These objects were crafted by removing a portion of the whorl adjacent to the aperture up to the shoulder and then extracting the columella (Webster 1970). The remaining portion can thus serve as a water-tight container. Most of these vessels in Late Archaic contexts show evidence of use over a fire and have been interpreted as cooking vessels. Variants of this object

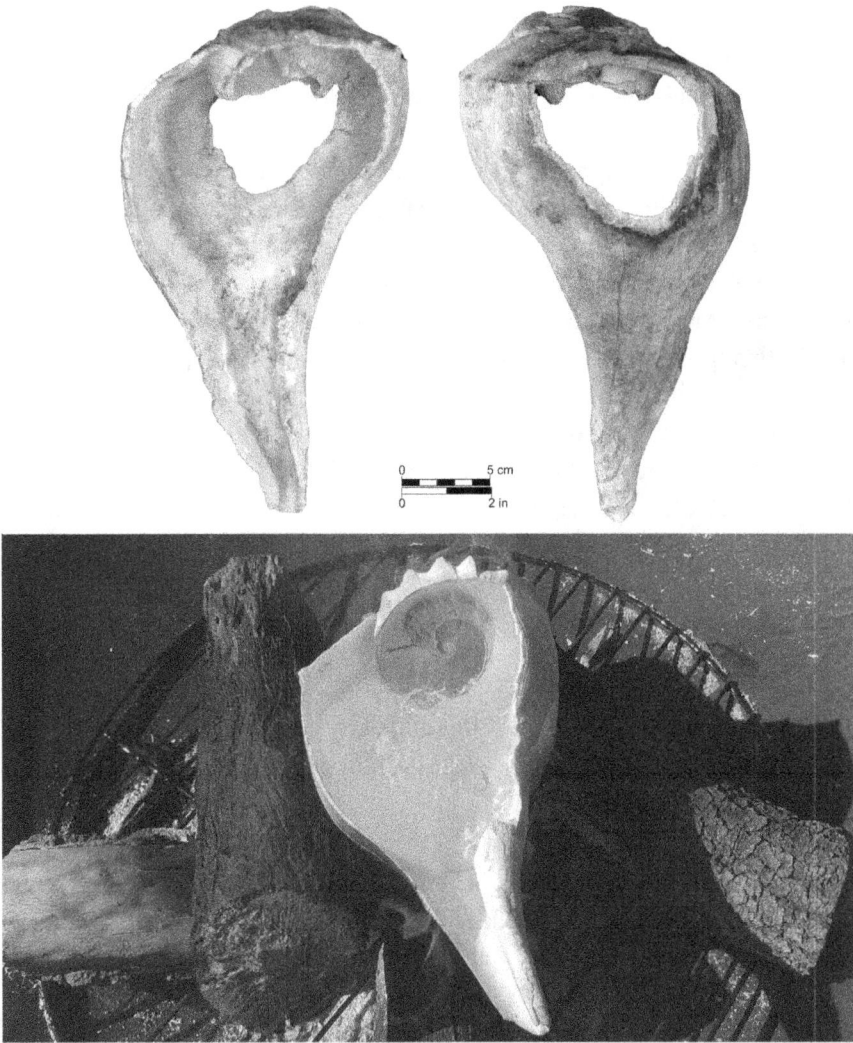

Figure 8.2. Marine shell vessels. *Top row:* front (*left*) and back (*right*) of vessel made from a *Busycon perversum* shell found at the Bluffton site (courtesy of the Collections of the Anthropology Division of the Florida Museum of Natural History, FLMNH Cat. No. FLMNH-ANT-95047); *bottom row:* boiling water in an experimental vessel.

are found throughout the St. Johns landscape, including nonmounded localities, shell mounds, and mortuaries. They have been found in contexts securely dated as early as 7,000 years ago and seemingly disappear from Late Archaic contexts at the cusp of pottery production 4,600 years ago.

The widespread distribution of these objects in different contexts suggests that they played a prominent role in the lives of Late Archaic Floridians. Yet to what extent were they involved in actual daily practice? Furthermore, what might their itineraries reveal about nonceramic containers and social process? If we look at the extended itinerary of the marine shell vessel, we should suspect that these objects might not register daily life at all. Southeastern archaeologists are no doubt familiar with this object, typically referred to as a cup, receptacle, or dipper. They are found in a variety of contexts throughout the southeast, often as mortuary offerings, including early Green River Shell Mound Archaic mortuaries (Marquardt and Kozuch 2016; Milanich 1979). In more recent millennia, this species was particularly valued for making vessels that appear to be serving wares for specific nonroutine events. Ethnohistorically, such cups were central to many purification rituals and were used to serve and consume cassina, the black drink, which is brewed from yaupon holly (papers in Hudson 1979). Without shells, the left-handed spiral can be found on a variety of media. As noted by Cheryl Claassen (2008), such shells, and their left-hand spiral, appear to be associated with origins, movement, and rejuvenation.

Although these observations from outside of the river valley would suggest a similar position of these objects during Late Archaic times—that is, not being everyday wares—we should be careful about upstreaming significance. What, then, might the itineraries of such vessels during Archaic times on the St. Johns River reveal about daily lives? There is much that we do not know, but we suggest means to resolve these issues.

Acquisition

Where objects come from is often central to their biography (Hahn and Weiss 2013). It is easy enough to state that these objects had their origins on a coastal strand. What remains unknown is from which coast these gastropods were collected. Furthermore, we do not have a good sense of whether these objects were acquired as some kind of embedded procurement as individuals seasonally traveled to the coast or whether special trips would be necessary. The relative abundance of marine shell in general certainly suggests that whatever means was used to acquire these shells (perhaps multiple pathways at the same time) was commonplace or unrestricted. Furthermore, no studies have looked at the production trajectory of marine shell vessels along the St. Johns River. Most lightning whelks recovered on the St. Johns River are in vessel form, although a handful of lightning whelks that have not been altered have been reported. The point is that we currently lack contextual data from Archaic sites on either coast to identify areas of acquisition or initial production. Ultimately the only way to resolve this issue will be through provenance studies. Sinistral whelks can be found along the Atlantic seaboard from New Jersey to the Florida Straits and then all throughout the Gulf of Mexico coast (Wise et al. 2004). Certain populations, particularly those on the Gulf strands, tend to attain the large sizes needed to be useful as vessels. The presence of lithic resources from Tampa Bay, just north of where the largest shells can be found today, would provide one network along which shells could move.

Manufacture, Use, and Deposition

A more detailed consideration of the manufacture and use of vessels can provide a sense for the social embeddedness of these objects (Wallis 2011). One standing pattern is that the largest assemblages come from the largest sites. At the Late Archaic Lake Monroe Outlet site, for example, Irvy Quitmyer (2001) identified eight vessels or vessel fragments from three excavation units. Similarly, Lawrence Aten (1999) reported at least twelve whole or fragmented vessels from the Middle Archaic mortuary at Harris Creek. Some were found within the mortuary, while others were emplaced on subsequent mound surfaces. Elsewhere, including saturated shell middens, large shell mounds, and small shell-bearing localities, they are found in smaller amounts, typically one or two examples only. The point is that this artifact type is widely distributed in low frequencies, and it would seem that these vessels were used in a range of social contexts.

As with ceramic vessels, wear from production and use can provide key insights (e.g., Hally 1983). Our sample of 15 whole vessels ranges in shell length from 17 to 32 cm. All are finished, but we cannot directly discern whether vessels were manufactured at the source or on the St. Johns. Their use is attested to by the presence of soot, which is concentrated on the base of the vessels, surrounding a hole ringed by thermally damaged shell (Figure 8.2). The basal breaks are often irregular and jagged, with some showing evidence of the shell body flaking off.

Although it is clear that these were used over fire, just how effective would they be as cooking vessels? A variety of opinions have been offered. William Webster (1970) suggested that they could be quite suitable for boiling, based on an experiment that he conducted. Noting their small size and volume, Kenneth Sassaman et al. (2011) argued that the vessels might be suited for brewing medicines, poisons, or other concoctions. Alternatively, Ryan Wheeler and Ray McGee (1994) suggested that the vessels were used instead to parch leaves, perhaps yaupon holly. A direct analysis of the residues adhering to shells or held within the shell vessel matrix would illuminate these possibilities.

While we might not be able to determine exactly what was cooked within one of these vessels, we can better delimit the role of these vessels by determining their performance characteristics. To this end, we conducted a pilot experimental study of purchased lightning whelks that we crafted into vessels (Figure 8.2). Four shells in the study encapsulate the size range of Archaic vessels, which could hold between 200 and 600 ml of liquid. Our experiments were designed to determine how long it took to boil water, how well the vessel would respond to being over heat, and whether we could replicate the breakage and sooting patterns associated with boiling or parching.

For brevity, we can reduce the results to a few important observations. First, we were able to boil water within three to five minutes in each case. Second, there is an evident upper limit on the duration that a shell vessel can be applied to a thermal source. In our tests, whelk shell begins to break down after 40 minutes of continuous use. By extension, the vessels were not likely to be used for processing large amounts of liquid. The maximum amount that could be boiled at one time was 600 ml, which might produce no more than 6 liters of boiled liquids over its life span. Finally, there is some important equifinality in our results. As a final test, we parched green holly leaves in an otherwise empty vessel. The leaves were nicely parched within four minutes, but the bottom of the vessel was burned out. In fact, the closest we came to replicating the final forms of the archaeological vessels was by parching leaves. It was not the parching of leaves but the lack of liquid within the vessel that led to the bottom being burned out.

So were these vessels used "every day"? Marine shell was certainly in use for a variety of occasions, from wood cutting to adornment. Based on our experimental data, however, it would seem that these vessels were not useful for extended durations and were not likely to have been used on a daily basis for food production. Moreover, certainly not enough of them have been found to have supported such usage. But does that mean that they were not invoked or did not loom large in daily concerns? At the largest scale, social networks extending from coast to coast are implied. Although the vessels were used in a similar fashion, moreover, their itineraries are distributed throughout the Late Archaic social landscape of the St. Johns River valley. They were embedded in socially poignant moments, as implied by their inclusion in larger numbers in mortuary contexts. Yet they also apparently were involved in the contexts of daily practice, perhaps used to brew medicines or other concoctions, which may be why they are found bundled in particular locations.

Late Archaic Ceramic Vessels

The persistence and widespread distribution of shell vessels is indicative, we think, of the complicated roles of these vessels in the social lives of Late Archaic communities. It is thus striking that these vessels disappear when Orange pottery, Florida's earliest ceramic container technology, was locally adopted at ca. 4600 cal B.P. by Late Archaic communities occupying the St. Johns River area and northern Atlantic Coast. Distinguished by their organic fiber-temper, Orange vessels consist primarily of shallow, straight-sided, and flat-bottomed bowls but also include rectangular trays and, rarely, cylindrical jars. Orange pottery is typically divided into three types based on differences in surface treatment (following Griffin 1945). These include Orange Plain, Orange Incised (characterized by rectilinear geometric motifs), and Tick Island Incised (distinguished by incised spirals surrounded by background punctations) (Figure 8.3).

Figure 8.3. Variation in Orange period ceramic decorations. Rows 1–3: Orange Incised; row 4: Tick Island Incised.

Differences among the types were long assumed to reflect successive stages in the evolution of Orange technology (following Bullen 1955, 1972). The coevalness of the full range of Orange stylistic and morphological variation is now widely accepted, however, strongly suggesting that ethnic and/or functional distinctions may have played a more prominent role than chronological ones (Sassaman 2003a).

Daily Life

Traditional accounts of incipient pottery use in Florida posit that the new technology came with few if any major changes in the basic lifeways of resident hunter-gatherers (e.g., Milanich 1994:86). Indeed, numerous studies of Late Archaic subsistence practices show apparent continuity between the late Thornhill Lake phase and early Orange period (e.g., Blessing 2011; Sassaman 2003b). Beyond subsistence, however, we now know that pottery's appearance coincided with a number of important transformations that cut across all facets of social life, from the everyday to the truly exceptional. This interval witnessed not only the disappearance of shell cups but also a marked decrease in the frequency of marine shell more generally, along with other exotics such as bannerstones and groundstone beads. Major shifts in settlement, mounding, and mortuary traditions also occurred. Village life centered on circular compounds that were either mounded or nonmounded. There is very little evidence for mortuary practice throughout the Orange period. However, ceremonial gatherings still took place at shell rings on the Atlantic Coast, along the St. Johns River, and along the southwestern Gulf Coast. As in the case of shell cups, we can gain a better understanding of pottery's role in these developments by more closely considering various stages in the itineraries of Orange vessels.

Production

Unfortunately, our grasp of Orange pottery production is rudimentary at best, beginning with the question of exactly who was involved in its manufacture. It is often assumed, based on ethnographic data from domestic contexts, that pottery was from the very beginning a technology executed and controlled by women (e.g., Brown 1989; Sassaman and Rudolphi 2001). Current radiocarbon data from St. Johns River sites, however, suggest that the first Orange vessels were not used domestically but instead were consumed and deposited during large-scale public events at shell mounds (Gilmore 2016). As detailed below, strong evidence also indicates that many vessels were conscripted into networks of long-distance exchange, traditionally assumed to be the purview of men. These factors make any firm conclusions regarding gendered production at this early stage of pottery use impossible. What does seem apparent is that Orange vessels were widely produced by individuals and communities with an exceedingly broad range of skill levels and aesthetic sensibilities. Virtually every Orange Incised pot exhibits a unique motif, with tremendous variability in the quality and symmetry of both incised designs and vessel morphology (Figure 8.3). Jon Endonino's (2013) research using X-ray images of Orange sherds from middle St. Johns River assemblages further indicates that early pots were crafted using a variety of different forming techniques, including slab construction, hand modeling, and coiling. When combined with the massive quantities of vessels deposited at many Orange sites, this array of stylistic and technological characteristics suggests that pottery was a technology accessible to most, if not all, members of Orange communities (cf. Saunders and Wrenn 2014).

Production and Circulation

Pottery's role in long-distance exchange has been largely downplayed, as archaeologists have typically focused on the circulation of rare and exotic materials as the basis for extralocal interaction networks. In fact, pottery is generally assumed to have tempered hunter-gatherer mobility and is linked directly to sedentism in most cultural evolutionary accounts (e.g., Arnold 1985; Braun 1987; Brown 1989). Nevertheless, recent research by Neill Wallis (2011) and Keith Ashley and others (Ashley et al. 2015) has demonstrated that Woodland period vessels from Florida were routinely transported over vast distances and played an important part in maintaining social and ritual ties among distant communities. Importantly, new provenance data from Silver Glen, one of four known Orange shell mound complexes in the St. Johns valley, indicate that pottery's role in extralocal interactions extends all the way back to the technology's nascent stages (Figure 8.4). A total of 288 Orange vessels were submitted for neutron activation analysis (NAA), of which 75 were also thin-sectioned and analyzed petrographically. The data yielded by these techniques link Silver Glen vessels not only to raw material sources throughout northeast Florida but also to some locations as far away as Tampa Bay and points further south (Gilmore 2016). These results provide convincing evidence that large numbers of Late Archaic pots were circulated across peninsular Florida, with some moving over a distance of hundreds of kilometers.

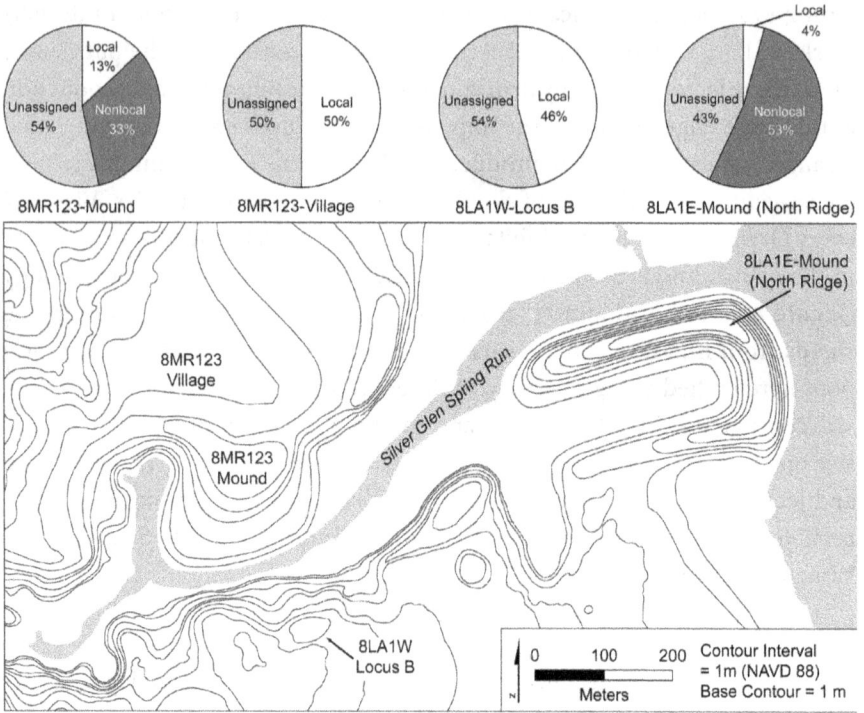

Figure 8.4. Results of provenance analysis of Orange pottery from the Silver Glen Springs watershed (note: the topography is reconstructed).

Use and Deposition

It is abundantly clear at this point that Orange pots were not consumed and deposited in the same manner across all types of places. Research by Rebecca Saunders (2004a, 2004b) and Kenneth Sassaman (2004) at both coastal and riverine sites has shown that shell rings and mounds received disproportionate quantities of ornately decorated Orange Incised vessels compared to the contemporary nonmound locales. This has led some to argue that mounds and rings were venues for special large-scale events such as public rituals and feasts where personal and social identities were displayed in ceramic form (e.g., Gilmore 2016; Russo 2004; Sassaman 2004; Saunders 2004a). This appears to indeed be the case at Silver Glen, where vessels from the complex's two massive shell mounds are differentiated not only by their elaborate decorative motifs but also by their significantly larger size, thicker walls, and greater frequency of sooting and mend holes. What is more, every one of the vessels identified as nonlocal in the provenance study described above was recovered from the two mounds, while all pottery from the complex's off-mound contexts was likely locally produced (Gilmore 2016) (Figure 8.4). Together, these data suggest that Orange cultural landscapes featured spatial and social boundaries that set mounds and rings apart as places of large-scale gathering. In all likelihood, this arrangement was both a result of and the primary reason for the highly structured patterns of pottery use and deposition observed throughout the region.

However, one type of Orange pottery, Tick Island Incised, seems to have regularly transcended these boundaries as well as many long established stylistic conventions of Archaic Floridians. In fact, these vessels may be skeuomorphs: copies of earlier marine shell vessels transposed into a new medium. As noted by John Blitz (2015), skeuomorphs are often crucial for the adoption and innovation of new technologies and provided a means for social memory to be promoted and the past to be retained in the present (Knappett 2013). As already noted, this variety is characterized by spiral motifs that stand in stark contrast to the more typical rectilinear decorations of Orange Incised (Figure 8.3). These rectilinear decorations are clearly reminiscent of carved designs found on any number of bone and wooden objects dating back to at least the Early Archaic period (Wheeler 1994), while the curvilinear elements of Tick Island Incised have no obvious historical precedents in the region. Tick Island Incised vessels seem to mirror the distribution of preceramic shell cups in that they occur broadly across all types of Orange contexts within the middle St. Johns valley but generally in very low frequency (Figure 8.1). At Silver Glen, for example, these pots are found sparingly at both shell mounds but also in larger quantities at an associated shellfish-processing locality and multiple nearby habitation sites. Outside of the middle St. Johns valley, Tick Island Incised is found almost exclusively along Florida's Gulf Coast, the suspected origin of many of the region's shell cups (e.g., McFadden and Palmiotto 2012). Moreover, in six out of the seven known examples with intact spiral centers, the orientation of the spiral is such that it opens to the left, the same direction as in lightning whelk shells (Figure 8.5). Tick Island Incised vessels are also more likely than other Orange types to exhibit lug handles, a feature that may have further enhanced their resemblance to the knobby gastropods. Together, these factors point to the intriguing possibility that Tick Island Incised pots were the ceramic equivalent of preceramic shell cups, simply reconstituted in a new medium.

Figure 8.5. Comparison of a lightning whelk (*left*) and Tick Island Incised vessel rim sherd (*right*), not to scale.

Late Archaic Vessel Itineraries and Everyday Matters

The everyday certainly invokes the mundane but also preparation for the more infrequent moments of life. Tracing the itineraries of vessels throughout the Archaic has revealed their varied participation in the everyday and the extraordinary. While many of these vessels eventually found their way into places of commemoration, it does not mean that they did not participate and impinge upon the time allotted to daily tasks by their makers and users (see also Pluckhahn et al., Chapter 9). During the Thornhill Lake phase, for example, shell vessels were acquired directly across extensive social networks that brought other items into the St. Johns River area. They were apparently not particularly useful for producing large quantities of consumables. Nonetheless, they were deposited and thus likely circulated throughout everyday and ritualized contexts and perhaps bundled and contained the social exchanges that they enabled through the production and consumption of beverages, whatever the recipe.

With the advent of ceramic technology, vessel itineraries illuminate how new containers impinged on both routine and relatively extraordinary facets of Late Archaic experience. Many vessels certainly appear to have been produced for the production of daily fare. The making, using, and repairing of those pots likely required their own attentions and tempo. Lest we assume that Orange pots served solely the needs of local inhabitants in their day-to-day lives, the remarkable scale of production of vessels apparent at numerous sites indicates that pottery production undoubtedly diverted a significant amount of labor from other tasks, a situation that would have been exacerbated by demand for ritual consumption. The crafting of each pot bundled not only a variety of different materials, styles, and technological attributes but also the traditions and identities of their makers. Hundreds of individual vessels—some of which had origins hundreds of kilometers away—were in turn bundled together in monumental contexts at places like Silver Glen, Tick Island, and Old Enterprise. In this way, communal bonds were created and periodically reaffirmed among the diverse constituents gathered at mound-centered feasts. The distant origins of many of these pots and dearth of other exotics suggest that, once adopted, pottery quickly supplanted other materials as the long-distance trade item of choice. This includes marine shell cups, whose material form and specialized function were apparently replaced by ceramic surrogates. In that sense, marine shell cups and their affordances never disappeared from everyday matters, but their itineraries extended through different substances (see also Knappett 2013). In this context, it would seem that they connected persons in daily life with other individuals, ancestors, and perhaps, if we rely on ethnohistory, even nonhuman forces.

9

Crafting Everyday Matters
in the Middle and Late Woodland Periods

THOMAS J. PLUCKHAHN, MARTIN MENZ, AND LORI O'NEAL

At first glance, the stated theme of this book—"an archaeology of everyday matters"—seemed to us synonymous with "the matters of everyday archaeology." The material record is, after all, arguably mostly about everyday life in the aggregate (Lucas 2012:183). Moreover, for more than two decades now many of us have operated from a perspective—practice theory (Bourdieu 1977, 1980)—that emphasizes "the structured and structuring role of material culture in everyday life" (Joyce 2008:71–72). Yet it seems clear that we frequently subsume the everyday in the extraordinary, as Price and Carr (Chapter 1) suggest in their framing of this volume.

Take, for example, archaeological treatments of craft production, specifically those for the Middle (ca. 100 B.C. to A.D. 500) and Late Woodland (ca. A.D. 500 to 1050) periods in the Southeast. A defining characteristic of these periods is the prevalence of craft goods of stone, bone, shell, and metal—frequently from exotic sources and often fashioned into nonutilitarian, symbolically charged products. In the processual heyday, archaeologists devoted considerable attention to the perceived control of the production and exchange of exotic goods for what this may say about the political and economic power of elites and by extension societal complexity. Sharon Goad (1978, 1979), for example, argued that the Crystal River site on the Florida Gulf Coast became organized as a chiefdom because elites were able to monopolize the import of copper from distant sources as well as the subregional distribution of these items to smaller mound centers in exchange for large marine gastropods from the Gulf (see also Anderson 1998). Similarly, for the Kolomoki site in southwestern Georgia, William Sears (1973) cited the unusual characteristics of Weeden Island excised effigy vessels found only in mortuary contexts as evidence for craft specialization supported by the community at large, a point that he offered in support of a broader argument that Kolomoki represented a state-level society (Sears 1956, 1973).

Interest in political economy did not fade with postprocessualism, but craft production was more often imbued with special importance for what it said about the ability of elites to enhance personal power and prestige through the control of ideological symbols and esoteric knowledge, as in Mark Seeman's (1995) discussion of select Hopewell artifacts from eastern North America. More recent interpretations turn increasingly to ritual economy, placing craft production in the context of periodic "gearing up" for ritual performances; Katherine Spielmann (1998, 2002, 2008; see also Miller 2015) has made this case for the Hopewell core, and Alice Wright and Erika Loveland (2015) have extended it to the Hopewellian societies of the Appalachian summit.

We do not disagree with any of these perspectives and have applied some of them in our own research. For example, along the lines of recent discussions of ritual economy, Pluckhahn et al. (2006) have argued that anomalies—including relatively large quantities of mica and limestone—in the fill from a house pit at Kolomoki may indicate preparation for ceremonies. But we suggest that the emphasis on the political- and ritual-economic contexts for craft production may obscure an important point: specifically, that crafting was rooted in the everyday rhythms of domestic life, by which we mean the networks of relationships with other people and other objects.

We develop three arguments in support of this thesis. First, reviewing the archaeological record for two of the largest Middle Woodland population and ceremonial centers in the region—Kolomoki in southwestern Georgia and Crystal River in west-central Florida (Figure 9.1)—we argue that a low level of craft production was common to domestic contexts. Next, based on recent middle range theory regarding cross-craft and multicraft specialization, we suggest that the production of some of the ritual objects that are most common to the region drew on the same skills and techniques that were employed in the manufacture of everyday utilitarian items.

We see the application of the perspective of everyday matters to craft production as typical not only of practice theory, as alluded to above, but also of more recent and specific extensions of this body of thought. First, our considerations of households and cross-craft production are consistent with relational archaeology, in that we are concerned with the relationships among things and among people and things in everyday life. On this point we find commonalities with the relational approach employed by Moore and Jefferies (Chapter 7), although their concern is primarily with relationships between people and animals. We also see parallels with Dumas's approach (Chapter 6) to salt production. Our emphasis on knowledge and skills and their transference to other contexts also resonates with recent interests in embodiment.

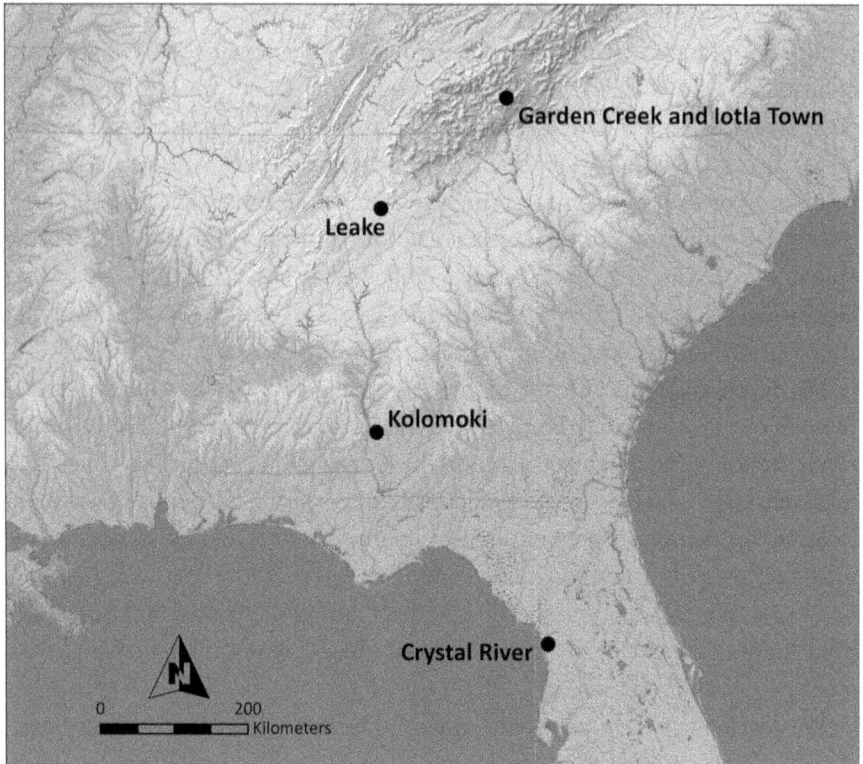

Figure 9.1. Location of Kolomoki, Crystal River, and other sites mentioned in the text.

Defining Domestic Craft Production

"Craft production" is most commonly used to refer to the manufacture of symbolically-charged objects. However, Cathy Costin (1998:4, 9; see also Costin 1991, 2001) provides a more expansive definition of crafting as the transformation of raw materials into "functional and valuable goods." We agree, and in the discussion below we include for consideration not only the production of ritual objects but also the intensified—perhaps specialized—production of utilitarian items.

Our perspective on craft production is in many ways dependent on reassessments of the concept of specialization, which has been the subject of considerable debate in archaeology (see Arnold and Munns 1994; Clark 1995, 2007; Clark and Parry 1990; Cobb 1993, 1996; Costin 1998, 2001; Flad and Hruby 2007; Muller 1984, 1997:291). A major focus of such debate is the degree to which the subsistence of specialists is dependent on exchange of the goods that they produce. Jon Muller (1984, 1997:291) characterizes specialization as near-total reliance on production and exchange as a means of subsistence, while others have acknowledged varying contexts and degrees of specialization ranging from independent part-time specialists engaged in cottage industries to full-time artisans producing goods at the behest of elite patrons or supporting themselves through exchange (Clark and Parry 1990; Cobb 1993; Costin 1991, 2001).

This broader understanding of specialization opens archaeological inquiry of the organization of specialized production beyond formal workshops and into domestic contexts. Middle and Late Woodland artisans probably fell into the category of part-time specialists as they negotiated the scheduling of crafting activities and subsistence tasks. The definition of craft production that we use here, considering our focus on crafting in domestic contexts, is the manufacture of items unrelated to, or at a level of intensity beyond, the subsistence needs of the "average" household (Arnold 1985; Costin 1991; Michaels 1989; Shafer and Hester 1991; Yerkes 2003).

The Production of Crafts in Domestic Contexts at Kolomoki and Crystal River

Regarding our argument that craft production was often conducted in domestic contexts in the Middle and Late Woodland Southeast, we point to evidence that some types of craft-related production debris are commonly found in small quantities in midden contexts. At Kolomoki, of the 18 test units that Pluckhahn (2003) excavated across the site, two-thirds produced mica. Some tests produced enough to suggest that households in these areas of the village may have been engaged in small-scale crafting of mica ornaments. This possibility was given greater credence with small-block excavations, where we recovered occasional masses of mica, such as the example from Block A pictured in Figure 9.2. Sears (1956) recovered similar masses in his excavations in the village. Small flecks of mica are common to the clays in this area, but the closest mapped mica deposits are located 50–100 miles north of Kolomoki (Sterrett 1923); thus these masses appear to have been brought to the site for the manufacture of ornaments. This is substantiated by the presence in the village of larger fragments that appear to have been cut (see Figure 9.2). The wide spatial distribution of mica in the village at Kolomoki suggests that the crafting of this material was not centralized in either time or space but was instead an activity that households undertook during day-to-day activities.

The same may be said of the production of crystalline quartz artifacts. Transparent quartz debitage, produced mainly from small river cobbles but occasionally

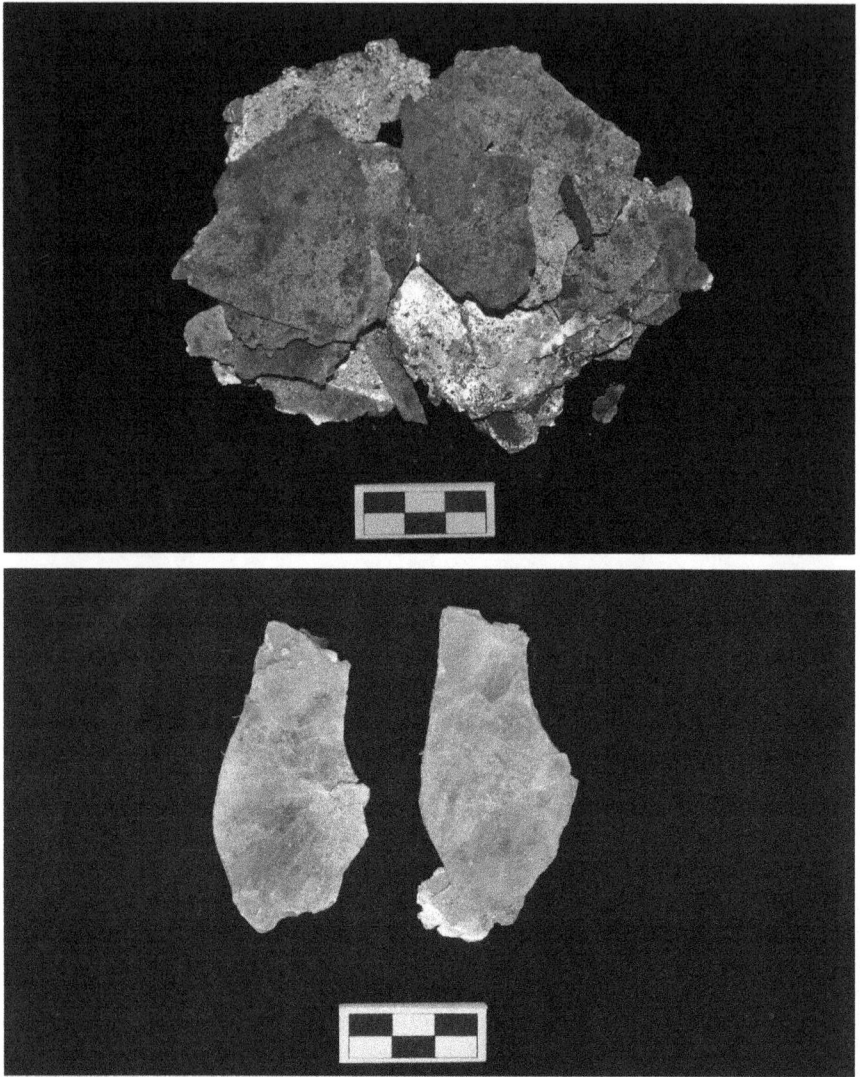

Figure 9.2. Sample of mica scraps from Excavation Unit A7, Feature 57, Zone A (*top*) and possible cut mica from Excavation Unit A29, Level 2 (*bottom*), recovered from excavations in Block A at Kolomoki. See Pluckhahn (2003).

also from quartz crystals, is ubiquitous at Kolomoki, as it is at many contemporaneous sites bearing Swift Creek Complicated Stamped pottery (Keith 2010; Menz 2015; Pluckhahn 2003) (Figure 9.3). In contrast, finished artifacts of crystalline quartz—in the sense of projectile points, plummets, or other formal tools or objects d'art—are almost nonexistent. Usewear analyses have thus far proven

Figure 9.3. Crystalline quartz debitage from a single level in a test unit at Kolomoki. Artifacts from Test Unit 6, Level 2. See Pluckhahn (2003).

inconclusive with regard to the use of quartz debitage (Menz 2015:59–64). However, statistical analyses of domestic assemblages from Kolomoki reveal strong correlations between quartz and Swift Creek ceramics and again between quartz and mica (Menz 2015:67, 87). This suggests that crystalline quartz may have been used either to carve the wooden paddles used to stamp Swift Creek pottery or to cut mica into forms for pendants or both. In any case, the distribution clearly suggests that quartz reduction was an activity common to domestic contexts.

Craft production at Kolomoki appears not to have been limited to the production of ritual objects. Thomas Pluckhahn and Ann Cordell (2011) have argued that the production of "sacred" or "prestige" ceramic vessels may have been limited to a subset of the population at Kolomoki. In addition, Martin Menz (2015) has recently argued that the disproportionately heavy concentration of chert debris, specifically debitage from bifacial and unifacial tool production, in some areas of the village at Kolomoki suggests that some households intensified the production of formal chert tools, perhaps for exchange during important ceremonies when visitors from lithic-poor areas within the region converged at Kolomoki.

Only very minute quantities of mica and crystal quartz, and only modest amounts of chert, have been recovered from domestic contexts at Crystal River,

Figure 9.4. Plummets recovered from test units at Crystal River. *From left*: Test Unit 8, Level 3; Test Unit 9, Level 8; Test Unit 9, Level 8, Locus G; Test Unit 6, Level 8. See O'Neal (2016).

as might be expected given that this site lies a considerable distance from potential sources of the two raw materials (O'Neal 2016). But there is evidence in village contexts for small-scale production of other craft items from raw materials available locally or subregionally. Plummets of stone, shell, and occasionally copper are abundant in mortuary contexts at Crystal River and other Middle Woodland sites in Florida (Moore 1903, 1907, 1918) and occasionally found at sites from this period elsewhere in the region (Keith 2010; Pluckhahn 2003). Our excavations at Crystal River have been limited, but we have nevertheless recovered a total of four plummets (including three of limestone and one of shell) from three of our four excavated trenches (O'Neal 2016) (Figure 9.4). One of these is clearly unfinished and another possibly so. In addition to these, we have found partially ground and pecked fragments of limestone and, less commonly, whelk columellae. Together, the evidence suggests that plummets were manufactured in the village at Crystal River.

Shell ornaments, especially beads, also appear to have been made and used in domestic contexts at Crystal River. We have recovered dozens of shell beads from four test units at Crystal River (O'Neal 2016). These beads appear to have been manufactured on-site, as evidenced by the common appearance of mollusk shells with holes. Other ornaments of shell were also produced; we have recovered a complete small shell ornament of the form that George Luer (2013) referred to as a Tabbed Circular Artifact (TCA) and a portion of what may be another, larger TCA (Figure 9.5). Larger shell ornaments such as these also appear to have been manufactured in the village at Crystal River, as evidence by the recovery of several gorget blanks reduced from the shoulder of a large gastropod (O'Neal 2016). Still, as Beth Blankenship (2013) has argued, the production of ornaments from marine shell appears to have been much less intensive than envisioned by Goad (1979).

Figure 9.5. Shell ornament and ornament blank recovered from test units at Crystal River. Ornament from Test Unit 9, Level 7, Locus A; blank from Test Unit 1, Level 6. See O'Neal (2016).

We have limited our discussion to Kolomoki and Crystal River, where we have data of our own to draw from, but evidence shows that the same pattern of low-level craft production in domestic contexts holds for other Middle and Late Woodland communities in the region. Mica and crystalline quartz, as well as copper, were abundant in domestic contexts at the Leake site in northwestern Georgia (Keith 2010). And, although Wright and Loveland (2015:148) cite the seemingly disproportionate amount of mica and crystalline quartz in the enclosure fill at the Garden Creek site in western North Carolina as contrary to the expectations for "comparatively unrestricted, household-based mica crafting documented at Middle Woodland hamlets," Tasha Benyshek and Paul Webb (2012) report that mica was plentiful in domestic contexts at the nearby and contemporaneous site of Iotla Town.

Cross-Craft Production at Kolomoki and Crystal River

Our second point, slightly more abstract than the first, is that craft production not only occurred in domestic contexts but was embedded in domestic lives at a more fundamental level, in that it drew on the knowledge and techniques that were employed in the manufacture of everyday utilitarian goods. Izumi Shimada (1996:30) has used the term "cross-craft interaction" to describe this process by which the production sequence for a given craft integrates material, knowledge, and techniques employed in the production of other crafts. For example, for the Middle Sicán and Inca periods in northern Peru, David Goldstein and Shimada (2010) suggest that the production of *chicha* (corn beer) and ceramics were linked both spatially and temporally as well as through the choice of fuels. Similarly, Verity Whalen and Luis Manuel González La Rosa (2014) argue that metal-working was accomplished in Late Nasca Peru using the same prevailing winds, fuel resources, and possibly even the same hearths as were used for preparing food and brewing *chicha*. They note: "Knowledge of how to control fires and generate high temperatures necessary for metallurgy was no doubt related to the expertise necessary for cooking and brewing activities" (2014:98). Extending the notion of cross-craft production even further, to the relation of materials, they observe that broken cooking vessels may have been used to make furnaces for the production of metal.

The crafts that were produced by Middle and Late Woodland artisans in the Southeast arguably required less specialized practical knowledge than metal working. Still, like the Peruvian examples, the production of craft items, like ornaments, drew on a repertoire of materials, technology, and techniques developed in the manufacture of the more mundane tools of everyday life. As we have already referenced, at Kolomoki crystalline quartz is strongly correlated with Swift Creek ceramics and mica debris; the stone tools and motions that were used to cut mica were probably the same as those used to carve paddles and other wooden tools as well as those employed for other utilitarian tasks like cutting leather. Consistent with this, Menz (2015:33, 45) has suggested that the use of quartz at Kolomoki consisted of a core reduction strategy focused on the production of expedient, informal, and generalized flake tools well suited for a wide variety of tasks. Additionally, it seems possible that waste mica from the production of ornaments could have been ground and added to pottery clays; much of the Swift Creek pottery at Kolomoki has a micaceous paste, despite a relatively low abundance of mica in the clay samples from the area that have thus far been tested (Pluckhahn and Cordell 2011).

Similarly, at Crystal River, the making of stone plummets undoubtedly drew on the same pecking and grinding technology and techniques that were used for making utilitarian ground stone tools of the same material, like celts and adzes. Likewise, the making of shell ornaments like gorgets and beads drew on many of the same scoring, snapping, and grinding techniques that were used for making shell tools like hammers, cutting tools, and net gauges.

We would suggest the possibility that craft production may have been more literally embodied in domestic tasks. The anthropologist Trevor Marchand (2007), drawing insights from neuroscience, suggests that crafting skills are learned in part through neural networks that fire when apprentices observe a process and again when they engage in the same manual activities. We suggest that this insight might be extended, to understand that some of the neural networks that are fired during crafting are the same as those that are fired while completing domestic tasks or the production of tools of everyday life. To draw an analogy from our own everyday matters, the process may be similar to the manner in which the skills that we learn and embody as archaeologists occasionally become useful for domestic tasks and vice versa. At the risk of sounding trivial, we have found that the skills we have developed leveling the floors and walls of our excavation units transfer well to household repairs like plumbing drain lines and leveling concrete.

The Embeddedness of Craft Production in Domestic Life at Kolomoki and Crystal River

Our final point is that our argument that craft production was embedded in everyday life is consistent with recent, higher-level theorizing regarding both household-based craft specialization and the ontology of objects. While our argument for the domestic organization of craft production in the Southeast is relatively novel, this approach is not new to archaeology beyond the confines of our region. Archaeologists working elsewhere in the Americas have recognized the household as the primary context of craft specialization for both ritual and utilitarian goods (see Hirth 2006, 2009; Mills 2007; Shimada 2007). Examples from these regions complicate our understanding of the relationship between craft specialization and elite control, placing the impetus for craft production with households themselves as strategies of economic diversification for purposes of risk-management (Hirth 2009) or identity creation and maintenance (Mills 2007; see also Costin 1998). We envision craft production by part-time specialists who produced goods for ceremony and exchange mainly as part of a seasonal cycle of domestic activities, as Charles Cobb (2003:70) suggests for the manufacture of chert hoes during the Mississippian period. At the same time, production may have increased, by devoting either more time or more people to the tasks, in preparation for special occasions. This "bottom-up," producer-centered view of craft production is a departure from political or ritual economic models that place political elites or ritual practitioners in charge of scheduling production, instead acknowledging the agency of households in determining where, when, and how they would engage in said production.

In her analysis of domestic craft specialization in the late prehistoric American Southwest, Barbara Mills (2007) notes that diverse domestic economies associated with craft production served as a means for social groups within aggregate villages to maintain and re-create particular identities. Our examples of household craft production at Kolomoki and Crystal River conform to a pattern of domestic craft production at civic-ceremonial centers and aggregate villages throughout North America. Whether it is a function of distinguishing class or other forms of social identity, the widespread pattern of economic differentiation and particularly household craft specialization within large prehistoric communities may be a natural outgrowth of the "coalescent society" (Kowalewski 2006), as social groups within these aggregate societies seek to set themselves apart socially and economically.

At a broader level, our argument for the embeddedness of craft production in the sociality and materiality of everyday life seems to us consistent with recent understanding of relational ontology of objects, from Tim Ingold (2000, 2013) to Bruno Latour (2005) and Bjørnar Olsen (2010), among others. In a passage that we consider appropriate to some previous treatments of craft items and their production in the Southeast, Ingold (2013:7) notes that anthropologists have tended to treat the work of art as an object of ethnographic analysis . . . to trace a chain of causal connections, in reverse, from the final object to the initial intention that allegedly motivated its production, or to the meanings that might be attributed to it. In a word, it is to place the object in a social and cultural context. In thus taking the artwork to be indexical of the social milieu and cultural values of its makers, the anthropology of art has merely taken on the mantle of art history . . . in so far as they continue to treat art as a compendium of works to be analysed, there can be no possibility of direct correspondence with the creative processes that give rise to them.

Likewise, we think that by focusing on craft goods as markers of social organization—whether framed in terms of politics or rituality—archaeologists have neglected an understanding of crafting as a creative process that necessarily involved networks of interactions with other people and materials. Olsen (2010:153) notes that the process of producing meaningful objects is complex and entangled with "The qualities that 'slumber' in the material used, the equipment involved in the processing, the 'ready-to-hand' knowledge of the human producer, [and] the effective history of former things and their production." We believe that in the small-scale, early-village societies of the Middle and Late Woodland periods the entanglements of craft production must have included the other people and materials that artisans interacted with in their everyday lives.

Although we argue that craft production in the Middle and Late Woodland periods was embedded in everyday matters, we do not assume that artisans enjoyed equal access to raw materials, the privileges to produce certain objects, or equivalent skills. Nor do we deny that the making of crafts was often—perhaps always—an act with religious or political significance or that the objects themselves should be understood as ritual objects or political symbols. But by focusing on these meanings to the exclusion of their connections with everyday life, archaeological treatments of craft production conjure images of artisans toiling secretly and in solitude, under the stern gaze of their chiefly patrons or with the solemnity of cloistered monks. We envision instead artisans working on craft goods during lulls in domestic chores (perhaps in the shade during hot afternoons or around fires in the evenings), generally in the company of others, and drawing on much the same knowledge, skills, and materials that they employed for other, more mundane tasks.

10

Stone Tool Life Meets Everyday Life

PHILIP J. CARR AND ANDREW P. BRADBURY

The intense interest in specimens per se is betrayed in many archaeological monographs, including those of the authors. We treat materials primarily as items to be described, listed, and arranged historically, but not as devices employed by human beings in important daily activities.

Steward and Seltzer (1938:6)

At times in our lives, we have examined lithic artifacts literally every day for weeks. The number of artifact types in an assemblage and questions regarding how best to complete the analysis dominated our thinking. These practical, present-day concerns left little room for imagining the everyday life of the past people who made and used those lithic artifacts. An assumption that the everyday life of the people in the past was invisible due to a coarse-grained archaeological record meant a lack of impetus for such a line of thinking. Present-day puzzles involving identifying lithic raw materials and applying the results of flintknapping experiments to infer reduction stages remained our focus.

A labeled and well-provenienced bag of lithics, which includes chipped-stone artifacts, does not for us immediately conjure images of the cultural identities of the makers, the activities in which those makers and others might have employed associated tools, or the intentions and ideologies of those makers. Our training dictates a more practical approach involving a focus on individual artifacts to make determinations such as cultural versus natural, type of material, tool versus debris, and so on. Ultimately, the questions that we answered concerned a people in the past and what we considered to be their practical concern of mapping onto resources, and not individuals conducting daily activities.

With our theoretical roots buried well into processual archaeology (e.g., Binford 1962, 1973; Kelly 1983, 1988; Schiffer 1972, 1983), consideration of "every day" is not something that feels comfortable, because the archaeological record as a palimpsest rarely allows us to "see" a single day or individuals. Yet stagnation of theory and archaeological thinking is more uncomfortable. We know the archaeological record consists of individuals making decisions on a daily basis, and individuals are arguably the unit of selection (Dunnell 1980:55; see also Dunnell 1995:41 for a shift in the unit of selection) as well as possessing agency (Hodder 1985:3; see also Dobres and Robb 2005:162 for collective forms of agency). How can this knowledge inform how we investigate the archaeological record and reconstruct the past, especially using lithic artifacts?

An archaeological site, however, even one of a short duration, undoubtedly witnessed a myriad of activities, some of which are driven by basic human needs. These activities include food preparation and consumption; socializing; resting/sleeping; and others such as fire building or shelter construction to support these pursuits. While not all of these activities leave direct traces in the archaeological record, their conduct reflects choices made by people in the past and impacts what we find archaeologically. In that respect an archaeological site, even one representing a single occupation, is a palimpsest of these daily choices and the actions carried out to achieve those needs.

Much of what we think of the human past comes from lithic artifacts. This is partially due to preservation; stone artifacts preserve even when other material classes do not. However, we are aware that people could do without lithic tools and survive just fine. On one hand, inferences that prehistoric people were tethered to a lithic raw material source, or that a settlement location was chosen primarily because of the availability of knappable rock, must be scrutinized due to the potential of allowing a large lithic assemblage with few other artifact types to blind us to additional activities and reasons for occupying a particular place. On the other hand, as humans born with an anatomy that does not provide biological answers to the need for something sharp (with weak nails and small teeth), a stone with a razor-sharp edge does make our problem-solving brain more useful. We study lithics not only because of survivability in the archaeological record but also because this material was important to some people in many cases in the past.

Here we explore modifying an Organization of Technology (OT) model, developed from processual archaeology, for examining daily activities of past peoples and how lithic materials recovered from a site articulate with those activities. Consideration is given to how a focus on past activities, conducted every day or on a similar scale, changes the way in which we view the archaeological record. We focus the approach of examining the everyday life of prehistoric people by combining artifact life histories with considerations of the activities necessary to meet everyday human needs. We conclude with implications for lithic analysis and making inferences regarding past human behavior from artifact assemblages largely consisting of lithics.

Lithic Artifact Life Histories

Prior to the widescale adoption of processual archaeology and continuing to-day in some reports of investigation (especially survey reports driven by Cultural Resources Management), the focus of lithic analyses has been finished tools and assigning temporal or functional inferences to those tools. Despite early work on reduction sequences by William Holmes (1890), the idea of changes in the form of a stone tool throughout its life cycle was not integrated into Americanist lithic studies until the 1970s and full-integration into Paleolithic archaeology continues to be discussed in the twenty-first century (see Bisson 2000; Bar-Yosef and Van Peer 2009) due to the dominance of typologies built on a finished-object approach. A brief overview of the concept of "artifact life history" demonstrates the fundamental manner in which it has and continues to impact archaeological method and theory. We later argue that such a reconceptualization is possible through adopting an "everyday" perspective on the past.

Specific use of the term "stone-tool life history" or its variants is uncommon in lithic analysis anywhere in the world (however, see McAnany 1988; Tomášková 2005); interestingly, the related term "Frison effect" (Jelinek 1976) is much more important in discussions of the Old World Paleolithic than in the Americas from which it derives. Arguably, the recent edited volume *Lithic Technology: Measures of Production, Use, and Curation* (Andrefsky 2008) has stone-tool life history as its focus. The authors are so dedicated to this concept that the chapters examine applications without the need for justifying the approach or term.

Through careful study of "retouch" flakes and refitting of lithic artifacts, as George Frison (1968:149) demonstrated, "Tools such as side scrapers, end scrapers, knives, and drills were continually modified throughout their lifetime of functional utility, and at the time when they were discarded or became non-functional, they were usually quite different than when originally completed," which is now readily accepted. At a time when artifact typology dominated analytical activity, however, a focus on artifact life cycles and processes of change was transformative. Frison (1968:154) readily recognized the implication of his findings: "Tool typology must consider these possibilities if typology is to have any value as a temporal, spatial, or functional indicator. Care must be taken to determine whether two or more different-appearing tools are not the same tool, functionally, at different stages of use."

Other researchers subsequently made similar observation, such as Dan Morse (1971) and Albert Goodyear (1974) regarding Dalton points. In a similar manner,

C. Marshall Hoffman (1985) used a variety of measurements and multivariate statistics to examine Late Archaic hafted biface types and determined the established types only represented resharpened versions of the same general form. Other researchers have examined the effect that resharpening and reworking have on hafted bifaces (e.g., Flenniken 1985; Flenniken and Raymond 1986; also see Titmus and Woods 1986; Towner and Warburton 1990). While the blade area is most often the focus of resharpening, in some cases the base may be reworked, causing the biface to be classified as a different type. David Thomas (1986), however, demonstrated (in response to Flenniken and Raymond 1986) that changes in biface type due to resharpening must be based on archaeological evidence and not on the "mental template" or simple convenience of the modern flintknapper.

In honor of the identification of the importance of changes occurring during the lifetime of a tool, Arthur Jelinek (1977:18) defined the "Frison effect" as a "tendency for a metamorphosis of tools through a succession of modifications." Instead of focusing on further investigation of artifact life history, Jelinek (1977:30) called for standardization in vocabulary for describing artifact variability. While such standardization certainly has utility, knowing what variation is relevant and how it is relevant should have been given equal attention. Importantly, this discussion concerned Paleolithic archaeology; the use of the term "Frison effect" can still be found on occasion in that literature today but only rarely in Americanist lithic literature (see Andrefsky 2008:xi).

While not discussed speaking in terms of stone-tool life history or the Frison effect, Michael Collins (1975:18) presented a "generalized flow model for the production of chipped stone tools" that described the stone-tool life history and incorporated the Frison effect. While it is of greater complexity, we can easily identify the more commonly used sequence in Americanist lithic studies since that time: raw material acquisition, tool manufacture, use, maintenance/reuse, and discard. While Collins did not refer directly to the Frison effect, he discussed the importance of "systemic context" and the work of Michael Schiffer (1972). This type of "life-history framework" is considered a core concept of behavioral archaeology (Schiffer et al. 2001) and is closely related to what Randall and Gilmore (Chapter 8) refer to as "itineraries." Focusing again on lithics, stone-tool life history can be investigated in part because of what Michael Shott (2005) has termed the "reduction thesis." In short, stone tools are not only reduced from larger pieces during manufacture but undergo further reduction during use and through resharpening (Shott and Nelson

2008:23). This continued resharpening affects the size and often the shape of the tool throughout its use-life. In some instances the resharpening or reworking of an existing tool is intended to change the function of that tool. "Recycling is a means of reclaiming and extending the lifespan of objects" (Amick 2015:15).

Adoption of an artifact life history approach so thoroughly by lithic specialists who were trained within the processualist paradigm made the value of the study of lithic raw materials, flake debris, experimental manufacture, and usewear studies clear. The relevance was demonstrated by relating patterning in one or more of these aspects of artifact form to mobility/settlement patterns (e.g., Beck et al. 2002; Carr 1994b; Kelly 1988). Much of this work concerns Paleoindian studies; for example, Robert Kelly and Larry Todd (1988) argue that Clovis people employed high residential and logistical mobility across an expansive territory and relied upon a transportable, complex technology that was highly curated. These inferences were based on several lines of evidence, including use of bifaces, focus on high-quality cryptocrystalline lithic material, and the similarities among Paleoindian fluted-point assemblages. Alternatively, Ashley Smallwood (2012) argues that the lack of homogeneity in hafted biface and biface manufacturing sequences data supports David Anderson's (1990b, 1996c) Staging Area Model (see Carr and Bradbury 2013 for an alternate view).

Due to the long history and dominance of lithic typology in Europe, the Frison effect can be said to still haunt certain aspects of Paleolithic archaeology. Harold Dibble (1995:360) has convincingly demonstrated the importance of resharpening and recycling for Middle Paleolithic scrapers and called for abandonment of "normative-empiricist frameworks." Others have argued for the necessity of replacing the Middle Paleolithic typology of François Bordes (Bisson 2000) and embracing artifact life histories as opposed to isolated artifact types as a "more productive research strategy" (Tomášková 2005:82). The chaîne opératoire method, which some contrast with an OT approach and others equate to reduction sequence (see Shott 2003; Tostevin 2011), is common in parts of Europe and starting to see some use in North America (e.g., Franklin et al. 2012; Sellet 1993). Frédéric Sellet (1993:106) defines chaîne opératoire as "a technological approach that attempts to reconstruct the organization of technology . . . it seeks to understand the cultural transformations that a specific raw material underwent. It is a chronological segmentation from material acquisition to discard of both the actions and mental processes that were required for the manufacture and maintenance of artifacts." The OT approach has concentrated on concepts such as curation and investigating hunter-gatherer land use, while chaîne opératoire has focused more on the individual and issues of intent, choice, preference, gesture, event, cognition, structure, symbolism, and agency (Bleed 2009).

Today lithic analysts working in an Americanist tradition employing an OT approach have wholly adopted the concept of artifact life history and are concerned with measures of aspects of it, such as retouch values, tool production effort, raw material constraints, and curation processes (Shott and Nelson 2008:25). Stone-tool life history is firmly embedded in the various definitions of OT (e.g., Kelly 1988; Nelson 1991) and is a major component of an OT model (Carr et al. 2012). Various methods have been proposed to determine the amount of resharpening observed on scrapers (e.g., Dibble 1995; Eren, Dominguez-Rodrigo, et al. 2015; Eren and Prendergast 2008; Kuhn 1990; Shott 1995), bifaces (e.g., Andrefsky 2006; Clarkson 2002; Miller and Smallwood 2012; Wilson and Andrefsky 2008; Shott and Ballenger 2007), and other tools (e.g., Bradbury et al. 2008; Shott and Sillitoe 2004, 2005). It must be cautioned that these various indices of reduction are not of interest in isolation: "The concepts of reduction, retouching, and resharpening are only important insofar as they provide information on the more complex concepts of prehistoric behavior, curation, and tool use-life" (Eren and Prendergast 2008:76).

Prior to thinking through an artifact life history approach, recognizing the impact of the Frison effect, or fully accepting the reduction thesis, archaeologists were unaware of the importance of certain kinds of variation in the archaeological record and lacked a framework to explain similarities and differences in artifact form, the presence/absence of certain kinds of flake debris, or the relationship between a Dalton point and a Dalton drill. The ability to imagine a stone tool transforming through everyday use and reduction during its life history has provided powerful insight. Are we blind to other aspects of assemblage variability today because we are not imagining the context of everyday life and activities in which artifact life histories play out?

We must consider that the continued focus on describing artifact form, whether through typology or through continuous measure, would be enriched by inferring the activities that represented the systemic context for these objects during their life history. Indeed, previously the "Activities" portion of the OT model (Figure 10.1) was limited to considerations of stone tool life history (Carr et al. 2012) and must be expanded to include the full range of activities conducted by people in the past that articulated with stone tool use either directly or indirectly.

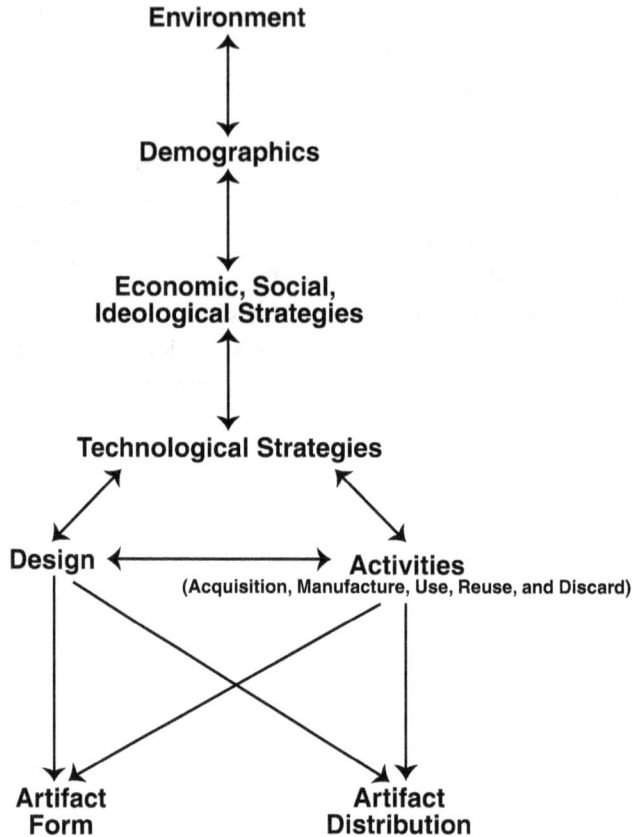

Figure 10.1. Organization of Technology (OT) model.

Everyday Life, Activities, and Lithics

Recognizing and explaining variation in human activities across space and time is what drives anthropology. However, an archaeological goal of fully reconstructing all aspects of this variation is unproductive. The archaeological record is often too coarse-grained for archaeologists to infer the actions of every individual every moment in the past. But limiting archaeological investigation to what our current theoretical perspectives allow us to "see" is also unproductive. We suggest starting with a consideration of the everyday lives of people in the past as constrained by the basic needs that those individuals needed to fulfill. People conduct certain minimal activities every day to meet their needs, and some of these activities leave traces in the archaeological record. Working back and forth between our understanding of these basic activities, the specific environment relevant to a site's occupants, and observations of the archaeological record should provide a means to achieve a more complete and accurate reconstruction employing a hypothesis-testing strategy.

Bronislaw Malinowski (1944) discussed seven basic human needs: metabolism, reproduction, bodily comfort, safety, movement, growth, and health. Not surprisingly, stone tools were not among these needs. These everyday needs provide us with a starting place for thinking about the activities that people in the past conducted at any site. For example, we envision people in the past choosing a campsite near a water source, as well as gathering and hunting for food to meet metabolic needs, constructing shelter for bodily comfort and safety, and so on. These activities cause us to consider how technology, and particularly stone tool technology, was employed by people in meeting these basic daily needs. Although activities obviously are carried out not only to meet needs, we suggest that we start with need-based activities and explore additional activities as our goals and the archaeological record warrant.

Organization of Technology

If we were to transport an individual 5,000 years into the past with no technology, the first order of business would *not* be to identify a source of tool stone. Immediate concerns (predators, water, food, shelter) would come first. As lithic analysts, we quickly think of how chert could help us in terms of making fire, shelter, and other tools, so our bias could lead us quickly to contemplate locating a stone tool source. The long-term and varied use of chipped-stone tools argues for some importance in the lives of people in the past. An OT model (see Figure 10.1) articulates the archaeological record (artifact form and distribution) with activities and the technological strategy as well as other considerations (Carr and Bradbury 2011; Carr et al. 2012).

Needs are derived from human biology and play out in relationship to particular environments. The activities to meet the needs of an individual in a particular environment are one consideration and the size of the population is another. Short- and long-term needs are addressed in the OT model through economic, ideological, and social strategies, which we combine for this discussion. (While it is necessary determine how these articulate, that is beyond the scope of this chapter.) We postulate that these are higher-order strategies than technology, meaning that a technological strategy is adopted to meet the demands of economic, ideological, and social strategies. This apparent subservient placement of technology might appear to lessen its importance in the lives of people in the past. To the contrary, this demonstrates that people do not directly go from economic strategy to activities performed in following that strategy, but rather that those activities adopted are performed with consideration of the available technology and as part of a technological strategy. In short, technology matters because it is so thoroughly integrated into everyday life.

The next level of the model consists of activities and design, which is where "everyday life" is most apparent. Activities in the model have been examined through a "lithic lens," particularly artifact life history (Carr et al. 2012). However, activities should encompass much more and are the means by which people meet everyday life needs: stone tool life cycle meets everyday life. Thinking about lithic tools in this way is similar to the itineraries discussed by Randall and Gilmore (Chapter 8) as the "wanderings of vessels and persons" when the vessel life history intersects with an activity. For lithic analysts using an OT approach, this leads to fresh directions for research by positing new questions or looking at old questions in novel ways. What activities conducted on a daily basis would involve a stone tool? What stone tools are best to have on hand for individuals to conduct their day-to-day activities? Do people flintknap daily, weekly, semiannually? Do only a few people make tools or certain types of tools? Is there a seasonality to stone tool manufacture and use? Are there gender-related differences in access to stone tools, learning to make stone tools, and what types of stone tools are needed or used on a regular basis?

The traditional "artifact-focused" approach includes an examination of artifact form and distribution to make inferences of design and activities and so on. Inferences of economic, ideological, and social strategies are further removed from the archaeological record and thus more tenuous. Importantly, the investigation of the environment and demography can be investigated by means other than lithics, so that we can work from both ends of the model to infer these strategies.

Further Investigating Activities as Life Cycles

Our current approach to a lithic assemblage is artifact-centered due to our training at a certain time in a processual paradigm, which engenders close adherence to data and a commitment to science. Yet, to realize fully the value of the data derived from an artifact life cycle approach, we cannot stop at the description of how a particular resharpened hafted biface of nonlocal chert was used to cut something hard in a certain motion. Inferring the specific activities allows greater insight into the lives of the person/people using the tool. Sitting in our lab, we could imagine any number of practical and fanciful activities that could result in the described artifact. Starting with basic needs and considering the specific environment, however, will provide a focus to our imagining certain activities at a site (fishing near water sources, gathering plants during certain times of the year) and the conduct (or not) of these activities could be tested with additional data. Importantly, activities also may be conducted unrelated to the basic needs of people that involve those aspects of culture that are meaningful in the lives of people: for example, carving a design in a bone pin. Stone tools will be used in a wide variety of these activities. Moving from an artifact-centered to an activity-centered approach results in two important realizations. First, activities have a life cycle. Second, when investigating hunter-gatherer mobility, consideration of activities provides more precise inferences regarding mobility.

Starting with our second point, most agree that foragers and collectors represent two ends of a continuum. It is common practice to infer a position on that continuum from a lithic assemblage; but, lacking precision, the dichotomy is employed in practice. By considering the activities likely to be conducted at a specific archaeological site based on the constraints of the environment and evidence from the archaeological record, a list of potential and probable activities could be constructed. These activities would allow a more nuanced and perhaps precise consideration of the social and economic strategies employed as well as mobility patterns.

As with artifact-life cycles, activity-life cycles can be viewed in stages. As a start, we suggest procurement, conduct, and distribution. Procurement includes gathering of materials, tools, and a person or people for the conduct of the activity. The conduct may involve a single person over a matter of minutes using personal gear to start a fire from curated wood or take place over months/years in a staged manner such as mound construction (see Kidder and Sherwood, Chapter 12). Finally, distribution leads to a consideration of the life-cycle of products and employed tools and discard of by-products.

Some chipped-stone tools were personal gear and might be personally carried most of the time or stored in personal space. Other tools might be more generic and could be left at the site of the activity because it is conducted over the course of several stages. These tools might be more likely to be lost, especially if something interrupts the activity. Thinking about the "life cycle of the activity" causes one to consider the life cycle of the tool in a different manner.

Identifying Everyday Activities

Using knowledge of the specific location of an archaeological site and the general environmental context, and hypothesizing the activities that took place there, is different from considering the archaeological evidence present and inferring activities for which there is evidence. A simplistic approach to lithic analysis employing the latter approach would lead to the inference that stone tools were manufactured and broken there based on flake debris and tool fragments. However, people conduct a vast array of activities daily for many different reasons, so we could become overwhelmed with possibilities for where to start. We suggest employing ethnography, special cases of archaeological preservation, and ethnohistory as means to expand the consideration of activities. Here we provide general examples that relate to our themes of activities and everyday life. For specific case studies, we would want to build an argument based on analogy as to why certain sources are useful for considering the activities at a specific site. We also note that we are not advocating the wholesale application of ethnographic or ethnohistoric data to the past. We are merely suggesting that such data sources can provide hypotheses for testing with archaeological data.

The Two Worlds of the Washo (Downs 1966) is a "reconstructed ethnography" that relies on memories of living people who experienced a more "traditional lifeway" in their youth. It remains useful for archaeologists to consider because of its focus on certain aspects of land use and material culture. This ethnography is divided into chapters such as "The Land," "Using the Land," "Society and Culture," and so on. Chapter 4, entitled "Using the Land," is divided into sections such as "The Fishing Year"; "Fishing Technology, Society, and Culture"; "The Gathering Year"; "Plants and the Patterns of Washo Life"; and so on. While this resource is imperfect because it is a reconstructed ethnography, it provides insight into activities and technologies employed to carry out those activities. For example, "Compared to hunting and gathering, fishing required immeasurably more tools and devices and an exceedingly high degree of skill. The making of fishhooks and spears was a complex job, equal to the making of bows and arrows, and their use required as much practice. Fish weirs, dams, traps, and even fishing platforms were all projects much more ambitious and complex than even the Washo winter house" (Downs 1966:16).

What is gained from ethnographies is a better understanding of the range of activities and material culture employed by people who are articulating with certain specific conditions. That is, given the ethnographic environment and demographics, people exhibited a lifeway involving economic, ideological, and social strategies. These include political and social organization as well as subsistence and mobility patterns. Archaeologists can then look to these ethnographies for inspiration regarding the activities that could have been conducted in the past, given similarities in certain conditions. This is *not* about the "!Kung San-itization" (Isaac 1990) of the archaeological record, but rather a more nuanced analogical approach that provides a range of possibilities. Ethnography helps us to think about possibilities and probabilities beyond the artifacts in front of us.

The second avenue of inquiry from which to gain insight into activities, stone tool use-life, and everyday life involves archaeological sites that have special preservation conditions. Evidence of material culture not commonly preserved at typical sites opens new windows into the lives of people in the past. For example, the Windover site is an "Early Archaic wet site, specifically a cemetery or charnel/mortuary pond near the southeast coast of Florida . . . artifacts . . . included a wide variety of bone, antler, wood and fabric specimens" (Doran 2002:281). Based on finds at Windover, we would suggest that a number of items of textile, bone, wood, and antler potentially are missing from our analyses of most Archaic sites in the Southeast. In the conclusion to Chapter 6 in the Windover volume, the authors make this point: "The fabrics and most related perishables . . . represent the end products of a labor-intensive non-durable technology, the potential roles of which have been drastically underestimated . . . As such, they have profound implications for group mobility, division and organization of labor, seasonality and subsistence practices, personal status, and a wide range of other issues virtually unapproachable through the medium of durable (i.e., lithic) technology" (Andrews et al. 2002:163–164). Of course here we are doing just that, working to "approach" the full range of aspects of prehistoric culture with lithic technology.

It is not only Windover that can provide insight but sites with excellent floral and faunal preservation, such as shell midden sites, that can bring focus to the range of daily activities and how those daily activities might change seasonally. Again, researchers can employ similarities in the site context to determine from which site with excellent preservation to draw specific inspiration, and in this case similarity in time might also be applicable.

A third source of data for consideration of activities in the past is ethnohistoric accounts. While potentially problematic due to observer bias, insights and observations of people using a chipped-stone technology do provide another means of thinking about possibilities and probabilities. For ethnohistoric accounts in the Americas, it is not too much of a stretch to postulate that certain technologies at the time of contact might have roots in the Archaic and beyond. Therefore we recommend something of a direct historical approach for the region under consideration and suggest drawing most heavily on those accounts. For the Southeast, an example is Charles C. Jones Jr., *Antiquities of the Southern Indians*, originally published in 1873. Jones combined archaeological investigation with ethnohistoric writings of early explorers and observers, so his book focuses on material culture. Consider the following quotation concerning mortars (Jones 1999:310):

To Adair are we indebted for the following account of the mortars which the women beat the flinty corn . . . The Indians always used mortars instead of mills, and they had them, with almost every other convellience [*sic*] . . . they cautiously burned a large log to a proper level and length, placed fire a-top, and wet mortar around it, in order to give the utensil a proper form; and when the fire was extinguished, or occasion required, they chopped the inside with their stone-instruments, patiently continuing the slow process till they finished the machine to the intended purpose.

Considering the full range of activities conducted in the past is daunting. In this chapter alone, by simply providing limited examples, we have considered fishing gear, wood/bone/antler tools, textile implements, and wooden mortars for which stone tools will be used in fashioning these items. Fishing, gathering, hunting, and other types of activities were conducted more efficiently with some type of sharp edge; in many cases, stone tools were an important means to conduct these activities.

These means (ethnography, ethnohistory, and special preservation archaeological sites) of approaching potential activities conducted by people in the past may provide more than just a range to consider and also lead to considering other aspects of how and why technology is organized, especially ethnographic accounts. We cannot forget that technological strategies are driven by economic, ideological, and social strategies, reflecting that culture is integrated. While we label all of these "strategies," optimality does not drive all aspects of culture.

Consider cultural norms and how these norms may impact decisions related to manufacturing. One material may be better suited to a particular task because of technological or functional concerns but that does not mean that it will be used in the manufacture of a particular item. An example can be found in the study of Thule material culture by Robert McGhee (1994). His analysis indicated an environmental opposition between land and sea mammals that was extended to the raw materials selected for tool manufacture. In the idealized cultural construct, weapons employed for hunting sea mammals were manufactured with materials obtained from the sea. In contrast, weapons used to hunt land mammals were made with materials procured from the land. These decisions were made regardless of their relative qualities of workability, use-efficiency, durability, and maintainability.

In trying to explore and understand this dichotomy, McGhee looked at other associations of ivory and antler in Thule culture. Ivory was used for items other than weapons associated with sea-mammal hunting: snow goggles, kayak mountings, and so on. Other items made from ivory were connected with women and with winter activities: needle cases, thimble holders, female ornaments, small bird-woman figures. Antler, in contrast, was linked to land mammals, particularly caribou, men, and summer life on land. A structured set of differences results in land/sea : summer/winter : man/woman : antler/ivory. This is what we would offer as an ideological strategy for a specific OT model dealing with Thule culture.

Activities and the Past

People make a wide-range of decisions related to daily activities to meet their needs. In combination with natural processes, these impact to a degree the manner in which the archaeological record accrues. Myopically considering only those activities directly inferred from surviving artifacts, such as lithics, leads to an extremely inadequate view of people's lifeways. Expanding the view of activities, even if limited to those derived from everyday needs, through analogy with ethnography, ethnohistory, and special preservation archaeological sites adds both depth and reality to the actual lived events in the past and new consideration of evidence contained within the archaeological record. That is, an activity-based approach enriches the investigation of the archaeological record (see the discussion of salt-making as an activity in Dumas, Chapter 6:Figure 6.1). However, we would caution against applying analogy uncritically. There are no constants of human behavior (Dunnell 1992:217); therefore we cannot simply apply information obtained from one culture and time to another. Working back and forth between various sources of hypothesis inspiration and the archaeological record has the potential to allow new insights and testing of those insights.

Building an Activity Approach

On the one hand, we can use our experience to fill in the daily events that occurred at a site. However, this naive and egotistical exercise leads to placing the present in the past in a counterproductive way. On the other hand, we can begin to imagine the daily activities required to meet basic human needs in the relevant environmental context that are inspired by pertinent ethnography, ethnohistory, and special preservation archaeological sites. These imagined daily activities provide hypotheses for testing with archaeological data. This approach complements the traditional, artifact-centered approach in which only activities directly inferred from archaeological materials are discussed. Here we provide only initial suggestions based on previous discussion to demonstrate potential paths for future research.

The seven basic human needs (metabolism, reproduction, bodily comfort, safety, movement, growth, and health) serve as a jumping-off point to consider site activities, given aspects of the environment and articulation with the archaeological record. In terms of the environment, we can determine when the site was occupied, the distance to water, and similar aspects of the site location. Food and water are the most basic resources needed for metabolism. Situating a site near a source of water provides easy access to meeting this need; a creek/ stream/river of sufficient size can provide a means of transportation by watercraft and in some cases gravel chert. Reproduction as a basic human need is perhaps best considered archaeologically in terms of maintaining families and access to potential mates, such as through aggregation sites for hunter-gatherers. Two aspects that readily come to mind in terms of Malinowski's third basic human need, bodily comfort, are shelter and clothing. Is there evidence for structures at the site through the presence of postholes and/or are adzes present? Are artifacts (such as scrapers) present that would indicate the production of clothing? Predators are threats to safety, and hearths, structures, and weaponry provide some protection. Movement or mobility can involve the search for resources to supply the current site occupied and consideration of the next residential move for hunter-gatherers. For growth, again, food is a key. The basic needs of children suggest that food must be regularly available. The health of the elderly also is especially dependent on a regular, daily food supply. This leads to a variety of considerations. What is the evidence for food processing at the site? What foods were eaten? How were they obtained?

These simple lines of inquiry engender hypothesis formation and consideration of means to test those hypotheses. On the one hand, equifinality remains a major problem for archaeology in that a number of possibilities remain as alternate explanations for the available data. On the other hand, these hypotheses serve to inspire new data collection in the field, such as use of certain screen sizes for collecting small flake debris (Price 2012) in order to investigate the location and type of activities at a site. We see the potential for new field and lab methods to develop as we push our consideration of everyday activities, generate hypotheses, and develop means to test those hypotheses.

Discussion

As archaeologists, we ultimately are devoted to the investigation of culture change; and as lithic analysts we examine variability in artifact form and distribution to investigate prehistoric behavior at archaeological sites. While it is clear today that the artifact life cycle impacts its form and distribution, the impact of an archaeology/artifact approach as opposed to a culture/activities approach is less obvious. An archaeology/artifact approach, while useful for describing archaeological assemblages, is limited in terms of generating new observations. Tradition and theory drive data collection. The complementary "culture/activities" approach advocated here places an emphasis on people and starts with biological needs. Fulfilling these human needs generates activities beyond those inferred directly from current observations of artifacts (such as material type worked and motion). Additionally, the environment provides opportunities and constraints for fulfilling needs. Technology plays a key role in articulating humans with the environment.

Mobility is a key means that hunter-gatherers adapt to their environment. The degree of dependence on residential mobility and how and when logistical mobility is employed by a group together dictate what resources are accessible. There is interplay with demographics as well. In examining these relationships, Kelly (1995:215) provides two conclusions: "First, when hunter-gatherers depend on evenly spaced, stable resources they are expected to live in small, evenly dispersed groups. Second, when relying on aggregated and mobile resources, they are expected to live in larger, centrally located groups." Due to the different daily activities for the two ends of the forager-collector continuum, the technology of the two groups will be organized differently. For example, in the case of residentially mobile groups, most aspects of food processing will occur at the residential base. In contrast, for logistically mobile groups, resource extraction is likely to take place at or near the resource. The processed materials would then be transported back to the main residential base for consumption. These aspects have an effect on the activities, conducted at residential bases, along with the stone tools employed. In the case of residentially mobile groups, we are likely to recover a wider assortment of stone tools related to food processing at the residential base. This would also be affected by the resources being targeted from that site. In contrast, we might expect to find a wide variety of botanical and faunal remains at a residential base occupied by logistically mobile groups, but a narrower range of stone tools used for processing these items because many of the foods would have been processed at the logistical camp. The same set of basic needs must be met whether or not people are residentially or logistically mobile. Mobility patterns and technology are two integrated means of meeting those needs. We would expect to see evidence of these differences in the activities conducted at a site and, by extension, the stone tools left behind there.

An OT model is useful for inferring certain aspects of prehistoric behavior by examining variation in artifact form and distribution, which form the base of the model. In a hierarchical model that includes various types of decision-making within a specific context, activities that generate the archaeological record are one level removed from design of tools for conducting those activities. Traditionally, activities minimally considered for lithic assemblages are derived from the artifact life cycle: procurement, manufacture, use/reuse, and discard. This "archaeology/artifact focused" model has served to generate inferences regarding prehistoric mobility patterns.

As we shift focus, a single occupation site of short duration due to high levels of residential mobility is a palimpsest of sorts, because the materials left behind reflect a myriad of decisions made by people on a daily basis. These decisions, in turn, reflect how the technology was organized. For example, the decision to use an expedient tool versus a formal tool for a specific task is based on raw material access, composition of the current toolkit, design of those tools, anticipated needs to meet social and economic needs, and so on. Over the time of site occupation, these daily decisions create the archaeological record. Given this, what are the possibilities for examining the everyday life of an individual in the past on the basis of the stone procured for the manufacture of chipped stone tools, used in various activities, discarded, sometimes reused, but eventually discarded, only to be recovered by us? This is the question that we have attempted to explore here, because we have been working on variations of it for our entire careers in archaeology. The scale generally has differed with a focus on prehistoric cultures versus the individual or, more specifically, cultural behaviors at a specific site. We are hopeful that varying the scale may provide a focus and perspective that we have lacked in the past. In this regard, simulations hold great promise for investigating lithic assemblages produced by everyday site activities.

Conclusions

Investigating daily activities and decisions made by people in the past is a complicated matter. Technology was integrated into those decisions, however, and lithic technology is a tangible link to those activities and decisions. To investigate what lithic assemblages can tell us about the everyday in the past, we would make several recommendations. First, we think that an OT model provides a means to think through what factors were important in the formation of those lithic assemblages.

Much work remains, however, especially in more fully developing ways to consider technological strategies and making activities robust. Hence our second recommendation is that considering stone tool use-life in the context of everyday life has great potential. Activities have a life cycle, which articulates with tool life history. Tool use for an activity might be prolonged due to the stages of conduct of that activity, which causes us to think about personal gear and site furniture in new ways as well as suggesting new implications for discard and loss of tools. Additionally, we envision lithic experimentation expanding beyond direct manufacture and use of tools such that it involves the full activity in which lithic tools were used. Instead of simply making a scraper and using that scraper on a hide for a certain amount of time to replicate usewear, we see archaeologists making a hide bag or clothing item to examine the various tools involved in this activity, especially when lithic tools intersect with the various aspects of the full activity.

Third, ethnography, special preservation archaeological sites, and ethnohistoric accounts can help us more completely hypothesize everyday life, though none of them can be applied uncritically. Ethnography also can help us gain insight into culture, especially those aspects not driven by strategies and optimality. In some ways, associations like "sea-winter-woman-ivory" are more straightforward to simulate. But we all know that culture is more complex than that and the exceptions can be as informative as the rule.

Finally, attaining the goals of archaeology is a difficult endeavor, so polarizing theoretical perspectives and insular thinking will do little to aid in making progress. We envision a balance: we will retain our practical, artifact-focused approach and attempt to balance it with an activity-based approach, while retaining a commitment to scientific archaeology.

Acknowledgments

We would like to thank our wives, KMAB and NTC, for putting up with the time we spent thinking through and working on this chapter. We want to thank Sarah Price for commenting on an early draft and for her thoughtful suggestions during the revision process. Comments provided by two anonymous reviewers helped us to strengthen our arguments.

11

The Role of Dogs in Everyday Life

RENEE B. WALKER

Anthropologists are increasingly exploring the relationships between animals and people (see Conklin, Chapter 14; Moore and Jefferies, Chapter 7). The relationship between dogs and human is certainly worth consideration in regard to everyday matters. Dogs are the earliest and most widespread domestic animal in the world and thus are potentially an everyday matter for some peoples in the past and in the present. Arriving in the Americas with humans at the end of the Pleistocene, dogs helped people hunt, protected their families, and carried wood, meat, and other household items. At sites throughout the Southeast, we see clear evidence that dogs were side by side with their human counterparts in life and in death, as dogs were frequently buried with humans in cemeteries. It is clear that dogs helped humans with their everyday tasks and greatly enhanced their quality of life. In return, dogs were fed and cared for by their humans. This chapter explores the integral everyday relationship between dogs and humans in the past.

The location and timing of dog domestication are still the subject of considerable debate and somewhat tangential in the context of this chapter. However, it bears mentioning that archaeologists have used studies of modern dog genetics and archaeological data to calculate the age of origin for domestic dogs. A recent study on dog and wolf genetics places the origins of dog domestication in Central Asia (Shannon et al. 2015), while a previous study places the origin in Europe (Thalmann et al. 2013). The European origin supported by Olaf Thalmann et al. (2013) corresponds to archaeological evidence from Goyet Cave in Belgium and Razboinichya Cave in Siberia, which suggests that people had domestic dogs at these sites as early as 36,000 years ago. However, work by Laura Shannon et al. (2015) and Darcy Morey and Rujana Jeger (2015) supports a later domestication date of 15,000–17,000 years ago. This debate will likely continue for some time as new evidence comes to light. Wherever and whenever dogs were domesticated, however, it is clear that they eventually accompanied humans as they migrated across the Old World and into the New World. So far researchers of both genetic and archaeological data conclude that dogs were not domesticated independently in the Americas from American gray wolves but were purely of Old World stock.

The earliest evidence of domestic dogs in the Americas dates to 9,400 years ago at Hinds Cave in Texas, where a dog bone was found in a human coprolite (Tito et al. 2012). Other early evidence of dogs comes from the Koster site, where three dogs were interred at levels dating to 8,500 years ago (Morey and Wiant 1992). Evidence of the earliest burials of dogs directly with humans is at the Braden site in Idaho, dating to around 6,600 years ago, where two dogs were interred with humans (Morey 2006, 2010).

There has been extensive research on the skeletal morphology of domestic dogs in the Americas. The prehistoric dogs appear to be very similar in size and shape, though we can only hypothesize about coat color (Morey 2010; Warren 2004). Mummified dogs from White Dog Cave in Arizona show much variation in coat color and hair length even within a small sample. The larger of the cave dogs is described as long-haired and about "the size of a small collie, with erect ears and a long bushy tail . . . [the] specimen is also described as yellowish in color" (Guernsey and Kidder 1921:44). Analyses from multiple sites in the southeastern United States indicate that dogs were much smaller in size than might be expected from a descendant of wolves. On average, the shoulder height of southeastern dogs is 42 cm for males and 38 cm for females. The average shoulder height of early American dogs is around 40 cm, which is about the same as the modern breed of the standard beagle but likely leaner, with a narrower face and longer legs.

Why Have Dogs?

In addition to questions about where and when dogs were domesticated, how they came to the Americas, and what early dogs looked like, there have long been questions about why people kept dogs around in the first place. What would have been the benefit of having other mouths to feed and care for? Human Behavioral Ecology (HBE) and Optimal Foraging Theory (OFT) go a long way toward explaining that the costs of keeping dogs are outweighed by the benefits that they bring. The main premise in HBE is that people respond to their environment in a way that increases their fitness (Borgerhoff Mulder and Schacht 2012). Under the broader principles of HBE, OFT is a cost-benefit analysis to identify why certain behaviors are carried out by humans.

The costs of including a dog in everyday life could be food, care, and management of the dog's activities. Depending on the situation, in modern times dogs can be extremely high-maintenance and require significant care. Special diets, brushing, and training all require time on the part of humans and can take away from other activities that are important parts of our daily lives. However, consideration of the most well-accepted domestication scenario suggests that prehistoric dogs were low maintenance. Dog domestication emerged from a symbiotic relationship between humans and wolves. Wolves scavenged from human dump areas and became accustomed to humans. Over time their phenotype changed to what we know of as dogs today (Morey and Jeger 2015). This "self-domestication" of dogs is a phenomenon that was re-created with silver foxes in Russia, where foxes were bred based on levels of aggressiveness (Hare et al. 2012). Over time, the nonaggressive foxes took on the phenotypic characteristics similar to those of modern dogs (Morey and Jeger 2015). If this self-domestication hypothesis is correct, then I see the costs of the dogs living among humans as minimal, because they largely took care of themselves. They could hunt and scavenge for themselves without taking away from human food. They were small-bodied, so they were easier to manage and required less food. Probably the most significant cost would be in training dogs to hunt, track, and carry packs. Their contributions to the lives of humans are many. I discuss specifics of the beneficial roles that dogs played at some sites in the Southeast here.

We have a substantial body of data supporting the presence of dogs from dozens of sites in the southeastern United States. In Alabama, for example, 20 sites contain dog remains, with a total of 144 individuals (Table 11.1). These sites range in age from the Archaic through Mississippian periods, but the majority of the remains date to the Archaic period. This chapter uses the case of Alabama to provide evidence of dogs and their behaviors, with a specific emphasis on the sites of Dust Cave and Spirit Hill, but the information from Alabama can be applied broadly to other sites in much of the Southeast. While some of the sites have relatively large numbers of dog remains, such as Spirit Hill, Perry, and Flint River, most sites have less than ten and usually one to two dogs at the sites. Also, most of the dogs come from burial contexts. While some sites mention dog remains in refuse middens (Haag 1948; Webb and Dejarnette 1942, 1948), the majority are from deliberate interment of dogs in cemeteries, by themselves, with other dogs, or with humans.

The Role of Dogs in Everyday Life

Domestic dogs contributed to the everyday lives of people through their assistance with accomplishing or improving everyday tasks. This everyday role is acknowledged in the symbolic and ritual interments of dogs at some sites. We should keep

Table 11.1. Dog Remains from Sites in Alabama

Site	Count	Site Date Range	Dates for Dogs
Whitesburg Bridge	9	Archaic	Archaic
Bear Creek Cave	1	Archaic	Archaic
Cedar Creek Reservoir	1	Archaic	Archaic
O'Neal	1	Archaic	Archaic
Mulberry Creek	3	Archaic	Archaic
Perry	55	Archaic	Archaic
Flint River	19	Archaic	Archaic
Flint Shop	2	Archaic	Archaic
Little Bear Creek	2	Archaic	Archaic
Mason Island	1	Archaic	Archaic
Ricker	1	Archaic	Archaic
Russell Cave	1	Archaic/Woodland	Archaic/Woodland
James Village	5	Mississippian	Mississippian
Bessemer	2	Mississippian	Mississippian
Henry Island	2	Mississippian	Mississippian
Dust Cave	4	Paleo/Archaic	Archaic
Spirit Hill	29	Woodland/Mississippian	Woodland/Mississippian
Deposit Landing	2	Woodland/Mississippian	Woodland/Mississippian
Riley	1	Woodland	Woodland
Stearns	3	Woodland	
Total	144		

in mind the caution advised by Darcy Morey (2010) on the issue of plausible supposition versus secure inference. While the links between the role that dogs played and continue to play in human lives are sometimes clear, such as their deliberate burial in cemeteries, the role that they played is less evident in the archaeological record in many cases. Under the heading of everyday tasks, I consider the roles that likely come under the auspices of plausible supposition. In this sense, despite the lack of clear archaeological evidence, dogs probably served to protect their humans on a daily basis. Dogs have a keen sense of hearing and smell and are adept at detecting when something is amiss and letting humans know. Ethnohistoric accounts of dogs protecting camps and people record the significance that the early warning dogs provided to their human owners (Schwartz 1997).

We know from historical accounts that dogs played a role in human hunting and most likely added to the success of hunts. Dogs are adept at tracking prey, catching smaller prey, and bringing larger prey to bay. In *The Invaders* Pat Shipman (2015) hypothesizes that dogs were so successful in helping modern humans in their hunting that the demise of Neanderthals was much faster than it would have been without the aid of dogs. For example, she cites studies by Jeremy Koster and Kenneth Tankersley in which modern foragers hunting with dogs were nine times more successful than those hunting without dogs (Shipman 2015:186). In addition, early ethnohistoric accounts mention the importance of dogs in hunting bears, deer, beavers, and other game (Schwartz 1997).

There may be some secure evidence for this activity in the prehistoric Southeast. For example, some dogs from southeastern sites have injuries that might be consistent with hunting accidents. Dog Burial #19 from the Spirit Hill site was severely injured in early adulthood but survived and was later interred in the cemetery. This dog was an adult, based on epiphyseal fusion of all long bones and was determined to be a female due to good preservation and the absence of a baculum (Walker and Windham 2014). Two pathologies included a healed fracture of the left pelvis and another of the left humerus. The break of the left humerus was so extreme, with both ends healing separately from each other, that the individual probably was not able to use that leg at all (Figure 11.1). There was

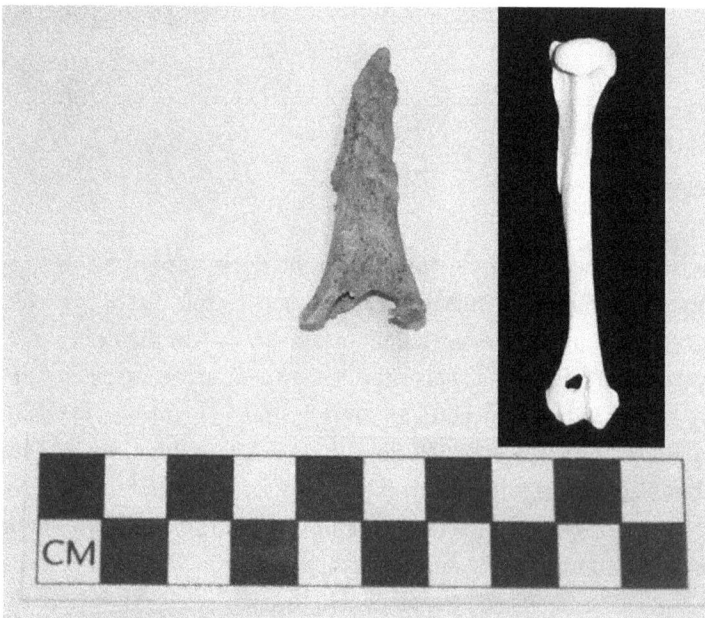

Figure 11.1. Left humerus of Dog Burial #19 from the Spirit Hill site, Alabama. A humerus with no pathology is shown on the right (modified from Walker and Windham 2014:113).

a large degree of bone resorption, indicating that the individual survived for a long time after the break. This type of injury may have occurred when hunting, particularly in the case of large game such as deer or bears that could kick out or swipe with great force. Certainly it can be postulated that the injury could have occurred when a human kicked or hit the dog; but the healing of the injury, the probability that the dog was only able to get around on three legs, and the later interment of the dog in a cemetery speak to the care that was afforded to this animal. In another example, Burial #4, an adult female has a fractured and healed rib, which could be associated with a hunting injury (Walker and Windham 2014). Again, this injury healed and the individual was later interred in the cemetery.

Dogs are also potential sources of useful by-products for humans for use in daily activities. Dog urine may have been used by horticultural groups to keep pests from raiding gardens. "Predator urine" is a product used today to keep pests out of people's gardens or off their property. The feces of dogs could also be applied to deer or other animal skins to tan the hides, similar to brain tanning. In the late eighteenth century, as mentioned in *The Art of Tanning and Currying Leather*, dog feces were added to vegetable material in the tanning process (Lalande 1774). In addition, dog skins could be utilized like the skins of other animals. Some dogs in burial contexts have cut marks consistent with skinning. One example is Burial #4 from the Spirit Hill site, which has skinning cut marks; they may be present on other dogs but perhaps were overlooked. For example, I have observed possible skinning cut marks on the tops of dog skulls but dismissed them because the dogs were interred and articulated and therefore not butchered. However, these dogs might have had their skins removed before interment as keepsakes for their human owners or for a ritual purpose. Another by-product is the hair or "wool" of dogs, which was combed from dogs and used in textiles. Susan Crockford (1997) refers to dogs in British Columbia that were specially bred for their hair, which was shaved and used to weave blankets.

There is evidence that dogs were consumed either habitually or for emergency purposes throughout the world. For example, it has been documented at sites in the Great Plains that dogs were often consumed in the late winter, possibly when other sources of stored food ran out (Snyder 1995). Dog bones are found in middens at sites across the Southeast, including sites mentioned in this analysis (Wing 1978). Interestingly, it is not mutually exclusive to find dog bones in midden contexts and at the same sites where dogs are deliberately buried. For example, at the Indian Knoll shell mound, William Webb (1946) noted dog bones in shell midden contexts but also found 24 dogs intentionally buried at the site. A dog bone was recovered in the midden at the Spirit Hill site, and

29 dogs were buried in the cemetery. The numbers of dog bones in middens is relatively slight for the early prehistoric Southeast. It has been suggested that dog bones in middens did not become more common until the late prehistoric and the early historic periods (Schwartz 1997; VanDerwarker 1996). Bones in middens may not be direct evidence for the consumption of dogs, though cut marks and burning provide some support for this activity. There is the case of the previously mentioned dog skull fragment from Hinds Cave in Texas that was found in a human coprolite, but no such evidence currently exists for the Southeast (Tito et al. 2012).

Another topic with substantial evidence to support secure inferences on the role of dogs is transportation of people or goods. Dogs have been documented ethnohistorically pulling a travois, which could have held household goods, such as wood, meat, and other items, from collection areas back to the campsite or village. Travois were probably more commonly used in open areas, such as the plains of the west or the river floodplains of the Southeast, and may not have been commonly used where dense trees or underbrush would have made dragging the poles difficult. It is more likely that in these areas dogs were loaded with packs that sat on their upper backs, between the shoulder blades. These packs probably draped like saddlebags over the dogs' backs and in some cases may have weighed as much as 50 pounds, more than most of the dogs themselves weighed.

Multiple sites offer evidence that dogs were carrying packs consistently and with a heavy enough load to cause damage to the vertebrae. The most common damage is the curvature of the vertebral spinous processes, caused by heavy loads pressing down on the backs of the animals. Fractures of the spinous processes were also observed and may have been caused by having animals carry loads that were too heavy or having very young dogs (less than a year old) carrying heavy packs. Finally, curvature of the scapular spine was also observed. At the Dust Cave site, three of the four dogs exhibit damage to the vertebra or scapula. Burial #1, a young female, exhibited curvature of the dorsal spinous processes and slight ossification of the right acetabulum. In addition, Burial #3, also a young female, had curvature of the dorsal spinous processes and caudal deviation of both spines of the scapulae. Of the 29 dogs recovered at the Spirit Hill site, 9 had some damage to the thoracic or lumbar vertebrae with either curved spinous processes or spinous processes with healed fractures (Walker and Windham 2014). It is interesting to note that Dog Burial #19, the adult female previously mentioned, had survived severe trauma to her left forelimb and also had extensive curvature of the thoracic and lumbar vertebral spinous processes

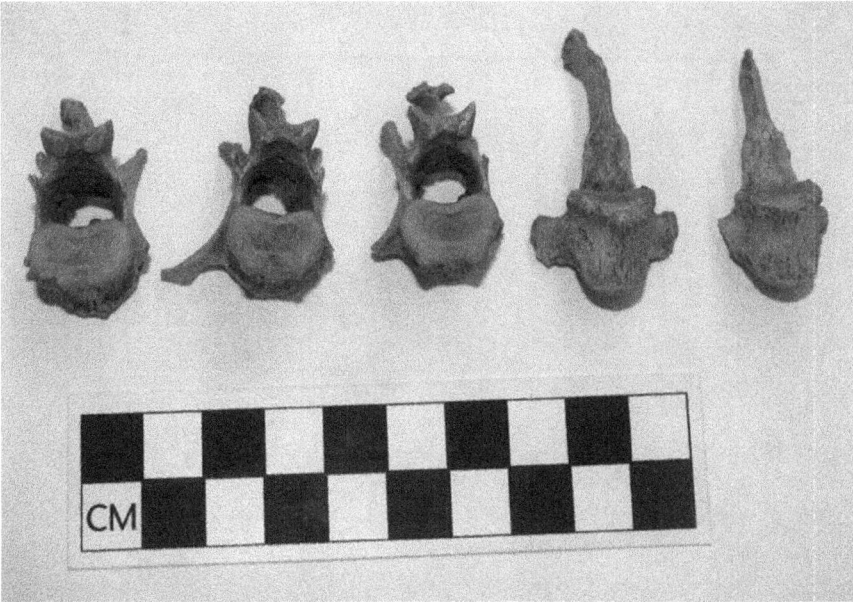

Figure 11.2. Vertebra of Dog Burial #19 from the Spirit Hill site, showing curvature of the spinous processes.

(Figure 11.2). Canine Burial #9 also had curvature of the spinous processes. At the other sites, not all dog burials were available for analysis, but a large number of the dogs have pathologies consistent with pack-carrying (Darwent and Gilliland 2001; Warren 2004).

Dogs were an integral part of people's daily lives, as can best be inferred from their burials in cemeteries with humans or close to humans. In many cases, dogs are buried with the same attention to care and detail seen in associated human burials and also buried with grave goods, though recognized instances of this are rare. At Dust Cave four dogs are buried in the northwest area of the main chamber of the cave (Walker et al. 2005). Of these, one dog was buried in the same pit as a human, and the other three were in the same area where most of the human burials are located. The dog burials at the Spirit Hill site are located among the human burials, adjacent to houses. Of the 29 dog burials at Spirit Hill, 25 are buried alone and four are buried with humans. One of the dogs is actually buried at the feet of one person and the head of another. In addition, Dog Burial #27 at Spirit Hill was buried with grave goods located between the paws, similar to a small medicine bundle (Figure 11.3) (Walker and Windham

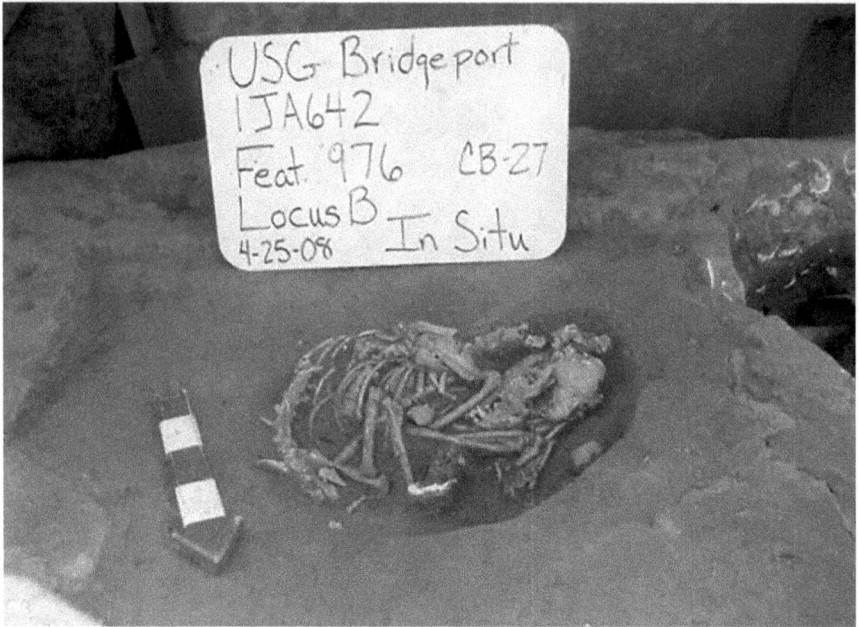

Figure 11.3. Dog Burial #27 from the Spirit Hill site with "medicine bundle" buried at mid-body, between the paws (modified from Walker and Windham 2014:115).

2014). This bundle included one nondiagnostic chert biface, a chert debitage specimen, a nonlocal greenstone fragment, and an unidentifiable shell specimen (Wettstaed and Windham 2009). The dogs' burial in cemeteries and treatment at death is a testament to the role that they played in humans' lives.

Looking back at theories of Human Behavioral Ecology (HBE) and Optimal Foraging Theory (OFT), the benefits listed above would certainly outweigh most of the costs of keeping dogs. One criticism of HBE and OFT, though, is that these applications tend to ignore cultural factors. That is certainly a problem when it comes to why people chose to associate with dogs, because those choices were not based on economics alone. Today the reasons why people "own" dogs are clearly entangled with social and cultural ideals and constructs. One strategy to explore the social and cultural reasons for keeping dogs is to use historical fiction, imagining the activities that dogs took part in and what they have meant for the people around them. So we join "Dog," a male dog living during the Archaic period in the Southeast, and follow him throughout year. Dog's activities were inspired by those of the young girl in the chapter by Hollenbach and Carmody (Chapter 5).

Dog Days

Second Day of the Strawberry Moon

Dog settled in the soft sand of the riverbank with a sigh. It had been a long haul to reach the wide river. Dog liked walking along with his girl and other humans, but the heavy poles strapped to his back made it hard to stop and smell all the good things along the way. He knew from the way his humans were moving around that they would stay at this place for a while. The smell of the nearby water made him think of fish. He drifted to sleep with his belly grumbling.

Dog could sense the humans moving as he woke. It was getting dark, but he was ready to hunt. The pack was hungry, because it had been cold for a long time and the prey had become harder to find. Dog liked to hunt the smaller animals—raccoon, opossum, squirrels. He could find them and corner them so his humans could shoot them down from the trees. Bringing them back meant scraps of meat or skin at the end of a long day.

Eighteenth Day of the Big Chestnut Moon

As the girl got the baskets ready, Dog knew that it was time to help the girl collect nuts from the grove. Dog could romp in the woods while the girl collected, then she would load the packs on his back with nuts. He didn't mind this so much—the packs weren't as heavy as they were when traveling and the journey was not as long. The people camped nearer to the nut groves. Even though the harvest lasted less than a moon, Dog knew that the nuts would provide food for the people to eat for many moons to come. He liked being with the girl, because she would share her scraps and her sleeping spot.

Second Day of the Bear Moon

Dog knew when the warm time started to turn to cold time that the humans would go for longer hunts for bigger animals: deer and bears, much more fun to track and corner. Dog would work with the girl's brother, uncle, and father and their dogs to find the deer, in groups of does and young. It was so easy to track and herd toward the humans who would hide in the underbrush then stand and shoot them. Dog liked the times when the pack all worked together to take down prey and bring back meat to feed the people. With bigger hunts, Dog would help carry the meat and skins back to camp. The smell sometimes distracted him, but he knew he that would get his share. Bears were harder to find but moved through the trees and left good signs. Taking them could be dangerous. Dog remembered the time he was hurt when a bear swung a huge paw and caught him on the side. It took most of the cold time to heal from that wound, but the girl cared for him. Dog was grateful to be back hunting again.

Seventh Day of the Deer Moon

Dog also liked the times when the people fished in the new warm time. The people would make nets from long, thin plants and tie heavy rocks to the bottom. Dog would help carry these nets to the river on his back. The people would toss these into the river, and Dog would help haul the nets full of fish back onto the river bank. The girl was always happy to see him when he returned to camp and would sneak him extra fish as they sat around the campfire. Dog spun around in circles then settled at the girl's feet and fell asleep with a full belly, content after a long day working with the humans.

Conclusions

Writing this piece of fiction was fun as well as informative, and I learned several things from this exercise that reflect how I think about the role of dogs in prehistoric life. One of the main things is to attempt to "read" the circumstances of the dogs and their burial with humans in the context of everyday life. I know from my research that dogs carried packs and helped humans, but how did that help come about? For example, my vision of "Dog" was a single dog tied to a particular family and a particular person in that family. But was that necessarily the case? Were early dogs tied to individuals or single family units or were they more communal? My take on the burial of dogs individually and with certain humans in cemeteries makes me think that the dogs were tied to families. Another aspect that I had not considered until this exercise was the extent to which dogs participated in the everyday lives of past peoples. I typically pictured them guarding camp, hunting, and sleeping until needed, but dogs were probably used in a large range of activities—including gathering. Gathering and hauling wood, water, and nuts would have been an integral part of human activities and would have carried over into the role of dogs as well.

Some other aspects were not considered in this piece, such as the ritual role of dogs, which is something connected to the everyday that can be pursued further. This lack is largely due to my writing from the dog's perspective. It could be revealing to consider writing from a dual perspective—the girl (from Chapter 5 by Hollenbach and Carmody) and the dog, perhaps bridging the everyday life with the symbolic and afterlife. In any case, considering dogs in an everyday setting helped me newly envision the role of dogs in prehistoric human society and bring the static archaeological record to life. While it is clear that dogs play a significant role in all aspects of human activities, from everyday tasks to ritual roles, it helped to consider how that role was manifested on a daily basis. Some aspects of their roles can only be assumed and imagined. We need to use our imaginations, which drove us to become archaeologists, to take "real" data and turn them into plausible interpretations about the people and animals that we study as well as develop new hypotheses that can be tested through new archaeological methods. The first step to achieving this is to shift from notions of what archaeologists consider exotic or rarely recovered archaeologically to conceptualizing how these "special finds" were part of the everyday lives of people in the past.

12

Mound Building as Daily Practice

TRISTRAM R. KIDDER AND SARAH C. SHERWOOD

Mounds and earthworks of various sorts are icons of southeastern archaeology. Indeed, they are the primary icon of southeastern Native American history in the eyes of archaeologists and the public (Knight 2010; Lindauer and Blitz 1997; Milner 2004a; Silverberg 1968; Wright and Henry 2013) (Figure 12.1). We suggest here that they were also the icon of pre-Contact Native American communities across the Southeast and Midwest and served in this capacity for the last 5,000 years. These communities did or thought about or planned or experienced mound building every day. Mounds were omnipresent and loomed over every community—sometimes in fact and often only in thought or memory. In this chapter, we explore the ways in which monumental earthworks were active in

Figure 12.1. John J. Egan, American (born Ireland), active mid-nineteenth century; "Huge Mound and the Manner of Opening Them," scene 20 from *Panorama of the Monumental Grandeur of the Mississippi Valley*, ca. 1850; distemper on cotton muslin; 25 scenes, full panoramic painting: 90 inches × 348 feet; Saint Louis Art Museum, Eliza McMillan Trust 34:1953.

the daily lives of the Southeast's indigenous people. Throughout this discussion, we neither present original data nor provide an exhaustive literature review but instead cite a sample of the studies that support these ideas or provide a basis from which to propose their potential. Thus this chapter explores the significance of these complex earthen structures in the rhythm of everyday life.

Until recently archaeologists gave little consideration to how mounds were built, because the construction process was seen as secondary to the finished product—a platform for a house or temple or a locus for human burial. Surveying the literature on mounds, we encounter a number of references to some processes (e.g., "basket loading"), but nothing we can find indicates that most of the archaeological community even tried to understand how a given community went from the idea of the mound to the construction and preservation of the edifice. Most often discussions of mound building assume that the process was uncomplicated and consisted only of piling up dirt into a heap and in some way shaping it into a final form. Hence it is hard to find significant engagement with the myriad issues of how to build a mound. Energetic studies of mound building come closest to discussing the physical and engineering aspects of erecting an earthen mound (Abrams and Bolland 1999; Abrams and Le Rouge 2008; Galaty 1996; Jeter 1984; Shenkel 1986), but few go beyond the moving of earth, because that is seen as the only significant effort required. Even the duration of mound building is rarely tackled (Bernardini 2004). Among Mississippian period mounds most acknowledge that the mound stages were erected relatively quickly. Even this allows for a great deal of relativity, however, because estimates mostly imply timing, which usually involves a generation or more (Cobb and King 2005; Hally 1996; King 2001). At Poverty Point, a Late Archaic mound in northeast Louisiana, estimates for the duration of construction of Mound A, the second largest mound in the United States, range from as little as "several generations" (Gibson 1986) to as much as a thousand years (Crothers 2004). In short, precious little in the literature specifically and explicitly discusses what mound building entailed for the Native American communities of the Southeast.

Our own approach has been to focus on mound building, specifically the processes of earth moving, preparation, emplacement, finishing, and rebuilding, as an activity (see Carr and Bradbury, Chapter 10) that can yield meaningful social and cultural evidence (Sherwood and Kidder 2011). We see sediments as being akin to artifacts and thus capable of being interpreted in many of the same ways. How a mound site is prepared, where the earth comes from, how it was moved, how it was prepared, and the ways in which it was built up, shaped, packed down, and repaired are all important considerations for understanding not just the engineering of the mounds (make no mistake: Native American mound builders were sophisticated earthen engineers) but also the organization and mobilization of labor, the deployment of resources, and the social, cultural, and symbolic values of the builders. In an earlier publication (Sherwood and Kidder 2011:84) we argued: "Mounds in the Mississippi River basin of North America are more than just piles of dirt and they are also more than just pedestals on which activities take place. We are convinced that . . . the Native American mound builders were far more than laborers, conscripted or otherwise, piling dirt with minimal effort or intentions. Mound building was an art and a science requiring considerable knowledge, skill and planning, hard work, and impressive aesthetic and symbolic expression." As we detail below, these skills were not "one-off" deployments of knowledge; rather, they are embedded in everyday behavior, in regular, repetitious actions, and are coded in the ritual, religious, and spiritual worldview of people through vast time and across large swaths of space.

Because mound building occurred over 5,000 or more years and is found in most every part of the Southeast, we do not offer a case study of mound building every day. Current literature contains many detailed examples (Anderson et al. 2013; Kassabaum et al. 2014; Knight 2010; Ortmann and Kidder 2013; Thompson et al. 2016; Van Nest 1998) and presenting only one would imply that the case study could embody the range of variation practiced by Native American peoples. In our discussion about the role of mound building in the daily consciousness of southeastern indigenous populations, we are not claiming that construction took place every day for five or more thousand years. It is probable that many members of a given community may not have even seen a mound or participated in the construction of a mound. But this does not mean that these mounds did not cast a long shadow over every community. Mounds are encoded in myth as the center of creation for some descendant communities (e.g., Galloway 1995; Gibson and Carr 2004; Rogers and Wilson 1993; Swanton 1911, 1928; Waring 1968), and it is hard to imagine that this mythic memory does not have deep roots.

Mounds were made for an array of purposes across time and through space. Mounds served as gathering places for people across large swaths of space at times and may have been places of pilgrimage where the mounds and mound building were a part of the process of community formation, negotiation, and identity. Even if mounds were only visited periodically or seasonally, they defined membership in society (Alt 2011; Buikstra and Charles 1999; Howey 2012; Thompson 2009). In other instances, mounds were the physical resting places of ancestors and arguably in some contexts places where the dead were gathered in body and in spirit so that the living community could affirm their own solidarity and sense of community. Mounds were powerful places that anchored a community and symbolized participation and belonging. They were also practical. At some times and in some places, mounds were places of habitation and locations elevated above floods, sea levels, and marshes (e.g., Russo 1996; Sassaman and Randall 2012; Schwadron 2010). They are terraformed parts of the environment where mound building and residential living were everyday experiences. In later pre-Contact times, mounds served as the platforms for perishable structures for elites and priests; these platform mounds were the everyday embodiment of politics, ritual, and power (Anderson 1994; Gibson and Carr 2004; Lindauer and Blitz 1997).

Mound building has a nearly 5,500-year history in the eastern United States, so mounds served a variety of purposes. For reasons of brevity in this overview we lump together the totality of earthen construction—mounds, embankments, linear features, shell heaps, plazas, and borrow pits. In short, we speak of the built environment, which evidence now shows is far more extensive and intensive than we once thought.

Mounds were incorporated into daily life in many ways, but we see four primary processes: mound building (including the organization and mobilization of labor, the selection of the site, the layout and plan of the mound, and the configuration of the community); mound use and the practices of encountering and viewing the mounds; mound maintenance and reconfiguration; and, finally, abandonment. These processes have counterparts in objects' life histories (Carr and Bradbury, Chapter 10) and itineraries (Randall and Gilmore, Chapter 8).

To begin, building earthworks requires extensive site preparation. In some circumstances through time this seems to involve dismantling or burning a structure or structures that lay beneath the footprint of the mound (Dickens 1976; Hally 1996). In other instances, it meant that the site area had to be stripped of underlying surface soil (e.g., Knight 2010; Sherwood 2013); in more radical conditions, undulating terrain had to be leveled (Knight 2010). And in almost every instance the mound or mounds were part of a larger architectural plan involving a plaza or plazas. More and more we are finding that plazas, once thought to be simply empty spaces around which architecture clustered, were constructed features that in some instances required massive labor efforts equal to or probably exceeding the energy required to build the mound (Alt et al. 2010; Barrier and Kassabaum, Chapter 13; Dalan 1997; Kidder 2004; Lewis et al. 1998).

All sites were built in accordance with an architectural grammar that dictated the formal rules of placement and organization. The complex rules of site layout—whether for a single mound or a mass of mounds—indicate that site planning was not haphazard. Sites and their associated spaces—especially their plaza spaces—had to be thought through, presumably debated, revised, rebuilt, and expanded. Because mound building was so central to these societies, we suspect that mound building and site layout plans and their execution were sharply contested and part of everyday conflicts and their resolution. Multiple instances of site reconfiguration, in some cases involving massive earth moving, show that these spaces were not static and immutable; they were surely shaped by daily practice and negotiation (e.g., Kidder 2011; Knight 2010; Lynott 2015; Morgan 2003).

Site preparation and layout, though, are only the beginning. Selecting soil, mining it, mixing it, and transporting it to the construction site were everyday tasks required to be able to build the mound. Studies show that not just any dirt will do when building a mound, for at least two reasons. First, building a mound is an engineering task of remarkable complexity. Earthen engineering (geotechnical engineering) today is quite literally a science, and there is no reason to think it was otherwise in the past. To make a mound, large or small, flat-topped or conical, was a feat of skill that is testified to by the enduring presence of these features on the modern landscape. Whether Poverty Point's Mound A or Cahokia's Monks Mound, these masses of earth have retained much of their integrity despite being built by hand and without the tools of modern earth movers. To put these ancient mounds in context, earthen engineered features today fail with startling regularity.

Not any dirt will do for another reason, which we can only dimly perceive but can document through repeated patterning (e.g., Schilling 2012; Sherwood 2013; Sherwood and Kidder 2011). Earth moving and emplacement is not random; in every mound, soil patterning is often marked by color changes, sometimes by texture changes, and not infrequently by both. We argue that these are not simply odd deposits but purposeful manipulation of soils and sediments to achieve a purposeful end (Kidder and Sherwood 2017). Earthen mounds were built as part of a ritual process; we feel that the act of construction was a significant part of the meaning of erecting a mound. This is not to say that the mounds' intended function was not important or the target of the construction process, but we want to emphasize that mound building itself is not just an afterthought. Mound building was purposeful, deliberate, ritualized, and functional. We should not forget the massive physical effort required even to erect a small mound. This experience and the participation in the act of building were reminders every day that these edifices were part and parcel of life (and often death).

Mound building every day is not just a slogan. Work over the last twenty years demonstrates the remarkable complexity of mound construction as a process. Mound building every day is far more than the routinized heaping of baskets and bags of earth to create a pile that is then shaped into a specified form. Instead, it clearly takes remarkable planning, complex logistics, skillful engineering, mobilization, organization, and direction of labor, and, perhaps most of all, motivation.

Although the focus of thinking is often on the physical labor to build the mounds (e.g., Blitz and Livingood 2004; Hammerstedt 2005), the logistics of this work effort was cause for everyday planning. The task of securing, preparing, and storing the food to feed workers must have consumed considerable time over the seasons. Making baskets, hide buckets, or cane mats would have been a frequent chore over the year that required acquiring materials and crafting the finished products. Finding wood for carving shovels or trays was probably embedded in daily life but was also a necessity to move the project forward. These labor requirements and the myriad tasks required to support mound building suggest that mound building was a practice that engaged the entire community, female and male, young and old, skilled or unskilled, and ritually adept or not.

The selection and mining of mound material reveal both a scientific understanding of materials and their strength and also the potential and limits of the local landscape. Areas where soils and sediments were removed and mixed were also a part of that place that was navigated on a daily basis. Mound building left a mark across a wide landscape and in some documented cases required builders to range wide and far over the terrain as well as deep to find the right soil for the right purpose (Sherwood and Kidder 2011).

Mound building did not stop once the construction was completed. Mounds are a physical presence on the landscape. By inscribing these features on the ground, members of the community were making a clear statement of their significance. In this way, the mounds loom over the everyday. Anyone who lived in a mound community, came to a mound community, encountered someone who had done so, or heard a tale about these monuments experienced the mounds as physical manifestations of this historical and cultural process. These were unambiguous statements spelled out in physical mass.

As elements of visual material culture, the mounds inherently signal information to those who see them. What messages were sent must have varied over time and across space. All mounds, no matter their size, shape, or number, were cues and clues to social practice, to status, to communal organization, and to history. These visual signals were encountered by residents every day and perhaps, like our encounters with contemporary ritual, religious, and political architecture, were assimilated at a variety of different levels, some perhaps barely at the level of consciousness. (How many places of worship, government buildings, banks, or monuments do you pass on your way to work and what meanings do these encounters convey or invoke?)

Mounds always serve as physical and architectural masses for displays of influence, wealth, and prestige of some sort. They are unambiguous signs of the social capacity to mobilize and organize labor for a limited and restricted end. Because of their everyday presence, the existence of mounds signals leadership and power (Knight 2001; Peacock and Rafferty 2013). In later pre-Contact times, this authority was available only to a select few who commanded political, economic, or social authority; in earlier contexts, the power may have been communal (Kidder 2010). In fact, it is likely that the social meanings inscribed on the land and ascribed by the participants varied depending on the viewers, their social and kinship position, their gender, and the time or place of viewing (Pursell 2012). Emphasis has typically been directed at the perishable architecture on the summit of these mounds, with little attention devoted to the practice of construction. However, it is evident that mounds are important for their mass, for the burials within them, and for the buildings on top of them.

Mound building every day was more than building the mounds. In some instances, it was recognizing what was buried beneath the mounds or what they contained and what was enacted in the process of interring people and objects within these earthen monuments. Mounds concentrated community and served to remind all members that they were part of a whole that could trace an ancestry back in time. In this sense, mounds (especially burial mounds but in fact, we think, all mounds) were historical documents. And history is always with us, consciously or not.

Like all architecture, mounds defined a moral order; perhaps more accurately, mounds reflected a moral order that was structured through myth that connected mounds with origin stories. These myths may have been taught by the example of building the mounds and were enacted in life through song, dance, and worship on or near the mound (Buikstra et al. 1998). This moral foundation was at some times and in many places especially made clear in death and the interment of corpses within the mound. The mounds were constant reminders of the moral order of many communities, much as the medieval cathedral crystallized the religious, ritual, ethical, and indeed political structure of its time. The mounds reminded community members of their role in society; of their membership in the social, political, and economic structure of the community; and of their place in a cosmological universe that was anchored in the physical mass of the mounds.

The mounds were never static. They were often reconfigured, reused, rebuilt, added to, and repaired (e.g., Schilling 2012; Sherwood 2013). Patterns of mound use practices vary considerably through time and surely depending on intended function. These reconfigurations or efforts at maintenance of mounds were likely a part of everyday life. In the temperate eastern United States, keeping the mounds from eroding, banishing burrowing animals, burning or cutting vegetation, and addressing inevitable slope failures, faults, and soil movement must have been a full-time task. Significant repairs and changes had to be envisioned, planned, and enacted. These activities must have required prolonged and sustained conversations. Some changes may have been initiated by calendrical events, some by life history events, and some by purposeful reconfigurations that rewrote existing historical narratives.

What was the appearance that communities were seeking to maintain or reenvision for these earthen monuments? Were they bare, covered in grass, shrouded in trees, or painted in colored sediments? We have limited data on their outward appearance; the way they appear to today's visitors, covered in manicured grass, was likely not how they appeared to those in pre-Contact times (Sherwood and Kidder 2011). Several mound studies reveal that the surfaces were kept clean with no vegetation and only limited artifact accumulation, if any (Anderson et al. 2013; Kassabaum et al. 2014). The mounds were used for a variety of activities that required regular upkeep and attention to purity and hygiene. Archaeological investigations of mound stage surfaces suggest that they were not only carefully prepared but kept clear of artifacts, organic debris, and even microartifacts. In some instances, fires were tended, renewed, and cleaned up. In other situations, structured middens containing the remains of feasts and/or destroyed buildings have been identified off the flanks of mounds (often as patterned disposal) and then buried in the next construction stage, creating a new and pristine surface (e.g., Knight 2004, 2010; McNutt et al. 2012; Price and Fox 1990; Smith and Williams 1994).

Ultimately mounds were abandoned. In many instances, abandonment itself was a complex act that required planning and sometimes significant labor. It also was not always or in fact often accidental or unintentional. Abandonment frequently was a purposeful and presumably meaningful activity that involved termination and capping of mounds (e.g., Poverty Point Mound B; Angel Mounds Mound F; Lake George Mound A; Anna Mound 3). In some cases, mound abandonment coincides with site abandonment; in other instances, it was selective and may, like Moundville, have to do with the site's life history (Knight 1998, 2010). But the end of a mound's life history was as everyday an event as the creation of the mound, because even when no longer being used the mounds had a mass that could not be ignored. Once abandoned, the mounds took on a new life; with every encounter they became a lesson in history, in morality, in genealogy, and in mythology. We have come to think of mounds for their architectural function. They were platforms for the living or vessels for the dead. But we wonder if some mounds were not built to be abandoned—to be monuments that rendered meaning by what they covered or what they meant as acts of construction. Even when abandoned, these mounds exert a powerful force as anchors of history and touch points of memory.

Mounds are central to the cultural landscape of the Southeast, in their placement, design, construction, use, maintenance, remodeling, and ultimately abandonment. Born out of the natural landscape and created as central places in the cultural landscape, they were essential parts of everyday actions, routines, planning, and memory. Situating mound construction and use as an everyday practice reminds us that we should be careful not to separate out earthen constructions as exclusively special monuments where only certain people lived and certain ceremonies emanated. Even in the times when they were special and where ritual was restricted, and when they were the locus of extraordinary and unique activities, they were also communal, public, open to interpretation, and part of the everyday.

Thinking about mound building every day compels us to understand that these icons of southeastern archaeology were more than masses of earth or a foundation or a sepulcher. Mounds are all these things and more. For us, the exercise of thinking about mound building every day opens up new vistas for considering how the processes of mound planning, engineering, building, repairing, and even abandoning were central to the rhythms and patterns of southeastern life for millennia. It means, then, that we need to step back from the notion that mound building and mounds themselves are "just": just a one-off event; just an effort aimed at a specific purpose; just a simple task; or just a big pile of dirt. With few exceptions (Collins and Chalfant 1993; Monaghan and Peebles 2010; Schilling 2012), the number of pages in site reports, articles, and monographs devoted to understanding mound building as a process is far, far smaller than the number of pages devoted to any other artifact class. Our approach suggests that excavated mounds need to be studied in the same way, and with the same effort and energy, as lithics, pottery, or plant and animal remains. However, we are not just advocating studying mounds as if they are artifacts. Our analysis suggests that mounds are central to understanding what it meant to be a Native American person. Thus mounds, as understood in both the past and in the present, cast long shadows that need to be examined.

We do not doubt that the specific practices, intentions, and meanings attached to mound building, every day and in every way, varied massively across the vast expanse of the Southeast and Midcontinent. We make no claim of uni-

Figure 12.2. The funeral procession of Serpent Piqué (Tattooed Serpent) by Le Page du Pratz (U.S. Public Domain).

formity of mound function, of purpose, or of meaning. We do, however, make a very explicit claim that mound building was an essence of being human in this part of the world for the last 5,000 years. To be was to be born out of a mound in myth and memory or to die and to be buried in a mound (Figure 12.2). To exist was to make a mound or to practice rituals and religion on a mound or in its shadow. To be part of a larger community required encountering the mounds, or laboring to build a mound, or simply experiencing their mass in the daily comings and goings of life. History was not made on a mound or around a mound; it was made from a mound. The past, the present, and the future were imagined, labored over, invoked in story, song, and dance, buried, and made real in the creation, use, and abandonment of mounds.

13

Gathering in the Late Woodland

Plazas and Gathering Places as Everyday Space

CASEY R. BARRIER AND MEGAN C. KASSABAUM

The practice of enclosing open spaces with earthen mounds begins in the Lower Mississippi Valley around 3500 B.C. As the earliest recognized monumentalized landscapes in eastern North America, these locations are thought to have provided periodic bases for the exploitation of natural resources and maintenance of social relationships. Archaeological work at these early plaza sites has focused on establishing the age and stratigraphy of the associated mounds, leaving little known about the everyday activities that occurred around or between them (Saunders 2012:26) and how their inclusion in the broader landscape structured communities, relationships, and movements. On the other end of the pre-Columbian temporal spectrum, Mississippian mound-and-plaza centers throughout the Eastern Woodlands are more heavily studied through excavation and survey. Archaeological work at these centers has likewise tended to focus on the mounds themselves, although studies of off-mound areas have become more common. The tendency to privilege earthworks, and particularly platform mounds understood to support elite or special-purpose structures, has created a mound-centric view that emphasizes a limited number of activities assumed to take place on their summits (but see Kidder and Sherwood, Chapter 12; Sherwood and Kidder 2011).

With that said, many researchers have recognized the importance of studying and understanding the plazas so often associated with earthen mounds (Alt et al. 2010; Boudreaux 2013; Cobb and Butler 2016; Dalan 1997; Dalan et al. 2003; Davis et al. 2015; Holley et al. 1993; Kidder 2004; Lewis et al. 1998; Nelson 2014; Rogers et al. 1982). We echo Kidder's (2004:515) sentiment that "plazas are not just empty spaces that developed because architecture enclosed an open area; they must be understood as one of the central design elements of community planning and intrasite spatial organization." Like others, we suggest that focusing on plazas can help balance the emphasis on discussions about social interactions taking place at mound-and-plaza centers with considerations of the everyday outcomes of communal social behavior, whether the interactions themselves occurred every day or only periodically. We also propose that a focus upon gathering places more generally (including those marked by means other than mounding) gives archaeologists a window into how groups constructed their various identities, institutions, and communities. The social practices that were conducted within open spaces were meant to be seen and experienced by others. The built environment—accessible to archaeologists—can provide evidence about what actions took place, who could have been present or seen, and the scales and tempos of interactions and events.

The archaeological record of the southeastern United States is replete with plazas and other gathering spaces. Herein we detail the use of such places from two areas within this region with particular focus on two sites dating to the Late Woodland period (A.D. 400–1000). Feltus (22JE500) in the Lower Mississippi Valley and Range (11S47) in the American Bottom portion of the Central Mississippi Valley have both been extensively surveyed and excavated (Kassabaum 2014; Kelly 1990a; Steponaitis et al. 2015). Both sites were locations of human activity over several centuries, but we focus on the use of their plazas and court-yards between the years A.D. 750 and 1000. Although the gathering places at these sites and the individuals that utilized them were contemporaries, we show that the open spaces at Feltus and Range were active in organizing different scales of communities, all of which had profound implications for the everyday lives of their members.

Price and Carr (Chapter 1) state that an archaeology of "everyday matters" can be a study of daily tasks or the seemingly ordinary concerns and actions of individuals, while also suggesting that it can be more than that. In this chapter we draw upon discussions of performance and its spatiality to address how the various actions and activities that took place in gathering places affected matters of daily life in the past. According to Monica Smith: "The human past is the collective story of individuals . . . using tools, acquiring resources, and discarding waste" as they operate "within a social context framed by family, community, and ideology." It is "the generative quality of individuals' decisions and actions" and the "relationship among people, material objects, and space" that produce the cultural patterns of the past and present that we detect as archaeologists (Smith 2010:1).

Influenced by theories of practice and materiality, archaeologists have variously considered how practices (from the ordinary to the extraordinary) and the co-mingling of humans and their material worlds affect cultural fields. In this chapter we emphasize that reconstructing the actions of individuals and understanding the social milieu in which they operate are both essential steps in evaluating the archaeology of everyday matters. More specifically, we approach the "everyday" by reference to how performance in places of gathering would have influenced how people perceived themselves and others as members of various communities (Hodder 2006; Inomata 2006; Inomata and Coben 2006). The spaces of plazas and courtyards at Feltus and Range were built forms that would have served to delimit and guide physical experiences through actions, the seeing, hearing, and feeling of others and the temporal rhythms of these occurrences (Smith 2003). Various institutions, from family to polity, were shaped over time through spatialized behaviors in a cultural landscape as "aggregate[s] of practices and representations of people orchestrated to continuously regenerate the perception of those institutions" (Pauketat 2007:40). Some practices occurred daily while others occurred sporadically, but all were uniquely shaped by the places in which they occurred and the built-up meanings attached to those places. Moreover, these institutions were undoubtedly a structuring component of identities that would have been perceivable every day, even while those identities were being played out in other places (Smith 2003:32).

This approach also allows us to link our consideration of spatialized practices and identities to other archaeologies of the everyday that focus more on the use of particular sets of artifacts (e.g., Carr and Bradbury, Chapter 10; Randall and Gilmore, Chapter 8) or certain routine tasks (e.g., Hollenbach and Carmody, Chapter 5; Pluckhahn et al., Chapter 9). Scholars using performance theory often deal with large-scale public spectacles or political theater (Holt 2009; Inomata 2006; Inomata and Coben 2006), but ordinary encounters, daily interactions, and the use and display of material things also can take on measures of performativity (DeMarrais 2014:157–158, 161; see also Christophersen 2015; Hodder 2006). Thus, although we do reference some of the material objects recovered at Feltus and Range and discuss a subset of the activities known to have taken place in their plazas and courtyards, our primary focus is how these spaces were active in shaping landscapes of community.

Theorizing Gathering

> When the night appears to have really mattered was for the extension of cultural institutions over time and space to link individuals . . . into larger "imagined communities" . . . In most hunter-gatherer societies, firelight hours drew aggregations of individuals . . . for ventures into such virtual communities . . . Stories conveyed unifying cosmologies and charters for rules

and rites governing behavior . . . Stories told by firelight put listeners on the same emotional wavelength, elicited understanding, trust, and sympathy . . . and built positive reputations for qualities like humor, congeniality, and innovation.

Wiessner (2014:14033)

The area directly in front of the White House was a mob scene. Women sat on shoulders waving flags. Everyone held their cameras aloft and tried to capture the magic. A man next to me said, "It's like a Who concert or something." But there was no band, no focal point to the celebration. No one had anything to wait for, and yet, it seemed like everyone was waiting for something.

Madrigal (2011)

Gathering spaces are ubiquitous. From athletic stadiums to places of religious practice to living-room sofas in front of flat-screen televisions, we create spaces for the formation of both permanent and momentary groups. Some of these gatherings have only fleeting effects on participants' interpersonal relationships—individuals may register some sense of groupness only because of their temporary shared spatial proximity or common experiences. Other gatherings, however, may have durable and persistent effects on perceptions of shared identity, from the co-residing family to the spiritual congregation to a "nation" of fans rooting for their favorite team. Regardless of the variable frequency and duration of gatherings, we suggest that the effects of both daily and periodic events can have consequences relating to the creation of imagined communities.

The quotations that begin this section highlight momentary gatherings from the last few decades. Although both reference contemporary societies, the events described reflect different scales of aggregation that have defined human sociality for millennia. The second quotation captures a scene that took place outside the White House during the midnight hours following Barack Obama's announcement of the death of Osama bin Laden. This large gathering was an unplanned and one-off event. The crowd was large and diverse, and thousands more watched the live televised broadcast or kept up with the news through social media. In many ways, this spontaneous gathering (and the gathering of thousands of others via modern technology) gets at the heart of Benedict Anderson's (1991) notion of an "imagined community." The plaza in front of the White House is a place traversed daily by many visitors and one permanently fixed among the institutional architecture of the American state. The events of the early morning hours of May 2, 2011, however, created a potent space (sensu Soja 2000) for the workings, if uneasy, of mixed emotions, nationalism, and tempered celebrations, memories of which continue to influence the daily lives of the broader American community.

The other opening quotation likewise allows us to consider the formative essence of human gatherings, small or large, urban or otherwise. Polly Wiessner (2014) describes nightly gatherings within the camps of Ju/'hoan (!Kung) foragers. Whereas daytime communication involved economic matters, airing of complaints, or discussion of conflicts, nighttime talk around central campfires shifted to the telling of stories, singing, dancing, and ceremony. For those gathered around the fire, these stories brought to life individuals in distant camps and from different bands, recounted long-distance journeys and social contracts, and illuminated memories of important events from earlier generations. The telling and reliving of these stories helped to reproduce (or create) expectations for social behaviors within the minds of those listening larger cultural institutions and fictive kinship networks. In these situations, acts of storytelling and subsequent discussion "keep cultural institutions alive, explicate relations between people, create *imaginary communities* . . . and trace networks for great distances" (Wiessner 2014:14032; emphasis added).

These recent gatherings let us consider some of the many ways that humans create imaginings of community and identity (Brubaker and Cooper 2000; Inomata and Coben 2006; Yaeger and Canuto 2000). Lest we be guilty of claiming that gatherings work only to produce congruity or shared isomorphic identities, we also acknowledge that places, technologies, material culture, and communicative and performative acts also serve to create distinction and divisions (Brumfiel 1992; Inomata and Coben 2006:24; Sassaman and Heckenberger 2004; Smith 2003:280; Wobst 1977). Social interactions create communities while also allowing groups and individuals to contest arrangements, reach temporary consensus, or induce innovations that shape and alter everyday lives through both time and space (Henry and Barrier 2016).

The built environment plays a role in determining who will participate in gatherings, who will be the spectators of events, and who will be excluded from seeing or knowing of certain undertakings (Inomata 2006). The arrangements of walls, buildings, mounds, or other monuments can serve to create more open and public or more closed-off and private venues for various activities, including feasts, ceremonies, religious rites, political maneuverings, or even daily domestic practices (Brown 2006; Dietler 2001; Knight 2004; Kurjack 1994; LeCount 2001; Pauketat and Alt 2005). Moreover, points on the landscape used for gatherings may shift purpose through time, serve numerous functions, or host diverse populations, with or without concomitant alterations to associated architecture or surroundings (Moore 2014; Nair 2015:65–87; Pluckhahn 2010; Smith

2008; Zucker 1959:5). Human modifications (intentional or unintentional) to the landscape can influence subsequent movements through these spaces and dictate future use to a specific range of activities with associated meanings (Nair 2015; Snead et al. 2011).

If the built environment plays a role in structuring the nature of social interactions between individuals and groups, then the systematic examination of places of gathering can provide for the study of social transformations associated with the use of space and the nature of interactions that spaces allow or encourage (Inomata and Tsukamoto 2014:5). Places intended for or repeatedly utilized for gatherings are often accessible to the archaeologist. When accompanied by monumental architecture these places are regularly theorized as important locations for community and identity construction. Here, however, we consider gathering spaces more broadly to examine how communities and identities can be crafted at varying spatial and temporal scales. From the sitting areas and dance grounds surrounding Ju/'hoansi central fires to the state's monumental public spaces like those in Washington, D.C., we are aware of the role that gathering places—and the performances that take place within them—play in structuring both daily life and the workings of variously scaled communities and institutions. Although gatherings can take many forms and do occur inside domestic structures or other buildings (e.g., Bowser 2000; McAnany 2002; Rodning 2009a), our focus in this chapter is on the open plaza, one of the primary gathering spaces at many prehistoric sites.

Living through Plazas

> The domain of the plaza is an arena for encounters.
>
> Da Matta (1984:210)

As gathering spaces, plazas are ubiquitous in the archaeological record. They are present at sites produced by ancient hunter-gatherers, were common components of the first villages and cities around the globe, and served prominently in the political machinations of the earliest states. Despite their use within many different social contexts and their various forms, scholars have demonstrated that a study of plazas can provide useful insights into the lives of the people who built and used them (Alt et al. 2010; Cobb and Butler 2016; Dalan 1997; Dalan et al. 2003; Holley et al. 1993; Kidder 2004; Lewis et al. 1998; Low 2000; Moore 1996; Nair 2015; Nelson 2014; Rogers et al. 1982; Sassaman and Heckenberger 2004; Smith 2008; Zucker 1959). Here we propose that plazas may be particularly useful in understanding the creation and maintenance of the imagined communities that form the day-to-day social environments in which people live.

The plaza is not always explicitly defined in archaeological literature. Plazas are usually considered spaces that remain free of substantial numbers of buildings, monuments, or other constructions but are often surrounded by and thus defined by their presence (Kidder 2004:515). Plazas often delineate public or communal spaces in which large segments of one or more communities can gather (Lewis et al. 1998:11). Archaeologists are aware that not all plazas were free of features, but their relative scarcity within a plaza (as opposed to around a plaza's boundaries) effectively allows the archaeologist to know a plaza when they see one.

In more general terms, a plaza "is nothing more than cultural meaning assigned to a defined space within a site" (Lewis et al. 1998:16). Although a looser concept, this more inclusive description captures the fact that plaza use can change from moment to moment, allowing for the congregation of various populations of different social composition through time (Nair 2015; Smith 2008). Plazas can thus host private and exclusive ceremonies and later shift to being spaces for large public and inclusive events. This flexibility is key to understanding how plazas form an integral part of the everyday lives of people (Low 2000).

The largest plazas can be viewed as spaces where entire communities could gather. However, it is equally important to note that multiple plazas within villages and urban centers may have had separate functions or served distinct populations or institutions. At these sites, effectual plaza spaces can be thought of as organizing the built environment into differentiated groups, including household groups around courtyards and patios, neighborhoods, and locations serving sodalities or specific interest groups (Nelson 2014; Smith 2008; Wilson 2008). The physicality of the smallest places of gathering would also have been part of the recursive structuring of interpersonal relationships, meanings, and perceptions (Smith 2008). As William Ringle (2014:169) points out, the Central American Nahuatl term cemithualtin means "those of a single patio" but is also defined as "family." "It is interesting that [the patio], rather than the house, was the architectural metaphor of choice, suggesting that the open common space between houses, the locus of daily socializing, visual contact, and task performance, was thought to better reflect the social bonds holding a household together" (Ringle 2014:169).

By emphasizing both the places wherein people interact and the acts themselves, we may productively consider the interplay of social spaces (the built environment), social interactions, and social organization (Moore 1996). Because "human sociality and identity are rooted in our sensory perceptions of the presence and actions of others" (Inomata 2006:805), the built environment can be an effective tool for considering how actions, and by extension institutions and communities, were structured through practice across various scales. The size and form of plazas, and their locations within sites relative to other components of the physical landscape, would have affected where people performed particular actions, who witnessed these actions, and even *how* those actions were perceived by others (Moore 1996). While acts are often considered political if conducted in monumental plazas in front of masses, they can take on "domestic" qualities if performed in the courtyard spaces in front of co-residing or visiting kin. But in terms of inscribing notions of groupness upon those who act, are seen, and do the seeing, even the institution of the co-residing family can be considered "imagined"—a community born of daily and routine, if not also politicized, performances (Hodder 2006; Sahlins 2011:2–3; see also Christophersen 2015).

We draw upon these ideas in framing how constructed gathering places in the southeastern United States were active components of the cultural act of community and identity construction. We consider contexts ranging from public to private and how various scales of community identities were likely enacted. The tempo, periodicity, and spatial scales at which individuals and groups interacted would have been important for community organization and social transformation, along with the actual events that took place within the physically constructed spaces that we examine. In this way, space and landscape are as much a part of the "everyday" archaeological record as the material items that we recover as artifacts. Plazas and courtyards, as places where people gather and interact, are one entryway into studying these everyday processes.

Plazas as Gathering Spaces in the Greater Southeastern United States

> Plazas . . . represent the social relations of the people who build, maintain, or simply appear in them. They are fixed, or marked, points that not only reflect social relations but also perpetuate or "sediment" these relations in place.
>
> Sassaman and Heckenberger (2004:229)

Central open areas at camps and aggregation sites have been used by Native American groups since Paleoindian times (Anderson 2012b; Kidder 2004:516). The act of enclosing a plaza with earthworks started in the Lower South during the Middle Archaic period. Mound building (and presumably plaza enclosure) was subsequently practiced in different subregions until the point of European contact, leaving a nearly unabated legacy of monumentalism that lasted roughly five millennia (Kassabaum 2015; Kidder and Sherwood, Chapter 12; Milner 2004b). Thus, since the initial "peopling" of the Eastern Woodlands through the moment of European contact and even up to the present, central spaces and plazas were and are utilized by communities as arenas for "activities that . . . served to promote group and cultural identity" (Anderson 2012b:80).

If relatively little is understood of Late Pleistocene and early Holocene gathering spaces, much more is known about later pre-Columbian plazas (Anderson 2012b:80–81). The mound-and-plaza site plan has a long history in the greater Southeast. "Plaza construction as a purposeful and planned element of site architecture is generally considered a diagnostic feature of the Mississippi period" (Kidder 2004:526; see also Holley et al. 1993:306; Lewis and Stout 1998). In the ethnohistoric record of southeastern Native American groups, plazas were publicly administered places dedicated to community celebrations, games, religious ceremonies, and diplomatic events (Black 1967:514–522; Knight 1989; Rogers et al. 1982:Tables 1 and 2). Prehistoric plazas have been interpreted through these accounts as well as through archaeological data, with a focus on what we know about plazas at Mississippian sites.

Though many accounts still focus on the role that mounds, as foundations for elite and special-purpose structures and thus stages for the exhibition of social status, played in determining plaza function, plazas are now commonly recognized to have served diverse social, economic, and political purposes. Many of these interpretations focus on the plaza's ability to hold large gatherings. For example, Cahokia's numerous open spaces, including its massive Grand Plaza, were locations where diverse populations, corporate kin groups and their followers, and members of various sodalities hosted public feasts, crafted and displayed ritually significant items, and likely hosted important ceremonies and games, among other things (Brown and Kelly 2015; Byers 2006; DeBoer 1993; Kelly 2001; Kelly 2006; Pauketat et al. 2002).

In the Midwest and Ohio River Valley, Middle Woodland Hopewell sites are known for their intricate patterning of mounds and geometric ditch-and-embankment earthworks and enclosures. Whether specific Hopewell centers served as "vacant" ceremonial centers or as aggregation sites for dispersed forager-farmers (see Bernardini 2004; Lynott 2015:72–25; Wright and Henry 2013:12), they are assumed to have hosted temporary gatherings where regional populations participated in the construction and maintenance of monuments, crafting, ceremonies, mate exchange, burial rite, and gifting (Charles and Buikstra 2002; Henry and Barrier 2016; Lynott 2015:40). Although Hopewell scholars rarely talk of formal plazas, this range of activities is similar to that posited for plaza sites throughout the American South. While mound-and-plaza settlements were places of residence for many sedentary groups in the Southeast, the pathways to village life differed across various subregions. We believe that it is important to take a temporally and spatially inclusive look at plazas.

In the last few decades, pre-Mississippian monumental spaces of the Southeast have received increased scholarly attention. Work at Archaic mound sites, shell rings, and ring middens in the lower South has provided a rich literature from which to consider the function and meaning of the earliest plazas in North America. The practice of creating monumental landscapes (including plazas) begins during the Middle Archaic period in the Lower Mississippi Valley at sites such as Watson Brake (Saunders et al. 1997), Hedgepeth (Saunders et al. 2006), Caney (Saunders et al. 2000), and possibly Frenchmen's Bend and Insley (Sassaman and Heckenberger 2004:225). We know very little about the use of early central spaces at these sites, but Kenneth Sassaman and Michael Heckenberger (2004) argue for their purposeful construction as part of the monumental process.

Evidence of activities was concentrated around the perimeter of a clean, central space at these earliest mound-and-plaza sites (Saunders 2012:37), meaning either that activity was not taking place within the plaza or that plazas were being actively swept free of debris. The latter explanation fits well with Vernon Knight's (1989:283–284) suggestion that mounds may have first developed due to the piling up of debris associated with periodic cleaning and purification of a central space, similar to the Muskogean term *tadjo*, referring to mounds or ridges formed during the cleaning of square grounds. Thus, everyday social practices that would have taken place during communal gatherings before or coincident with the advent of earthworks were likely constitutive of emergent monumentality (see Joyce 2004).

Late Archaic coastal shell rings provide evidence for other early monumental landscapes that developed around central spaces. Shell rings consist of curvilinear arrangements of shell-bearing sediment surrounding areas of little to no shell (Russo 2006). These sites have been variously interpreted as relating to feasting behavior (e.g., Russo 2004), purposeful monumentality (e.g., Saunders and Russo 2002), burial ceremonialism (e.g., Elliott and Sassaman 1995), identity signaling (e.g., Russo 2006), domestic habitation (e.g., Trinkley 1985), and water management (e.g., Marquardt 2010). Many recent analyses of shell rings accept a middle-of-the-road approach that emphasizes the various and dynamic functions that these locations may have served (e.g., Thompson and Andrus 2011).

Some attention has also been given to early nonshell ring middens in the Lower Southeast (Belmont 1967; Phillips 1970; Pluckhahn 2010; Russo et al. 2014; Stephenson et al. 2002). As curvilinear arrangements of organically stained soils intermixed with uneven amounts of shell and other cultural material, these ring middens also surround open and relatively clean plazas (Russo et al. 2014:127). Although these middens are sometimes interpreted as villages throughout both the Archaic and Woodland periods, archaeologists have considered the function and use of these middens' central plazas. Pluckhahn (2010) argues that plazas would have been necessary to early village groups because, as corporately organized ritual spaces, they served to reduce tensions in growing communities and provide locations for symbolic bonding that strengthened social ties (cf. Sassaman and Heckenberger 2004). While some plazas could have served village communities, large ring middens may also have served integrative purposes for dispersed regional populations.

Some of the larger ring middens of the later Middle to Late Woodland period have associated monuments, including platform mounds at Late Woodland sites such as Kolomoki (Pluckhahn 2003) and McKeithen (Milanich et al. 1984). These mounds, while closely resembling Mississippian platforms in final form, differ in dramatic ways, such as lacking structures on the summits and having unrestricted visual access from plazas (Knight 2001). Pluckhahn (2010) argues that the separation between sacred and profane (or public and private) space that took place early in the development of sites like these is key to understanding the social dynamics that eventually develop at later Mississippian mound-and-plaza centers.

Living through Gatherings in the Late Woodland

In this section we discuss two case studies from separate areas of the Late Woodland Southeast. Through these case studies, we hope to highlight how gathering spaces were actively used to organize different scales of pre-Columbian Native American communities. Due to the rise in popularity in the lower South of site layouts consisting of large platform mounds surrounding open plazas, the Late Woodland has recently garnered increasing attention as a time of changing community organization (Anderson and Sassaman 2012; Nassaney 2000). Though these early platform mounds and their associated plazas are often discussed as precursors to Mississippian mounds, their functions were variable and undoubtedly included both the continuation of long-standing traditions and the development of new ones.

Late Woodland Plazas in the Lower Mississippi Valley

Throughout the Late Woodland, flat-topped mounds become increasingly common in the Lower Mississippi Valley, culminating in the Coles Creek tradition of building two or more large platform mounds arranged around open plazas. These sites do not appear to have been permanently occupied. Instead, it appears that people lived in dispersed hamlets and used mound sites as central gathering places. Like earlier groups, they hunted, fished, and gathered wild plant and animal resources and eventually adopted a number of domesticated indigenous seed crops, though corn agriculture was not adopted until later (Fritz 2000; Fritz and Kidder 1993; Kidder and Fritz 1993; Listi 2008). Evidence concerning mound summit use is variable: some show formal buildings, others show periodic use of temporary structures, and still others show no evidence of buildings at all (e.g., Belmont 1967; Ford 1951; Fuller and Fuller 1987; Kassabaum 2014; Roe 2010; Williams and Brain 1983). While it is possible that some individuals in these societies earned status through their participation in activities associated with these mounds, it is likely that this power was impermanent and not inherited, ascribed, or made visible in the mortuary program (Kassabaum 2011).

Despite the now-common recognition that plazas are not just empty spaces but rather meaningful and purposefully constructed locations of activity, discussions of them still rely heavily on the presence of mounds. That is, without mounds, we do not often talk about plazas. However, a great deal of evidence from Late Woodland sites in the Lower Mississippi Valley suggests that plazas predate mounds at many sites. For example, John Belmont (1967) identified the "Black River site plan" at Greenhouse, and Philip Phillips (1970) identified the Tchula Lake pattern in his study of the Lower Yazoo Basin. These site plans consist of oval plazas flanked by midden accumulations. This general layout was common throughout the Lower Mississippi Valley during the Baytown period (A.D. 400–750). Only later were mounds constructed atop the ring of midden at some of these sites.

The Feltus site (22JE500), located in southwestern Mississippi, is a prime example of this pattern. Excavations were undertaken at Feltus from 2006 to 2012 under the direction of Vincas Steponaitis and John O'Hear. The site shows a traditional mound-and-plaza arrangement with four mounds surrounding a central open space (Steponaitis et al. 2015:Figure 2.4).

Surface collections suggested that the mounds were built on top of a midden similar to that identified by Belmont (1967:Figure 1) at Greenhouse. Shovel tests confirmed the presence of this oval midden, and artifact density maps indicated the plaza's extent relative to the midden (Kassabaum 2014:Figure 2.6; Steponaitis and O'Hear 2008). Geophysical survey of the off-mound areas further supported this pattern by showing features along the edges of the plaza with the center entirely clear of suggestive anomalies (Haley and Johnson 2008). The pattern of features and debris at Feltus indicates that the site was not used haphazardly before the construction of the mounds but rather that the premound occupation was a planned use of space, which already included the purposeful creation of the central plaza. Research at other Coles Creek sites such as Goldmine (Belmont 1982), Fredericks (Girard 2000), and Mazique (LaDu 2013) suggests that the presence of distinct, ring-shaped, premound middens might represent a broader Coles Creek pattern.

Five seasons of excavation at Feltus have provided a great deal of information about the activities that took place at the site both before and after mounds were constructed and hint at how periodic activities were active in structuring the daily lives of Coles Creek people. In general, Coles Creek plazas were carefully curated, being kept free of debris and at times artificially leveled or otherwise modified to form the desired size, shape, and grade (Kidder 2004). With the possible exception of ritual specialists, mound centers themselves were vacant, with the surrounding populations gathering at them only periodically. If central gathering places are not viewed as material components of peoples' cultural landscapes, then these sites might be considered of little value for understanding the everyday lives of Coles Creek people. However, the social relationships and imagined communities that were forged at these gathering places determined the everyday experiences of those involved, even, we argue, while groups were dispersed across the landscape (see Hollenbach and Carmody, Chapter 5, for a similar view of hunting-gathering communities; and Kidder and Sherwood, Chapter 12, for a similar view of mounds and earthworks).

The area immediately surrounding the Feltus plaza hosted periodic large-scale ritual events focused on communal food consumption, a repeated process of setting and removing large standing posts, and burial of the dead (Kassabaum 2014; Kassabaum and Nelson 2016; Nelson and Kassabaum 2014). While mound building eventually became part of these events, much of the activity at Feltus took place before mounds were constructed. This provides the important opportunity to take a less mound-centric view of the activities occurring at Coles Creek sites.

In evaluating the nature of the premound eating events at Feltus, Kassabaum (2014) concludes that the open communal location, large size of vessels, and sheer amount of food found at Feltus all imply the involvement of large groups of people drawn from throughout the surrounding region. Work at Feltus has also shown little to no evidence of high-quality vessels, prestige items, or any of the other traditional markers for competitive feasting. There are, however, large amounts of bear bone and pipe fragments, both materials used by Native American groups in rituals associated with community building through establishing, maintaining, and strengthening relationships (Bieder 2006; Black 1998; Brown 1953; Paper 1988; Rockwell 1991).

Combined, this evidence suggests that the primary function of the premound events was to gather the scattered Coles Creek population and provide an opportunity for communal reinforcement of social bonds. In other words, the Feltus events fostered the creation of an imagined community that persisted and structured relationships even when people returned to their daily lives in rural scattered homesteads. While we are merely speculating, we can imagine dispersed groups throughout the year at hamlets or camp sites sharing memories of past gatherings or envisioning and preparing for future festivities and sharing stories about those that they are likely to meet again.

The conclusion that the premound activities at Feltus centered on social integration is further supported by the repeated cycle of setting and removing nonstructural posts associated with the feasting events (Kassabaum and Nelson 2016; Nelson and Kassabaum 2014). Nonstructural standing posts were common on Woodland period sites (Milanich et al. 1984; Knight 1990, 2001; Kimball et al. 2010), including those in the American Bottom that are discussed below (Kelly 1990b). The interpretations of such posts are largely based on traditional Native American beliefs regarding the structure of the world as consisting of multiple layers connected by an axis mundi, commonly represented as a pole or a tree (Lankford 2007; Reilly 2004). This axis is seen as a "portal" through which certain beings can travel. The idea of opening lines of communication with the spirit world is further supported by the material inclusions in the Feltus postholes, which represent substances commonly associated with the upper and lower worlds (see also Kelly 1990b).

Megan Kassabaum and Erin Nelson (2016; see also Nelson and Kassabaum 2014) have argued that the standing posts at Feltus may therefore represent locations where beings could move and communicate between the worlds, thereby extending the social network being created at the Feltus events beyond the people physically attending to those who inhabited different spatial and temporal domains. The inclusion of the act of human burial within the ritual cycle further supports this conclusion, as previous generations of individuals were actively included in the Feltus gatherings. The spatial and temporal breadth of the imagined community formed during the events at Feltus quite literally created the social world inhabited by Coles Creek people every day, allowing individuals to structure their mundane decisions and day-to-day tasks around the knowledge that they were a part of something much larger than their co-habiting group (see also Hollenbach and Carmody, Chapter 5).

Importantly, after mound construction began, the nature of the activities taking place at Feltus shows remarkable stability (Kassabaum 2014; Kassabaum and Nelson 2016; Nelson and Kassabaum 2014). Continuity between the premound and postmound uses of the site suggests that the act of constructing and using platform mounds did not in and of itself change the nature of the social relationships being negotiated in and around the Feltus plaza and enacted in the daily lives of Coles Creek people. To the contrary, a strong focus on gathering and an ethos of communalism characterized the activities taking place during both the premound and mounded phases of Feltus's occupation.

Late Woodland Plazas and Courtyards in the American Bottom

The American Bottom portion of the Central Mississippi Valley is well known for its plazas. The roughly 20-hectare Grand Plaza at the Mississippian site of Cahokia is one of the largest constructed plazas in pre-Columbian North America (Alt et al. 2010; Dalan 1997; Dalan et al. 2003; Holley et al. 1993; see Cobb and Butler 2016:Table 1). The Grand Plaza, together with several other expansive plazas, dozens of mounds, and numerous neighborhoods, formed the central core of an urban settlement that stretched more than 15 km^2 (Kelly and Brown 2014; Pauketat 2004).

The construction of monumental plazas at Mississippian Cahokia points to a precocious history of plaza use and enlargement in the American Bottom (Kelly and Brown 2014). Unlike those in the Lower South, communities here did not construct earthen mounds or mound-and-plaza centers for much of the Late Woodland (Pauketat 2004:53). Small plazas were incorporated into early village settlements only during a few centuries before the start of the Mississippian period. These gathering places initially were not adjoined by mounds.

In general, the Late Woodland in the Upper South/Midwest is a time of steady population growth, reduced zones of resource acquisition, commitments toward sedentism (although not large villages until rather late), increased intergroup violence, the introduction and spread of bow-and-arrow technologies, and intensified use of indigenous seed crops (Anderson and Sassaman 2012; Blitz and Porth 2013; Buikstra et al. 1986; Emerson et al. 2000; Gremillion 2002; McElrath et al. 2000; Nassaney and Cobb 1991; Simon 2000). Maize, although present in small amounts throughout much of the period, becomes abundant in the American Bottom after A.D. 900 (Simon and Parker 2006). Settlement patterns suggest small groups were gradually "filling in" the region by increasingly utilizing upland and prairie zones.

Permanent and nucleated villages were present in the American Bottom by the end of the ninth century (Kelly 1990a; Koldehoff and Galloy 2006; Pauketat 1994:48–52). Numerous sites dating just prior to the start of the Mississippian period (circa A.D. 1050) have been studied, many of these under the auspices of the FAI-270 project (see Emerson et al. 2006). One of the better-known sites with pre-Mississippian occupations is Range (11S47) (Kelly 1990a:Figure 59). John Kelly directed year-round excavations there from 1978 to 1981. The resulting reports and publications provide the information used here (e.g., Kelly 1990b, 2000; Kelly et al. 2007).

From the Late Woodland through early Mississippi periods Range was the center of intense and repeated activities. More than 5,000 features dating to this time were delineated during excavations, including approximately 600 structures (Kelly 1990b:73–74). The initial structures at Range, built between A.D. 650 and 850, consist of dozens of rectilinear and keyhole-shaped structures (Kelly 1990b:Figure 20). Temporally distributed clusters of features bespeak occupations ranging from short-term encampments to small hamlets and larger clusters of buildings. The first "semisedentary" villages at Range may have developed at this time (cf. Kelly 1990b, 2000; Koldehoff and Galloy 2006), and occupations were likely short-term bases for pre-maize forager-farmer groups.

Between roughly A.D. 850 and 1050, Late Woodland (or emergent Mississippian) occupations consisted of multiple villages that formed and morphed through the fission and fusion of co-resident groups. These groups constructed their permanent domiciles around small, open courtyards. Together, each handful of structures ringing a central space is called a "courtyard group." Courtyard groups and their central places appear as built forms that would have increasingly focused the everyday activities of household members around a shared intimate space.

But everyday activities apparently involved more than subsistence-related tasks or a group of concerns that are often glossed as the domestic sphere. Excavations of courtyard groups reveal practices relating to both domestic and ceremonial activities (Kelly 1990b; Kelly et al. 2007). At villages like Range, courtyard groups were becoming the locus of daily life for individuals increasingly tethered to new domestic (and politicized) spaces, interpersonal relations with kin and corporate group members, and the emerging demands of the maize agricultural cycle (see Barrier 2011:215; Beck and Brown 2012; Brown and Kelly 2015; Cobb and Nassaney 2002:537–538; Koldehoff and Galloy 2006:278).

Analyses of materials recovered from courtyard groups at Range show that the importance of both deer and nut resources declines through time and that the frequency of projectile points (likely used for hunting) also decreases. There is evidence for increasing utilization of maize as well as indigenous starchy seed crops. Also increasing is the presence of Mill Creek chert hoes, which were used as digging and agricultural implements (Cobb 2000), and polished flakes. Changes seen in ceramic assemblages include substantial increases in the numbers of jars having restricted and plain necks, handles, and limestone tempering (instead of grog or grit), among other things. These ceramic attributes may have been associated with maize processing (Kelly 1990a:76; see also Briggs 2016).

In addition to the residential structures surrounding them, courtyards were typically marked by the placement of central features of probable ceremonial significance. These include four pits in a quadrilateral arrangement, a central post, or the occasional rectangular structure (Kelly 2000:Figure 7.3; Kelly and Brown 2014:Figure 9.3; Kelly et al. 2007). Kelly (1990a, 2007b) discusses the potential symbolic importance of these courtyard facilities, linking the courtyards with four pits (and the often associated gourd effigy vessels) to notions of the earth and fertility; and courtyards with central posts (and the sometimes associated chunky stones) to the upper world.

The actual relationships that reproduced (and were reproduced by) courtyard groups are not fully understood, but many archaeologists believe they represent the spatial and material expression of corporate kin groups, potentially akin to matrilineages (Kelly 2000:167; Pauketat 2003:43; see also Wilson 2008:136). The occurrence of daily domestic activities within courtyard spaces that also housed important ceremonial facilities signals the ritual proclivities of the emerging corporate entity. The range of practices taking place within these enclosed "domestic" spaces was seemingly as important to the coherence of the local family/corporate group as large plazas were for the creation of larger imagined communities (sensu Hodder 2006).

Between A.D. 950 and 1000 the village at Range was occupied by at least nine courtyard groups (Kelly 1990b:Figure 40, 2007c). With an estimated 105 individuals living within about 1.2 hectares (Barrier and Horsley 2014:Figure 6), this occupation marked the largest population that would be seen at the site. For the first time at Range, villagers also built formal plazas, around which they organized their courtyard groups that still contained internal ritual facilities. Two separate plazas, each covering about 0.04 hectares, created another scale of public space for the local village community (Kelly 2007a). It has been argued that, as the Range village's population grew, the shared public spaces would have been active in integrating the numerous courtyard groups into a larger and more nucleated community (Barrier and Horsley 2014; Kelly 1990a, 1990b, 1992, 2007b). Several courtyard groups were abandoned after about A.D. 1000, and the villagers at Range reorganized their courtyard groups now around one public plaza (Kelly 1990b:Figure 42).

Throughout the approximately two centuries of village life at Range, inhabitants made gathering places central components of their settlements. By viewing these places as part of the material record of their everyday lives, we could likewise say that these spaces also "made" the individuals and social groups that lived and moved through them. At least two types of central spaces are recognized: courtyards and public plazas. These spaces were stages for daily practices that would have brought these new communities and identities to life. The activities taking place within these spaces would also have served to integrate at least two scales of community: the co-residential corporate group and the local village.

As an aside, all of this was completed without earthen mounds. Platform mound construction would not begin in the American Bottom until near the transition to the Mississippi period around A.D. 1050 (Barrier and Horsley 2014; Horsley et al. 2014; Kelly 1990a; Milner 1998; Pauketat 2004). Mounds became important monuments for many Mississippian communities, but the history of community alterations at Range (as at Feltus, described above) draws our attention also to the role of gathering places as active spaces for the structuring of everyday lives.

Discussion

> It may be that we should identify ritual not as a separate sphere of practice, but as a distinct *mode of conduct*, which people move into and out of in the course of their day.
>
> Thomas (2011:379; emphasis in the original)

We hope that this chapter demonstrates that gathering spaces have played a significant role in the everyday lives of eastern Native American groups since initial colonization. Certain gathering spaces in the Lower South were monumentalized by the Middle and Late Archaic—literally leaving a more permanent record—by the raising of earth or shell around open plazas. Whether initial mounding happened unintentionally through acts of cleaning and refuse deposition or through purposeful monumentality, mounds and earthworks would go on to become icons of Native American communities (Kidder and Sherwood, Chapter 12). Indeed, mounds at different times and places became repositories for the ancestors, markers of significant places on the landscape, locations for community building and identity creation, and eventually platforms for important persons, temples, and political institutions.

We have highlighted instances where plazas were created and used before mounds, and where plazas developed as integral parts of the built environment alongside mounds, not coincidentally with them (see also Belmont 1967; Kidder 2004; Pluckhahn 2010; Schilling 2010:285, 2012). The presence of a ring midden at Feltus that only later was capped by mounds indicates an intense history of social gatherings surrounding a plaza where feasting and other important ritual activity occurred. The placement of permanent earthen monuments did not significantly alter the daily lives or organization of the scattered populations that congregated there but instead further memorialized an already important place of gathering, providing permanence to the collective memory inscribed there. A dispersed community was created and maintained through periodic acts of gathering, feasting, setting and pulling ritual posts, and eventually burial and mound building. People lived their daily lives in the context of this imagined community. It is likely that the details that were worked out at events like those at Feltus had effects that endured long after the events had concluded.

Concurrently, at places like Range in the American Bottom we see the transition to permanent and nucleated village life in the centuries leading up to the Mississippian period. These villages contained at least two types of gathering spaces: public plazas that would have served numerous corporate groups and held large public gatherings; and central courtyards that fixed new forms of domestic space and groupings. As at Feltus, these initial villages did not include mounds. Mounds in the American Bottom were not incorporated into towns and urban communities until the Mississippian transition around A.D. 1050 (and they were never built at Range).

There are both distinct similarities and clear differences between the patterns that we have identified at Feltus and Range. Though both represent locations for gathering, and we suggest also for the formation and maintenance of social bonds, the scale of the relationships forged differed between these two sites. The periodic gatherings around the Feltus plaza united a spatially (and perhaps temporally) expansive community. Gatherings in the numerous courtyards at Range emphasized new co-residential (and corporate) kin relations that were reinforced by the everyday rhythms of doing and seeing and the sharing of things and tasks with those often present within the permanent courtyard space. These groups at Range also struck new bonds with others in their village through the literal material gathering of their corporate bodies around more public and formal inclusive plazas.

Charles Cobb and Michael Nassaney (2002:538) note that during the Woodland period "there was very little formalization of domestic space through the use of either substantial houses or planned living communities. Thus, despite the veneer of formality suggested by earthworks . . . the discipline of the domestic world as seen in the Eurasian Neolithic did not seem to take hold during the Woodland era . . . until extremely late." They discuss the built landscape to consider how individuals would have altered the ways in which they envisioned themselves and their societies. In their view, most Woodland communities were visualized through the ritual world of mounds and earthworks long before they were organized through the domestic household. Our case studies support this assessment, although we wish to highlight that this communal orientation developed initially at many southeastern sites around the built environment of plazas, and gathering spaces more broadly, that served as arenas for the transformation of society.

As should be evident in our review of southeastern plazas, we do not see strong evidence for permanently nucleated settlements throughout most of the Archaic and Woodland Southeast. However, this settlement pattern becomes the norm at Range and other Upper South/Midwestern sites and would soon become what archaeologists consider definitional for most Mississippian societies. Only at occasional and often debated moments in the pre-Mississippian lower South do temporary gatherings appear to have taken on more permanence in residential and village form at monumental settings (see Pluckhahn 2010; Thompson and Moore 2015:252–254; Thompson and Pluckhahn 2010). This reminds us that those historical trajectories involving "settling down" were not singular evolutionary pathways but rather moments of creative response to particular realities (Quinn and Barrier 2014; Yoffee et al. 1999). Complex societies (i.e., societies with many parts) developed in both cases, just at different spatial and temporal scales. Only at Feltus were mounds eventually constructed, yet at both Feltus and Range gathering places were spaces for the active construction of complex communities.

Conclusion

Despite their apparent differences, our case studies emphasize the roles that open spaces played in creating different scales and temporalities of communities. The gathering places at both Feltus and Range created and housed multiple overlapping imagined communities. No matter what the size or character of these gatherings, the performances enacted in the central spaces created the social worlds in which pre-Columbian people lived. Participants in the large-scale rituals occurring in the Feltus plaza spent much of their time spatially separated, but the periodic moments of aggregation quite literally created the personal relationships, social structure, and ritual system in which they lived their daily lives. In contrast, participants in the daily activities that occurred in the Range courtyards co-resided, but the particular relationships that they shared with other individuals were negotiated in outside spaces and the very presence and structure of the courtyard itself tied them—every day—into a much larger local community around formal central plazas.

14

Matters and Mattering

BETH A. CONKLIN

It is striking how much life comes into focus through this volume's project of tracking the "everyday." Archaeologists work with materials associated with people who are long dead. But in tracing daily experience through its many forms of matter and mattering, these case studies bring vivid immediacy to the biomaterial, biosocial life—humans' engagements with other living beings in place-based ecological contexts.

Some of this presages the rapprochement between ecological anthropology and material culture studies that Tim Ingold (2012:428) called for, highlighting how material culture scholars "have sought to recapture the physicality of the material world that had been neglected by the post-processualists in their quest for free-floating 'meanings' that had seemed only arbitrarily attached to their signifiers." In seeking to capture the world's tangible physicality as well as human sociality, channels for analysis open up around sensory experience, affect, and contrasts between familiar, everyday events and less-common events and between human and nonhuman actors.

Empathy is crucial to making archaeology more accessible to the public, by creating a bridge of imaginative identification between people of the past and people today (Price and Carr, Chapter 15). Empathy grows through storytelling, and narratives come to life when they bring readers and visitors closer to the feel (and smells, taste, sight, sounds, and social pleasures and anxieties) of moments imagined as they might have been lived by specific people in a specific past with whom we can identify. Close attention to the body and bodily experience is central to developing more comprehensive understandings of human experiences in particular times and places. This requires treating the "body" not just as an abstraction but as the specific corporeal affordances that shape experience and the emotional register of senses, feelings, and habits through which humans participate in the reversibility of energies between bodies and worlds (Whatmore 2002:7). The phenomenology of everyday experience includes the many small, habitual, repetitive, taken-for-granted perceptions, responses, and emotions that make up most of social life, but these also define baselines against which the meanings of nonordinary experiences such as rituals, crises, and encounters with strangers are interpreted.

In my ethnographic work with indigenous people in the rainforest of western Brazil, most days bring a flow and rhythm of activities that is like the flow and rhythm of many other days. When a ritual or celebration takes place, or a crisis erupts, the sensory textures and routines of everyday life are the baseline and backdrop against which the nonordinary events' meanings and impacts are experienced. The people with whom I work, the Wari', live in settlements that vary in size from two or three households to villages of several hundred people. Until recently, they did not store much food other than maize and cooked and consumed fish and game immediately. Each day thus brings movements of going out and coming back, as people leave the village to hunt, fish, plant, or harvest and return home with food and news of what they encountered in the forest. The temporal unfolding of ordinary days follows familiar patterns in each register of bodily sensations.

Among Wari', sound and smell are especially salient in defining differences between ordinary everyday life and extraordinary ritual events. Except during storms, each morning begins in a hushed gray dawn that transitions into an explosion of exuberant birdsong then quiets again as the sun moves higher. Wari' seldom shout, and they have none of the loud daily orations and haranguing with which leaders in some other Amazonian groups motivate their followers. The chopping of wood and cries of children playing are the main sounds that echo across village space during the day. There is a familiar pattern to smells as well, dominated by the wood smoke that surrounds each hearth and clings to the skin so that people literally carry the scent of home with them. In the rainy season, mildew and mold add a distinctive edge. Wari' are acutely aware of odors; they smell the approach of rainstorms, track peccaries by their scent, and detest the smell of rot and decay.

With this baseline of the sensory patterns of everyday routines, it is striking to experience how dramatically ritual events interrupt and contradict these sensory regimes. Among the Wari', every collective ritual or celebration—parties, festivals, funerals, and today Christian church services—centers on loud group singing, drumming, or keening that goes on for hours or days, echoing off the surrounding forest and reverberating back into the village center. The entire community is immersed in a shared pulse of rising and falling sound. Funerals are a cacophony of high-pitched crying and expressions of grief recited in a loud, singsong pattern of keening that traditionally continues nonstop for three days. In both funerals and festivals, the force of constant, overwhelming sonic immersion is difficult to convey; it becomes almost trance-like. The aural contrast to daily life is a striking marker of the collective vitality and focused energies of the social group that has come together for a common purpose.

In traditional funerals, similarly dramatic sensory contrasts happened in the registers of smell and taste. Until the 1960s, Wari' disposed of the bodies of almost all their dead by roasting them and consuming the flesh, brain, heart, liver, and sometimes ground bones. They did not begin preparing the body until the three days of crying and keening had passed, so decay was usually well advanced. Elders describe how the putrid odor surrounded the gathering and clung to everyone's skin and hair and how the taste of decayed flesh was often almost too revolting to stomach. The contrast to daily life, in which Wari' studiously avoid anything contact with anything foul-smelling and would never touch rotten meat, could hardly be stronger. At a deep, visceral level of experience, it marked the radical change in the dead person's condition and the imperative for mourners to let go of the old relationship (see Conklin 2001).

For archaeological studies that project past lives in a sensory mode, the relational sensibilities that Ingold highlighted in his call for attunement to flows of materials are especially germane to processes of crafting that, as Pluckhahn et al. (Chapter 9) show, are based in close attention to the qualities of materials, such as stones and shells and the techniques for working them. Ingold and other theorists of the "new materialisms" such as Jane Bennett (2010) tend to focus on the phenomenology of individual consciousness and subjective perceptions. But there are equally powerful social dimensions in how groups and collectivities make meaning and organize their practices around interactions with materials beyond the human (cf. Rival 2012:133) and carry out activities of crafting and creating in the interstices of other activities and the sociability of a community's daily life.

Focusing on sociality, sensation, and emotion also can help move archaeology beyond the limitation that Ingold (2012:428) sees persisting in approaches to material culture studies that are biased by our own cultural categories—by "a conception of the material world, and of the nonhuman, that focuses on the artifactual domain at the expense of living organisms." Animals, plants, and other life forms and life forces are humanity's constant and intimate consociates in ways that matter every day. The attention that cultural anthropologists and archaeologists increasingly pay to biological life beyond the merely human resonates with directions in which some of the most refreshing developments in cultural theory are moving. The "ontological turn" and perspectival models that have consumed so much recent theoretical energy would be a dead end if they led only to abstractions about static categories of body and spirit and reversals of human and animal positions. But thinking concretely about how people experience more-than-human relationships in daily life opens into projects that move thinking forward.

Among the many diverse theoretical efforts to rupture the terms in which "nature" has been defined in the West, one strategy has been to redistribute social agency to accommodate nonhumans. Challenging the binary of nature and society connects to also challenging the exclusively human framing of the social fabric of these spaces and the privileging of the optical over other sensory registers that "evacuates the bodily presence of living creatures from the si(gh)ting of the wild" (Whatmore 2002:14). Ostensibly, critical theory too often erases all but humans as agents in the making of places and histories. The diverse energies of other earthly inhabitants (and the earth itself) get rolled into a lumpen "nature," a tabula rasa for the inscription of human history (Whatmore 2002:14).

We seem to be talking about animals more these days than ever before in social science. Donna Haraway (2008:2) has contributed some of the most useful thinking about relations that develop in the "contact zone" where different species meet and influence each other. Haraway adapted this idea of interspecies contact zones from Mary Louise Pratt's (1992:4) concept of cultural contact zones, the "social spaces where disparate cultures meet, clash, and grapple with each other, often in highly asymmetrical relations of domination and subordination." These are often spaces of violence and exploitation, and much of the interdisciplinary animal theory literature is preoccupied with critiquing human-animal hierarchies and disregard. Yet as Christopher Moore and Richard Jefferies (Chapter 7) remind us, hunting societies tend to approach their prey less in the language of extractivism and more in horizontal relations of wary entanglements—entanglements of exchange, negotiation, and sometimes partnerships of mutual obligation. Renee Walker (Chapter 11) offers an eye-opening account of social ties between dogs and people that challenges us to imagine how these might have played out in intimate, affective bonds that are hinted at by the care taken with dog burials. The meshwork of human-animal entanglements, as she observes, is as much social as it is economic.

Exploring mutual entanglements between animals and people shows the productivity of more symmetrical analysis that thinks beyond the merely human. Ethnography and ethnohistory show that indigenous people recognize animals as active agents with whom hunters strive to develop partnerships. Reciprocity is a structuring dynamic, and emotions are a bridge among the social, symbolic, and practical/ecological. Grounding empathy and imagination in close attention to the specificity of place and social arrangements, the intertwining of human and animal lives suggests connections and kinship beyond the human that may have been enacted in myriad everyday encounters and negotiations.

The attention that archaeologists accord to specific local environments and historical contexts offer models from which cultural anthropologists could learn to see more complexity, including the potential effects of small changes in interactions among landscape, cultural topologies, climate, and the actions of people and animals. I am reminded of the astonishing video that went viral in 2014–2015, called "How Wolves Change Rivers." This short film recounts how the reintroduction of wolves into Yellowstone National Park by wildlife ecologists started a "trophic cascade" that is rapidly changing the landscape. The story (which has its critics) is that humans set the process in motion by bringing back the wolves, then the animals (and plants) themselves became agents of change. Confronted with new predators, deer quickly modified their behavior to avoid browsing in the open. Consequently, tree seedlings are now left undisturbed. Seedlings can grow in the open, young trees can grow taller, meadows are being reforested, and newly stabilized riverbanks are altering watercourses. Human, nonhuman, and bioecological processes are inextricably intertwined in ways that can reshape the land itself.

Thinking about how animals respond to humans' actions that modify their circumstances, and vice versa, raises interesting questions about the earthen mounds that are so prominent in southeastern archaeology. Shane Miller and Jesse Tune (Chapter 2) suggest that spring floods may have concentrated deer and other game on islands of higher ground, which echoes findings in Amazonian archaeology. Our picture of South American prehistory has been rocked by mounting discoveries of vast networks of giant earthworks in lowland areas formerly thought to have always been sparsely inhabited. In eastern Bolivia, where rainy-season floods inundate vast areas, Clark Erickson (2001) and John Walker (2008) have shown that some earthworks served as giant fish farms and islands on which game congregated. By channeling animals' movements, these Amazonian earthworks made it easier to hunt game and harvest fish. In a charmingly reciprocal feedback loop in this contact zone where species meet, well-drained earthworks in flooded areas set in motion self-organizing processes driven by nonhuman "ecosystem engineers"—ants, termites, earthworms, and woody plants that prefer dry locations. The insects and roots burrow into the mounds, increasing the soil's porosity and thus reducing erosion. The insect "engineers" constantly build and rebuild their homes by transporting bits of earth to the top of the mounds, where this soil helps maintain the earthen mounds' structures over time. Termite mounds may improve soil quality and increase plant biodiversity (McKey et al. 2010).

Attention to engagements with other living beings also relates to the question of whether material culture is about relations to objects or relations with "things." In indigenous Amazonia, the imperative to treat certain carcasses respectfully—as special things, not objects—and to return bones to their rightful place in the cultural spatial landscape may correlate with patterned traces in ancient material remains. In excavating precontact Wari' settlement sites, for example, the contrasting treatment of human and animal bones would offer a major to clue to decipher ritual life and cosmology. At the end of a traditional funeral, Wari' burned the human bones along with all the funeral artifacts of mats, roasting rack, and ceramic pots. They then dug a deep hole in the house floor, pushed the charred remains into it, used the end of a log to pound everything into bits, filled in the hole, swept the floor clean, and went on living in the home above this burial site. Excavating old house sites would uncover a concentration of charred remains and perhaps chemical traces of human bone.

In contrast, the bones of animals that Wari' eat receive no special treatment; they are burned or discarded casually. In the past, the one exception was the boar-like white-lipped peccary, which has a special place in Wari' cosmology. White-lipped peccaries are the only terrestrial mammal in Amazonia that congregates in large social groups; a herd may number a hundred or more individuals. Wari' believe that when a person dies, his or her spirit travels to an underwater realm, from which the ancestors periodically return embodied as living peccaries. The coming of the herd is thus a visit from the ancestors. Individual ancestral spirits present themselves to hunters who are their own relatives, so that their peccary meat will go to feed the loved ones that they left behind. This idea that dead people become animals who continue to care for and nourish their kin is an emotionally powerful continuation of the bonds of feeding and being fed that are the essence of Wari' family life. This image of the dead becoming food for the living was central to the meanings evoked in the funeral act of consuming the corpse.

White-lipped peccaries' unique spiritual role in Wari' social life and cosmology was marked materially by the fact that they were the only animal whose bones were not simply tossed away. Hunters saved peccary skulls and stacked them in a column outside their houses. The contrasting ways in which Wari' treated the bones of peccaries, other animals, and people in everyday and ritual contexts thus map onto key cosmological categories and ritual ideas and practices.

In tracing the ways that animals and other nonhuman things participate in the spaces of social life, the archaeology of everyday life speaks to the larger theoretical concerns to which anthropology, more than any discipline, should be speaking: about the shape of future life in the Anthropocene. Rather than replicate analytic approaches that subsume biology under "society" or vice versa, some of the most promising approaches aim for truly integrated, biosocial understandings that take into account nonhuman as well as human actors and sensory experience as well as social arrangements and symbolism. The challenge, always, is to keep sight of all these dimensions simultaneously. This is especially difficult to do in a discipline whose subdisciplines, theoretical allegiances, and methodological specializations gravitate toward one pole or the other—toward either a focus on the social, symbolic, psychological, and cognitive or a focus on the biological, material, and ecological. However much we proclaim our commitments to the power of integrative, even four-field, holism, it is notably difficult to keep the full range of life-matters in focus. The project nonetheless is well worth pursuing. Welcoming diverse approaches to thinking deeper into the data, drawing out inferences in order to reconstruct daily life as it might have been lived long ago, brings home the power of the observation by Ashley Dumas (Chapter 6) that empathetic imagination is germane both to good science and, regardless of differences in methods or theory, to the question that we all want to answer: what was it like back then?

15

The Everyday Archaeologist Matters

SARAH E. PRICE AND PHILIP J. CARR

As practitioners, we commonly decry the Hollywood portrayal of archaeologists, while a few of us secretly smile and think: "Wow, I am a professional archaeologist." Most modern, professional, everyday archaeologists are far from these cinematic versions. Instead of wrestling with Nazis, we wrestle with other problems, both abstract and tangible. The contributions by the "everyday" archaeologists in this volume provide insight into a number of these dilemmas. First, there is the question of theory and consilience among researchers across diverse topics. Within this disparate sample of everyday archaeologists, we do see a capacity for consilience. We see a glimmer of where archaeological theory may be headed, at least in the Southeast. Second, through exploring everyday archaeology through the variety of approaches in this volume, we gained insight into what matters to archaeologists and what should matter. Finally, and perhaps most importantly, we can suggest ways in which archaeologists can overcome a crisis of relevance that is facing our discipline. Here we draw inspiration from the theme, everyday matters, and essays in this volume to address these three areas.

Theory Every Day

By not insisting on a particular theoretical perspective or giving a directive to consider everyday matters in a specific way, we ran the risk of a discordant hodgepodge of research that would have had the opposite impact of our intent by further emphasizing individual silos and talking past one another (sensu Harris 1980). Thankfully, Kuhnian incommensurability was not the result. We see threads of connection that with continuing efforts, primarily working to reconcile similarities and differences in jargon (i.e., artifact life histories, biographies, entanglements, and itineraries), may lead to greater consilience.

So does theory matter to an archaeologist every day? This is a loaded question and would receive an emphatic knee-jerk "yes" from most archaeologists. Theory is heavily emphasized in academic training but often fades to the background in real-life application. For those of us in Cultural Resource Management, the practice of CRM is something of a theoretical paradigm in and of itself (Dunnell 1990:16; see also Verhagen and Whitley 2012). In the Southeast, theory is reserved for plenary sessions at conferences or special publications. In short, theory is not explicitly the everyday or every day. Much like archaeological reports, theoretical writing is most often dry and full of esoteric terminology, rendering it uninteresting or inaccessible to most outside of a classroom. To add to the theoretical discordance, there are practitioners of various paradigms in southeastern archaeology (culture history, evolutionary, processual, and postprocessual) as well as those that are theoretically eclectic or in the "squishy middle ground" (Cobb 2014:215; see also White 2014:255, 259–261). Polemics between ardent theoreticians add to the disinterest in theory of those practicing archaeology.

There is, and has been for some time, an underlying discomfort in discussions of current theory in the Southeast (Brose 1993). This unrest is underscored by the numerous "taking stock" or reflexive publications regarding southeastern archaeology's history and development (e.g., Anderson and Sassaman 2012; Johnson 1993; Tushingham et al. 2002). Even in light of all the self-examination, we do not seem to be making much progress in furthering archaeological theory or contributing to its development. Perhaps this unease stems from an inability to apply theoretical paradigms to our everyday archaeologies. Our discipline, from a theoretical standpoint, is on the verge of change and likely in the middle of that shift (sensu Kristiansen 2014). From the perspective of Thomas Kuhn (1962), we are in a scientific crisis, a process of transition, and have not yet arrived at a comfortable theoretical place of normal science.

One approach is to develop a compromise, a middle ground between the extremes of sterile science and idiosyncratic humanities (Hegmon 2003; Van-Pool and VanPool 1999). These attempts at compromise have resulted in a variety of theoretical views, even in the Southeast, as evidenced by the papers in a thematic section of volume 33, issue 2, of *Southeastern Archaeology*, which address theory. Another factor is eclecticism, the mixing of theories or picking and choosing certain elements from one paradigm or another. Eclecticism may or may not be a bad thing. An adverse outcome would be that we can no longer effectively communicate with one another and spend more time thinking about archaeology than doing archaeology. Or it might mean that independent research can converge with similar exemplars, resulting in a concordance of evidence and ideas (sensu Wilson 1998). In reality, southeastern archaeologists might just be "science friendly," meaning that they do not particularly subscribe to any paradigm, but rather to science: "if you're not studying material remains and aren't asking questions about the human past, then you're not doing archaeology" (Rundkvist 2008).

The authors of this chapter spent an inordinate amount of time discussing eclecticism and the contributions to this volume. One is rather firmly against the practice of eclecticism following Knight (2014:206), while the other discovered that she was in fact eclectic (Cobb 2014; White 2014; see also Conkey 2007:288). After working on projects in productive tandem for over ten years, and not doing each other bodily harm as Lewis Binford and Robert Dunnell might have done if they had worked together, it seems we are not as incommensurable as our theoretical leanings might imply. The presence of eclectics in southeastern archaeology may be an indicator of where we are heading in the future. Or perhaps we will converge on processual-plus (Hegmon 2003) or postprocessual light (Sassaman 2010). Certainly, the work by Sassaman has potential for incorporating the everyday. It is possible that the next paradigm will be something parallel to Edward O. Wilson's consilience or Big History (Hesketh 2014), in that our individual datasets and research interests will begin to converge, achieving a concordance of evidence, and from that foundation we can begin to synthesize with strong conclusions.

However, we provide a caution regarding an eclectic theoretical approach. There is a danger of becoming so specialized that research and communication are no longer in step. This is already an issue in archaeology in general. Michael Shott (2014:1) remarked on this very topic concerning lithic analyses: "As a result, the analytical diversity that characterizes stone tool research is often experienced by archaeologists in disconnected fragments that do not impart a sense of a coherent field of study." We think that this is an accurate characterization of today's archaeology. Ideally, theory should be driving the questions we ask and therefore the data we collect. If we do not agree to collect the same data before we specialize (i.e., measure what matters), then we cannot build useful datasets. We end up with a big mess instead of big data. Perhaps the broad perspective allowed by everyday as a theme makes it possible to transcend theory, paradigms, individual sites, space, and professionals and nonprofessionals through its use as a scale for discourse.

Although many approaches and theoretical frameworks were adopted for or draped around the essays in this volume, they are unified underneath their various verbiages by a "big picture" approach. Whether it is labeled entanglements, organization of technology, itineraries and biographies, or just simply "mounds every day," southeastern archaeologists are seeking to investigate the archaeological record to answer questions other than simply the "when" and "what" that our culture history inheritance dictates. These authors employ and incorporate a sundry of information sources in addition to the archaeological data: ethnography, ethnohistory, ethnoarchaeology, experiments, and so forth. They are asking how the environment, social and technological situations, and decisions interact to shape the archaeological record, how do all the pieces fit together, and how did people think about and organize their everyday activities (see also Conklin, Chapter 14)?

A strong commitment to science is evidenced by the approaches adopted in this volume. It appears that southeastern archaeologists remain dedicated to empirical data collection as a way of knowing the past. Systematic observations and experimentations, inductive and deductive reasoning, and hypothesis formulation and testing (and retesting) are all hallmarks of good science and, explicitly or implicitly, present to one degree or another in these essays. For example, Randall and Gilmore (Chapter 8) demonstrate this most clearly in their incorporation of experimental archaeology in testing shell cup function. Even those contributors who chose to take what could be cursorily construed as a postmodern approach by composing narratives remain committed to an empirical and pragmatic study of the past in their close alignment of data with their reconstructions. The narratives force consideration of questions not always asked when working from the archaeological record that become hypotheses for testing when collecting new data. In some cases we may not know how some of these hypotheses could be tested due to the coarse-grained nature of the archaeological record, but assuming that this is the case is to damn the discipline to frustration and stagnation.

The essays in this volume represent a spectrum of what could be termed microstudies because of their use of site-specific examples/case studies, but they are underlain by a common theme—everyday life. This unifying theme allows us to see the underlying connections and disjoints among the various specializations and geographies represented by this sample of southeastern archaeologists. The everyday is certainly not a scale considered consciously by many archaeologists, but it is a useful heuristic for structuring and thinking about what we do know about the archaeological record and taking stock of what we still do not know. As Greene and Dumas found independently, having to distil even one site into the events of one day caused them to truly think (and rethink) about their respective sites' assemblages and features. This approach to thinking about archaeology in terms of everyday is also valuable in that it is fun (see Walker, Chapter 11), it utilizes one of the most powerful tools of our species—imagination—and allows us to be specialized researchers and theoretically eclectic, but not in a way that is counterproductive. It may even provide the common ground needed to begin communicating across restrictive cultural and archaeological barriers of our own construction. Time, space, and material classes continue to encumber southeastern archaeology, while infusing thinking about the everyday can lead us to forge new theoretical paths.

The Matters of Everyday Archaeology

Archaeology has many goals, which may differ depending on our theoretical paradigm. Our objectives vary: bringing order to an incomplete and imperfect record of people in the past, distilling the actions of the past to see cultural changes and the reasons changes occurred, synthesizing to predict human behavior through laws, and using the past to better the future of humanity. David Thomas and Robert Kelly (2016:14) state: "All archaeologists today are concerned with learning something new about the past, with communicating that knowledge to the public, and with protecting archaeological sites." We could also say that what matters to any archaeologist every day is having a job and doing something worthwhile or productive with it.

Archaeologists work in academia, government, and the private sector and all have everyday goals that shape how their archaeologies are produced. Thus there is an emphasis on a subset of the goals stated by Thomas and Kelly (2016:14–15). Academics are pushed to publish (or perish, as the popular saying goes). Tenure and promotions are often based on rates of publication, which encourages repetitive output. Archaeologists in government positions are bound to standards that often do not encourage creativity in recovery, or new initiatives in interpretation and preservation, and must operate within strict budgets, which encourages repetitive output due to gains in efficiency. The methods of achieving the everyday goals of current archaeology are homogenizing both the archaeology that is being produced and the way in which we view the archaeological record and thus past peoples and cultures.

National Public Radio (2015) discussed an examination of popular country songs and detailed how these songs are fundamentally the same lyrics over almost identical melodies. (Todd Block broke down six songs and then combined the parts to make one seamless song.) This repetitiveness in current pop culture is often explained as cost effective and guarantees success (e.g., movie reboots and sequels), in that people find the predictable appealing, particularly in times of economic uncertainty (Kaynak et al. 2014). Unfortunately, we think that we could say the same of archaeological reporting, conference papers, journal articles, grants, and the myriad of other products derived from current archaeological research. An example is the canned CRM report, which is cost effective from a production standpoint and (since the format was previously accepted by reviewers) will not result in revisions or delays. As a demonstration, an examination of the 1994 and 2014 Southeastern Archaeological Conference (SEAC) programs show a disturbing and remarkable similarity in paper abstracts (Figure 15.1). Twenty years of research has not diminished the popularity of Mississippian site-centric and date-centric conference presentations.

The issue of specialization and fragmentation (and thus homogenization due to the necessity of communicating between specialties at such a general level) among southeastern archaeologists is somewhat a question of scale. One solution may be to acknowledge that we are asking questions at different scales but to relate how results and interpretations can be scaled to be applicable across geographies

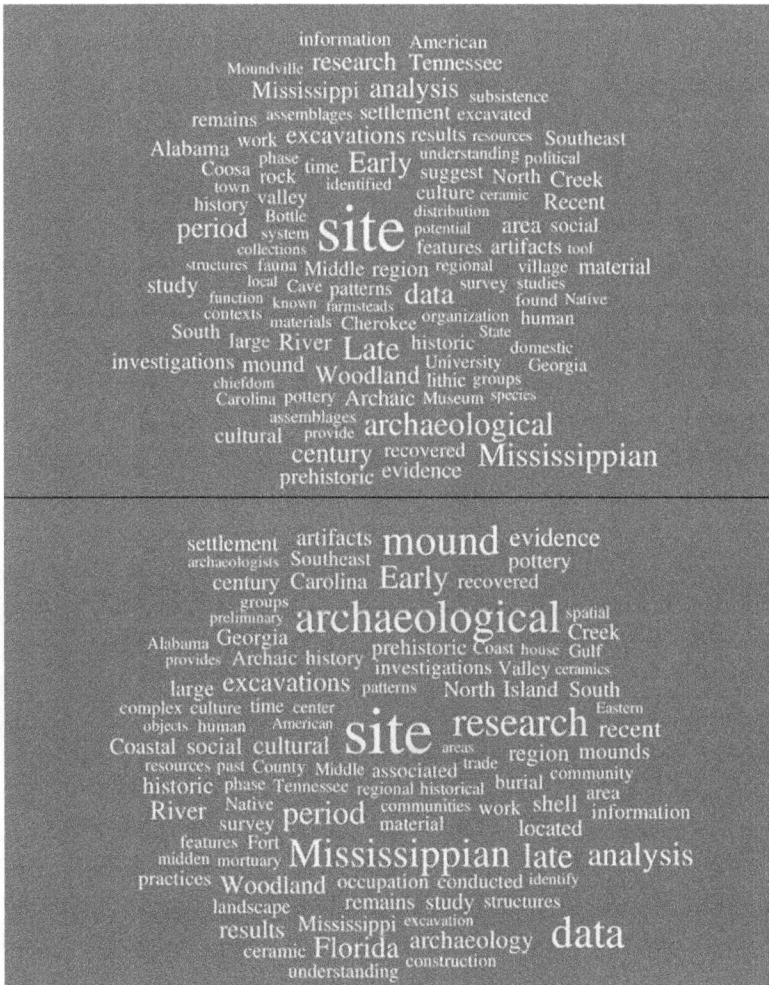

Figure 15.1. Word cloud comparison of 1994 and 2014 SEAC programs.

and time. Consideration of scale when framing questions, looking for answers, developing datasets, and interpreting results has a profound effect on the outcome (sensu Beck 2014; Kuhn 2013; Robb and Pauketat 2012; also Rodning et al. Chapter 2). Although it is perhaps not directly applicable to everyone's everyday archaeologies, chaos theory can help us rethink how we think about the past (Rodning et al., Chapter 3). Humans, and human cultures, are nonlinear systems; what often seems like chaos at one scale can be orderly and predictable at another. Similarly, disruptors to a system can seem chaotic but taken together have predictability.

Archaeologists have always excelled at successfully exploiting and incorporating methods and theories from other disciplines. Perhaps physics, and specifically chaos theory, can contribute to synthesizing our divergent views and scales of an ever-growing archaeological dataset and help us to refine our goals. We are certainly not the first to suggest that physics theories might be applicable to archaeology: David Brose (1993) proposed this very idea over twenty years ago. He concludes his discussion of the state of theory at that time with this statement: "Let's hope a bit of archaeological pessimism may be alleviated, not by rejecting all of those older approaches that have brought southeastern archaeology partial success, but by thinking about how they might be modified by paradigms that employ the concepts of location, simultaneity, and cause and effects in physics" (Brose 1993:14). Chaos seeks to bridge the understanding of individual processes and how those millions of processes behave and the patterns inherent in all scales. Is this not what we as archaeologists strive to achieve? Study of past individual behaviors within a culture that add up to culture change? Miller and Tune (Chapter 2) address this indirectly by examining behavioral consequences of repetitive environmental occurrences during the Paleoindian period. Rodning et al. (Chapter 3) consider the various responses to European contact with Native American cultures across the Southeast, a process usually treated on a site-by-site, culture-by-culture scale. Rather, they look to chaos theory to see how different responses were occurring in different places and different points in time are in reality very similar.

Another solution to scaling, and perhaps the hardest to accomplish for archaeologists, is removing specifics about time and place when addressing a topic (e.g., Kidder and Sherwood, Chapter 12). Scale is an issue because many of us think from our temporal and geographic areas of expertise, which makes it difficult to communicate to someone about Late Woodland when pottery types change across state borders. A popular remodeling television show purposefully does not reveal episode locations: "We don't emphasize the geographic location of the houses, as we want to focus on the informative aspects that could be applicable to a house in any city" (thescottbrothers.com 2015). This is the approach taken by Kidder and Sherwood as well as Barrier and Kassabaum, who discuss built landscapes. We think that this is useful more broadly in archaeology because it aids identification of similarities in behavior and culture when we remove the mantles of time and place. A simple example to consider is conference attendance. Lithic specialists might not attend a session entitled "Mississippian I and II," not necessarily seeing the application to their area of expertise/interest. But if sessions are organized around a method or broader theme, atypical attendance would occur, because specialists would not be predisposed to think that the topic is not applicable to their area of interest or expertise.

Regardless of archaeological goals, archaeologists are and have always been very good at one thing: generating data. Massive amounts of data are produced every day by archaeologists. There are currently many efforts to bring existing data into manageable and, more importantly, usable formats. The Digital Archaeological Record (tDAR) and the Paleoindian Database of the Americas (PIDBA) are two of the better-known examples. There is even a database, the Journal of Online Archaeological Data, for finding databases. Unfortunately, American archaeology is slightly behind the curve on "big data" analyses and applications compared to major businesses and European archaeologists. Target can successfully predict a pregnancy (Hill 2012), Netflix can deduce what movies customers would like to watch (and takes it a step further by using the data to develop new content—which has been wildly successful) (Bulygo 2013), and Pandora can recommend what music to listen to (Layton 2006), all using big data. Every day archaeologists are generating new data, and yet we are doing little in the way of putting these data to work for us to achieve any of the possible goals of archaeology. Gabriele Gattiglia (2015) provides an insightful discussion on the use of big data in archaeology as a tool for informing archaeological research as well as issues and limitations, such as incommensurable datasets.

Aside from issues with comparable datasets and accessing these data, the lack of meaningful syntheses of existing data is an everyday archaeological matter. After forty-some years of contract archaeology, we have not significantly modified our cultural frameworks to reflect the information gleaned from the archaeological record in the Southeast (sensu Kristiansen 2014:18). A promotional video for the reissue of a classic synthesizer provides an interesting parallel to our lack of synthesis. Back to the Future Sounds (Moog Music Inc. 2015) describes thesis, antithesis, and synthesis (see also Immanuel Kant, Karl Marx, and G. W. F. Hegel). Thesis is understanding that which is, to the extent possible. Antithesis is the opposite: imagination without restraint (which, incidentally, was one of the directives to the volume contributors). Out of thesis and antithesis comes synthesis, which is the creation of something new, and the process repeats ad infinitum. In archaeology today, we are too quick to move on to the next technological innovation or site, with little appreciation and understanding of the extant archaeological data. At the end of the Moog promotional video, Malcolm Cecil states that "we have not even scraped the surface of all the sounds synthesizers can make—they are infinite." In turn, archaeologists have not even scraped the surface of what the existing dataset contains. We are decent at thesis but not so good at antithesis and meaningful synthesis. Until we begin to imagine and examine what we cannot necessarily know, using existing methods and data, we cannot exploit the potential of the archaeological record.

While the general goals of archaeology are worthwhile, perhaps the everyday goals of the twenty-first-century archaeologist should be modified. Archaeology is in a crisis: we are, at best, marginally relevant to current questions and concerns of the modern world. Archaeology is irrelevant to most anyone outside of the profession. This is evident every time someone asks what kind of dinosaurs we dig up, although at least they get the digging part right. Or when our colleagues with a bachelor's degree in biology or Geographic Information Systems (GIS) bill out at three times the rate of archaeologists with a master's degree, for less work, but clients feel that this is justified. Or when local historical societies are more interested in scheduling Christmas parties at their historical houses than in promoting nonvisible resources, much less preserving them.

It is obvious that most people do not exactly know what we do; why we do it; why they should care; and especially why they should *pay* for it. Who can blame them? The crisis in archaeology that goes beyond looting, destruction of archaeological sites, and lack of funding. There is a crisis of relevance, particularly in demonstrating the utility of the study of the past to current issues and problems. So what can we, as everyday archaeologists, potentially do to change our current course?

Making Archaeology Relevant Every Day

It does not seem that sweeping changes in the practice of archaeology will occur anytime soon, and such changes most likely will not happen from the top down. Therefore we challenge every archaeologist to make small changes, every day. We see three opportunities: palatable writing, scaling interactions, and engaging people with their past by bringing archaeology into their everyday lives.

Palatable Writing

Even as archaeologists, we find most archaeological writing to be dry and overly complicated by jargon, which leaves us wondering "what is the point, or how is this relevant to me?" Archaeology is by its very nature fascinating. We love learning about ourselves, but the information should be conveyed in a way that is understandable and relatable. There is a general push in science (see Clayton 2015) to address the need for better science-to-public writing, so this is not an issue restricted to archaeology. Many writers of science do not "think about the average person" (Deborah S. Bosley in Clayton 2015). This is a real deficit in a field, such as archaeology, that thinks about people.

An excellent example of relatable archaeological writing is Ian Brown's *Bottle Creek Reflections: The Personal Side of Archaeology in the Mobile-Tensas Delta* (2012). The book takes the reader behind the scenes of archaeology, recounting stories of conducting archaeological fieldwork, interwoven with archaeological data and interpretation. Contrasting with Brown's depiction of fieldwork and archaeology, *Lives in Ruins: Archaeologists and the Seductive Lure of Human Rubble* (number 18 seller on Amazon in the Archaeology category) by Marilyn Johnson (2014) attempts to convey what it is like to be an archaeologist. (The title of this book is telling of her perception of archaeologists.) There are some high points, but the takeaways for any nonarchaeologist are that we work in foreign places, are highly guarded about our research and results, and will do just about anything to dig up sites. That is not the best message to be sending to the 91 percent of reviewers who thought it was a "great book that taught them a lot about doing archaeology and being an archaeologist" (Amazon 2015).

Not all of us have the time or experience of working on a site for sufficient time to write a Brown-style book, so what can we do every day to make archaeological writing more palatable? The senior author has addressed this issue by no longer writing canned CRM reports, particularly "recycled" cultural contexts. Every project report, no matter what the size, receives individual narratives of people and events that may be pertinent to archaeological findings. Approaching each project as unique does require (slightly) more time and effort but is more rewarding and engaging for the author who writes hundreds of these reports every year and (we hope) more intriguing and stimulating for reviewers. On occasion this style of writing engages clients in understanding and appreciating their local archaeology.

Scaling Everyday Interactions

Our second challenge, which is related to the first, is to begin scaling our writing and interactions to a wider variety of audiences who are potentially interested in and even have an impact on our daily archaeology. Schoolchildren, tribal nations, and local archaeological societies are groups that we are accustomed to making presentations to and interacting with on a regular basis. These relationships are important and must continue. At the same time, we should be putting more effort into interacting with law enforcement (e.g., Archaeological Resources Protection Act implementation), landowners and developers (developing stewardship), local and state level politicians (taking a proactive approach rather than being reactive when historic preservation laws come under fire), and tourism bureaus (developing and promoting heritage tourism and preservation awareness). These should not be just static, one-sided relationships. As archaeologists, we should be developing meaningful relationships with all of these groups. This is where building social capital with a broader network of consumers would greatly benefit archaeology, every day and in everyday ways. The everyday presents a scale that is relevant, interesting, and comprehensible to these various factions of archaeology consumers.

Engaging with the Everyday

Our third challenge to every archaeologist is to bring archaeology into the everyday lives of everyone. The everyday is certainly a scale that nonarchaeologists find interesting, because it is the most relatable. Our job is to keep the past alive in a way that people in the present can understand and appreciate and perhaps learn from and apply to their everyday lives. Confucius (2015) said: "A true teacher is one who, keeping the past alive, is also able to understand the present."

The romance of our profession and the archaeological sites that we investigate rarely meet public expectations, so the bridge that we must create is empathy, between the past and its people and people today. Carl Wernicke (2014) noted that "how little we seem to learn from a past we don't ourselves experience." He was referring to the thousands killed by the 2011 tsunami because modern people built homes seaward of ancient stone markers that indicate historical tsunami crests. People in the present had never experienced catastrophic flooding; therefore they ignored the very (explicit) warnings of past peoples' experience. If we can provide compelling experiences of the past to people today, we think that people will better understand, learn from, and more importantly care about preserving our collective heritage. If you can show people in the twenty-first century how removal from their homes for construction of a military base is akin to removal of Native Americans in the early nineteenth century, they may start to see that experiences and people that seem entirely different are in reality not that different. As anthropologists, are we not supposed to take the unfamiliar, strange, and weird and make it familiar?

So how can we make archaeology a more engaging experience? There is no one-size-fits-all answer, but several tactics are accessible to the everyday archaeologist. The first is publishing in accessible forums (using palatable writing) like

The Conversation (theconversation.com) or *Sapiens* (www.sapiens.org). *Sapiens* is an online publication, which promotes itself as "dedicated to popularizing anthropological research." The stories are not "look at this new, unique thing": they are in-depth yet digestible stories about all aspects of anthropology. According to Alexa (2016), *Sapiens* is doing moderately well in terms of number of visitors, but engagement with the website is not as good. The range of archaeology topics covers Acheulean handaxes, climate change in Fiji, and the Stone Age in Africa. We would like to believe that maybe if more articles were aimed at the everyday archaeology in their backyards, there might be more interest and engagement from the 51.7 percent of the visitors who are from the United States (Alexa 2016). So far it appears that no contributions have been made by southeastern archaeologists. We hope that this will change.

We see another opportunity in online gaming. Simulations and gamers are being exploited in other fields to conduct scientific research, usually through an online interface. "Foldit" players resolved the structure of an enzyme that causes a disease in monkeys in three weeks; researchers had been working on it for thirteen years. Players of "Planet Hunters" are tasked with identifying exoplanets from the Kepler spacecraft dataset. To date, they have discovered over forty planets that could support life that were previously missed by professional astronomers. These "citizen science" projects expand the knowledge base exponentially, as anyone can be a researcher. Zooniverse, a platform that supports many of these people-powered research projects, even includes a handful of archaeological and historical research games (e.g., "Ancient Lives").

The third engaging experience has had success in Europe but not so much in the United States yet: crowd-funded archaeology. Thomas Van Damme (2014) studied crowd-funded archaeological projects to identify what separated successful projects from unsuccessful projects. Some of the conclusions are not unexpected (such as that 88 percent of funded campaigns have a video; this is generally true of all successful crowd-fund-raising projects). Other insights were more surprising. For example, "GoFundMe" has the worst success rate: successful campaigns are large groups seeking full funding of an entire project, including salaries. Some of the rewards from successful archaeological projects are site tours, presentations, acknowledgments, and hard copies of the final product.

Conclusion

If asked at this point whether we have accomplished our goals, our answer would be yes. The symposium and this resulting volume are well outside the norm for southeastern archaeology. Through the efforts of the contributors, this was accomplished in a way that helps their results further the potential for consilience and growth in archaeology.

In regard to understanding where southeastern archaeology is theoretically, and where we may be headed, we see commitment to data and empirical studies. But beyond that we are working in theoretical frameworks that may not best be serving the discipline. Theory is certainly not an everyday matter in southeastern archaeology, and perhaps it does not need to be. But theory should be driving the questions we ask and the data that we collect. If we continue to specialize (and it does not seem feasible not to specialize, as the sheer amount of information is on an exponential upward trajectory), however, then perhaps nonarchaeological, nonlinear paradigms can provide the background structure that unites us. We need theory (otherwise archaeology would be a never-ending litany of "first-finds"), but we may need to restructure how we develop and disseminate paradigms in order to make them more accessible and applicable to our everyday archaeologies.

A rethinking of archaeological goals and how we achieve those goals is in order as well. If archaeologists want to contribute productively to the present and future, then we must work every day to be relevant. The scale of everyday may help get us there. A long-running critique of our discipline is information about the past and artifacts are locked away in ivory towers (or dusty museum boxes). We must work harder, every day, to put this knowledge front and center, in ways that can be related to and understood by the nonarchaeological population. We propose that the scale of everyday and the exemplars produced here are a fruitful approach to achieving this goal.

Although public tax dollars support a good portion of what we currently do, the end results and products only rarely or in special cases engage with or compel the public to care about their heritage. This is disappointing, considering that protection of archaeological sites is mandated. It is "our" collective heritage, yet many do not take ownership of their stake in the past. Static, detached products will not keep preservation laws in place and certainly do not lead to better funding of archaeology. We need to change how we approach archaeology, both within and outside of our profession. The change will have to occur at the scale of everyday actions by every one of us, every day.

References Cited

Abrams, Elliot M., and Thomas W. Bolland

1999   Architectural Energetics, Ancient Monuments, and Operations Management. *Journal of Archaeological Method and Theory* 6:263–291.

Abrams, Elliot M., and Mary F. Le Rouge

2008   Political Complexity and Mound Construction among the Early and Late Adena of the Hocking Valley, Ohio. In *Transitions: Archaic and Early Woodland Research in the Ohio Country*, edited by Martha P. Otto and Brian G. Redmond, pp. 214–231. Ohio University Press in association with the Ohio Archaeological Council, Athens.

Adair, James

2005 [1775]   *The History of the American Indians*, edited by Kathryn E. Holland Braund. University of Alabama Press, Tuscaloosa.

Adhead, S. A. M.

1992   *Salt and Civilization*. St. Martin's Press, New York.

Alexa (www.alexa.com)

2016   Site Overview of Sapiens.org. http://www.alexa.com/siteinfo/sapiens.org.

Alt, Susan

2011   Histories of Mound Building and Scales of Explanation in Archaeology. In *Ideologies of Archaeology*, edited by Reinhard Bernbeck and Randall H. McGuire, pp. 194–211. University of Arizona Press, Tucson.

Alt, Susan, Jeffery D. Kruchten, and Timothy R. Pauketat

2010   The Construction and Use of Cahokia's Grand Plaza. *Journal of Field Archaeology* 35:131–146.

Amazon (www.amazon.com)

2015   Customer Reviews. https://www.amazon.com/Lives-Ruins-Archaeologists-Seductive-Rubble/dp/0062127195.

Amick, Daniel S.

2015   The Recycling of Material Culture Today and during the Paleolithic. *Quaternary International* 361:4–20.

Anderson, Benedict

1991   *Imagined Communities: Reflections on the Origins and Spread of Nationalism*. Verso, London.

Anderson, David G.

1990a   Stability and Change in Chiefdom-Level Societies: An Examination of Mississippian Political Evolution on the South Atlantic Slope. In *Lamar Archaeology: Mississippian*

Chiefdoms in the Deep South, edited by Mark Williams and Gary Shapiro, pp. 187–213. University of Alabama Press, Tuscaloosa.

1990b   The Paleoindian Colonization of Eastern North America: A View from the Southeastern United States. In *Early Paleoindian Economies of Eastern North America*, edited by Kenneth Tankersley and Barry Isaac, pp. 163–216. Research in Economic Anthropology Supplement 5. JAI Press, Greenwich.

1994a   *The Savannah River Chiefdoms: Political Change in the Late Prehistoric Southeast*. University of Alabama Press, Tuscaloosa.

1994b   Factional Competition and the Political Evolution of Mississippian Chiefdoms in the Southeastern United States. In *Factional Competition and Political Development in the New World*, edited by Elizabeth Brumfiel and Timothy Earle, pp. 61–76. Cambridge University Press, Cambridge.

1995   Paleoindian Interaction Networks in the Eastern Woodlands. In *Native American Interaction: Multiscalar Analyses and Interpretations in the Eastern Woodlands*, edited by Michael S. Nassaney and Kenneth E. Sassaman, pp. 1–26. University of Tennessee Press, Knoxville.

1996a   Chiefly Cycling and Large-Scale Abandonments as Viewed from the Savannah River. In *Political Structure and Change in the Prehistoric Southeastern United States*, edited by John F. Scarry, pp. 150–191. University Press of Florida, Gainesville.

1996b   Fluctuations between Simple and Complex Chiefdoms: Cycling in the Late Prehistoric Southeast. In *Political Structure and Change in the Prehistoric Southeastern United States*, edited by John F. Scarry, pp. 231–252. University Press of Florida, Gainesville.

1996c   Models of Paleoindian and Early Archaic Settlement in the Lower Southeast. In *The Paleoindian and Early Archaic Southeast*, edited by David G. Anderson and Kenneth E. Sassaman, pp. 29–57. University of Alabama Press, Tuscaloosa.

1998   Swift Creek in a Regional Perspective. In *A World Engraved: Archaeology of the Swift Creek Culture*, edited by Mark Williams and Daniel T. Elliott, pp. 274–300. University of Alabama Press, Tuscaloosa.

2001   Climate and Culture Change in Prehistoric and Early Historic Eastern North America. *Archaeology of Eastern North America* 29:143–186.

2012a   Comments on "The Anonymity of the Hunt: A Critique of Hunting as Sharing" by John Knight. *Current Anthropology* 53(3):345–346.

2012b   Monumentality in Eastern North America during the Mississippian Period. In *Early New World Monumentality*, edited by Richard L. Burger and Robert M. Rosenwig, pp. 78–108. University of Florida Press, Gainesville.

Anderson, David G., John E. Cornelison, Jr., Sarah C. Sherwood (editors)

2013   *Archeological Investigations at Shiloh Indian Mounds National Historic Landmark (40hr7) 1999–2004, Volumes 1 and 2*. National Park Service, Southeast Archeological Center, Tallahassee, Florida: http://pidba.org/anderson/cv/2013.Anderson.Shiloh.pdf.

Anderson, David G., and J. Christopher Gillam

2000   Paleoindian Colonization of the Americas: Implications from an Examination of Physiography, Demography, and Artifact Distribution. *American Antiquity* 65(1):43–66.

Anderson, David G., Albert C. Goodyear, James Kennett, and Allen West

2011   Multiple Lines of Evidence for a Possible Human Population Decline during the Early Younger Dryas. *Quaternary International*:570–583.

Anderson, David G., and Glen T. Hanson

1988   Early Archaic Settlement in the Southeastern United States: A Case Study from the Savannah River Valley. *American Antiquity* 53:262–286.

Anderson, David G., and Kenneth E. Sassaman

1996   *The Paleoindian and Early Archaic Southeast.* University of Alabama Press, Tuscaloosa.

2012   *Recent Developments in Southeastern Archaeology: From Colonization to Complexity.* Society for American Archaeology Press, Washington, D.C.

Anderson, David G., Ashley M. Smallwood, and D. Shane Miller

2015   Pleistocene Human Settlement in the Southeastern United States: Current Evidence and Future Directions. *PaleoAmerica* 1(1):7–51.

Anderson, Derek T., Ashley M. Smallwood, Albert C. Goodyear, and Sarah E. Walters

2016   The Paleoindian and Early Archaic Hilltop Occupations at the Topper Site. *Tennessee Archaeology* 8(1–2):102–113.

Andrefsky, William, Jr.

2006   Experimental and Archaeological Verification of an Index of Retouch for Hafted Bifaces. *American Antiquity* 71:743–758.

2008   *Lithic Technology: Measures of Production, Use, and Curation.* Cambridge University Press, Cambridge.

Andrews, Anthony P.

1983   *Maya Salt Production and Trade.* University of Arizona Press, Tucson.

Andrews, R. L., James M. Adovasio, B. Humphrey, David C. Hyland, J. S. Gardner, and D. G. Harding

2002   Conservation and Analysis of Textile and Related Perishable Artifacts. In *Windover: Multidisciplinary Investigations of an Early Archaic Cemetery*, edited by Glen H. Doran, pp. 121–165. University Press of Florida, Gainesville.

Archaeological Consultants and Janus Research

2001   Phase III Mitigative Excavations at Lake Monroe Outlet Midden (8VO53), Volusia County, Florida. Report Submitted to U.S. Department of Transportation Federal Highway Administration and Florida Department of Transportation District Five. Archaeological Consultants, Inc., and Janus Research, Tampa.

Arnold, Dean

1985   *Ceramic Theory and Cultural Process.* Cambridge University Press, Cambridge.

Arnold, Jeanne E., and Ann Munns

1994   Independent or Attached Specialization: The Organization of Shell Bead Production in California. *Journal of Field Archaeology* 21(4):473–489.

Ashley, Keith, Neill J. Wallis, and Michael D. Glascock

2015   Forager Interactions on the Edge of the Early Mississippian World: Neutron Activation Analysis of Ocmulgee and St. Johns Pottery. *American Antiquity* 80(2):290–311.

Associated Press

2011   Corps to Repair Birds Point Levee: http://thesouthern.com/news/local/article_6a0dc750-9832-11e0-8967-001cc4c002e0.html.

Aten, Lawrence E.

1999   Middle Archaic Ceremonialism at Tick Island, Florida: Ripley P. Bullen's 1961 Excavations at the Harris Creek Site. *Florida Anthropologist* 52(3):131–200.

Barker, Gary, and John B. Broster
1996   The Johnson Site (40Dv400): A Dated Paleoindian and Early Archaic Occupation in Tennessee's Central Basin. *Journal of Alabama Archaeology* 42(2):97–153.

Barnard, Andrew
1840   Letter to Governor Edward Dudley, April 6, 1840. Governors' Papers, State Archives, Raleigh, North Carolina.

Barnett, James F.
2007   *The Natchez Indians: A History to 1735.* University Press of Mississippi, Jackson.

Baron, Nancy
2010   *Escape from the Ivory Tower: A Guide to Making Your Science Matter.* Island Press, Washington, D.C.

Barrier, Casey R.
2011   Storage and Relative Surplus at the Mississippian Site of Moundville. *Journal of Anthropological Archaeology* 30:206–219.

Barrier, Casey R., and Timothy J. Horsley
2014   Shifting Communities: Demographic Profiles of Early Village Population Growth and Decline in the Central American Bottom. *American Antiquity* 79:295–313.

Barton, C. Michael, Steven Schmich, and Steven R. James
2004   The Ecology of Human Colonization in Pristine Landscapes. In *The Settlement of the American Continents: A Multidisciplinary Approach to Human Biogeography*, edited by C. Michael Barton, Geoffrey A. Clark, David R. Yesner, and Georges A. Pearson, pp. 138–161. University of Arizona Press, Tucson.

Bar-Yosef, Ofer, and Philip Van Peer
2009   The Chaîne Opératoire Approach in Middle Paleolithic Archaeology. *Current Anthropology* 50:103–131.

Beahm, Emily L., and Kevin E. Smith
2006   New Insights from Castalian Springs: A Mississippian Chiefdom in the Nashville Basin of Tennessee. Paper presented at the 63rd Annual Meeting of the Southeastern Archaeological Conference, Little Rock, Arkansas.

Beauchamp, Gary K.
1993   Mammalian Salt Perception and Preference. In *Seventh Symposium on Salt*, Vol. 2, edited by Hidetake Kakihana, pp. 345–349. Elsevier Science Publishers, B. V., Amsterdam.

Beck, Charlotte, and George T. Jones
2011   The Role of Mobility and Exchange in the Conveyance of Toolstone during the Great Basin Paleoarchaic. In *Perspectives on Prehistoric Trade and Exchange in California and the Great Basin*, edited by Richard E. Hughes, pp. 55–82. University of Utah Press, Salt Lake City.

Beck, Charlotte, Amanda Taylor, George T. Jones, Cynthia M. Fadem, Caitlyn R. Cook, and Sara A. Millward
2002   Rocks Are Heavy: Transport Costs and Paleoarchaic Quarry Behavior in the Great Basin. *Journal of Anthropological Archaeology* 21:481–507.

Beck, Robin A., Jr.
2013   Appropriating Community: Platforms and Power on the Formative Taraco Peninsula, Bolivia. In *From Prehistoric Villages to Cities: Settlement Aggregation and Community Transformation*, edited by Jennifer Birch, pp. 87–110. Routledge Press, London.

2014   What I Believe: Structure and the Problem of Microsociality. *Southeastern Archaeology* 33(2):208–213.

Beck, Robin A., Jr., and James A. Brown

2012   Political Economy and the Routinization of Religious Movements: A View from the Eastern Woodlands. *Archaeological Papers of the American Anthropological Association* 21:72–88.

Beck, Robin A., Jr., and David G. Moore

2002   The Burke Phase: A Mississippian Frontier in the North Carolina Foothills. *Southeastern Archaeology* 21:192–205.

Beck, Robin A., Jr., David G. Moore, and Christopher B. Rodning

2006   Identifying Fort San Juan: A Sixteenth–Century Spanish Occupation at the Berry Site, North Carolina. *Southeastern Archaeology* 25:65–77.

Beck, Robin A., Christopher B. Rodning, and David G. Moore

2010   Limiting Resistance: Juan Pardo and the Shrinking of Spanish La Florida, 1566–1568. In *Enduring Conquests: Rethinking the Archaeology of Resistance to Spanish Colonialism in the Americas*, edited by Matthew Liebmann and Melissa S. Murphy, pp. 19–39. School for Advanced Research Press, Santa Fe, New Mexico.

Beck, Robin A., Christopher B. Rodning, and David G. Moore (editors)

2016   *Fort San Juan and the Limits of Empire: Colonialism and Household Practice at the Berry Site*. University Press of Florida, Gainesville.

Bell, Philip, Bruce Lewenstein, Andrew W. Shouse, and Michael A. Feder

2009   *Learning Science in Informal Environments: People, Places, and Pursuits*. National Academies Press, Washington, D.C.

Belmont, John

1967   The Culture Sequence at the Greenhouse Site, Louisiana. *Southeastern Archaeological Conference Bulletin* 6:27–34.

1982   The Troyville Concept and the Gold Mine Site. *Louisiana Archaeology* 9:65–98.

Bennett, Jane

2010   *Vibrant Matter: A Political Ecology of Things*. Durham, NC: Duke University Press.

Bentley, R. Alexander, and Herbert D. G. Maschner

2008   Complexity Theory. In *Handbook of Archaeological Theories*, edited by R. Alexander Bentley and Herbert D. G. Maschner, pp. 245–272. AltaMira Press, Lanham, Maryland.

Benyshek, Tasha, and Paul Webb

2012   Recent Excavations at Iotla Town. Paper presented at the 69th Annual Meeting of the Southeastern Archaeological Conference, Baton Rouge.

Bernardini, Wesley

2004   Hopewell Geometric Earthworks: A Case Study in the Referential and Experiential Meaning of Monuments. *Journal of Anthropological Archaeology* 23:331–356.

Bertino, M., Gary K. Beauchamp, and K. Engelman

1982   Long-term Reduction in Dietary Sodium Alters the Taste of Salt. *American Journal of Clinical Nutrition* 36(6):1134–1144.

Bieder, Robert E.

2006   The Imagined Bear. *Current Writing* 18(1):163–173.

Binford, Lewis R.

1962   Archaeology as Anthropology. *American Antiquity* 28:217–225.

1973   Interassemblage Variability—The Mousterian and the "Functional" Argument. In *The Explanation of Culture Change: Models in Prehistory*, edited by Colin Renfrew, pp. 227–253. Duckworth, London.

1981   Behavioral Archaeology and the "Pompeii Premise." *Journal of Anthropological Research* 37:195–208.

Bird, Rebecca

1999   Cooperation and Conflict: The Behavioral Ecology of the Sexual Division of Labor. *Evolutionary Anthropology* 8(2):65–75.

Bisson, Michael S.

2000   Nineteenth Century Tools for Twenty-First Century Archaeology? Why the Middle Paleolithic Typology of François Bordes Must Be Replaced. *Journal of Archaeological Method and Theory* 7:1–48.

Black, Glenn A.

1967   *Angel Site, An Archaeological, Historical and Ethnological Study*. Indiana Historical Society, Indianapolis.

Black, Lydia T.

1998   Bear in Human Imagination and in Ritual. *Ursus* 10:343–347.

Blake, William

1860   Report upon the Property of the Valley River Gold Company. North Carolina Collection, University of North Carolina at Chapel Hill.

Blankenship, Beth

2013   The Hopewellian Influence at Crystal River, Florida: Testing the Marine Shell Artifact Production Hypothesis. Unpublished MA thesis, Department of Anthropology, University of South Florida, Tampa.

Bleed, Peter

2009   Comment to Bar-Yosef and Van Peer's "The Chaîne Opératoire Approach in Middle Paleolithic Archaeology." *Current Anthropology* 50(1):117–118.

Blessing, Meggan E.

2011   Zooarchaeological Assemblage. In *Cultural Resource Assessment Survey of Silver Glen Springs Recreational Area in the Ocala National Forest, Florida*, edited by Asa R. Randall, Meggan E. Blessing, and Jon C. Endonino, pp. 173–194. Technical Report 13. Laboratory of Southeastern Archaeology, Department of Anthropology, University of Florida, Gainesville.

Blitz, John H.

2015   Skeuomorphs, Pottery, and Technological Change. *American Anthropologist* 117:665–678.

Blitz, John H., and Patrick Livingood

2004   Sociopolitical Implications of Mississippian Mound Volume. *American Antiquity* 69:291–301.

Blitz, John H., and Karl G. Lorenz

2006   *The Chattahoochee Chiefdoms*. University of Alabama Press, Tuscaloosa.

Blitz, John H., and Erik S. Porth

2013   Social Complexity and the Bow in the Eastern Woodlands. *Evolutionary Anthropology* 22:89–95.

Boldurian, Anthony T., and John L. Cotter

1999   *Clovis Revisited: New Perspectives on Paleoindian Adaptations from Blackwater Draw,*

New Mexico. University Museum Monograph 103. University Museum, University of Pennsylvania, Philadelphia.

Booker, Karen M., Robert L. Rankin, and Charles M. Hudson

1992   Place Name Identification and Multilingualism in the Sixteenth-Century Southeast. *Ethnohistory* 39:399–451.

Borgerhoff Mulder, Monique, and Ryan Schacht

2005   Human Behavioural Ecology. In *Encyclopedia of Life Sciences (eLS).* Wiley Online Library: http://www.els.net/WileyCDA/ElsArticle/refId-a0003671.html.

Boudreaux, Edmond A., III

2013   Community and Ritual within the Mississippian Center at Town Creek. *American Antiquity* 78:483–501.

Boulware, Tyler

2011   *Deconstructing the Cherokee Nation: Town, Region, and Nation among Eighteenth-Century Cherokees.* University Press of Florida, Gainesville.

Bourdieu, Pierre

1977   *Outline of a Theory of Practice.* Cambridge University Press, Cambridge.

1980   *The Logic of Practice.* Stanford University Press, Stanford.

Bowser, Brenda J.

2000   From Pottery to Politics: An Ethnoarchaeological Study of Political Factionalism, Ethnicity, and Domestic Pottery Style in the Ecuadorian Amazon. *Journal of Archaeological Method and Theory* 7:219–248.

Brackenridge, G. Robert

1984   Alluvial Stratigraphy and Radiocarbon Dating along the Duck River, Tennessee: Implications Regarding Flood-plain Origin. *Geological Society of America Bulletin* 95(1):9–25.

Bradbury, Andrew P., Philip J. Carr, and D. Randall Cooper

2008   Raw Material and Retouched Flakes. In *Lithic Technologies: Measures of Production, Use, and Curation,* edited by William Andrefsky Jr., pp. 233–254. Cambridge University Press, Cambridge.

Brain, Jeffrey P.

1978   Late Prehistoric Settlement Patterning in the Yazoo Basin and Natchez Bluffs Regions of the Lower Mississippi Valley. In *Mississippian Settlement Patterns,* edited by Bruce D. Smith, pp. 331–368. Academic Press, New York.

1988   *Tunica Archaeology.* Peabody Museum of Archaeology and Ethnology Papers 78, Harvard University, Cambridge, Massachusetts.

Braun, David P.

1987   Coevolution of Sedentism, Pottery Technology, and Horticulture in the Central Midwest, 200 B.C.–A.D. 600. In *Emergent Horticultural Economies of the Eastern Woodlands,* edited by William Keegan, pp. 153–181. Center for Archaeological Investigations, Southern Illinois University, Carbondale.

Braund, Kathryn E. Holland

2008   *Deerskins and Duffels: The Creek Indian Trade with Anglo–America, 1685–1815.* University of Nebraska Press, Lincoln.

Breitburg, Emanuel

1982   Analysis of Area A Fauna. In *The Carrier Mills Archaeological Project: Human Adaptation in the Saline Valley, Illinois,* edited by Richard W. Jefferies and Brian M. Butler, pp.

861–957. Center for Archaeological Investigations Research Paper. Southern Illinois University at Carbondale, Carbondale.

Briggs, Rachel V.

2016   The Civil Cooking Pot: Hominy and the Mississippian Standard Jar in the Black Warrior Valley, Alabama. *American Antiquity* 81:316–332.

Brose, David S.

1993   Changing Paradigms. In *The Development of Southeastern Archaeology*, edited by Jay K. Johnson, pp. 1–17. University of Alabama Press, Tuscaloosa.

Broster, John B., and Mark R. Norton

1993   The Carson-Conn-Short Site (40BN190): An Extensive Clovis Habitation in Benton County, Tennessee. *Current Research in the Pleistocene* 10:3–5.

1996   Recent Paleoindian Research in Tennessee. In *The Paleoindian and Early Archaic Southeast*, edited by David G. Anderson and Kenneth E. Sassaman, pp. 288–297. University of Alabama Press, Tuscaloosa.

Broster, John B., Mark R. Norton, Bobby Hulan, and Ellis Durham

2006   Paleoamerican and Early Archaic Occupations of the Widimeier Site (40Dv9), Davidson County, Tennessee. *Current Research in the Pleistocene* 25:64–65.

Broster, John B., Mark R. Norton, D. Shane Miller, Jesse W. Tune, and Jonathan Baker

2013   Tennessee's Paleoindian Record: The Cumberland and Lower Tennessee River Watersheds. In *The Eastern Fluted Point Tradition*, edited by Joseph A. M. Gingerich, pp. 299–314. University of Utah Press, Salt Lake City.

Brown, Ian W.

1980   *Salt and the Eastern North American Indian: An Archaeological Study*. Lower Mississippi Survey Bulletin No. 6. Peabody Museum, Harvard University, Cambridge, Massachusetts.

1981   *The Role of Salt in Eastern North American Prehistory*. Anthropological Study No. 3. Department of Culture, Recreation, and Tourism, Louisiana Archaeological Survey and Antiquities Commission, Baton Rouge.

1989   Natchez Indians and the Remains of a Proud Past. In *Natchez before 1830*, edited by Noel Polk, pp. 8–28. University Press of Mississippi, Jackson.

1990   Historic Indians of the Lower Mississippi Valley: An Archaeologist's View. In *Towns and Temples along the Mississippi*, edited by David H. Dye and Cheryl Anne Cox, pp. 227–238. University of Alabama Press, Tuscaloosa.

2008   Culture Contact along the I-69 Corridor: Protohistoric and Historic Use of the Northern Yazoo Basin, Mississippi. In *Time's River: Archaeological Syntheses from the Lower Mississippi Valley*, edited by Janet Rafferty and Evan Peacock, pp. 357–394. University of Alabama Press, Tuscaloosa.

2010   The Archaeology of Salt Springs in the Eastern Woodlands of the United States. In *Salt Archaeology in China*, Vol. 2: *Comparative Studies*, edited by Shuicheng Li and Lothar von Falkenhausen, pp. 375–409. Science Press, Beijing.

2012   *Bottle Creek Reflections: The Personal Side of Archaeology in the Mobile-Tensas Delta*. Borgo Publishing, Tuscaloosa.

Brown, James A.

1989   The Beginnings of Pottery as an Economic Process. In *What's New? A Closer Look at the Process of Innovation*, edited by Sander E. van der Leeuw and Robin Torrence, pp. 203–224. Unwin Hyman, London.

1990 Archaeology Confronts History at the Natchez Temple. *Southeastern Archaeology* 9:1–9.

2006 Where's the Power in Mound Building? An Eastern Woodlands Perspective: Leadership and Polity in Mississippian Society. In *Leadership and Polity in Mississippian Society*, edited by Brian M. Butler and Paul D. Welch, pp. 197–213. Occasional Paper No. 33, Center for Archaeological Investigations, Southern Illinois University, Carbondale.

Brown, James A., and John E. Kelly

2015 Surplus Labor, Ceremonial Feasting, and Social Inequality at Cahokia: A Study in Process. In *Surplus: The Politics or Production and the Strategies of Everyday Life*, edited by Christopher T. Morehart and Kristin De Lucia, pp. 221–244. University Press of Colorado, Boulder.

Brown, Joseph Epes (editor)

1953 *The Sacred Pipe: Black Elk's Account of the Seven Rites of the Oglala Sioux.* University of Oklahoma Press, Norman.

Brubaker, Rogers, and Frederick Cooper

2000 Beyond "Identity." *Theory and Society* 29:1–47.

Brück, Joanna

2007 Ritual and Rationality: Some Problems of Interpretation in European Archaeology. In *The Archaeology of Identities: A Reader*, edited by Timothy Insoll, pp. 281–307. Routledge, New York.

Brumfiel, Elizabeth M.

1992 Breaking and Entering the Ecosystem—Gender, Class, and Faction Steal the Show. *American Anthropologist* 94:551–567.

Buikstra, Jane E., and Douglas K. Charles

1999 Centering the Ancestors: Cemeteries, Mounds, and Sacred Landscapes of the Ancient North American Midcontinent. In *Archaeologies of Landscape: Contemporary Perspectives*, edited by Wendy Ashmore and A. Bernard Knapp, pp. 201–228. Blackwell Publishers, Oxford.

Buikstra, Jane E., Douglas K. Charles, and Gordon F. M. Rakita

1998 *Staging Ritual: Hopewell Ceremonialism at the Mound House Site, Greene County, Illinois.* Kampsville Studies in Archeology and History 1. Center for American Archeology Press, Kampsville, Illinois.

Buikstra, Jane E., Lyle W. Konigsberg, and Jill Bullington

1986 Fertility and the Development of Agriculture in the Prehistoric Midwest. *American Antiquity* 51:528–546.

Bullen, Ripley P.

1955 Stratigraphic Tests at Bluffton, Volusia County Florida. *Florida Anthropologist* 8(1):1–16.

1972 The Orange Period of Peninsular Florida. In *Fiber-Tempered Pottery in Southeastern United States and Northern Columbia: Its Origins, Context, and Significance*, edited by Ripley P. Bullen and James B. Stoltman, pp. 9–33. Florida Anthropological Society Publications, No. 6. Florida Anthropological Society, Gainesville.

Bulygo, Zach

2013 How Netflix Uses Analytics to Select Movies, Create Content, and Make Multimillion Dollar Decisions. https://blog.kissmetrics.com/how-netflix-uses-analytics/.

Butler, Brian M., and Charles R. Cobb

2002 The Vacant Quarter Revisited: Late Mississippian Abandonment of the Lower Ohio Valley. *American Antiquity* 67(4):325–641.

Byers, A. Martin

2006   *Cahokia: A World Renewal Cult Heterarchy.* University Press of Florida, Gainesville.

Cambron, James W., and David C. Hulse

1960   The Transitional Paleo-Indian in North Alabama and South Tennessee. *Journal of Alabama Archaeology* 6(1):7–23.

Card, Jeb (editor)

2013   *The Archaeology of Hybrid Material Culture.* Carbondale, Center for Archaeological Investigations Occasional Paper No. 39, Southern Illinois University, Carbondale.

Carmody, Stephen

2009   Hunter/Gatherer Foraging Adaptations during the Middle Archaic Period at Dust Cave, Alabama. Unpublished master's thesis, Department of Anthropology, University of Tennessee, Knoxville, Tennessee.

2014   From Foraging to Food Production on the Southern Cumberland Plateau of Alabama and Tennessee, U.S.A. Unpublished Ph.D. dissertation, Department of Anthropology, University of Tennessee, Knoxville.

Carr, Philip J.

1994a   The Organization of Technology: Impact and Potential. In *The Organization of North American Prehistoric Chipped Stone Tool Technologies,* edited by Philip J. Carr, pp. 1–8. Archaeological Series No. 7. International Monographs in Prehistory, Ann Arbor, Michigan.

1994b   Technological Organization and Prehistoric Hunter-Gatherer Mobility: Examination of the Hayes Site. In *The Organization of North American Prehistoric Chipped Stone Tool Technologies,* edited by Philip J. Carr, pp. 35–44. Archaeological Series No. 7. International Monographs in Prehistory, Ann Arbor, Michigan.

Carr, Philip J., and Andrew P. Bradbury

2011   Learning from Lithics: A Perspective on the Foundation and Future of the Organization of Technology. Special Issue: Reduction Sequence, Chaîne Opératoire, and Other Methods: The Epistemologies of Different Approaches to Lithic Analysis, edited by Gilbert B. Tostevin. *PaleoAnthropology* 2011:305–319.

2013   Evaluating Descriptions of Clovis Migration and Lifeways by Applying an Organization of Technology Model. Under review.

Carr, Philip J., Andrew P. Bradbury, and Sarah E. Price

2012   Introduction. In *Contemporary Lithic Analysis in the Southeast: Problems, Solutions, and Interpretations,* edited by Philip J. Carr, Andrew P. Bradbury, and Sarah E. Price, pp. 1–12. University of Alabama Press.

Cattell, Maria G., and Jacob J. Climo

2002   Meaning in Social Memory and History: Anthropological Perspectives. In *Social Memory and History,* edited by Jacob J. Climo and Maria G. Cattell, pp. 1–36. AltaMira Press, Washington, D.C.

Chapman, Jefferson

1973   *The Icehouse Bottom Site (40MR23).* Report of Investigations 13. Department of Anthropology, University of Tennessee, Knoxville.

1975   *The Rose Island Site and the Bifurcate Point Tradition.* Report of Investigations 14. Department of Anthropology, University of Tennessee, Knoxville.

1977   *Archaic Period Research in the Lower Little Tennessee River Valley, 1975: Icehouse Bot-*

> tom, Harrison Branch, Thirty Acre Island, Calloway Island. Report of Investigations 18. Department of Anthropology, University of Tennessee, Knoxville.

1978　*The Bacon Farm Site and a Buried Site Reconnaissance.* Report of Investigations 23. Department of Anthropology, University of Tennessee, Knoxville.

1985　The Archaeology and the Archaic Period in the Southern Ridge and Valley Province. In *Structure and Process in Southeastern Archaeology*, edited by Roy S. Dickens Jr. and H. Trawick Ward, pp. 137–153. University of Alabama Press, Tuscaloosa.

Chapman, Jefferson, and Andrea Shea

1981　The Archaeobotanical Record: Early Archaic to Contact in the Lower Little Tennessee River Valley. *Tennessee Anthropologist* 6:61–84.

Charles, Douglas K., and Jane E. Buikstra

2002　Siting, Sighting, and Citing the Dead. *Archaeological Papers of the American Anthropological Association* 11:13–25.

Chittenden, Dave, Graham Farmelo, and Bruce Lewenstein (eds.)

2004　*Creating Connections: Museums and the Public Understanding of Current Research.* AltaMira Press, Walnut Creek, California.

Christophersen, Axel

2015　Performing Towns. Steps towards an Understanding of Medieval Urban Communities as Social Practice. *Archaeological Dialogues* 22(2):109–132.

Claassen, Cheryl

2008　Shell Symbolism in Pre-Columbian North America. In *Early Human Impact on Megamolluscs*, edited by Andrzej Antczak and Roberto Cipriani, pp. 231–236. BAR International Series 1865. Archaeopress, Oxford.

Clark, John E.

1995　Craft Specialization as an Archaeological Category. *Research in Economic Anthropology* 16:267–294.

2007　In Craft Specialization's Penumbra: Things, Persons, Action, Value, and Surplus. *Archaeological Papers of the American Anthropological Association* 17(1):20–35.

Clark, John E., and William J. Parry

1990　Craft Specialization and Cultural Complexity. *Research in Economic Anthropology* 12:289–346.

Clarkson, Chris

2002　An Index of Invasiveness for the Measurement of Unifacial and Bifacial Retouch: A Theoretical, Experimental, and Archaeological Verification. *Journal of Archaeological Science* 29:65–75.

Clayton, Victoria

2015　The Needless Complexity of Academic Writing. *Atlantic* October 26, 2015: http://www.theatlantic.com/education/archive/2015/10/complex-academic-writing/412255/.

Cobb, Charles R.

1996　Specialization, Exchange, and Power in Small-Scale Societies and Chiefdoms. *Research in Economic Anthropology* 18:251–294.

2000　*From Quarry to Cornfield: The Political Economy of Mississippian Hoe Production.* University of Alabama Press, Tuscaloosa.

2003　Mississippian Chiefdoms: How Complex? *Annual Review of Anthropology* 32:63–84.

2005　Archaeology and the "Savage Slot": Displacement and Emplacement in the Premodern World. *American Anthropologist* 107:563–574.

2014 What I Believe: A Memoir of Processualism to Neohistorical Archaeology. *Southeastern Archaeology* 33(2):214–225.

Cobb, Charles R., and Brian M. Butler

2016 Mississippian Plazas, Performances, and Portable Histories. *Journal of Archaeological Method and Theory*, March 8, 2016. https://link.springer.com/article/10.1007/s10816-016-9281-3.

Cobb, Charles R., and Adam King

2005 Re-Inventing Mississippian Tradition at Etowah, Georgia. *Journal of Archaeological Method and Theory* 12:167–192.

Cobb, Charles R., and Michael S. Nassaney

2002 Domesticating Self and Society in the Woodland Southeast. In *The Woodland Southeast*, edited by David G. Anderson and Robert C. Mainfort Jr., pp. 525–539. University of Alabama Press, Tuscaloosa.

Collins, James M., and Michael L. Chalfant

1993 A Second-Terrace Perspective on Monks Mound. *American Antiquity* 58:319–332.

Collins, Michael B.

1975 Lithic Technology as a Means of Processual Inference. In *Lithic Technology: Making and Using Stone Tools*, edited by Earl H. Swanson, pp. 15–34. Aldine, Chicago.

Confucius

2015 Analects 2.11. http://www.azquotes.com/quote/434394.

Conkey, Margaret W.

2007 Questioning Theory: Is There a Gender of Theory in Archaeology? *Journal of Archaeological Method and Theory* 14(3):285–310.

Conklin, Beth A.

2001 *Consuming Grief: Compassionate Cannibalism in an Amazonian Society*. University of Texas Press, Austin.

Conley, Robert

1992 *Mountain Windsong: A Novel of the Trail of Tears*. University of Oklahoma Press, Norman.

Connah, Graham

1996 *Kibiro: The Salt of Bunyoro, Past and Present*. British Institute in Eastern Africa Memoir 13. British Institute in Eastern Africa, London.

Conneller, Chantal

2004 Becoming Deer: Corporeal Transformations at Star Carr. *Archaeological Dialogues* 11(1):37–56.

Cordell, Linda S.

2000 Aftermath of Chaos in the Pueblo Southwest. In *Environmental Disaster and the Archaeology of Human Response*, edited by Garth Bawden and Richard Martin Reycraft, pp. 179–193. Anthropological Papers 7. Maxwell Museum of Anthropology, Albuquerque, New Mexico.

Costin, Cathy L.

1991 Craft Specialization: Issues in Defining, Documenting, and Explaining the Organization of Production. In *Archaeological Method and Theory*, Vol. 3, edited by Michael B. Schiffer, pp. 1–56. University of Arizona Press, Tucson.

1998 Introduction: Craft and Social Identity. In *Craft and Social Identity*, edited by Cathy

L. Costin and Rita P. Wright, pp. 3–16. Archaeological Papers, 8. American Anthropological Association, Arlington, Virginia.

2001   Craft Production Systems. In *Archaeology at the Millennium: A Sourcebook*, edited by Gary M. Feinman and T. Douglas Price, pp. 273–327. Kluwer Academic/Plenum Press, New York.

Crockford, Susan J.

1997   *Osteometry of Makah and Coast Salish Dogs*. Archaeology Press, Simon Fraser University, Burnaby, British Columbia.

Crothers, George M.

1999   Prehistoric Hunters and Gatherers, and the Archaic Period Green River Shell Middens of Western Kentucky. Unpublished PhD dissertation, Department of Anthropology, Washington University, St. Louis, Missouri.

2004   The Green River in Comparison to the Lower Mississippi Valley during the Archaic: To Build Mounds or Not to Build Mounds. In *Signs of Power: The Rise of Complexity in the Southeast*, edited by Jon L. Gibson and Philip J. Carr, pp. 86–96. University of Alabama Press, Tuscaloosa, Alabama.

2005   Vertebrate Fauna from the Carlston Annis Site. In *Archaeology of the Middle Green River Region, Kentucky*, edited by W. H. Marquardt and Patty Jo Watson, pp. 295–314. Florida Museum of Natural History Institute of Archaeology and Paleoenvironmental Studies Monograph No. 5. University of Florida, Gainesville.

Crumley, Carole L.

2002   Exploring Venues of Social Memory. In *Social Memory and History*, edited by Jacob J. Climo and Maria G. Cattell, pp. 39–52. AltaMira Press, Washington, D.C.

Currier, R.

1966   The Hot-Cold Syndrome and Symbolic Balance in Mexican and Spanish-American Folk Medicine. *Ethnology* 5:251–263.

Dalan, Rinita A.

1997   The Construction of Mississippian Cahokia. In *Cahokia: Domination and Ideology in the Mississippian World*, edited by Timothy R. Pauketat and Thomas E. Emerson, pp. 89–102. University of Nebraska Press, Lincoln.

Dalan, Rinita A., George R. Holley, William I. Woods, and John. A. Koepke

2003   *Envisioning Cahokia: A Landscape Perspective*. Northern Illinois University Press, DeKalb.

Da Matta, Roberto

1984   Carnival in Multiple Planes. In *Rite, Drama, Festival, Spectacle: Rehearsals toward a Theory of Cultural Performance*, edited by John J. MacAloon, pp. 208–240. Institute for the Study of Human Issues, Philadelphia.

Daniel, I. Randolph

1998   *Hardaway Revisited: Early Archaic Settlement in the Southeast*. University of Alabama Press, Tuscaloosa.

2001   Stone Raw Material Availability and Early Archaic Settlement in the Southeastern United States. *American Antiquity* 66(2):237–266.

Darwent, Crystyann M., and J. Eric Gilliland

2001   Osteological Analysis of Domestic Dogs from Burials in Southern Missouri. *Missouri Archaeologist* 62:149–169.

Davis, Jera R., Chester A. Walker, and John H. Blitz
2015   Remote Sensing as Community Settlement Analysis at Moundville. *American Antiquity* 80:161–169.

Davis, R. P. Stephen, Jr.
2002   The Cultural Landscape of the North Carolina Piedmont at Contact. In *The Transformation of the Southeastern Indians, 1540–1760*, edited by Robbie Ethridge and Charles Hudson, pp. 135–154. University Press of Mississippi, Jackson.

DeBoer, Warren R.
1993   Like a Rolling Stone: The Chunkey Game and Political Organization in Eastern North America. *Southeastern Archaeology* 12(2):83–92.

Deetz, James
1977   *In Small Things Forgotten: The Archaeology of Early American Life*. Anchor Press/Doubleday, New York.

DeMarrais, Elizabeth
2014   Introduction: The Archaeology of Performance. *World Archaeology* 46:155–163.

Denton, Derek
1982   *The Hunger for Salt: An Anthropological, Physiological, and Medical Analysis*. Springer-Verlag, New York.

DePratter, Chester B.
1994   The Chiefdom of Cofitachequi. In *The Forgotten Centuries: Indians and Europeans in the American South, 1521–1704*, edited by Charles Hudson and Carmen Chaves Tesser, pp. 197–226. University of Georgia Press, Athens.

Dethier, Vincent G.
1977   The Taste of Salt. *American Scientist* 65(6):744–751.

Dibble, Harold L.
1995   Middle Paleolithic Scraper Reduction: Background, Clarification, and Review of the Evidence to Date. *Journal of Archaeological Method and Theory* 2(4):299–368.

Dickens, Roy S., Jr.
1976   *Cherokee Prehistory: The Pisgah Phase in the Appalachian Summit Region*. University of Tennessee Press, Knoxville.

1978   Mississippian Settlement Patterns in the Appalachian Summit Area: The Pisgah and Qualla Phases. In *Mississippian Settlement Patterns*, edited by Bruce D. Smith, pp. 115–139. Academic Press, New York.

1979   The Origins and Development of Cherokee Culture. In *The Cherokee Indian Nation: A Troubled History*, edited by Duane H. King, pp. 3–32. University of Tennessee Press, Knoxville.

Dietler, Michael
2001   Theorizing the Feast: Rituals of Consumption, Commensal Politics, and Power in African Contexts. In *Feasts: Archaeological and Ethnographic Perspectives on Food, Politics, and Power*, edited by Michael Dieter and Brian Hayden, pp. 65–114. Smithsonian Institution Press, Washington, D.C.

Dobres, Marcia-Anne, and John E. Hoffman
1994   Social Agency and the Dynamics of Prehistoric Technology. *Journal of Archaeological Method and Theory* 1(3):211–258.

Dobres, Marcia-Anne, and John Robb
2005   "Doing" Agency: Introductory Remarks on Methodology. *Journal of Archaeological Method and Theory* 12:159–166.
Doran, Glen
2002   *Windover: Multidisciplinary Investigations of an Early Archaic Florida Cemetery.* Florida Museum of Natural History: Ripley P. Bullen Series. University Press of Florida, Gainesville.
Downs, James F.
1966   *The Two Worlds of the Washo: An Indian Tribe of California and Nevada. Case Studies in Cultural Anthropology Series.* Holt, Rinehart & Winston, New York.
Dumas, Ashley A.
2007   The Role of Salt in the Late Woodland to Early Mississippian Transition in Southwest Alabama. Unpublished Ph.D. dissertation. Department of Anthropology, University of Alabama, Tuscaloosa.
Duncan, Barbara R., and Brett H. Riggs
2003   *Cherokee Heritage Trails Guidebook.* University of North Carolina Press, Chapel Hill.
Dunnell, Robert C.
1980   Evolutionary Theory and Archaeology. *Advances in Archaeological Method and Theory* 3:35–99.
1990   The Role of the Southeast in American Archaeology. *Southeastern Archaeology* 9:11–22.
1992   Archaeology and Evolutionary Science. In *Quandaries and Quests: Visions of Archaeology's Future*, edited by LuAnn Wandsnider, pp. 209–224. Center for Archaeological Investigations, Occasional Paper No. 20. Southern Illinois University, Carbondale.
1995   What Is It That Actually Evolves? In *Evolutionary Archaeology: Methodological Issues*, edited by Patrice A. Teltser, pp. 33–50. University Press of Arizona, Tucson.
Dye, David H.
1990   Warfare in the Sixteenth-Century Southeast: The de Soto Expedition in the Interior. In *Columbian Consequences, Volume 2: Archaeological and Historical Perspectives on the Spanish Borderlands East*, edited by David Hurst Thomas, pp. 211–222. Smithsonian Institution Press, Washington, D.C.
2002   Warfare in the Protohistoric Southeast, 1500–1700. In *Between Contacts and Colonies: Archaeological Perspectives on the Protohistoric Southeast*, edited by Cameron B. Wesson and Mark A. Rees, pp. 126–141. University of Alabama Press, Tuscaloosa.
2004   Art, Ritual, and Chiefly Warfare in the Mississippian World. In *Hero, Hawk, and Open Hand: Ancient Indian Art of the Midwest and South*, edited by Richard F. Townsend, pp. 191–205. Yale University Press, New Haven, Connecticut.
2009   *War Paths, Peace Paths: An Archaeology of Cooperation and Conflict in Native Eastern North America.* AltaMira Press, Walnut Creek, California.
Dyson, John P.
2006   "Salt-Grass" of the Inland Southeast. Paper presented at the 63rd Annual Meeting of the Southeastern Archaeological Conference, Little Rock, Arkansas.
Eckert, Allan
1995   *That Dark and Bloody River: Chronicles of the Ohio River Valley.* Bantam Books, New York.

Eliade, Mircea
1964   *Shamanism: Archaic Techniques of Ecstasy.* Translated by Willard R. Trask. Princeton University Press, Princeton, New Jersey.

Elliott, Daniel T., and Kenneth E. Sassaman
1995   Archaic Period Archaeology of the Georgia Coastal Plain and Coastal Zone. University of Georgia Laboratory of Archaeology Series Report No. 35, Georgia Archaeological Research Design Paper No. 11. University of Georgia, Athens.

Elston, Robert G., and David W. Zeanah
2002   Thinking outside the Box: A New Perspective on Diet Breadth and Sexual Division of Labor in the Prearchaic Great Basin. *World Archaeology* 34(1):103–130.

Emerson, Thomas E., Dale L. McElrath, and Andrew C. Fortier (editors)
2000   *Late Woodland Societies: Tradition and Transformation across the Midcontinent.* University of Nebraska Press, Lincoln.

Emerson, Thomas E., John A. Walthall, Andrew C. Fortier, and Dale L. McElrath
2006   Advances in American Bottom Prehistory: Illinois Transportation Archaeology Two Decades after I-270. *Southeastern Archaeology* 25(2)155–159.

Endonino, Jon C.
2008   The Thornhill Lake Archaeological Research Project: 2005–2008. *Florida Anthropologist* 61(3–4):149–165.
2010   Thornhill Lake: Hunter-Gatherers, Monuments, and Memory. Unpublished PhD dissertation, Department of Anthropology, University of Florida, Gainesville.
2013   Examining Orange Period Vessel Forming Methods through Experiment and Radiography: Implications for Chronology, Technology, and Function. *Florida Anthropologist* 66:5–21.

Eren, Metin I., Briggs Buchanan, and Michael J. O'Brien
2015   Social Learning and Technological Evolution during the Clovis Colonization of the New World. *Journal of Human Evolution* 80:159–170.

Eren, Metin I., Manuel Dominguez-Rodrigo, Steven L. Kuhn, Daniel S. Adler, Ian Le, Ofer Bar-Yosef
2015   Defining and Measuring Reduction in Unifacial Stone Tools. *Journal of Archaeological Science* 32:1190–1201.

Eren, Metin I., and Mary E. Prendergast
2008   Comparing and Synthesizing Lithic Reduction Indices. In *Lithic Technology: Measures of Production, Use, and Curation*, edited by William Andrefsky Jr., pp. 49–85. University of Cambridge Press, Cambridge.

Erickson, Clark L.
2001   Pre-Columbian Fish Farming in the Amazon. *Expedition* 43(3):7–8.

Eskew, Garnett L.
1948   *Salt: The Fifth Element.* J. G. Ferguson and Associates, Chicago.

Ethridge, Robbie F.
2003   *Creek Country: The Creek Indians and Their World.* University of North Carolina Press, Chapel Hill.
2006   Creating the Shatter Zone: Indian Slave Traders and the Collapse of the Southeastern Chiefdoms. In *Light on the Path: The Anthropology and History of Southeastern Indians*, edited by Robbie Ethridge and Thomas J. Pluckhahn, pp. 207–218. University of Alabama Press, Tuscaloosa.

2010   *From Chicaza to Chickasaw: The European Invasion and the Transformation of the Mississippian World, 1540–1715.* University of North Carolina Press, Chapel Hill.

Eubanks, Paul N.

2015   A Reconstruction of the Caddo Salt Making Process at Drake's Salt Works. *Caddo Archaeology Journal* 25:145–166.

2016   Salt Production in the Southeastern Caddo Homeland. Unpublished Ph.D. dissertation. Department of Anthropology, University of Alabama, Tuscaloosa.

Ewen, Charles R.

1990   Soldier of Fortune: Hernando de Soto in the Territory of the Apalachee, 1539–1540. In *Columbian Consequences, Volume 2: Archaeological and Historical Perspectives on the Spanish Borderlands East,* edited by David Hurst Thomas, pp. 83–91. Smithsonian Institution Press, Washington, D.C.

1996   Continuity and Change: De Soto and the Apalachee. *Historical Archaeology* 30(2):41–53.

Fenner, Jack N.

2005   Cross-Cultural Estimation of the Human Generation Interval for Use in Genetics-Based Population Divergence Studies. *American Journal of Physical Anthropology* 128:415–423.

Fiedel, Stuart J.

2015   The Clovis-Era Radiocarbon Plateau. In *Clovis: On the Edge of a New Understanding,* edited by Ashley M. Smallwood and Thomas A. Jennings, pp. 11–20. Texas A&M University Press, College Station.

Finger, John

1984   *The Eastern Band of Cherokees, 1819–1900.* University of Tennessee Press, Knoxville.

Flad, Rowan

2004   Specialized Salt Production and Changing Social Structure at the Prehistoric Site of Zhongba in the Eastern Sichuan Basin, China. Unpublished Ph.D. dissertation, Department of Anthropology, University of California, Los Angeles.

Flad, Rowan K., and Zachary X. Hruby

2007   *Rethinking Craft Specialization in Complex Societies: Archaeological Analysis of the Social Meaning of Production.* Archaeological Papers of the American Anthropological Association, 17. American Anthropological Association, Arlington, Virginia.

Flenniken, J. Jeffery

1985   Stone Tool Reduction Techniques as Cultural Markers. In *Stone Tool Analysis: Essays in Honor of Don. E. Crabtree,* edited by Mark G. Plew, James C. Woods, and Max G. Pavesic, pp. 265–276. University of New Mexico Press, Albuquerque.

Flenniken, J. Jeffery, and Anan W. Raymond

1986   Morphological Projectile Point Typology: Replication, Experimentation, and Technological Analysis. *American Antiquity* 51:603–614.

Flores, Martha Monzón

2015   Huixtocihuatl: The Goddess of Salt. Paper presented at the First International Congress on the Anthropology of Salt, Iasi, Romania.

Fogelin, Lars

2007   Inference to the Best Explanation: A Common and Effective Form of Archaeological Reasoning. *American Antiquity* 72(4):603–625.

Fogelson, Raymond D.

1989   The Ethnohistory of Events and Nonevents. *Ethnohistory* 36:133–147.

Fogelson, Raymond D., and Paul Kutsche
1961   Cherokee Economic Cooperatives: The Gadugi. In *Symposium on Cherokee and Iroquois Culture*, edited by William N. Fenton and John Gulick, pp. 83–123. Smithsonian Institution Bureau of American Ethnology, Bulletin 180. U.S. Government Printing Office, Washington D.C.

Ford, James A.
1951   *Greenhouse: A Troyville-Coles Creek Period Site in Avoyelles Parish, Louisiana*. Anthropological Papers 11(1). American Museum of Natural History, New York.

Franklin, Jay D, Maureen A. Hays, Sarah C. Sherwood, and Lucinda M. Langston
2012   An Integrated Approach: Lithic Analysis and Site Function, Eagle Drink Bluff Shelter, Upper Cumberland Plateau, Tennessee. In *Contemporary Lithic Analysis in the Southeast: Problems, Solutions, and Interpretations*, edited by Philip J. Carr, Andrew P. Bradbury, and Sarah E. Price, pp. 128–145. University of Alabama Press, Tuscaloosa.

French, Laurence, Jim Hornbuckle, Karen French Owl, Herbert Wachacha, Yvonne Wachacha, Richard Crowe, Amy Walker, Reuben Teesatuskie, Elsie Martin, and Patricia Panther
1981   Cherokee Perspective: Written by Eastern Cherokees. Appalachian Consortium Press, Boone North Carolina. http://ehrafworldcultures.yale.edu/document?id=nn08-031.

Frison, George C.
1968   Functional Analysis of Chipped Stone Tools. *American Antiquity* 33(2):149–155.
1974   *The Casper Site: A Hell Gap Bison Kill on the High Plains*. Studies in Archeology. Academic Press, New York.

Fritz, Gayle J.
2000   Native Farming Systems and Ecosystems in the Mississippi River Valley. In *Imperfect Balance: Landscape Transformations in the Precolumbian Americas*, edited by David L. Lentz, pp. 225–250. Columbia University Press, New York.
2001   Ethnobotany of Ku-Nu-Che: Cherokee Hickory Nut Soup. *Journal of Ethnobiology* 21(2):1–27.

Fritz, Gayle J., and Tristram R. Kidder
1993   Recent Investigations into Prehistoric Agriculture in the Lower Mississippi Valley. *Southeastern Archaeology* 12(1):1–14.

Fuller, Richard S., and Diane S. Fuller
1987   *Excavations at Morgan: A Coles Creek Period Mound Complex in Coastal Louisiana*. Lower Mississippi Survey Bulletin 11. Peabody Museum of Archaeology and Ethnology, Harvard University, Cambridge, Massachusetts.

Galaty, Michael L
1996   Labor, Population, and Social Complexity. *Chicago Anthropology Exchange* 32:33–49.

Galloway, Patricia
1994   Confederacy as a Solution to Chiefdom Dissolution: Historical Evidence in the Choctaw Case. In *The Forgotten Centuries: Indians and Europeans in the American South, 1521–1704*, edited by Charles Hudson and Carmen Chaves Tesser, pp. 393–420. University of Georgia Press, Athens.
1995   *Choctaw Genesis, 1500–1700*. University of Nebraska Press, Lincoln.
1998   Where Have All the Menstrual Huts Gone? The Invisibility of Menstrual Seclusion in the Late Prehistoric Southeast. In *Reader in Gender Archaeology*, edited by Kelley Hays-Gilpin and David S. Whitley, pp. 197–211. Routledge, London.
2002   Colonial Period Transformations in the Mississippi Valley: Disintegration, Alliance,

Confederation, Payoff. In *The Transformation of the Southeastern Indians, 1540–1760*, edited by Robbie Ethridge and Charles Hudson, pp. 225–247. University Press of Mississippi, Jackson.

Gardner, Paul S.
1997   The Ecological Structure and Behavioral Implications of Mast Exploration Strategies. In *People, Plants and Landscapes: Studies in Paleoethnobotany*, edited by Kristen J. Gremillion, pp. 161–178. University of Alabama Press, Tuscaloosa.

Gattiglia, Gabriele
2015   Think Big about Data: Archaeology and the Big Data Challenge. Archäologische Informationen 38:1–12.

Gibson, Jon L.
1986   Earth Sitting: Architectural Masses at Poverty Point, Northeastern Louisiana. *Louisiana Archaeology* 13:201–237.

Gibson, Jon L., and Philip J. Carr
2004   Big Mounds, Big Rings, Big Power. In *Signs of Power: The Rise of Cultural Complexity in the Southeast*, edited by Jon L. Gibson and Philip J. Carr, pp. 1–9. University of Alabama Press, Tuscaloosa.

Gifford-Gonzales, Diane
1993   You Can Hide, But You Can't Run: Representation of Women's Work in Illustration of Paleolithic Life. *Visual Anthropology Review* 9:3–21.

Gilbert, William Harlen
1978   "Eastern Cherokees." *Bulletin: Anthropological Papers*: 171–314. New York: AMS Press. http://ehrafworldcultures.yale.edu/document?id=nn08-023.

Gillam, J. Christopher
2015   The Early Archaic Cultural Landscape of the Coastal Plain. *South Carolina Antiquities* 47(1–2):3–12.

Gilmore, Zackary I.
2011   Locus B. In *St. Johns Archaeological Field School 2007–2010: Silver Glen Run*, edited by Kenneth E. Sassaman, Zackary I. Gilmore and Asa R. Randall. Technical Report 12, Laboratory of Southeastern Archaeology, Department of Anthropology, University of Florida, Gainesville. http://lsa.anthro.ufl.edu/publications/LSATechReport12.pdf.
2016   *Gathering at Silver Glen: Community and History in Late Archaic Florida*. University Press of Florida, Gainesville. Girard, Jeffrey S.

Girard, Jeffrey S.
2000   Excavations at the Fredericks Site (16NA2), Natchitoches Parish, Louisiana. *Louisiana Archaeology* 24:1–106.

Gladwell, Malcolm
2000   *The Tipping Point: How Little Things Can Make a Big Difference*. Little Brown, New York.

Gleick, James
1987   *Chaos: Making a New Science*. Penguin Books, New York.

Glore, Michael T.
2005   Vertebrate Faunal Remains from the Carlston Annis Site (15Bt5): An Evaluation of Cultural Stratigraphy. In *Archaeology of the Middle Green River Region, Kentucky*, edited by William H. Marquardt and Patty Jo Watson, pp. 315–337. Florida Museum

of Natural History Institute of Archaeology and Paleoenvironmental Studies Monograph No. 5. University of Florida, Gainesville.

Goad, Sharon

1978   *Exchange Networks in the Prehistoric Southeastern United States.* Ph.D. dissertation, University of Georgia, Athens. University Microfilms, Ann Arbor.

1979   Middle Woodland Exchange in the Prehistoric Southeastern United States. In *Hopewell Archaeology: The Chillicothe Conference,* edited by David S. Brose and N'omi B. Greber, pp. 239–246. Kent State University Press, Kent, Ohio.

Goldstein, David J., and Izumi Shimada

2010   Feeding the Fire: Food and Craft Production in the Middle Sicán Period (AD 950–1050). In *Inside the Kitchen: New Directions in the Study of Daily Meals and Feasts,* edited by Elizabeth A. Klarich, pp. 161–190. University Press of Colorado, Boulder.

Goodwin, Gary C.

1977   *Cherokees in Transition: A Study of Changing Culture and Environment Prior to 1775.* Research Paper 181, Department of Geography. University of Chicago, Chicago.

Goodyear, Albert C.

1974   *The Brand Site: A Techno-Functional Study of a Dalton Site in Northeast Arkansas.* Research Series No. 7. Arkansas Archeological Survey, Fayetteville.

1999   The Early Holocene Occupation of the Southeastern United States: A Geoarchaeological Summary. In *Ice Age People of North America,* edited by Robson Bonnichsen and Karen L. Turnmire, pp. 432–481. Oregon State University Press, Corvallis.

Gorey, Megan

2013   *15th Anniversary of Deadly Flash Flood in Carter County.* http://www.wcyb.com/news/15th-anniversary-of-deadly-flash-flood-in-Carter-County/18040970.

Gosden, Chris, and Yvonne Marshall

1999   The Cultural Biography of Objects. *World Archaeology* 31:169–178.

Gouletquer, Pierre, and Olivier Weller

2015   Techniques of Salt Making: From China (Yangtze River) to Their World Context. In *Archaeology of Salt: Approaching an Invisible Past,* edited by Robin Brigand and Olivier Weller, pp. 13–27. Sidestone Press, Leiden.

Gramly, Richard M.

1982   *The Vail Site: A Paleoindian Encampment in Maine.* Buffalo Society of Natural Sciences, Buffalo, New York.

Gray, Ernest

1945   Notes on the Salt-Making Industry of the Nyanja People near Lake Shirwa. *South African Journal of Science* 41:465–475.

Greene, Lance

2009   A Struggle for Cherokee Community: Excavating Identity in Post-Removal North Carolina. Unpublished PhD dissertation, Department of Anthropology, University of North Carolina, Chapel Hill.

Gremillion, Kristen J.

2002   The Development and Dispersal of Agricultural Systems in the Woodland Period Southeast. In *The Woodland Southeast,* edited by David G. Anderson and Robert C. Mainfort Jr., pp. 483–501. University of Alabama Press, Tuscaloosa.

Griffin, James B.

1945   The Significance of Fiber-Tempered Pottery of the St. Johns Area in Florida. *Journal of the Washington Academy of Sciences* 35(7):218–223.

Grimm, Eric C., William A. Watts Jr., George L. Jacobson, Barbara C. S. Hansen, Heather R. Almquist, and Ann C. Dieffenbacher-Krall

2006   Evidence for Warm Wet Heinrich Events in Florida. *Quaternary Science Reviews* 25 (17–18):2197–2211.

Grinnell, George Byrd

1940   The Salt Story of Laguna Pueblo, New Mexico. *Masterkey*: 80–81.

Guernsey, Samuel J., and Alfred V. Kidder

1921   *Basket-Maker Caves of Northeastern Arizona*. Papers of the Peabody Museum of American Archaeology and Ethnology, Harvard University, Cambridge, Massachusetts.

Haag, William G.

1948   An Osteometric Analysis of Some Aboriginal Dogs. *Reports in Anthropology* (University of Kentucky, Lexington) 7 (3):107–264.

Hahn, Hans Peter, and Hadas Weiss

2013   Introduction: Biographies, Travels and Itineraries of Things. In *Mobility, Meaning and the Transformations of Things: Shifting Contexts of Material Culture through Time and Space*, edited by Hans Peter Hahn and Hadas Weiss, pp. 1–14. Oxbow, Oxford.

Haley, Brian S., and Jay K. Johnson

2008   Geophysics at Feltus. Paper presented at the 65th annual meeting of the Southeastern Archaeological Conference, Charlotte, North Carolina.

Hall, Robert L.

1997   *An Archaeology of the Soul: North American Indian Belief and Ritual*. University of Illinois Press, Urbana.

Hally, David J.

1983   Use Alteration of Pottery Surfaces: An Important Source of Evidence for the Identification of Vessel Function. *North American Archaeologist* 4(1):3–26.

1994a   The Chiefdom of Coosa. In *The Forgotten Centuries: Indians and Europeans in the American South, 1521–1704*, edited by Charles Hudson and Carmen Chaves Tesser, pp. 227–253. University of Georgia Press, Athens.

1994b   An Overview of Lamar Culture. In *Ocmulgee Archaeology, 1936–1986*, edited by David J. Hally, pp. 144–174. University of Georgia Press, Athens.

1996   Platform-Mound Construction and the Instability of Mississippian Chiefdoms. In *Political Structure and Change in the Prehistoric Southeastern United States*, edited by John F. Scarry, pp. 92–127. University Press of Florida, Gainesville.

2006   The Nature of Mississippian Regional Systems. In *Light on the Path: The Anthropology and History of the Southeastern Indians*, edited by Thomas J. Pluckhahn and Robbie Ethridge, pp. 26–42. University of Alabama Press, Tuscaloosa.

2007   Mississippian Shell Gorgets in Regional Perspective. In *Southeastern Ceremonial Complex: Chronology, Content, Context*, edited by Adam King, pp. 185–231. University of Alabama Press, Tuscaloosa.

Hamel, Paul B., and Mary Ulmer Chiltoskey

1975   *Cherokee Plants and Their Uses: A 400 Year History*. Herald Pub. Co., Sylva, North Carolina. http://ehrafworldcultures.yale.edu/document?id=nn08-003.

Hamilton, Marcus J., and Briggs Buchanan

2007   Spatial Gradients in Clovis-Age Radiocarbon Dates across North America Suggest Rapid Colonization from the North. *Proceedings of the National Academy of Sciences* 104(40):15625–15630.

Hammerstedt, Scott W.

2005   Mississippian Construction, Labor, and Social Organization in Western Kentucky, Unpublished Ph.D. thesis, Department of Anthropology, Pennsylvania State University, State College, Pennsylvania.

Hann, John H.

1988   *Apalachee: The Land between the Rivers.* University Press of Florida, Gainesville.

1994   The Apalachee of the Historic Era. In *The Forgotten Centuries: Indians and Europeans in the American South, 1521–1704,* edited by Charles Hudson and Carmen Chaves Tesser, pp. 327–354. University of Georgia Press, Athens.

1996   *A History of the Timucua Indians and Missions.* University Press of Florida, Gainesville.

Hann, John H., and Bonnie G. McEwan

1998   *Apalachee Indians and Mission San Luis.* University Press of Florida, Gainesville.

Haraway, Donna

2008   *When Species Meet.* University of Minnesota Press, Minneapolis.

Hardin, Garret

1968   The Tragedy of the Commons. *Science* 162(3859):1243–1248.

Harding, Anthony

2013   *Salt in Prehistoric Europe.* Sidestone Press, Leiden.

Hare, Brian, Victoria Wobber, and Richard Wrangham

2012   The Self-Domestication Hypothesis: Evolution of Bonobo Psychology Is Due to Selection against Aggression. *Animal Behavior* 83:573–585.

Harrington, M. R.

1927   Prehistoric Salt Workings. *El Palacio* 23(3):48.

Harris, Marvin

1980   *Cultural Materialism: The Struggle for a Science of Culture.* Vintage Books, New York.

Hatley, M. Thomas

1989   The Three Lives of Keowee: Loss and Recovery in Eighteenth-Century Cherokee Villages. In *Powhatan's Mantle: Indians in the Colonial Southeast,* edited by Peter H. Wood, Gregory A. Waselkov, and M. Thomas Hatley, pp. 223–248. University of Nebraska Press, Lincoln.

1993   *The Dividing Paths: Cherokees and South Carolinians through the Era of Revolution.* Oxford University Press, Oxford.

Haury, Emil W., E. B. Sayles, and William W. Wasley

1959   The Lehner Mammoth Site, Southeastern Arizona. *American Antiquity* 25(1):2–32.

Hawkes, Kristen

1993   Why Hunter-Gatherers Work: An Ancient Version of the Problem of Public Goods. *Current Anthropology* 34(4):341–361.

1996   Foraging Difference between Men and Women: Behavioral Ecology of the Sexual Division of Labor. In *The Archaeology of Human Ancestry: Power, Sex and Tradition,* edited by James Steele and Stephen Shennan, pp. 283–305. Routledge, New York.

Hawkins, Benjamin

2003   *The Collected Works of Benjamin Hawkins, 1796–1810.* Edited and with an introduction by H. Thomas Foster II. University of Alabama Press, Tuscaloosa.

Heffernan, Margaret

2015   *Beyond Measure: The Big Impact of Small Changes.* Simon & Schuster, New York.

Hegmon, Michelle

2003   Setting Theoretical Egos Aside: Issues and Theory in North American Archaeology. *American Antiquity* 68(2):213–243.

Henry, Edward R., and Casey R. Barrier

2016   The Organization of Dissonance in Adena-Hopewell Societies of Eastern North America. *World Archaeology* 48(1):87–109.

Hesketh, Ian

2014   The Story of Big History. *History of the Present* 4(2):171–202.

Hill, J. D.

2001   Can We Recognise a Different European Past? A Contrastive Archaeology of Later Prehistoric Settlements in Southern England. In *Interpretive Archaeology: A Reader*, edited by J. Thomas, pp. 431–444. A & C Black, London.

Hill, Kashmir

2012   How Target Figured Out a Teen Girl Was Pregnant Before Her Father Did. *Forbes*, February 16, 2012. http://www.forbes.com/sites/kashmirhill/2012/02/16/how-target-figured-out-a-teen-girl-was-pregnant-before-her-father-did/.

Hill, Sarah H.

1997   *Weaving New Worlds: Southeastern Cherokee Women and Their Basketry.* University of North Carolina Press, Chapel Hill.

Hill, Willard W.

1940   *Navajo Salt Gathering. University of New Mexico Bulletin* 359:1–25.

Hirth, Kenneth G.

2006   Modeling Domestic Craft Production at Xochicalco. In *Obsidian Craft Production in Ancient Central Mexico*, edited by Kenneth G. Hirth, pp. 275–286. University of Utah Press, Salt Lake City.

2009   Craft Production, Household Diversification, and Domestic Economy in Prehispanic Mesoamerica. In *Housework: Craft Production and Domestic Economy in Ancient Mesoamerica*, edited by Kenneth G. Hirth, pp. 13–32. Archaeological Papers of the American Anthropological Association No. 19. American Anthropological Association, Washington, D.C.

Hodder, Ian

1985   Postprocessual Archaeology. *Advances in Archaeological Method and Theory* 8:1–26.

2006   The Spectacle of Daily Performance at Catalhoyuk. In *Archaeology of Performance: Theaters of Power, Community, and Politics*, edited by Takeshi Inomata and Lawrence S. Coben, pp. 81–102. AltaMira, Lanham, Maryland.

2011   Human-Thing Entanglement: Towards an Integrated Archaeological Perspective. *Journal of the Royal Anthropological Institute* 17:154–177.

Hoffman, C. Marshall

1985   Projectile Point Maintenance and Projectile Point Typology: Assessment with Factor and Canonical Correlation. In *For Concordance in Archaeological Analysis: Bridging*

Data Structure, Quantitative Technique, and Theory, edited by Christopher Carr, pp. 566–612. Westport Publishers, University of Arkansas, Fayetteville.

Hofman, Jack L., and James G. Enloe (editors)

1992 *Piecing Together the Past: Applications of Refitting Studies in Archaeology.* BAR International Series 578. Tempus Referatum, Oxford, United Kingdom.

Holland, John

1995 *Hidden Order: How Adaptation Builds Complexity.* Basic Books, New York.

Hollenbach, Kandace D.

2005 Gathering in the Late Paleoindian and Early Archaic Periods in the Middle Tennessee River Valley, Northwest Alabama. Ph.D. dissertation. Department of Anthropology, University of North Carolina, Chapel Hill. https://www.academia.edu/1188486/Gathering_in_the_Late_Paleoindian_and_Early_Archaic_Periods_in_the_Middle_Tennessee_River_Valley_Northwest_Alabama.

2007 Gathering in the Late Paleoindian Period: Archaeobotanical Remains from Dust Cave, Alabama. In *Foragers of the Terminal Pleistocene in North America*, edited by Boyce N. Driskell and Renee B. Walker, pp. 132–147. University of Nebraska Press, Lincoln.

2009 *Foraging in the Tennessee River Valley, 12,500 to 8,000 Years Ago.* University of Alabama Press, Tuscaloosa.

Holley, George R., Rinita A. Dalan, and Philip A. Smith

1993 Investigations in the Cahokia Site Grand Plaza. *American Antiquity* 58:306–319.

Holmes, William H.

1890 A Quarry Workshop of the Flaked Stone Implement Makers in the District of Columbia. *American Anthropologist* 3:1–26.

Holt, Julie Zimmermann

2009 Rethinking the Ramey State: Was Cahokia the Center of a Theater State? *American Antiquity* 74:231–254.

Hooley, Bruce A., and Sanek Terit

1972 Preparation of Salt among the Buang, New Guinea. *Man* (new series) 7(2):319–322.

Hornborg, Anne-Christine

2006 Visiting the Six Worlds: Shamanistic Journeys in Canadian Mi'kmaq Cosmology. *Journal of American Folklore* 119(473):312–336.

Horsley, Timothy, Alice Wright, and Casey Barrier

2014 Prospecting for New Questions: Integrating Geophysics to Define Anthropological Research Objectives and Inform Excavation Strategies at Monumental Sites. *Archaeological Prospection* 21:75–86.

Howey, Meghan C.L.

2012 *Mound Builders and Monument Makers of the Northern Great Lakes, 1200–1600.* University of Oklahoma Press, Norman.

Hudson, Charles M.

1979 *Black Drink: A Native American Tea.* University of Georgia Press, Athens.

1997 *Knights of Spain, Warriors of the Sun: Hernando de Soto and the South's Ancient Chiefdoms.* University of Georgia Press, Athens.

2003 *Conversations with the High Priest of Coosa.* University of North Carolina Press, Chapel Hill.

2005   *The Juan Pardo Expeditions: Exploration of the Carolinas and Tennessee, 1566–1568.* University of Alabama Press, Tuscaloosa.

2009   *The Packhorseman.* University of Alabama Press, Tuscaloosa.

2014   *The Cow-Hunter: A Novel.* University of South Carolina Press, Columbia.

Hunter, Helen Virginia

1940   The Ethnography of Salt in Aboriginal North America. Unpublished master's thesis, Department of Anthropology, University of Pennsylvania, Philadelphia.

Hutchinson, Dale L.

1990   Postcontact Biocultural Change: Mortuary Site Evidence. In *Columbian Consequences, Volume 2: Archaeological and Historical Perspectives on Spanish Borderlands East,* edited by David Hurst Thomas, pp. 61–70. Smithsonian Institution Press, Washington, D.C.

2006   *Tatham Mound and the Bioarchaeology of European Contact: Disease and Depopulation in Central Gulf Coast Florida.* University Press of Florida, Gainesville.

Hutchinson, Dale L., and Jeffrey M. Mitchem

2001   Correlates of Contact: Epidemic Disease in Archaeological Context. *Historical Archaeology* 35(2):58–72.

Ingold, Tim

1993   The Temporality of the Landscape. *World Archaeology* 25(2):152–174.

1996   Hunting and Gathering as Ways of Perceiving the Environment. In *Redefining Nature: Ecology, Culture, and Domestication,* edited by Roy Ellen and Katsuyoshi Fukui, pp. 117–155. Berg, Oxford.

2000   *The Perception of the Environment: Essays in Livelihood, Dwelling and Skill.* Routledge, London.

2006   Rethinking the Animate, Re-animating Thought. *Ethnos* 71(1):9–20.

2007   Materials against Materiality. *Archaeological Dialogues* 14(1):1–16.

2012   Toward an Ecology of Materials. *Annual Review of Anthropology* 41:427–442.

2013   *Making: Anthropology, Archaeology, Art and Architecture.* Routledge, London.

Inomata, Takeshi

2006   Plazas, Performers, and Spectators: Political Theaters of the Classic Maya. *Current Anthropology* 47:805–842.

Inomata, Takeshi, and Lawrence S. Coben

2006   Overture: An Invitation to the Archaeological Theater. In *Archaeology of Performance: Theaters of Power, Community, and Politics,* edited by Takeshi Inomata and Lawrence S. Coben, pp. 11–44. AltaMira, Lanham, Maryland.

Inomata, Takeshi, and Kenichiro Tsukamoto

2014   Gathering in an Open Space: Introduction to Mesoamerican Plazas. In *Mesoamerican Plazas: Arenas of Community and Power,* edited by Kenichiro Tsukamoto and Takeshi Inomata, pp. 3–15. University of Arizona Press, Tucson.

Intersalt Cooperative Research Group

1988   Intersalt: An International Study of Electrolyte Excretion and Blood Pressure, Results for 24 Hour Urinary Sodium and Potassium Excretion. *British Medical Journal* 297(6644):319–328.

Isaac, Barry L.

1990   Economy, Ecology, and Analogy: The !Kung San and the Generalized Foraging Model.

In *Early Paleoindian Economies of Eastern North America*, edited by Barry L. Isaac and Kenneth G. Tankersley, pp. 323–335. Research in Economic Anthropology Supplement 5. JAI Press, Greenwich, Connecticut.

Iseminger, William
2010   *Cahokia Mounds: America's First City*. The History Press, Charleston, South Carolina.

Jacobson, Harry, Bronson Strickland, Steve Demarans, and Chad Dacus
2011   Potential Impact of the 2011 Flood on Deer in the Mississippi Delta. *Delta Wildlife* Fall:20–23.

Jefferies, Richard W.
1982   Archaeological Overview of the Carrier Mills District. In *The Carrier Mills Archaeological Project: Human Adaptation in the Saline Valley, Illinois*, edited by Richard W. Jefferies and Brian M. Butler, pp. 1459–1509. Center for Archaeological Investigations Research Paper. Southern Illinois University at Carbondale, Carbondale, Illinois.

Jelinek, Arthur J.
1976   Form, Function, and Style in Lithic Analysis. In *Cultural Change and Continuity: Essays in Honor of James Bennett Griffin*, edited by Charles E. Cleland, pp. 19–33. Academic, New York.
1977   The Lower Paleolithic: Current Evidence and Interpretations. *Annual Review of Anthropology* 6:11–32.

Jeter, Marvin D.
1984   Mound Volumes, Energy Ratios, Exotic Materials, and Contingency Tables: Comments on Some Recent Analyses of Copena Burial Practices. *Midcontinental Journal of Archaeology* 9:91–104.

Johnson, Jay K.
2000   The Chickasaws. In *Indians of the Greater Southeast: Historical Archaeology and Ethnohistory*, edited by Bonnie G. McEwan, pp. 85–121. University Press of Florida, Gainesville.

Johnson, Jay K. (editor)
1993   *The Development of Southeastern Archaeology*. University of Alabama Press, Tuscaloosa.
2003   *The Development of Southeastern Archaeology*. University of Alabama Press, Tuscaloosa.

Johnson, Jay K., John W. O'Hear, Robbie Ethridge, Brad R. Lieb, Susan L. Scott, and H. Edwin Jackson
2008   Measuring Chickasaw Adaptation on the Western Frontier of the Colonial South: A Correlation of Documentary and Archaeological Data. *Southeastern Archaeology* 27:1–30.

Johnson, Marilyn
2014   *Lives in Ruins: Archaeologists and the Seductive Lure of Human Rubble*. Harper Collins Publishers, New York.

Jones, Charles C. Jr.
1999   *Antiquities of the Southern Indians, Particularly of the Georgia Tribes*. University of Alabama Press, Tuscaloosa. Originally published by D. Appleton and Company, New York, in 1873.

Jones, George T., Charlotte Beck, Eric E. Jones, and Richard E. Hughes
2003   Lithic Source Use and Paleoarchaic Foraging Territories in the Great Basin. *American Antiquity* 68:5–38.

Jones, George T., Lisa M. Fontes, Rachel A. Horowitz, Charlotte Beck, and David G. Bailey
2012   Reconsidering Paleoarchaic Mobility in the Central Great Basin. *American Antiquity* 77:351–367.

Jones, J. Scott, John B. Broster, and Mark R. Noron
2010   Paleoindian Lithic Raw Material Use in the Tennessee River Valley. *Current Research in the Pleistocene* 27:105–106.

Jordan, Peter
2001   The Materiality of Shamanism as a "World-View": Praxis, Artefacts and Landscape. In *The Archaeology of Shamanism*, edited by Neil Price, pp. 87–104. Routledge, London.
2003   Investigating Post-Glacial Hunter Gatherer Landscape Enculturation: Ethnographic Analogy and Interpretive Methodologies. In *Mesolithic on the Move: Papers Presented at the Sixth International Conference on the Mesolithic in Europe, Stockholm 2000*, edited by Lars Larsson, Hans Kindgren, Kjel Knutsson, David Loeffler, and Agneta Akerlund, pp. 128–138. Oxbow Books, Oxford.

Joyce, Rosemary
2004   Unintended Consequences? Monumentality as a Novel Experience in Formative Mesoamerica. *Journal of Archaeological Method and Theory* 11:5–29.
2008   *The Languages of Archaeology: Dialogue, Narrative, and Writing*. John Wiley & Sons, New York.

Joyce, Rosemary A., and Susan D. Gillespie
2015   Making Things Out of Objects That Move. In *Things in Motion: Object Itineraries in Anthropological Practice*, edited by Rosemary A. Joyce and Susan D. Gillespie, pp. 3–20. School for Advanced Research Press, Santa Fe.

Kapches, Mima
1995   Chaos Theory and Social Movements: A Theoretical View of the Formation of the Northern Iroquoian Longhouse Cultural Pattern. In *Origins of the People of the Longhouse*, edited by André Bekerman and Gary A. Warrick, pp. 86–96. Proceedings of the 21st Annual Symposium of the Ontario Archaeological Society, Toronto, 1994.

Kassabaum, Megan C.
2011   Looking beyond the Obvious: Identifying Patterns in Coles Creek Mortuary Data. *Southeastern Archaeology* 30(2):215–225.
2014   Feasting and Communal Ritual in the Lower Mississippi Valley, AD 700–1000. Unpublished Ph.D. dissertation, Department of Anthropology, University of North Carolina, Chapel Hill.
2015   "Monumental Grandeur of the Mississippi Valley": The Mounds of Native North America. *Expedition* 57(2):6–16.

Kassabaum, Megan C., Edward R. Henry, Vincas P. Steponaitis, and John W. O'Hear
2014   Between Surface and Summit: The Process of Mound Construction at Feltus. *Archaeological Prospection* 21(1):27–37.

Kassabaum, Megan C., and Erin S. Nelson
2016   Standing Posts and Special Substances: Gathering and Ritual Deposition at Feltus (22Je500), Jefferson County, Mississippi. *Southeastern Archaeology* 35(2):134–154.

Kauffman, Stuart A., and Sonke Johnsen
1991   Coevolution to the Edge of Chaos: Couple Fitness Landscapes, Poised States, and Coevolutionary Avalances. *Journal of Theoretical Biology* 149(4):467–505.

Kaynak, Erdener, Jung-Hee Lee, and John Dawson
2014   *International Retailing Plans and Strategies in Asia.* Routledge, New York.

Keegan, William
2007   *Taíno Indian Myth and Practice: The Arrival of the Stranger King.* University Press of Florida, Gainesville.

Keel, Bennie C.
1976   *Cherokee Archaeology: A Study of the Appalachian Summit.* University of Tennessee Press, Knoxville.

Keith, Scot J.
2010   Archaeological Data Recovery at the Leake Site, Bartow County, Georgia, Volume I, Final Report. Southern Research, Historic Preservation Consultants, Ellerslie, Georgia. Submitted to Georgia Department of Transportation, Office of Environmental Services, Atlanta.

Kellert, Stephen
1993   *In the Wake of Chaos.* University of Chicago Press, Chicago.

Kelly, John E.
1990a   Range Site Community Patterns and the Mississippian Emergence. In *The Mississippian Emergence*, edited by Bruce D. Smith, pp. 67–112. Smithsonian Institution Press, Washington, D.C.

1990b   The Emergence of Mississippian Culture in the American Bottom Region. In *The Mississippian Emergence*, edited by Bruce D. Smith, pp. 113–152. Smithsonian Institution Press, Washington, D.C.

1992   The Impact of Maize on the Development of Nucleated Settlements: An American Bottom Example. In *Late Prehistoric Agriculture: Observations from the Midwest*, edited by William I. Woods, pp. 167–197. Studies in Illinois Archaeology 8. Illinois Historic Preservation Agency, Springfield.

2000   The Nature and Context of Emergent Mississippian Cultural Dynamics in the Greater American Bottom. In *Late Woodland Societies: Tradition and Transformation across the Midcontinent*, edited by Thomas E. Emerson, Dale L. McElrath, and Andrew C. Fortier, pp. 163–175. University of Nebraska Press, Lincoln.

2006   The Ritualization of Cahokia: The Structure and Organization of Early Cahokia Crafts. In *Leadership and Polity in Mississippian Society*, edited by Brian M Butler and Paul D. Welch, pp. 236–263. Occasional Paper No. 33. Center for Archaeological Investigations, Southern Illinois University, Carbondale.

2007a   An Interpretation of the George Reeves Phase Occupation of the Range Site. In *The Range Site 4: Emergent Mississippian George Reeves and Lindeman Phase Occupations*, edited by John E. Kelly, Steven J. Ozuk, and Joyce A. Williams, pp. 223–233. Transportation Archaeological Research Reports No. 18. Illinois Transportation Archaeological Research Program. University of Illinois, Urbana-Champaign.

2007b   Conclusions. In *The Range Site 4: Emergent Mississippian George Reeves and Lindeman Phase Occupations*, edited by John E. Kelly, Steven J. Ozuk, and Joyce A. Williams, pp. 491–494. Transportation Archaeological Research Reports No. 18. Illinois Transportation Archaeological Research Program. University of Illinois, Urbana-Champaign.

2007c   George Reeves Phase Features. In *The Range Site 4: Emergent Mississippian George Reeves and Lindeman Phase Occupations*, edited by John E. Kelly, Steven J. Ozuk, and Joyce A. Williams, pp. 25–87. Transportation Archaeological Research Reports No. 18. Illinois Transportation Archaeological Research Program. University of Illinois, Urbana-Champaign.

Kelly, John E., and James A. Brown

2014   Cahokia: The Processes and Principles of the Creation of an Early Mississippian City. In *Making Ancient Cities: Space and Place in Early Urban Societies*, edited by Andrew T. Creekmore, and Kevin D. Fisher, pp. 292–336. Cambridge University Press, Cambridge.

Kelly, John E., Steven J. Ozuk, and Joyce A. Williams (editors)

2007   *The Range Site 4: Emergent Mississippian George Reeves and Lindeman Phase Occupations*. Transportation Archaeological Research Reports No. 18. Illinois Transportation Archaeological Research Program. University of Illinois, Urbana-Champaign.

Kelly, Lucretia S.

2001   A Case of Ritual Feasting at the Cahokia Site. In *Feasts: Archaeological and Ethnographic Perspectives on Food, Politics, and Power*, edited by Michael Dietler and Brian Hayden, pp. 334–367. Smithsonian Institution Press, Washington D.C.

Kelly, Robert L.

1983   Hunter-Gatherer Mobility Strategies. *Journal of Anthropological Research* 39:277–306.

1988   The Three Sides of a Biface. *American Antiquity* 53:717–734.

1995   *The Foraging Spectrum: Diversity in Hunter-Gatherer Lifeways*. Smithsonian Institution Press, Washington, D.C.

2013   *The Lifeways of Hunter-Gatherers: The Foraging Spectrum*. Cambridge University Press, New York.

Kelly, Robert L., and Larry C. Todd

1988   Coming into the Country: Early Paleoindian Hunting and Mobility. *American Antiquity* 53(2):231–244.

Kelton, Paul

2002   The Great Southeastern Smallpox Epidemic, 1696–1700: The Region's First Major Epidemic. In *The Transformation of the Southeastern Indians, 1540–1760*, edited by Robbie Ethridge and Charles Hudson, pp. 21–37. University Press of Mississippi, Jackson.

2004   Avoiding the Smallpox Spirits: Colonial Epidemics and Southeastern Indian Survival. *Ethnohistory* 51:45–71.

2007   *Epidemics and Enslavement: Biological Catastrophe in the Native Southeast, 1492–1715*. University of Nebraska Press, Lincoln.

Kennett, Douglas J., and Bruce Winterhalder (editors)

2006   *Behavioral Ecology and the Transition to Agriculture*. University of California Press, Berkeley.

Kidder, Tristram R.

1992   Excavations at the Jordan Site (16MO1), Morehouse Parish, Louisiana. *Southeastern Archaeology* 11:109–131.

1998   Mississippi Period Mound Groups and Communities in the Lower Mississippi Valley. In *Mississippian Towns and Sacred Spaces: Searching for an Architectural Grammar*, edited by R. Barry Lewis and Charles Stout, pp. 123–150. University of Alabama Press, Tuscaloosa.

2002 Woodland Period Archaeology of the Lower Mississippi Valley. In *The Woodland Southeast*, edited by David G. Anderson and Robert C. Mainfort Jr., pp. 65–91. University of Alabama Press, Tuscaloosa.

2004 Plazas as Architecture: An Example from the Raffman Site, Northeast Louisiana. *American Antiquity* 69:514–532.

2010 Hunter-Gatherer Ritual and Complexity: New Evidence from Poverty Point, Louisiana. In *Ancient Complexities: New Perspectives in Precolumbian North America*, edited by Susan M. Alt, pp. 32–51. University of Utah Press, Salt Lake.

2011 Transforming Hunter-Gatherer History at Poverty Point. In *Hunter-Gatherer Archaeology as Historical Process*, edited by Kenneth E. Sassaman and Donald H. Holley Jr., pp. 95–119. University of Arizona Press, Tucson.

Kidder, Tristram R., and Gayle J. Fritz

1993 Subsistence and Social Change in the Lower Mississippi Valley: The Reno Brake and Osceola Sites, Louisiana. *Journal of Field Archaeology* 20(3):281–297.

Kidder, Tristram R., and Sarah C. Sherwood

2017 Look to the Earth: The Search for Ritual in the Context of Mound Construction. *Journal of Archaeological and Anthropological Sciences* 9(1):1–23. https://link.springer.com/article/10.1007/s12520-016-0369-1.

Kimball, Larry R.

1996 Early Archaic Settlement and Technology: Lessons from Tellico. In *The Paleoindian and Early Archaic Southeast*, edited by David G. Anderson and Kenneth E. Sassaman, pp. 149–186. University of Alabama Press, Tuscaloosa.

Kimball, Larry R., Thomas R. Whyte, Thomas, and Gary D. Crites

2010 The Biltmore and Hopewellian Mound Use in the Southern Appalachians. *Southeastern Archaeology* 29(1):44–58.

King, Adam

2001 Long-Term Histories of Mississippian Centers: The Developmental Sequence of Etowah and Its Comparison to Moundville and Cahokia. *Southeastern Archaeology* 20:1–17.

2002 Creek Chiefdoms at the Temporal Edge of the Mississippian World. *Southeastern Archaeology* 21:221–226.

2003a *Etowah: The Political History of a Chiefdom Capital*. University of Alabama Press, Tuscaloosa.

2003b Over a Century of Explorations at Etowah. *Journal of Archaeological Research* 11:279–306.

2006 The Historic Period Transformation of Mississippian Societies. In *Light on the Path: the Anthropology and History of the Southeastern Indians*, edited by Thomas J. Pluckhahn and Robbie Ethridge, pp. 179–195. University of Alabama Press, Tuscaloosa.

Knappett, Carl

2013 Imprints as Punctuations of Material Itineraries. In *Mobility, Meaning and the Transformations of Things: Shifting Contexts of Material Culture through Time and Space*, edited by Hans Peter Hahn and Hadas Weiss, pp. 37–49. Oxbow, Oxford.

Kneberg, Madeline

1951a An Archaic Autobiography. *Tennessee Archaeologist* 7(1):1–5.

1951b An Early Woodland Autobiography. *Tennessee Archaeologist* 7(2):31–38.

1952a The Autobiography of a Memorial Mound Builder. *Tennessee Archaeologist* 8(1):1–9.

1952b The Autobiography of a "Bone House" Indian. *Tennessee Archaeologist* 8(2):37–41.

Knight, John

2012   The Anonymity of the Hunt: A Critique of Hunting as Sharing. *Current Anthropology* 53(3):334–355.

Knight, Vernon J., Jr.

1989   Symbolism of Mississippian Mounds. In *Powhatan's Mantle: Indians in the Colonial Southeast*, edited by Peter H. Wood, Gregory A. Waselkov, and M. Thomas Hatley, pp. 279–291. University of Nebraska Press, Lincoln.

1990   *Excavation of the Truncated Mound at the Walling Site: Middle Woodland Culture and Copena in the Tennessee Valley.* Report of Investigations 56. Division of Archaeology, Alabama State Museum of Natural History, University of Alabama, Tuscaloosa.

1994a   The Formation of the Creeks. In *The Forgotten Centuries: Indians and Europeans in the American South, 1521–1704*, edited by Charles Hudson and Carmen Chaves Tesser, pp. 373–392. University of Georgia Press, Athens.

1994b   Ocmulgee Fields Culture and the Historical Development of Creek Ceramics. In *Ocmulgee Archaeology, 1936–1986*, edited by David J. Hally, pp. 181–189. University of Georgia Press, Athens.

1998   Moundville as a Diagrammatic Ceremonial Center. In *Archaeology of the Moundville Chiefdom*, edited by Vernon J. Knight Jr. and Vincas P. Steponaitis, pp. 44–62. Smithsonian Institution Press, Washington, D.C.

2001   Feasting and the Emergence of Platform Mound Ceremonialism in Eastern North America. In *Feasts: Archaeological and Ethnographic Perspectives on Food, Politics, and Power*, edited by Michael Dietler and Brian Hayden, pp. 311–333. Smithsonian Institution Press, Washington, D.C.

2004   Characterizing Elite Midden Deposits at Moundville. *American Antiquity* 69(2):304–321.

2010   *Mound Excavations at Moundville: Architecture, Elites and Social Order.* University of Alabama Press, Tuscaloosa.

2014   Taking Stock of Social Theory in Southeastern Archaeology. *Southeastern Archaeology* 33(2):206–207.

Knight, Vernon J., Jr., and Sheree L. Adams

1981   A Voyage to the Mobile and Tomeh in 1700, with Notes on the Interior Regions of Alabama. *Journal of Alabama Archaeology* 27(1):32–56.

Kohler, Tim

2011   *Complex Systems and Archaeology.* Sante Fe Institute Working Papers, #11-06-023. Sante Fe Institute, Santa Fe, New Mexico.

Koldehoff, Brad, and Joseph M. Galloy

2006   Late Woodland Frontiers in the American Bottom Region. *Southeastern Archaeology* 25:275–300.

Koldehoff, Brad, and Thomas Loebel

2009   Clovis and Dalton: Unbounded and Bounded Systems in the Midcontinent of North America. In *Lithic Materials and Paleolithic Societies*, edited by Brian Adams and Brooke S. Blades, pp. 270–286. Wiley-Blackwell, Hoboken, New Jersey.

Kooyman, Brian, Len V. Hills, Paul McNeil, and S. Tolman

2006   Late Pleistocene Horse Hunting at the Wally's Beach Site (DhPg-8), Canada. *American Antiquity* 71(1):101–121.

Kowalewski, Stephen A.

2006   Coalescent Societies. In *Light on the Path: The Anthropology and History of the Southeastern Indians*, edited by Thomas J. Pluckhahn and Robbie Ethridge, pp. 94–122. University of Alabama Press, Tuscaloosa.

Kristiansen, Kristian

2014   Towards a New Paradigm?: The Third Science Revolution and Its Possible Consequences in Archaeology. *Current Swedish Archaeology* 22:11–29.

Kroeber, Alfred L.

1942   *Culture Element Distributions XV: Salt, Dogs, Tobacco*. University of California Publications in Anthropological Records, Vol. 6, 1941–1942. University of California Press, Berkeley and Los Angeles.

Kuhn, Steven L.

1990   A Geometric Index of Reduction for Unifacial Stone Tools. *Journal of Archaeological Science* 17(5):583–593.

2013   Questions of Complexity and Scale in Explanations for Cultural Transitions in the Pleistocene: A Case Study from the Early Upper Paleolithic. *Journal of Archaeological Method and Theory* 20:194–211.

Kuhn, Steven L., and D. Shane Miller

2015   Artifacts as Patches: The Marginal Value Theorem and Stone Tool Life Histories. In *Lithic Technological Systems: Evolutionary Approaches to Understanding Stone Technologies as a Byproduct of Human Behavior*, edited by Nathan Goodale and William Andrefsky, pp. 173–197. Cambridge University Press, New York.

Kuhn, Thomas S.

1962   *The Structure of Scientific Revolutions*. University of Chicago Press, Chicago.

Kurjack, Edward B.

1994   Political Geography of the Yucatecan Hill Country. In *Hidden among the Hills: Maya Archaeology of the Northwest Yucatan Peninsula*, edited by Hanns Prem, pp. 308–315. Verlag Von Flemming, Möckmühl, Germany.

Kurlansky, Mark

2002   *Salt: A World History*. Penguin Books, New York.

LaDu, Daniel A.

2013   The 2013 Excavations at the Mazique Mounds (22Ad502). Paper presented at the 70th annual meeting of the Southeastern Archaeological Conference, Tampa, Florida.

Lalande, J. J.

1774   *The Art of Tanning and of Currying Leather, With the Processes for Dying [sic] Leather Red and Yellow, as Practiced in Turkey, Collected from the French of Monsieur De La Lande and Others*. Dublin Society, Dublin.

Lane, Leon, and David G. Anderson

2001   Paleoindian Occupations of the Southern Appalachians. In *Archaeology of the Appalachian Highlands*, edited by Lynne P. Sullivan and Susan C. Prezzano, pp. 88–102. University of Tennessee Press, Knoxville.

Langton, Chris G.

1991   Computation at the Edge of Chaos: Phase Transitions and Emergent Computation. Unpublished Ph.D. dissertation, Computer and Communication Sciences Department, University of Michigan, Ann Arbor.

Lankford, George E.
2007   Some Cosmological Motifs in the Southeastern Ceremonial Complex. In *Ancient Objects and Sacred Realms: Interpretations of Mississippian Iconography*, edited by F. Kent Riley III and James Garber, pp. 8–38. University of Texas Press, Austin.

Lansing, J. Stephen
2003   Complex Adaptive Systems. *Annual Review of Anthropology* 23:183–204.

Laszlo, Pierre
2001   *Salt, Grain of Life*. Columbia University Press, New York.

Latour, Bruno
2005   *Reassembling the Social: An Introduction to Actor-Network-Theory*. Oxford University Press, Oxford, United Kingdom.

Layton, Julia
2006   How Pandora Radio Works. May 23, 2006. http://computer.howstuffworks.com/internet/basics/pandora.htm.

LeCount, Lisa J.
2001   Like Water for Chocolate: Feasting and Political Ritual among the Late Classic Maya at Xunantunich, Belize. *American Anthropologist* 103(4):935–953.

Leigh, David S.
2008   Late Quaternary Climates and River Channels of the Atlantic Coastal Plain, Southeastern United States. *Geomorphology* 101:90–108.

Lewis, R. Barry, and Charles Stout
1998   The Town as Metaphor. In *Mississippian Towns and Sacred Spaces*, edited by R. Barry Lewis and Charles Stout, pp. 227–241. University of Alabama Press, Tuscaloosa.

Lewis, R. Barry, Charles Stout, and Cameron B. Wesson
1998   The Design of Mississippian Towns. In *Mississippian Towns and Sacred Spaces*, edited by R. Barry Lewis and Charles Stout, pp. 1–21. University of Alabama Press, Tuscaloosa.

Lewis, Thomas M. N., and Madeline Kneberg
1958   The Nuckolls Site: A Possible Dalton-Meserve Chipped Stone Complex in the Kentucky Lake Area. *Tennessee Archaeologist* 14(2):60–79.

Lewis, Thomas M. N., Madeline D. Kneberg Lewis, and Lynne P. Sullivan
1995   *The Prehistory of the Chickamauga Basin in Tennessee*. University of Tennessee Press, Knoxville.

Lindauer, Owen, and John H. Blitz
1997   Higher Ground: The Archaeology of North American Platform Mounds. *Journal of Archaeological Research* 5:169–207.

Listi, Ginesse A.
2008   Bioarchaeological Analysis of Diet and Nutrition during the Coles Creek Period in the Lower Mississippi Valley. Unpublished Ph.D. dissertation, Department of Anthropology, Tulane University, New Orleans, Louisiana.

Logan, Michael H.
1973   Humoral Medicine in Guatemala and Peasant Acceptance of Modern Medicine. *Human Organization* 32:385–395.

Lorenz, Edward
1996   *The Essence of Chaos*. University of Washington Press, Seattle.

Lorenz, Karl G.

1997   Re-Examination of Natchez Sociopolitical Complexity: A View from the Grand Village and Beyond. *Southeastern Archaeology* 16:97–112.

2000   The Natchez of Southwest Mississippi. In *Indians of the Greater Southeast: Historical Archaeology and Ethnohistory*, edited by Bonnie G. McEwan, pp. 142–177. University Press of Florida, Gainesville.

Lovejoy, Paul E.

1986   *Salt of the Desert Sun: A History of Salt Production and Trade in the Central Sudan.* African Studies Series No. 46. Cambridge University Press, Cambridge, United Kingdom.

Low, Setha M.

2000   *On the Plaza: The Politics of Public Space and Culture.* University of Texas Press, Austin.

Lowenthal, David

1975   Past Time, Present Place: Landscape and Memory. *Geographical Review* 65(1):1–37.

Lucas, Gavin

2012   *Understanding the Archaeological Record.* Cambridge University Press, New York.

Luer, George M.

2013   Tabbed Circular Artifacts in Florida: An Intriguing Type of Gorget and Pendant. *Florida Anthropologist* 66(3):103–128.

Lynch, B. Mark

1982   Mortuary Behavior in the Carrier Mills Archaeological District. In *The Carrier Mills Archaeological Project: Human Adaptation in the Saline Valley, Illinois*, edited by Richard W. Jefferies and Brian M. Butler, pp. 1115–1231. Center for Archaeological Investigations Research Paper. Southern Illinois University at Carbondale.

Lynott, Mark J.

2015   *Hopewell Ceremonial Landscapes of Ohio: More Than Mounds and Geometric Earthworks.* Oxbow Books, Oxford.

McAnany, Patricia A.

1988   The Effects of Lithic Procurement Strategies on Tool Curation and Recycling. *Lithic Technology* 17:3–11.

2002   Rethinking the Great and Little Tradition Paradigm from the Perspective of Domestic Ritual. In *Domestic Ritual in Ancient Mesoamerica*, edited by Patricia A. Plunket, pp. 115–119. Cotsen Institute of Archaeology, University of California, Los Angeles.

McCullough, John M.

1973   Human Ecology, Heat Adaptation, and Belief Systems: The Hot-Cold Syndrome of Yucatan. *Journal of Anthropological Research* 29(1):32–36.

MacDonald-Beyers, Kristi, and Ronald F. Labisky

2005   Influence of Flood Waters on Survival, Reproduction, and Habitat Use of White-Tailed Deer in the Florida Everglades. *Wetlands* 35(3):659–666.

McElrath, Dale L., Thomas E. Emerson, and Andrew C. Fortier

2000   Social Evolution or Social Response? A Fresh Look at the "Good Gray Cultures" after Four Decades of Midwest Research. In *Late Woodland Societies: Tradition and Transformation Across the Midcontinent*, edited by Thomas E. Emerson, Dale L. McElrath, and Andrew C. Fortier, pp. 3–36. University of Nebraska Press, Lincoln.

McFadden, Paulette S., and Andrea Palmiotto

2012   *Archaeological Investigations at Bird Island (8di52), Dixie County, Fl.* Technical Report

14. Laboratory of Southeastern Archaeology, Department of Anthropology, University of Florida, Gainesville.

McGhee, Robert

1994   Ivory for the Sea Woman: The Symbolic Attributes of a Prehistoric Technology. In *Interpreting Objects and Collections*, edited by Susan M. Pearce, pp. 59–66. Routledge, New York.

McKey, Doyle, Stéphen Rostain, José Iriarte, Bruno Glaser, Jago Jonathan Birk, Irene Holst, and Delphine Renard

2010   Pre-Columbian Agricultural Landscapes, Ecosystem Engineers, and Self-Organized Patchiness in Amazonia. *Proceedings of the National Academy of Sciences* 107(17):7823–7828.

McKillop, Heather

2002   *Salt: White Gold of the Ancient Maya*. University Press of Florida, Gainesville.

McNutt, Charles H., John Broster, and Mark Norton

2008   A Surface Collection from the Kirk Type Site (40HS174), Humphreys County, Tennessee. *Tennessee Archaeology* 3(1):25–75.

McNutt, Charles H., Jay D. Franklin, and Edward R. Henry

2012   New Perspectives on Mississippian Occupations in Western Tennessee and Northwestern Mississippi: Recent Chronological and Geophysical Investigations at Chucalissa (40SY1), Shelby County, Tennessee. *Southeastern Archaeology* 31:231–250.

McShea, William J., H. Brian Underwood, and John H. Rappole

1997   Deer Management and the Concept of Overabundance. In *The Science of Overabundance: Deer Ecology and Population Management*, edited by William J. McShea, H. Brian Underwood and John H. Rappole, pp. 1–10. Smithsonian Institution, Washington, D.C.

Madrigal, Alexis C.

2011   Outside the White House, A Celebration of Osama Bin Laden's Death. *Atlantic*. May 2, 2011. http://www.theatlantic.com/politics/archive/2011/05/outside-the-white-house-a-celebration-of-osama-bin-ladens-death/238141/.

Maggard, Greg, and Kacy Stackelbeck

2008   Paleoindian Period. In *The Archaeology of Kentucky: An Update: Volume One*, edited by David Pollack, pp. 109–192. Preservation Plan Report No. 3. Kentucky Heritage Council, Frankfurt.

Mainfort, Robert C., Jr.

2001   The Late Prehistoric and Protohistoric Periods in the Central Mississippi Valley. In *Societies in Eclipse*, edited by David S. Brose, C. Wesley Cowan, and Robert C. Mainfort Jr., pp. 173–189. Smithsonian Institution Press, Washington D.C.

Majewski, Teresita

2000   "We Are All Storytellers": Comments on Storytelling, Science, and Historical Archaeology. *Historical Archaeology* 34:17–19.

Malinowski, Bronislaw

1944   *A Scientific Theory of Culture and Other Essays*. Vol. 10. Routledge, London.

Marchand, Trevor

2007   Crafting Knowledge: The Role of "Parsing and Production" in the Communication of Skill-Based Knowledge among Masons. In *Ways of Knowing: Anthropological Ap-*

proaches to Crafting Experience and Knowledge, edited by Mark Harris, pp. 181–202. Berghahn Books, New York.

Marcoux, Jon Bernard

2010   Pox, Empire, Shackles, Hides: The Townsend Site, 1670–1710. University of Alabama Press, Tuscaloosa.

Marquardt, William H.

2010   Shell Mounds in the Southeast: Middens, Monuments, Temple Mounds, Rings, or Works? American Antiquity 75(3):551–570.

Marquardt, William H., and Laura Kozuch

2016   The Lightning Whelk: An Enduring Icon of Southeastern North American Spirituality. Journal of Anthropological Archaeology 42:1–26.

Marquardt, William H., and Patty Jo Watson

2005   The Green River Shell Mound Archaic: Conclusions. In Archaeology of the Middle Green River Region, Kentucky, edited by William H. Marquardt and Patty Jo Watson, pp. 629–647. Florida Museum of Natural History Institute of Archaeology and Paleoenvironmental Studies Monograph No. 5. University of Florida, Gainesville.

Martin, Paul S.

1984   Prehistoric Overkill: The Global Model. In Quaternary Extinctions: A Prehistoric Revolution, edited by Paul S. Martin and Richard G. Klein, pp. 354–403. University of Arizona Press, Tucson.

Mason, Carol I.

2005   The Archaeology of Ocmulgee Old Fields, Macon, Georgia. University of Alabama Press, Tuscaloosa.

Meeks, Scott C., and David G. Anderson

2012   Evaluating the Effect of the Younger Dryas on Human Population Histories in the Southeastern United States. In Hunter-Gatherer Behavior: Human Responses during the Younger Dryas, edited by Metin I. Eren, pp. 111–138. Left Coast Press, Walnut Creek, California.

Mehta, Jayur Madhusudan

2013   Spanish Conquistadores, French Explorers, and Natchez Great Suns in Southwestern Mississippi, 1542–1729. Native South 6:33–69.

Mehta, Jayur Madhusudan, David Abbott, and Charlotte D. Pevny

2016   Mississippian Craft Production in the Yazoo Basin: Thin-Section Analysis of a Mississippian Structure Floor on the Summit of Mound D at the Carson Site. Journal of Archaeological Science: Reports 5:471–484.

Mehta, Jayur Madhusudan, Kelsey M. Lowe, Rachel Stout-Evans, and John Connaway

2012   Moving Earth and Building Monuments at the Carson Mounds Site, Coahoma County, Mississippi. Journal of Anthropology 2012:1–21.

Meltzer, David J.

2004   Modeling the Initial Colonization of the Americas: Issues of Scale, Demography, and Landscape Learning. In The Settlement of American Continents: A Multidisciplinary Approach to Human Biogeography, edited by C. Michael Barton, Geoffrey A. Clark, David R. Yesner, and Georges A. Pearson, pp. 123–137. University of Arizona Press, Tucson.

2009   The First Peoples in a New World: Colonizing Ice Age America. University of California Press, Berkeley.

Meltzer, David J., and Vance T. Holliday

2010   Would North American Paleoindians Have Noticed the Younger Dryas Age Climate Change? *Journal of World Prehistory* 23:1–41.

Menz, Martin W.

2015   Like Blood from a Stone: Teasing Out Social Difference from Lithic Production Debris at Kolomoki (9ER1). Unpublished MA thesis, Department of Anthropology, University of South Florida, Tampa.

Merrell, James H.

1989   *The Indians' New World: Catawbas and Their Neighbors from European Contact through the Era of Removal.* University of North Carolina Press, Chapel Hill.

2006   "Our Bond of Peace": Patterns of Intercultural Exchange in the Carolina Piedmont, 1650–1750. In *Powhatan's Mantle: Indians in the Colonial Southeast*, edited by Gregory A. Waselkov, Peter H. Wood, and Tom Hatley, pp. 267–304. Revised and expanded edition. University of Nebraska Press, Lincoln.

Meyers, Maureen

2002   The Mississippian Frontier in Southwestern Virginia. *Southeastern Archaeology* 21(2): 178–191.

Michaels, George H.

1989   Craft Specialization in the Early Postclassic of Colha. *Research in Economic Anthropology*, Supplement 4:139–183.

Milanich, Jerald T.

1979   Origins and Prehistoric Distribution of Black Drink and the Ceremonial Shell Drinking Cup. In *Black Drink: A Native American Tea*, edited by Charles M. Hudson, pp. 83–119. University of Georgia Press, Athens.

1990   The European Entrada into La Florida: An Overview. In *Columbian Consequences, Volume 2: Archaeological and Historical Perspectives on Spanish Borderlands East*, edited by David Hurst Thomas, pp. 3–29. Smithsonian Institution Press, Washington, D.C.

1994   *Archaeology of Precolumbian Florida.* University Press of Florida, Gainesville.

2000   The Timucua Indians of Northern Florida and Southern Georgia. In *Indians of the Greater Southeast: Historical Archaeology and Ethnohistory*, edited by Bonnie G. McEwan, pp. 1–25. University Press of Florida, Gainesville.

Milanich, Jerald T., Ann S. Cordell, Vernon James Knight Jr., Timothy K. Kohler, and Brenda J. Sigler-Lavelle

1984   *McKeithen Weeden Island: The Culture of Northern Florida, A.D. 200–900.* Academic Press, New York.

Miller, D. Shane

2014   From Colonization to Domestication: A Historical Ecological Analysis of Paleoindian and Archaic Subsistence and Landscape Use in Central Tennessee. Unpublished Ph.D. dissertation, School of Anthropology, University of Arizona, Tucson.

Miller, D. Shane, and Stephen B. Carmody

2016   Colonization after Clovis: Using the Ideal Free Distribution to Interpret the Distribution of Late Pleistocene and Early Holocene Archaeological Sites in the Duck River Valley, Tennessee. *Tennessee Archaeology* 8:78–101.

Miller, D. Shane, and Joseph A. M. Gingerich

2013   Regional Variation in the Terminal Pleistocene and Early Holocene Radiocarbon Record of Eastern North America. *Quaternary Research* 79:175–188.

Miller, D. Shane, and Ashley M. Smallwood

2012   Beyond Stages: Modeling Clovis Biface Production at the Topper Site, South Carolina. In *Contemporary Lithic Analysis in the Southeast: Problems, Solutions, and Interpretations*, edited by Philip J. Carr, Andrew P. Bradbury, and Sarah E. Price, pp. 28–41. University of Alabama Press, Tuscaloosa.

Miller, G. Logan

2015   Ritual Economy and Craft Production in Small-scale Societies: Evidence from Microwear Analysis of Hopewell Bladelets. *Journal of Anthropological Archaeology* 39:124–138.

Mills, Barbara J.

2007   Multicrafting, Migration, and Identity in the American Southwest. In *Craft Production in Complex Societies: Multicraft and Producer Perspectives*, edited by Izumi Shimada, pp. 25–43. University of Utah Press, Salt Lake City.

Milner, George R.

1996   Development and Dissolution of a Mississippian Society in the American Bottom, Illinois. In *Political Structure and Change in the Prehistoric Southeastern United States*, edited by John F. Scarry, pp. 27–52. University Press of Florida, Gainesville.

1998   *The Cahokia Chiefdom: The Archaeology of a Mississippian Society*. Smithsonian Institution Press, Washington, D.C.

2004a   Old Mounds, Ancient Hunter-Gatherers, and Modern Archaeologists. In *Signs of Power: The Rise of Complexity in the Southeast*, edited by Jon. L. Gibson and Philip J. Carr, pp. 300–315. University of Alabama Press, Tuscaloosa, Alabama.

2004b   *The Moundbuilders: Ancient Peoples of Eastern North America*. Thames & Hudson, London.

Missouri Department of Conservation

2011   *Wildlife Will Survive Flood Conditions*. http://mdc.mo.gov/node/13901.

Mollat, Michel (ed.)

1968   *Le rôle du sel dans l'histoire*. Publications de la Faculté des Lettres et Sciences Humaines de Paris-Sorbonne, Vol. 37. Presses Universitaires de France, Paris.

Monaghan, G. William, and Christopher S. Peebles

2010   The Construction, Use, and Abandonement of Angel Site Mound A: Tracing the History of a Middle Mississippian Town through Its Earthworks. *American Antiquity* 75:935–953.

Moog Music, Inc.

2015   Back to the Future Sounds. https://www.youtube.com/watch?v=3w6qWiEx8BQ.

Mooney, James

1982   *Myths of the Cherokee and Sacred Formulas of the Cherokees*. C. Elder-Bookseller, Nashville, Tennessee. http://ehrafworldcultures.yale.edu/document?id=nn08-021.

Mooney, James K., and Frans M. Olbrechts

1932   *The Swimmer Manuscript: Cherokee Sacred Formulas and Medicinal Prescriptions*. Bureau of American Ethnology Bulletin 99. Smithsonian Institution, Washington, D.C.

Moore, Christopher R.

2011   Production, Exchange and Social Interaction in the Green River Region of Western Kentucky: A Multiscalar Approach to the Analysis of Two Shell Midden Sites. Unpublished Ph.D. dissertation, Department of Anthropology, University of Kentucky, Lexington.

2015 Hunter-Gatherer Histories: The Role of Events in the Construction of the Chiggerville Shell Midden. In *The Archaeology of Events: Cultural Change and Continuity in the Pre-Columbian Southeast*, edited by Zackary I. Gilmore and Jason M. O'Donoughue, pp. 62–76. University of Alabama Press, Tuscaloosa.

Moore, Christopher R., and Victoria G. Dekle

2010 Hickory Nuts, Bulk Processing, and the Advent of Early Horticultural Economies in Eastern North America. *World Archaeology* 42(4):595–608.

Moore, Christopher R., and Victor D. Thompson

2012 Animism and Green River Persistent Places: A Dwelling Perspective of the Shell Mound Archaic. *Journal of Social Archaeology* 12(2):264–284.

Moore, Clarence Bloomfield

1903 Certain Aboriginal Mounds of the Central Florida West-Coast. *Journal of the Academy of Natural Sciences of Philadelphia* 12:361–438.

1907 Crystal River Revisited. *Journal of the Academy of Natural Sciences of Philadelphia* (second series) 13(3):406–425.

1918 The Northwestern Florida Coast Revisited. *Journal of the Academy of Natural Sciences of Philadelphia* (second series) 16(4):514–581.

Moore, David G.

2002 *Catawba Valley Mississippian: Ceramics, Chronology, and Catawba Indians.* University of Alabama Press, Tuscaloosa.

Moore, Jerry D.

1996 The Archaeology of Plazas and the Proxemics of Ritual, Three Andean Traditions. *American Anthropologist* 98:789–802.

2014 Ancient Plazas: Spaces of Inquiry in Mesoamerica and Beyond. In *Mesoamerican Plazas: Arenas of Community and Power*, edited by Kenichiro Tsukamoto and Takeshi Inomata, pp. 213–223. University of Arizona Press, Tucson.

Moorehead, Warren K.

1910 *The Stone Age in North America: An Archaeological Encyclopedia of the Implements, Ornaments, Weapons, Utensils, etc., of the Prehistoric Tribes of North America.* Vol. 2. Houghton Mifflin Co., New York.

Morey, Darcy F.

2006 Burying Key Evidence: The Social Bond between Dogs and Humans. *Journal of Archaeological Science* 33(2):158–175.

2010 *Dogs: Domestication and the Development of a Social Bond.* Cambridge University Press, New York.

Morey, Darcy F., and Rujana Jeger

2015 Paleolithic Dogs: Why Sustained Domestication Then? *Journal of Archaeological Science: Reports* 3:420–428.

Morey, Darcy F., and Michael D. Wiant

1992 Early Holocene Domestic Dog Burials from the North American Midwest. *Current Anthropology* 33(2):224–229.

Morgan, David W.

2003 A Proposed Construction Sequence of the Mound B Terrace at Bottle Creek. In *Bottle*

Creek: A Pensacola Culture Site in South Alabama, edited by Ian W. Brown, pp. 63–83. University of Alabama Press, Tuscaloosa.

Morse, Dan F.

1971   Recent Indications of Dalton Settlement Pattern in Northeast Arkansas. *Southeastern Archaeological Conference Bulletin* 13:5–10.

1973   Dalton Culture in Northeast Arkansas. *Florida Anthropologist* 26:23–38.

1975   Reply to Schiffer. In *The Cache River Archaeological Project: An Experiment in Contract Archaeology*, edited by Michael B. Schiffer and John H. House, pp. 113–120. Research Series 8. Arkansas Archaeological Survey, Fayetteville.

1990   The Nodena Phase. In *Towns and Temples along the Mississippi*, edited by David H. Dye and Cheryl Ann Cox, pp. 69–97. University of Alabama Press, Tuscaloosa.

Morse, Dan F., and Phyllis A. Morse

1983   *Archaeology of the Central Mississippi Valley*. Academic Press, New York.

1997   An Overview of the Dalton Period in Northeastern Arkansas and in the Southeastern United States. In *Sloan: A Paleoindian Dalton Cemetery in Arkansas*, edited by Dan F. Morse, pp. 123–139. Smithsonian Institution Press, Washington D. C.

Morse, Phyllis A.

1990   The Parkin Site and the Parkin Phase. In *Towns and Temples along the Mississippi*, edited by David H. Dye and Cheryl Ann Cox, pp. 118–134. University of Alabama Press, Tuscaloosa.

Morse, Phyllis A., and Dan F. Morse

1990   The Zebree Site: An Emerged Early Mississippian Expression in Northeast Arkansas. In *The Mississippian Emergence*, edited by Bruce D. Smith, pp. 51–66. Smithsonian Institution Press, Washington, D.C.

Mouer, Daniel

1998   Thomas Harris, Gent., as Related by His Second Sonne. *Historical Archaeology* 32:4–14.

Muller, Jon

1984   Mississippian Specialization and Salt. *American Antiquity* 49(3):489–507.

1986   *Archaeology of the Lower Ohio Valley*. Academic Press, New York.

1997   *Mississippian Political Economy*. Plenum Press, New York.

1998   Towns along the Lower Ohio. In *Mississippian Towns and Sacred Spaces: Searching for an Architectural Grammar*, edited by R. Barry Lewis and Charles B. Stout, pp. 179–199. University of Alabama Press, Tuscaloosa.

Multhauf, Robert P.

1978   *Neptune's Gift: A History of Common Salt*. Johns Hopkins University Press, Baltimore.

Nair, Stella

2015   Pampa | Plaza. In *At Home with the Sapa Inca: Architecture, Space, and Legacy at Chinchero*, pp. 65–87. University of Texas Press, Austin.

Nassaney, Michael S.

2000   The Late Woodland Southeast. In *Late Woodland Societies: Tradition and Transformation across the Midcontinent*, edited by Thomas E. Emerson, Dale L. McElrath, and Andrew C. Fortier, pp. 713–730. University of Nebraska Press, Lincoln.

Nassaney, Michael S., and Charles R. Cobb (editors)

1991   *Stability, Transformation, and Variation: The Late Woodland Southeast*. Plenum Press, New York.

Nassaney, Michael S., and Kenneth E. Sassaman
1995   Introduction: Understanding Native American Interactions. In *Native American Interactions: Multiscalar Analyses and Interpretations in the Eastern Woodlands*, edited by Michael S. Nassaney and Kenneth E. Sassaman, pp. xix–xxxviii. University of Tennessee Press, Knoxville.

National Public Radio (NPR)
2015   You Know Exactly What These Six Country Songs Have in Common. January 9, 2015. http://www.npr.org/2015/01/09/376145745/you-know-exactly-what-these-six-country-songs-have-in-common.

National Weather Service
2010   *May 1 & 2 2010 Epic Flood Event for Western and Middle Tennessee.* http://www.srh.noaa.gov/ohx/?n=may2010epicfloodevent.

Nelson, Erin S.
2014   Intimate Landscapes: The Social Nature of the Spaces Between. *Archaeological Prospection* 21:49–57.

Nelson, Erin S., and Megan C. Kassabaum
2014   Expanding Social Networks through Ritual Deposition: A Case Study from the Lower Mississippi Valley. *Archaeological Review from Cambridge* 29(1):103–128.

Nelson, Margret C.
1991   The Study of Technological Organization. In *Archaeological Method and Theory*, edited by Michael B. Schiffer, pp. 57–100. University of Arizona Press, Tucson.

Nenquin, Jacques A. E.
1961   *Salt: A Study in Economic Prehistory.* Dissertationes Archaeologicae Gandenses VI. De Tempel, Bruges, Belgium.

Neumann, Thomas W.
1977   A Biocultural Approach to Salt Taboos: The Case of the Southeastern United States. *Current Anthropology* 18(2):289–307.

Norton, Mark R., and John B. Broster
1992   40HS200: The Nuckolls Extension Site. *Tennessee Anthropologist* 17:13–32.
1993   Archaeological Investigations at the Puckett Site (40SW228): A Paleoindian/Early Archaic Occupation on the Cumberland River, Stewart County, Tennessee. *Tennessee Anthropologist* 18:45–58.

Olsen, Bjørnar
2003   Material Culture after Text: Re-Membering Things. *Norwegian Archaeological Review* 36(2):87–104.
2010   *In Defense of Things: Archaeology and the Ontology of Objects.* AltaMira Press, Lanham, MD.

Olson, Randy
2015   *Houston, We Have Narrative: Why Science Needs Story.* University of Chicago Press, Chicago.

O'Neal, Lori L.
2016   What's in Your Toolbox? Examining Tool Choices at Two Middle and Late Woodland Period Sites on Florida's Gulf Coast, Citrus County, Florida. Unpublished MA thesis, Department of Anthropology, University of South Florida, Tampa.

Ortmann, Anthony L., and Tristram R. Kidder
2013 Building Mound A at Poverty Point, Louisiana: Monumental Public Architecture, Ritual Practice, and Implications for Hunter-Gatherer Complexity. *Geoarchaeology* 28:66–86.

Panter-Brick, Catherine
2002 Sexual Division of Labor: Energetic and Evolutionary Scenarios. *American Journal of Human Biology* 14:627–640.

Panter-Brick, Catherine, Robert H. Layton, and Peter Rowley-Conwy
2001 *Hunter-Gatherers: An Interdisciplinary Perspective.* Cambridge University Press, Cambridge.

Paper, Jordan
1988 *Offering Smoke: The Sacred Pipe and Native American Religion.* University of Idaho Press, Moscow.

Parsons, Jeffrey R.
2001 *The Last Saltmakers of Nexquipayac, Mexico: An Archaeological Ethnography.* Anthropological Papers, No. 92. Museum of Anthropology, University of Michigan, Ann Arbor.

Pauketat, Timothy R.
1994 *The Ascent of Chiefs: Cahokia and Mississippian Politics in Native North America.* University of Alabama Press, Tuscaloosa.
2003 Resettled Farmers and the Making of a Mississippian Polity. *American Antiquity* 68:39–66.
2004 *Ancient Cahokia and the Mississippians.* Cambridge University Press, Cambridge, United Kingdom.
2007 *Chiefdoms and Other Archaeological Delusions.* AltaMira, Lanham, Maryland.

Pauketat, Timothy R., and Susan M. Alt
2005 Agency in a Postmold? Physicality and the Archaeology of Culture-Making. *Journal of Archaeological Method and Theory* 12:213–236.

Pauketat, Timothy R., Lucretia S. Kelly, Gayle J. Fritz, Neal H. Lopinot, Scott Elias, and Eve Hargrave
2002 The Residues of Feasting and Public Ritual at Early Cahokia. *American Antiquity* 67(2):257–279.

Peacock, Evan, and Janet Rafferty
2013 The Bet-Hedging Model as an Explanatory Framework for the Evolution of Mound Building in the Southeastern United States. In *Beyond Barrows: Current Research on the Structuration and Perception of the Prehistoric Landscape through Monuments*, edited by David Fontijn, Arjan J. Louwen, Sasja van der Vaart, and Karsten Wentink, pp. 253–279. Sidestone Press, Leiden.

Perdue, Theda
1995 Women, Men and American Indian Policy: The Cherokee Response to "Civilization." In *Negotiators of Change: Historical Perspectives on Native American Women*, edited by Nancy Shoemaker, pp. 90–114. Routledge, New York.

Pétrequin, Pierre, Olivier Weller, Émilie Gauthier, Alexa Dufraisse, and Jean-François Piningre
2001 Salt Springs Exploitation without Pottery during Prehistory, from New Guinea to the French Jura. In *Ethno-Archaeology and Its Transfers: Papers from a Session Held at the European Association of Archaeologists Fifth Annual Meeting in Bournemouth 1999,*

edited by Sylvie Beyries and Pierre Pétrequin, pp. 37–53. BAR International Series 983. British Archaeological Reports, Oxford, United Kingdom.

Phillips, Philip
1970   Archaeological Survey in the Lower Yazoo Basin, Mississippi, 1949–1955. Papers of the Peabody Museum of Archaeology and Ethnology, Vol. 60. Harvard University, Cambridge, Massachusetts.

Phillips, Philip, James A. Ford, and James B. Griffin
1951   Archaeological Survey in the Lower Mississippi Alluvial Valley, 1940–1947. Papers of the Peabody Museum of American Archaeology and Ethnology. Harvard University, Vol. 25. Cambridge, Massachusetts.

Pluckhahn, Thomas J.
2003   Kolomoki: Settlement, Ceremony, and Status in the Deep South, A.D. 350 to 750. University of Alabama Press, Tuscaloosa.
2010   The Sacred and the Secular Revisited: The Essential Tensions of Early Village Society in the Southeastern United States. In Becoming Villagers: Comparing Early Village Societies, edited by Matthew S. Bandy and Jake R. Fox, pp. 100–118. University of Arizona Press, Tucson.

Pluckhahn, Thomas J., J. Matthew Compton, and Mary Theresa Bonhage-Freund
2006   Archaeological Correlates of Small-Scale Feasting: Evidence from the Woodland Period Site of Kolomoki in Georgia. Journal of Field Archaeology 31(3):263–284.

Pluckhahn, Thomas J., and Ann S. Cordell
2011   Paste Characterization of Weeden Island Pottery from Kolomoki and Its Implications for Specialized Production. Southeastern Archaeology 30(2):288–310.

Pratt, Mary Louise
1992   Imperial Eyes: Travel Writing and Transculturation. London: Routledge.

Price, James E., and Gregory L. Fox
1990   Recent Investigations at Towosahgy State Historic Site. Missouri Archaeologist 51:1–71.

Price, Sarah E.
2012   Omnipresent? We Don't Recover the Half of It! In Contemporary Lithic Analysis in the Southeast: Problems, Solutions, and Interpretations, edited by Philip J. Carr, Andrew P. Bradbury, and Sarah E. Price, pp. 13–27. University of Alabama Press, Tuscaloosa.

Pursell, Corin C.
2012   Colored Monuments and Sensory Theater among the Mississippians. In Making Senses of the Past: Toward a Sensory Archaeology, edited by Jo Day, pp. 69–89. Center for Archaeological Investigations, Occasional Paper No. 40. Southern Illinois University Press, Carbondale.

Quinn, Colin P., and Casey R. Barrier
2014   Early Regional Centers: Evolution and Organization. In Encyclopedia of Global Archaeology, edited by Claire Smith, pp. 2248–2260. Springer, New York.

Quitmyer, Irvy R.
2001   Zooarchaeological Analyses. In Phase III Mitigative Excavations at Lake Monroe Outlet Midden (8VO53), Volusia County, Florida, pp. 1–25. Report Submitted to U.S. Department of Transportation Federal Highway Administration and Florida Department of Transportation District Five by Archaeological Consultants and Janus Research, Sarasota, Florida.

Randall, Asa R.

2013   The Chronology and History of Mount Taylor Period (ca. 7400–4600 cal B.P.) Shell Sites on the Middle St. Johns River, Florida. *Southeastern Archaeology* 32(2):193–217.

2015   *Constructing Histories: Archaic Freshwater Shell Mounds and Social Landscapes of the St. Johns River, Florida.* University Press of Florida, Gainesville.

Randall, Asa R., Meggan E. Blessing, and Jon C. Endonino

2011   *Cultural Resource Assessment Survey of Silver Glen Springs Recreational Area in the Ocala National Forest, Florida* Technical Report 13. Laboratory of Southeastern Archaeology, Department of Anthropology, University of Florida, Gainesville. http://lsa. anthro.ufl.edu/publications/LSATechReport13.pdf.

Redfield, Robert, and Margaret P. Redfield

1940   Disease and Its Treatment in Dzitás, Yucatán. In *Contributions to American Anthropology and History* No. 32, pp. 49–81. Publication 523. Carnegie Institution of Washington, Washington, D.C.

Reidhead, Van A.

1981   *A Linear Programming Model of Prehistoric Subsistence Optimization: A Southeastern Indiana Example.* Prehistory Research Series, Vol. 6, No. 1. Indiana Historical Society, Indianapolis.

Reilly, F. Kent, III

2004   People of Earth, People of Sky: Visualizing the Sacred in Native American Art of the Mississippian Period. In *Hero, Hawk, and Open Hand: American Indian Art of the Ancient Midwest and South,* edited by Richard F. Townsend and Robert V. Sharp, pp. 125–137. Art Institute of Chicago in Association with Yale University Press, New Haven.

Reina, Rueben E., and John Monaghen

1981   The Ways of the Maya: Salt Production in Sacapulas, Guatemala. *Expedition* 23:13–33.

Ridington, Robin

1982   Technology, World View, and Adaptive Strategy in a Northern Hunting Society. *Canadian Review of Sociology and Anthropology* 19:469–481.

1988   *Trail to Heaven: Knowledge and Narrative in a Northern Native Community.* University of Iowa Press, Iowa City.

Riggs, Brett H.

2012   Reconsidering Chestowee: The 1713 Raid in Regional Perspective. In *Yuchi Indian Histories before the Removal Era,* edited by Jason B. Jackson, pp. 43–71. University of Nebraska Press, Lincoln.

Ringle, William M.

2014   Plazas and Patios of the Feathered Serpent. In *Mesoamerican Plazas: Arenas of Community and Power,* edited by Kenichiro Tsukamoto and Takeshi Inomata, pp. 168–192. University of Arizona Press, Tucson.

Rival, Laura

2012   The Materiality of Life: Revisiting the Anthropology of Nature in Amazonia. *INDIANA* 29:127–143.

Robb, John, and Timothy R. Pauketat

2012   From Moments to Millennia: Theorizing Scale and Change in Human History. In *Big Histories, Human Lives: Tackling Problems of Scale in Archaeology,* edited by John Robb and Timothy R. Pauketat, pp 3–34. SAR Press, Santa Fe.

Rockwell, David

1991   *Giving Voice to Bear: North American Indian Rituals, Myths, and Images of the Bear.* Roberts Rinehart, Niwot, Colorado.

Rodning, Christopher B.

2009a   Mounds, Myths, and Cherokee Townhouses in Southwestern North Carolina. *American Antiquity* 74:627–663.

2009b   Domestic Houses at Coweeta Creek. *Southeastern Archaeology* 28:1–26.

2010a   Architectural Symbolism and Cherokee Townhouses. *Southeastern Archaeology* 29:59–79.

2010b   European Trade Goods at Cherokee Settlements in Southwestern North Carolina. *North Carolina Archaeology* 59:1–84.

2011   Mortuary Practices, Gender Ideology, and the Cherokee Town at Coweeta Creek. *Journal of Anthropological Archaeology* 30:45–73.

2014   Cherokee Towns and Calumet Ceremonialism in Eastern North America. *American Antiquity* 79:425–443.

2015   *Center Places and Cherokee Towns: Archaeological Perspectives on Native American Architecture and Landscape in the Southern Appalachians.* University of Alabama Press, Tuscaloosa.

Roe, Lori M.

2010   Social Complexity and Mound Ceremony in the Coles Creek Culture: Research at the Raffman Mound Center in Madison Parish, Louisiana. Unpublished Ph.D. dissertation, Department of Anthropology, Tulane University, New Orleans, Louisiana.

Rogers, J. Daniel

1995   Dispersed Communities and Integrated Households: A Perspective from Spiro and the Arkansas Basin. In *Mississippian Communities and Households*, edited by Bruce D. Smith and J. Daniel Rogers, pp. 110–132. University of Alabama Press, Tuscaloosa.

1996   Markers of Social Integration: The Development of Centralized Authority in the Spiro Region. In *Political Structure and Change in the Prehistoric Southeastern United States*, edited by John F. Scarry, pp. 53–68. University Press of Florida, Gainesville.

Rogers, J. Daniel, Michael C. Moore, and Rusty Greaves

1982   *Spiro Archaeology: The Plaza.* Studies in Oklahoma's Past 10. Oklahoma Archaeological Survey, Norman.

Rogers, J. Daniel, and Samuel M. Wilson (editors)

1993   *Ethnohistory and Archaeology: Approaches to Postcontact Change in the Americas.* Plenum Press, New York.

Rundkvist, Martin

2008   Classifying an Archaeologist. *Aardvarchaeology.* October 27, 2008. http://scienceblogs.com/aardvarchaeology/2008/10/27/classifying-an-archaeologist/.

Russo, Michael

1996   Southeastern Preceramic Archaic Ceremonial Mounds. In *Archaeology of the Mid-Holocene Southeast*, edited by Kenneth E. Sassaman and David G. Anderson, pp. 259–287. University Press of Florida, Gainesville.

2004   Measuring Shell Rings for Social Inequality. In *Signs of Power: The Rise of Cultural Complexity in the Southeast*, edited by Jon L. Gibson and Philip J. Carr, pp. 26–70. University of Alabama Press, Tuscaloosa.

2006   Archaic Shell Rings of the Southeast U.S.: National Historic Landmarks, Historic Context. Southeast Archeological Center, National Park Service, Tallahassee, Florida. https://www.nps.gov/nhl/learn/themes/ArchaicShellRings.pdf.

Russo, Michael, Craig Dengel, and Jeffrey Shanks
2014   Northwest Florida Woodland Mounds and Middens: The Sacred and Not So Secular. In *New Histories of Pre-Columbian Florida*, edited by Neill J. Wallis and Asa R. Randall, pp. 121–142. University Press of Florida, Gainesville.

Russo, Michael, Barbara Purdy, Lee A. Newsom, and Ray M. McGee
1992   A Reinterpretation of Late Archaic Adaptations in Central-East Florida: Groves' Orange Midden (8VO2601). *Southeastern Archaeology* 11(2):95–108.

Sahlins, Marshall
2011   What Kinship Is (Part One). *Journal of the Royal Anthropological Institute* 17:2–19.

Sanchez, Guadalupe, Vance T. Holliday, Edmund P. Gaines, Joaquin Arroyo-Cabrales, Natalia Martínez-Tagüeña, Andrew Kowler, Todd Lange, Gregory W. L. Hodgins, Susan M. Mentzer, and Ismael Sanchez-Morales
2014   Human (Clovis)-Gompothere (*Cuvieronius* sp.) Association ~13,390 Calibrated yBP in Sonora, Mexico. *Proceedings of the National Academy of Sciences* 111(30):10972–10977.

Sassaman, Kenneth E.
2003a   New AMS Dates on Orange Fiber-Tempered Pottery from the Middle St. Johns Valley and Their Implications for Culture History in Northeast Florida. *Florida Anthropologist* 56:5–13.
2003b   *St. Johns Archaeological Field School 2000–2001: Blue Spring and Hontoon Island State Parks*. Technical Report 4. Laboratory of Southeastern Archaeology, Department of Anthropology, University of Florida, Gainesville.
2004   Common Origins and Divergent Histories in the Early Pottery Traditions of the American Southeast. In *Early Pottery: Technology, Function, Style, and Interaction in the Lower Southeast*, edited by Rebecca Saunders and Christopher T. Hays, pp. 23–39. University of Alabama Press, Tuscaloosa.
2010   *The Eastern Archaic, Historicized*. AltaMira Press, Lantham, Maryland.

Sassaman, Kenneth E., and Michael J. Heckenberger
2004   Crossing the Symbolic Rubicon in the Southeast. In *Signs of Power: The Rise of Cultural Complexity in the Southeast*, edited by John L. Gibson and Philip. J. Carr, pp. 214–233. University of Alabama Press, Tuscaloosa.

Sassaman, Kenneth E., Jason M. O'Donoughue, and Julie Byrd
2011   Material Culture. In *Archaeological Investigations at Salt Springs (8MR2322), Marion County, Florida*, edited by Jason M. O'Donoughue, Kenneth E. Sassaman, Meggan E. Blessing, Johanna B. Talcott, and Julie Byrd, pp. 49–64. Technical Report 11. Laboratory of Southeastern Archaeology, Department of Anthropology, University of Florida, Gainesville.

Sassaman, Kenneth E. and Asa R. Randall
2012   Shell Mounds of the Middle St. Johns Basin, Northeast Florida. In *Early New World Monumentality*, edited by Richard L. Burger and Robert M. Rosenswig, pp. 53–77. University Press of Florida, Gainesville.

Sassaman, Kenneth E., and Victoria Rudolphi
2001   Communities of Practice in the Early Pottery Traditions of the American Southeast. *Journal of Anthropological Research* 57:407–425.

Saunders, Joe

2012   Early Mounds in the Lower Mississippi Valley. In *Early New World Monumentality*, edited by Richard L. Burger and Robert M. Rosenswig, pp. 25–52. University Press of Florida, Gainesville.

Saunders, Joe W., Thurman Allen, Reca Jones, and Gloria Swoveland

2000   Caney Mounds (16CT5). *Louisiana Archaeological Society Newsletter* 27:14–21.

Saunders, Joe, Reca Bamburg Jones, and Thurman Allen

2006   Annual Report for Management Unit 2: Regional Archaeology Program, Department of Geosciences, Northeast Louisiana University. Report submitted to Division of Archaeology, Louisiana Department of Culture, Recreation and Tourism, Baton Rouge.

Saunders, Joe W., Rolfe D. Mandel, Roger T. Saucier, E. Thurman Allen, C. T. Hallmark, Jay K. Johnson, Edwin H. Jackson, Charles M. Allen, Gary L. Stringer, Douglas S. Frink, James K. Feathers, Stephen Williams, Kristen J. Gremillion, Malcolm F. Vidrine, and Reca Jones

1997   A Mound Complex in Louisiana at 5400–5000 Years B.P. *Science* 277 (5333):1796–1799.

Saunders, Rebecca

2000a   *Stability and Change in Guale Indian Pottery, A.D. 1300–1702.* University of Alabama Press, Tuscaloosa.

2000b   The Guale Indians of the Lower Atlantic Coast: Change and Continuity. In *Indians of the Greater Southeast: Historical Archaeology and Ethnohistory*, edited by Bonnie G. McEwan, pp. 26–56. University Press of Florida, Gainesville.

2002   Seasonality, Sedentism, Subsistence, and Disease in the Protohistoric. In *Between Contacts and Colonies: Archaeological Perspectives on the Protohistoric Southeast*, edited by Cameron B. Wesson and Mark A. Rees, pp. 32–48. University of Alabama Press, Tuscaloosa.

2004a   Spatial Variation in Orange Culture Pottery: Interaction and Function. In *Early Pottery: Technology, Function, Style, and Interaction in the Lower Southeast*, edited by Rebecca Saunders and Christopher T. Hays, pp. 40–62. University of Alabama Press, Tuscaloosa.

2004b   The Stratigraphic Sequence at Rollins Shell Ring: Implications for Ring Function. *Florida Anthropologist* 57(4):249–268.

Saunders, Rebecca, and Christopher T. Hays

2004   Introduction: Themes in Early Pottery Research. In *Early Pottery: Technology, Function, Style, and Interaction in the Lower Southeast*, edited by Rebecca Saunders and Christopher T. Hays, pp. 1–22. University of Alabama Press, Tuscaloosa.

Saunders, Rebecca, and Michael Russo

2002   *The Fig Island Ring Complex (38CH42): Coastal Adaptation and the Question of Ring Function in the Late Archaic.* Grant No. 45-01-16441, South Carolina Department of Archives and History, Columbia. http://shpo.sc.gov/research/Documents/FigIsland.pdf.

Saunders, Rebecca, and Margaret K. Wrenn

2014   Crafting Orange Pottery in Early Florida: Production and Distribution. In *New Histories of Pre-Columbian Florida*, edited by Neill J. Wallis and Asa R. Randall, pp. 183–202. University Press of Florida, Gainesville.

Scarry, C. Margaret

2003   Patterns of Wild Plant Utilization in the Prehistoric Eastern Woodlands. In *People and Plants in Eastern North America*, edited by Paul E. Minnis, pp. 50–104. Smithsonian Books, Washington, D.C.

Scarry, C. Margaret, and Kandace D. Hollenbach

2012   What Can Plants and Plant Data Tell Us about Seasonality? In *Seasonality and Human Mobility along the Georgia Bight: Proceedings of the Fifth Caldwell Conference, St. Catherines Island, Georgia, May 14–16, 2010*, pp. 187–198. Anthropological Papers of the American Museum of Natural History, No. 97. American Museum of Natural History, New York.

Scarry, John F.

1990   Mississippian Emergence in the Fort Walton Area: The Evolution of the Cayson and Lake Jackson Phases. In *The Mississippian Emergence*, edited by Bruce D. Smith, pp. 227–250. Smithsonian Institution Press, Washington, D.C.

1994a   The Late Prehistoric Southeast. In *The Forgotten Centuries: Indians and Europeans in the American South, 1521–1704*, edited by Charles Hudson and Carmen Chaves Tesser, pp. 17–35. University of Georgia Press, Athens.

1994b   The Apalachee Chiefdom: A Mississippian Society on the Fringe of the Mississippian World. In *The Forgotten Centuries: Indians and Europeans in the American South, 1521–1704*, edited by Charles Hudson and Carmen Chaves Tesser, pp. 156–178. University of Georgia Press, Athens.

1996a   The Nature of Mississippian Societies. In *Political Structure and Change in the Prehistoric Southeastern United States*, edited by John F. Scarry, pp. 12–24. University Press of Florida, Gainesville.

1996b   Stability and Change in the Apalachee Chiefdom. In *Political Structure and Change in the Prehistoric Southeastern United States*, edited by John F. Scarry, pp. 192–227. University Press of Florida, Gainesville.

Schiffer, Michael B.

1972   Archaeological Context and Systemic Context. *American Antiquity* 37:156–165.

1983   Toward the Identification of Formation Processes. *American Antiquity* 48:675–706.

Schiffer, Michael B., James M. Skibo, Janet Griffits, Kacy Hollenback, and William A. Longacre

2001   Behavioral Archaeology and the Study of Technology. *American Antiquity* 66:729–738.

Schilling, Timothy M.

2010   An Archaeological Model of the Construction of Monks Mound and Implications for the Development of Cahokian Society (800–1400 A.D.). Unpublished Ph.D. dissertation, Department of Anthropology, Washington University, Saint Louis, Missouri.

2012   Building Monks Mound, Cahokia, Illinois, A.D. *Journal of Field Archaeology* 37(4):302–313.

Schroedl, Gerald F.

1978   *The Patrick Site (40MR40), Tellico Reservoir, Tennessee.* Report of Investigations No. 25, Department of Anthropology, University of Tennessee, Knoxville.

1998   Mississippian Towns in the Eastern Tennessee Valley. In *Mississippian Towns and Sacred Spaces: Searching for an Architectural Grammar*, edited by R. Barry Lewis and Charles B. Stout, pp. 64–92. University of Alabama Press, Tuscaloosa.

2000 Cherokee Ethnohistory and Archaeology from 1540 to 1838. In *Indians of the Greater Southeast: Historical Archaeology and Ethnohistory*, edited by Bonnie G. McEwan, pp. 204–241. University Press of Florida, Gainesville.

Schwadron, Maro

2010 Prehistoric Landscapes of Complexity: Archaic and Woodland Period Shell Works, Shell Rings, and Tree Islands of the Everglades, South Florida. In *Trend, Tradition, and Turmoil: What Happened to the Southeastern Archaic?*, edited by David H. Thomas and Matthew C. Sanger, pp. 113–146. Anthropological Papers, American Museum of Natural History, Vol. 89, Pt. 2. American Museum of Natural History, New York.

Schwartz, Marion

1997 *A History of Dogs in the Early Americas*. Yale University Press, New Haven, Connecticut.

Searcy, Margaret

1981 *The Charm of the Bear Claw Necklace* (1971). University of Alabama Press, Tuscaloosa.

1991 *Wolf Dog of the Woodland Indians*. Firebird Press, Gretna, Louisiana.

1995 *Eye the Hunter: A Story of Ice-Age America*. Pelican Publishing Company, Gretna, Louisiana.

2009 *Ikwa of the Mound-Builder Indians* (1974). Pelican Publishing Company, Gretna, Louisiana.

Sears, William H.

1956 *Excavations at Kolomoki: Final Report*. University of Georgia Press, Athens.

1973 The Sacred and the Secular in Prehistoric Ceramics. In *Variation in Anthropology: Essays in Honor of John C. McGregor*, edited by Donald W. Lathrop and Jody Douglas, pp. 31–42. Illinois Archaeological Survey, Urbana.

Seeman, Mark F.

1995 When Words Are Not Enough: Hopewell Interregionalism and the Use of Material Symbols at the GE Mound. In *Native American Interactions*, edited by Michael S. Nassaney and Kenneth E. Sassaman, pp. 122–143. University of Tennessee Press, Knoxville.

Sellet, Frédéric

1993 Chaîne Opératoire: The Concept and Its Application. *Lithic Technology* 18(21–22):106–112.

Shafer, Harry J., and Thomas R. Hester

1991 Lithic Craft Specialization and Product Distribution at the Maya Site of Colha, Belize. *World Archaeology* 23:79–97.

Shannon, Laura M., Ryan H. Boyko, Marta Castelhano, Elizabeth Corey, Jessica J. Hayward, Corin McLean, Michelle E. White, Mounir Abi Said, Baddley A. Anita, Nono Ikombe Bondjengo, Jorge Calero, Ana Galov, Marius Hedimbi, Bulu Imam, Rajashree Khalap, Douglas Lally, Andrew Masta, Kyle C. Oliveira, Lucía Pérez, Julia Randall, Nguyen Minh Tam, Francisco J. Trujillo-Cornejo, Carlos Valeriano, Nathan B. Sutter, Rory J. Todhunter, Carlos D. Bustamante, and Adam R. Boykoa

2015 Genetic Structure in Village Dogs Reveals a Central Asian Domestication Origin. *Proceedings of the National Academy of Sciences* 112(44):13417–13418.

Shenkel, J. Richard

1986 An Additional Comment on Volume Calculations and a Comparison of Formulae using Several Southeastern Mounds. *Midcontinental Journal of Archaeology* 11:201–220.

Sherwood, Sarah C.

2013   Geoarchaeological Study of the Mound A Stratigraphy. In *Archaeological Investigations at Shiloh Indian Mounds National Historic Landmark (40HR7), 1999–2004*, edited by David G. Anderson, John E. Cornelison Jr., and Sarah C. Sherwood, pp. 526–645. National Park Service, Southeastern Archeological Center, Tallahassee.

Sherwood, Sarah C., Boyce N. Driskell, Asa R. Randall, and Scott C. Meeks

2004   Chronology and Stratigraphy at Dust Cave, Alabama. *American Antiquity* 69(3):533–554.

Sherwood, Sarah C., and Tristram R. Kidder

2011   The DaVincis of Dirt: Geoarchaeological Perspectives on Native American Mound Building in the Mississippi River Basin. *Journal of Anthropological Archaeology* 30:69–87.

Shimada, Izumi

1996   Sicán Metallurgy and Its Cross-Craft Relationships. *Boletín del Museo del Oro* 41:27–61.

Shimada, Izumi (editor)

2007   *Craft Production in Complex Societies: Multicraft and Producer Perspectives*. University of Utah Press, Salt Lake City.

Shipman, Pat

2015   *The Invaders: How Humans and Their Dogs Drove Neanderthals to Extinction*. Harvard University Press, Cambridge, Massachusetts.

Shott, Michael J.

1995   How Much Is a Scraper? Curation, Use Rates, and the Formation of Scraper Assemblages. *Lithic Technology* 20:52–72.

2003   Reduction Sequence and *Chaîne Opèratoire*. *Lithic Technology* 28:95–105.

2005   Representativity of the Midwestern Paleoindian Site Sample. *North American Archaeologist* 25:189–212.

2014   *Works in Stone: Contemporary Perspectives on Lithic Analysis*. University of Utah Press, Salt Lake City.

Shott, Michael J., and Jesse Ballenger

2007   Biface Reduction and the Measurement of Dalton Curation: A Southeastern Case Study. *American Antiquity* 72:153–175.

Shott, Michael J., and Margaret C. Nelson

2008   Lithic Reduction, Its Measurements, and Implications. In *Lithic Technologies: Life-Cycles of Production and Retouch*, edited by William Andrefsky, pp. 23–45. Cambridge University Press, Cambridge.

Shott, Michael J., and Paul Sillitoe

2001   The Mortality of Things: Correlates of Use Life in Wola Material Culture Using Age-at-Census Data. *Journal of Archaeological Method and Theory* 8:269–302.

2004   Modeling Use-Life Distributions in Archaeology Using New Guinea Wola Ethnographic Data. *American Antiquity* 69:339–355.

2005   Use Life and Curation in New Guinea Experimental Used Flakes. *Journal of Archaeological Science* 32:653–663.

Silverberg, Robert

1968   *Mound Builders of Ancient America*. New York Graphic Society, Greenwich.

Simon, Mary L.

2000   Regional Variations in Plant Use Strategies in the Midwest during the Late Woodland. In *Late Woodland Societies: Tradition and Transformation across the Midcontinent*, edited by Thomas E. Emerson, Dale L. McElrath, and Andrew C. Fortier, pp. 37–75. University of Nebraska Press, Lincoln.

Simon, Mary L., and Kathryn E. Parker

2006   Prehistoric Plant Use in the American Bottom: New Thoughts and Interpretations. *Southeastern Archaeology* 25:212–257.

Simonton, Dean K

1999   *Origins of Genius: Darwinian Perspectives on Genius.* Oxford University Press, New York.

Smallwood, Ashley M.

2012   Clovis Technology and Settlement in the American Southeast Using Biface Analysis to Evaluate Dispersal Models. *American Antiquity* 77(4):689–713.

2014   Introduction. In *Clovis: On the Edge of a New Understanding*, edited by Ashley M. Smallwood and Thomas A. Jennings, pp. 1–10. Texas A&M University Press, College Station.

Smallwood, Ashley M., Thomas A. Jennings, David G. Anderson, and Jerald Ledbetter

2015   Testing for Evidence of Paleoindian Responses to Environmental Changes during the Younger Dryas Chronozone in Georgia. *Southeastern Archaeology* 34(1):23–45.

Smith, Adam T.

2003   *The Political Landscape: Constellations of Authority in Early Complex Polities.* University of California Press, Berkeley.

Smith, Betty Anderson

1979   Distribution of Eighteenth-Century Cherokee Settlements. In *The Cherokee Indian Nation: A Troubled History*, edited by Duane H. King, pp. 46–60. University of Tennessee Press, Knoxville.

Smith, Bruce D.

1986   The Archaeology of the Southeastern United States: From Dalton to de Soto, 10,500–500 B.P. *Advances in World Archaeology* 5:1–92.

Smith, Eric A., Monique Borgerhoff Mulder, and Kim Hill

2001   Controversies in the Evolutionary Social Sciences: A Guide for the Perplexed. *Trends in Ecology and Evolution* 16(3):128–135.

Smith, Kevin E.

2015   Long before Salt Peanuts Appeared on the Ballpark Menu, Salt Was Significant at Nashville's Sulphur Dell. *Tennessee Conservationist* (March/April 2015):32–35.

Smith, Marvin T.

1987   *Archaeology of Aboriginal Change in the Interior Southeast: Depopulation during the Early Historic Period.* University Press of Florida, Gainesville.

2000   *Coosa: The Rise and Fall of a Southeastern Mississippian Chiefdom.* University Press of Florida, Gainesville.

2001   The Rise and Fall of Coosa, A.D. 1350–1700. In *Societies in Eclipse: Archaeology of the Eastern Woodlands Indians, A.D. 1400–1700*, edited by David S. Brose, C. Wesley Cowan, and Robert C. Mainfort, Jr., pp. 143–155. Smithsonian Institution Press, Washington, D.C.

2002   Aboriginal Population Movements in the Postcontact Southeast. In *The Transformation of the Southeastern Indians, 1540–1760*, edited by Robbie Ethridge and Charles Hudson, pp. 3–20. University Press of Mississippi, Jackson.

2006   Aboriginal Population Movements in the Early Historic Period Interior Southeast. In *Powhatan's Mantle: Indians in the Colonial Southeast*, edited by Gregory A. Waselkov, Peter H. Wood, and Tom Hatley, pp. 43–56. Revised and expanded edition. University of Nebraska Press, Lincoln.

Smith, Marvin T., and Julie Barnes Smith

1989   Engraved Shell Masks in North America. *Southeastern Archaeology* 8:9–18.

Smith, Marvin T., and Mark Williams

1994   Mississippian Mound Refuse Disposal Patterns and Implications for Archaeological Research. *Southeastern Archaeology* 13:27–35.

Smith, Monica L.

2008   Urban Empty Spaces: Contentious Places for Consensus Building. *Archaeological Dialogues* 15(2):216–231.

2010   *A Prehistory of Ordinary People*. University of Arizona Press, Tucson.

Smith, Peter

1998   *Explaining Chaos*. Cambridge University Press, Cambridge.

Snead, James E., Clark L. Erickson, and J. Andrew Darling (editors)

2011   *Landscapes of Movement: Trails, Paths, and Roads in Anthropological Perspective*. University of Pennsylvania Press, Philadelphia.

Snyder, Lynn M.

1995   Assessing the Role of the Domestic Dog as a Native American Food Resource in the Middle Missouri Subarea A.D. 1000–1840. Unpublished Ph.D. dissertation, Department of Anthropology, University of Tennessee, Knoxville.

Soday, Frank J.

1954   The Quad Site: A Paleo-Indian Village in North Alabama. *Tennessee Archaeologist* 10:1–20.

Soja, Edward W.

2000   *Postmetropolis: Critical Studies of Cities and Regions*. Blackwell, Oxford.

Speck, Frank B.

2004   *Ethnology of the Yuchi Indians*. University of Oklahoma Press, Norman.

Spector, Janet

1993   *What This Awl Means: Feminist Archaeology at a Wahpeton Dakota Village*. Minnesota Historical Society Press, St. Paul.

Spielmann, Katherine A.

1998   Ritual Craft Specialists in Small-scale Societies. In *Craft and Social Identity*, edited by Cathy Lynne Costin and Rita Wright, pp. 153–159. Archaeological Papers, 8. American Anthropological Association, Arlington, Virginia.

2002   Feasting, Craft Specialization, and the Ritual Mode of Production in Small-scale Societies. *American Anthropologist* 104:195–207.

2008   Crafting the Sacred: Ritual Places and the Paraphernalia in Small-scale Societies. In *Dimensions of Ritual Economy*, edited by E. Christian Wells and Patricia Ann McAnany, pp. 37–72. Research in Economic Anthropology, Vol. 27. Emerald Group Publishing, Bingley, United Kingdom.

Stephenson, Keith, Judith A. Bense, and Frankie Snow

2002   Aspects of Deptford and Swift Creek of the South Atlantic and Gulf Coastal Plains. In *The Woodland Southeast*, edited by David G. Anderson and Robert C. Mainfort Jr., pp. 318–351. University of Alabama Press, Tuscaloosa.

Steponaitis, Vincas P.

1986   Prehistoric Indians of the Southeastern United States, 1970–1985. *Annual Review of Anthropology* 15:363–404.

1991   Contrasting Patterns of Mississippian Development. In *Chiefdoms: Power, Economy, and Ideology*, edited by Timothy K. Earle, pp. 193–228. Cambridge University Press, New York.

2009   *Ceramics, Chronology, and Community Patterns: An Archaeological Study at Moundville*. New edition (reprint of 1983 edition with new preface). University of Alabama Press, Tuscaloosa.

Steponaitis, Vincas P., Megan C. Kassabaum, and John W. O'Hear

2015   Coles Creek Antecedents. In *The Medieval Mississippians*, edited by Timothy R. Pauketat and Susan M. Alt, pp. 12–19. School for Advanced Research Press, Santa Fe.

Steponaitis, Vincas P., and John W. O'Hear

2008   Recent Excavations at the Feltus Mounds: Preliminary Findings and Comparisons. Paper presented at the 65th annual meeting of the Southeastern Archaeological Conference, Charlotte, North Carolina.

Sternberg, George M.

1876   Indian Burial Mounds and Shellheaps near Pensacola, Florida. In *Proceedings of the American Association for the Advancement of Science*, 24th meeting, Detroit, pp. 282–292. Published by the Permanent Secretary, Salem, Massachusetts.

Sterrett, Douglas B.

1923   *Mica Deposits of the United States*, Bulletin 740. United States Geological Survey, Department of the Interior. Government Printing Office, Washington, D.C.

Steward, Julian H. and Frank M. Seltzer

1938   Function and Configuration in Archaeology. *American Antiquity* 4:4–10.

Stojanowski, Christopher M.

2005   *Biocultural Histories in La Florida: A Bioarchaeological Perspective*. University Press of Florida, Gainesville.

2008   The Bioarchaeology of Identity in Spanish Colonial Florida: Social and Evolutionary Transformation before, during, and after Demographic Collapse. *American Anthropologist* 107:417–431.

Stone, Lyle

1974   Fort Michilimackinac 1715–1781: An Archaeological Perspective on the Revolutionary Frontier. Publications of the Museum, Michigan State University, East Lansing.

Stone, Tammy

1999   The Chaos of Collapse: Disintegration and Reintegration of Inter-Regional Systems. *Antiquity* 73:110–118.

Styles, Bonnie W., and Walter Klippel

1996   Mid-Holocene Faunal Exploitation in the Southeastern United States. In *Archaeology of the Mid-Holocene Southeast*, edited by Kenneth E. Sassaman and David G. Anderson, pp. 115–133. University Press of Florida, Gainesville.

Sullivan, Lynne P.
2007   Shell Gorgets, Time, and the Southeastern Ceremonial Complex in Southeastern Tennessee. In *Southeastern Ceremonial Complex: Chronology, Content, Context*, edited by Adam King, pp. 88–106. University of Alabama Press, Tuscaloosa.

Surovell, Todd A.
2000   Early Paleoindian Women, Children, Mobility, and Fertility. *American Antiquity* 65(3): 493–508.

2003   Simulating Coastal Migration in New World Colonization. *Current Anthropology* 44(4):580–591.

Swanton, John R.
1911   *Indian Tribes of the Lower Mississippi Valley and Adjacent Coast of the Gulf of Mexico.* Bulletin 43. Bureau of American Ethnology, Washington, D.C.

1928   *Social Organization and Social Usages of the Indians of the Creek Confederacy.* 42nd Annual Report of the Bureau of American Ethnology. Smithsonian Institution, Washington, D.C.

1946   *The Indians of the Southeastern United States.* Bureau of American Ethnology Bulletin, No. 137. Government Printing Office, Washington, D.C.

Talalay, Laurie, Donald R. Keller, and Patrick J. Munson
1984   Hickory Nuts, Walnuts, Butternuts, and Hazelnuts: Observations and Experiments Relevant to Their Aboriginal Exploitation in Eastern North America. In *Experiments and Observations on Aboriginal Wild Plant Food Utilization in Eastern North America*, edited by Patrick J. Munson, pp. 338–359. Prehistory Research Series Vol. 6 (No. 2). Indiana Historical Society, Indianapolis.

Thaler, Wolfgang (director)
2012   *Ants!—Nature's Secret Power.* Adi Mayer-Film.

Thalmann, O., B. Shapiro, P. Cui, V. J. Schuenemann, S. K. Sawyer, D. L. Greenfield, M. B. Germonpré, M. V. Sablin, F. López-Giráldez, X. Domingo-Roura, H. Napierala, H.-P. Uerpmann, D. M. Loponte, A. A. Acosta, L. Giemsch, R. W. Schmitz, B. Worthington, J. E. Buikstra, A. Druzhkova, A. S. Graphodatsky, N. D. Ovodov, N. Wahlberg, A. H. Freedman, R. M. Schweizer, K.-P. Koepfli, J. A. Leonard, M. Meyer, J. Krause, S. Pääbo, R. E. Green, and R. K. Wayne
2013   Complete Mitochondrial Genomes of Ancient Canids Suggest a European Origin of Domestic Dogs. *Science* 342 (6160):871–874.

thescottbrothers.com (The Scott Brothers)
2015   FAQ: Where Is the Show Filmed? They Never Mention Where They Are Located. http://www.thescottbrothers.com/faq/.

Thomas, David H.
1986   Contemporary Hunter-Gatherer Archaeology in America. In *American Archaeology Past and Future: A Celebration of the Society of American Archaeology 1935–1985*, edited by David J. Meltzer, Don D. Fowler, and Jeremy A. Sabloff, pp. 237–276. Smithsonian Institution Press, Washington, DC.

Thomas, David H., and Robert L. Kelly
2016   *Archaeology.* 7th ed. Cengage Learning, Boston.

Thomas, Julian
2011   Ritual and Religion in the Neolithic. In *The Oxford Handbook of the Archaeology of*

Ritual and Religion, edited by Timothy Insoll, pp. 371–386. Oxford University Press, Oxford.

Thomas, William Holland
1840 Census of the North Carolina Cherokees, 1840. Manuscript copy in the William Holland Thomas Papers, Duke University Special Collections, Durham, North Carolina.
1871 Letter to Cherokee Council. Unbound volumes, William Holland Thomas Papers, Duke University Special Collections, Durham, North Carolina.

Thompson, Victor D.
2009 The Mississippian Production of Space through Earthen Pyramids and Public Buildings on the Georgia Coast, USA. *World Archaeology* 41(3):445–470.

Thompson, Victor D., and C. Fred T. Andrus
2011 Evaluating Mobility, Monumentality, and Feasting at the Sapelo Island Shell Ring Complex. *American Antiquity* 76:315–343.

Thompson, Victor D., William H. Marquardt, Alexander Cherkinsky, Amanda D. Roberts-Thompson, Karen J. Walker, Lee A. Newsom and Michael Savarese
2016 From Shell Midden to Midden Mound: The Geoarchaeology of Mound Key, an Anthropogenic Island in Southwest Florida, USA. *PLoS ONE* 11(4):1–22.

Thompson, Victor D., and Christopher R. Moore
2015 The Sociality of Surplus among Late Archaic Hunter-Gatherers of Coastal Georgia. In *Surplus: The Politics or Production and the Strategies of Everyday Life*, edited by Christopher T. Morehart and Kristin De Lucia, pp. 245–266. University Press of Colorado, Boulder.

Thompson, Victor D., and Thomas J. Pluckhahn
2010 History, Complex Hunter-Gatherers, and the Mounds and Monuments of Crystal River, Florida, USA: A Geophysical Perspective. *Journal of Island and Coastal Archaeology* 5:22–51.

Thulman, David K.
2006 A Reconstruction of Paleoindian Social Organization in North Central Florida. Unpublished Ph.D. dissertation, Department of Anthropology, Florida State University, Tallahassee.

Titiev, Mischa
1937 A Hopi Salt Expedition. *American Anthropologist* 39(2):244–258.

Titmus, Gene L., and James C. Woods
1986 An Experimental Study of Projectile Point Fracture Patterns. *Journal of California and Great Basin Anthropology* 8(1):37–49.

Tito, Raul Y., Samuel L. Belknap, Kristin D. Sobolik, Robert C. Ingraham, Lauren M. Cleeland, and Cecil M. Lewis Jr.
2012 Brief Communication: DNA from Early Holocene American Dog. *American Journal of Physical Anthropology* 145:653–657.

Tomášková, Silvia
2005 What Is a Burin? Typology, Technology, and Interregional Comparison. *Journal of Archaeological Method and Theory* 12:79–115.

Tostevin, Gilbert B.
2011 Levels of Theory and Social Practice in the Reduction Sequence and Chaîne Opératoire Methods of Lithic Analysis. Special Issue: Reduction Sequence, Chaîne Opéra-

toire, and Other Methods: The Epistemologies of Different Approaches to Lithic Analysis. *PaleoAnthropology*:351–375.

Towner, Ronald H., and Miranda Warburton
1990   Projectile Point Rejuvenation: A Technological Analysis. *Journal of Field Archaeology* 17:311–321.

Tringham, Ruth
1991   Households with Faces: The Challenge of Gender in Prehistoric Architectural Remains. In *Engendering Archaeology: Women and Prehistory*, edited by Joan Gero and Meg Conkey, pp. 93–131. Blackwell Press, Cambridge, Massachusetts.

Trinkley, Michael B.
1985   The Form and Function of South Carolina's Early Woodland Shell Rings. In *Structure and Process in Southeastern Archaeology*, edited by Roy S. Dickens Jr. and H. Trawick Ward, pp. 102–118. University of Alabama Press, Tuscaloosa.

Tucker, Bram T., and Alyson G. Young
2005   Growing Up Mikea: Children's Time Allocation and Tuber Foraging in Southwestern Madagascar. In *Hunter-Gatherer Childhoods*, edited by Barry S. Hewlett and Michael E. Lamb, pp. 147–171. Transaction Publishers, Somerset, New Jersey.

Tucker, Bryan D.
2009   Isotopic Investigations of Archaic Period Subsistence and Settlement in the St. Johns River Drainage, Florida. Unpublished Ph.D. dissertation, Department of Anthropology, University of Florida, Gainesville.

Tune, Jesse W.
2015   Settling into the Younger Dryas: Human Behavioral Adaptations during the Pleistocene to Holocene Transition in the Midsouth United States. Unpublished Ph.D. dissertation, Department of Anthropology, Texas A&M University, College Station.

Tune, Jesse W., Nathan Allison, Aaron Deter-Wolf, Adam Finn, and Ryan Parish
2015   The Parris Collection: A Life-Long Dedication to Archaeology. Paper presented at the Current Research in Tennessee Archaeology Annual Meeting, Nashville, Tennessee.

Tushingham, Shannon, Jane Hill, and Charles McNutt (editors)
2002   *Histories of Southeastern Archaeology*. University of Alabama Press, Tuscaloosa.

Van Damme, Thomas
2014   Crowdfunding Archaeology: Exploring the Potential of Crowdfunding in Archaeological Research. https://www.academia.edu/8541754/Crowdfunding_Archaeology_Exploring_the_Potential_of_Crowdfunding_in_Archaeological_Research.

VanDerwarker, Amber M.
1996   Domestic Dogs in the Diet: An Analysis of Canid Fauna from the Halliday Site, an Early Mississippian Upland Village in the American Bottom. Paper presented at the 53rd Annual Southeastern Archaeological Conference, Birmingham, Alabama.

Van Nest, Julieann
1998   The 1994 Geological Investigations at the Mound House Site. In *Staging Ritual: Hopewell Ceremonialism at the Mound House Site, Greene County, Illinois*, edited by Jane E. Buikstra, Douglas K. Charles, and Gordon F. M. Ratika, pp. 118–173. Kampsville Studies in Archaeology and History, Vol. 1. Center for American Archeology, Kampsville, Illinois.

VanPool, Christine S.
2009   The Signs of the Sacred: Identifying Shamans Using Archaeological Evidence. *Journal of Anthropological Archaeology* 28:177–190.

VanPool, Christine S., and Elizabeth Newsome
2012   The Spirit in the Material: A Case Study of Animism in the American Southwest. *American Antiquity* 77(2):243–262.

VanPool, Christine S., and Todd L. VanPool
1999   The Scientific Nature of Postprocessualism. *American Antiquity* 64(1):33–53.

Verhagen, Philip, and Thomas G. Whitley
2012   Integrating Archaeological Theory and Predictive Modeling: A Live Report from the Scene. *Journal of Archaeological Method and Theory* 19:49–100.

Viveiros de Castro, Eduardo
1998   Cosmological Deixis and Amerindian Perspectivism. *Journal of the Royal Anthropological Institute* 4(3):469–488.

2004   Exchanging Perspectives: The Transformation of Objects into Subjects in Amerindian Ontologies. *Common Knowledge* 10(3):463–484.

Walker, John H.
2008   The Llanos de Mojos. In *The Handbook of South American Archaeology*, edited by Helaine Silverman and William Isbell, 927–939. Springer, New York.

Walker, Renee
1998   The Late Paleoindian through Middle Archaic Evidence from Dust Cave, Alabama. Unpublished Ph.D. dissertation, Department of Anthropology, University of Tennessee, Knoxville.

2007   Hunting in the Late Paleoindian Period: Faunal Remains from Dust Cave, Alabama. In *Foragers of the Terminal Pleistocene*, edited by Renee B. Walker and Boyce N. Driskell, pp. 99–115. University of Alabama Press, Tuscaloosa.

Walker, Renee B., Darcy F. Morey, and John H. Relethford
2005   Early and Mid-Holocene Dogs in Southeastern North America: Examples from Dust Cave. *Southeastern Archaeology* 24 (1):83–92.

Walker, Renee B., and Paul W. Parmalee
2004   A Noteworthy Cache of Goose Humeri from Late Paleoindian Levels at Dust Cave, Northwestern Alabama. *Journal of Alabama Archaeology* 50(1):18–35.

Walker, Renee B., and R. Jeannine Windham
2014   The Dogs of Spirit Hill: An Analysis of Domestic Dog Burials from Jackson County, Alabama. In *Trends and Tradition in Southeastern Zooarchaeology*, edited by Tanya M. Peres, pp. 105–124. Florida Museum of Natural History: Ripley P. Bullen Series. University Press of Florida, Gainesville.

Wallis, Neill J.
2011   *The Swift Creek Gift*. University of Alabama Press, Tuscaloosa.

Walthall, John A.
1998   Rockshelters and Hunter-Gatherer Adaptation to the Pleistocene/Holocene Transition. *American Antiquity* 63(2):223–238.

Ward, H. Trawick, and R. P. Stephen Davis, Jr.
1993   *Indian Communities on the North Carolina Piedmont, A.D. 1000 to 1700*. Monograph 2, Research Laboratories of Anthropology, University of North Carolina, Chapel Hill.

1999   *Time before History: The Prehistory of North Carolina*, University of North Carolina Press, Chapel Hill.

2001   Tribes and Traders on the North Carolina Piedmont, A.D. 1000–1700. In *Societies in Eclipse: Archaeology of the Eastern Woodlands Indians, A.D. 1400–1700*, edited by David S. Brose, C. Wesley Cowan, and Robert C. Mainfort Jr., pp. 125–141. Smithsonian Institution Press, Washington, D.C.

Waring, Antonio J., Jr.

1968   The Southern Cult and Muskhogean Ceremonial. In *The Waring Papers: The Collected Works of Antonio J. Waring, Jr.*, edited by Stephen Williams, pp. 30–69. Papers of the Peabody Museum of Archaeology and Ethnology, Vol. 58. Harvard University, Cambridge, Massachusetts.

Warren, Diane M.

2004   Skeletal Biology and Paleopathology of Domestic Dogs from Prehistoric Alabama, Illinois, Kentucky, and Tennessee. Unpublished Ph.D. dissertation, Department of Anthropology, Indiana University, Bloomington.

Waselkov, Gregory A.

1989   Seventeenth-Century Trade in the Colonial Southeast. *Southeastern Archaeology* 12: 117–133.

1994   The Macon Trading House and Early European-Indian Contact in the Colonial Southeast. In *Ocmulgee Archaeology, 1936–1986*, edited by David H. Hally, pp. 190–196. University of Georgia Press, Athens.

2006   Indian Maps of the Colonial Southeast. In *Powhatan's Mantle: Indians in the Colonial Southeast*, edited by Gregory A. Waselkov, Peter H. Wood, and Tom Hatley, pp. 435–502. Revised and expanded edition. University of Nebraska Press, Lincoln.

Waselkov, Gregory A., and Bonnie L. Gums

2000   *Plantation Archaeology at Rivière aux Chiens, ca. 1725–1848.* University of South Alabama Monograph 7. Center for Archaeological Studies, University of South Alabama, Mobile.

Waselkov, Gregory A., and Marvin T. Smith

2000   Upper Creek Archaeology. In *Indians of the Greater Southeast: Historical Archaeology and Ethnohistory*, edited by Bonnie G. McEwan, pp. 242–264. University Press of Florida, Gainesville.

Waters, Michael R., and Thomas W. Stafford

2007   Redefining the Age of Clovis: Implications for the Peopling of the Americas. *Science* 315:1122–1126.

Waters, Michael R., Thomas W. Stafford Jr., Brian Kooyman, and L. V. Hills

2015   Late Pleistocene Horse and Camel Hunting at the Southern Margin of the Ice-Free Corridor: Reassessing the Age of Wally's Beach, Canada. *Proceedings of the National Academy of Sciences* 112(14):4263–4267.

Webb, William S.

1946   *Indian Knoll, Site OH 2, Ohio County, Kentucky.* Reports in Archeology and Anthropology 4(3), part 1. University of Kentucky, Lexington.

1950a   *The Carlson Annis Mound, Site 5, Butler County, Kentucky.* Reports in Anthropology 7, no. 4. University of Kentucky, Lexington.

1950b   *The Read Shell Midden, Site 10, Butler County, Kentucky.* Reports in Anthropology
7(5). University of Kentucky, Lexington.

1951   *The Parrish Village Site, Site 45, Hopkins County, Kentucky.* Reports in Anthropology
7(6). University of Kentucky, Lexington.

1974   *Indian Knoll.* University of Tennessee Press, Knoxville.

Webb, William S., and David L. DeJarnette

1942   *An Archaeological Survey of Pickwick Basin and Adjacent Portions of the States of Alabama, Mississippi, and Tennessee.* Bulletin 129. Smithsonian Institution, Bureau of
American Ethnology, Washington, D.C.

1948   *The Flint River Site.* Museum Paper 23. Geological Survey of Alabama, Tuscaloosa.

Webb, William S., and William G. Haag

1939   *The Chiggerville Site, Site 1, Ohio County, Kentucky.* Reports in Anthropology 4(1).
University of Kentucky, Lexington.

1947   *Archaic Sites in McLean County, Kentucky.* Reports in Anthropology 7(1). University
of Kentucky, Lexington.

Webster, Gary S.

2008   Culture History: A Culture-Historical Approach. In *Handbook of Archaeological Theories*, edited by R. Alexander Bentley, Herbert D. G. Maschner, and Christopher Chip-
pindale, pp. 11–27. AltaMira Press, Lanham, Maryland.

Webster, William J.

1970   A New Concept for the *Busycon* Shell Receptacle. *Florida Anthropologist* 23(1):1–7.

Welch, Elizabeth

1855   Letter to the Commissioner of Indian Affairs, October 15, 1853. In Letters Received
by the Office of Indian Affairs, 1824–1881, microfilm M-234, roll 97, p. 43. National
Records and Archives, Washington, D.C.

Welch, William, and Nimrod Jarrett

1837   Valuations of Cherokee Property in North Carolina. Manuscript, Record Group 75,
United States National Archives, Washington, D.C.

Wernicke, Carl

2014   Ivan, Nature, and History. September 17, 2014. http://wuwf.org/post/ivan-nature-and-
history#stream/0.

Wesson, Cameron B.

2002   Prestige Goods, Symbolic Capital, and Social Power in the Protohistoric Southeast.
In *Between Contacts and Colonies: Archaeological Perspectives on the Protohistoric
Southeast*, edited by Cameron B. Wesson and Mark A. Rees, pp. 110–125. University of
Alabama Press, Tuscaloosa.

2008   *Households and Hegemony: Early Creek Prestige Goods, Symbolic Capital, and Social
Power.* University of Nebraska Press, Lincoln.

Wettstaed, Judith, and R. Jeannine Windham

2009   Secular and Sacred: Zooarchaeological Remains from the Spirit Hill Site (1Ja642),
Jackson County, Alabama. Report prepared by New South Associates and submitted
to TRC Companies, Nashville, Tennessee.

Whalen, Verity H., and Luis Manuel González La Rosa

2014   Late Nasca Food and Craft Production in the Tierras Blancas Valley, Peru. *Ñawpa
Pacha, Journal of Andean Archaeology* 34(1):79–106.

Whatmore, Sara
2002   *Hybrid Geographies: Natures, Cultures, Spaces*. London: SAGE Publications.
Wheeler, Ryan J.
1994   Early Florida Decorated Bone Objects: Style and Aesthetics from Paleo-Indian through Archaic. *Florida Anthropologist* 47(1):47–60.
Wheeler, Ryan J., and Ray M. McGee
1994   Technology of Mount Taylor Period Occupation, Groves' Orange Midden (8VO2601), Volusia County, Florida. *Florida Anthropologist* 47(4):350–379.
White, Andrew A.
2015   Changing Scales of Lithic Raw Material Transport among Early Hunger-Gatherers in Midcontinental North America. *Archaeology of Eastern North America* 42:51–75.
White, Karli
1990   An Analysis of Bone Tools from the Carlston Annis Site (15Bt5), Kentucky. Unpublished thesis in anthropology, Washington University, St. Louis, Missouri.
2005   Bone Artifacts from the Carlston Annis Site. In *Archaeology of the Middle Green River Region, Kentucky*, edited by William H. Marquardt and Patty Jo Watson, pp. 339–350. Florida Museum of Natural History Institute of Archaeology and Paleoenvironmental Studies Monograph No. 5. University of Florida, Gainesville.
White, Nancy Marie
2014   What I Believe about the Useful Diversity of Theory in Southeastern Archaeology. *Southeastern Archaeology* 33(2):255–268.
Wiessner, Polly W.
2014   Embers of Society: Firelight Talk among the Ju/'hoansi Bushmen. *Proceedings of the National Academy of Sciences* 111:14027–14035.
Willey, Gordon R.
1949   *Archaeology of the Florida Gulf Coast*. Smithsonian Miscellaneous Collections, Vol. 113. Smithsonian Institution Press, Washington, D.C.
Williams, Eduardo
2015   The Salt of the Earth: Ethnoarchaeology of Salt Production in Michoacán, Western Mexico. BAR International Series 2725. Archaeopress, Oxford, England.
Williams, Mark
1994   The Origins of the Macon Plateau Site. In *Ocmulgee Archaeology, 1936–1986*, edited by David Hally, pp. 130–143. University of Georgia Press, Athens.
Williams, Mark, and Gary Shapiro
1996   Mississippian Political Dynamics in the Oconee Valley, Georgia. In *Political Structure and Change in the Prehistoric Southeastern United States*, edited by John F. Scarry, pp. 92–127. University Press of Florida, Gainesville.
Williams, Stephen
1990   The Vacant Quarter and Other Late Events in the Lower Valley. In *Towns and Temples along the Mississippi*, edited by David H. Dye and Cheryl Anne Cox, pp. 170–180. University of Alabama Press, Tuscaloosa.
2001   The Vacant Quarter Hypothesis and the Yazoo Delta. In *Societies in Eclipse: The Archaeology of the Eastern Woodlands Indians, A.D. 1400–1700*, edited by David S. Brose, C. Wesley Cowan, and Robert C. Mainfort Jr., pp. 191–203. Smithsonian Institution Press, Washington, D.C.

Williams, Stephen, and Jeffrey P. Brain

1983   *Excavations at the Lake George Site, Yazoo County, Mississippi, 1958–1960*. Papers of the Peabody Museum of Archaeology and Ethnology, Vol. 74. Harvard University Press, Cambridge, Massachusetts.

Wilson, Edward O.

1998   *Consilience: The Unity of Knowledge*. Vintage Books, Random House, New York.

Wilson, Gregory D.

2008   *The Archaeology of Everyday Life at Early Moundville*. University of Alabama Press, Tuscaloosa.

Wilson, Jennifer, and William Andrefsky

2008   Exploring Retouch on Bifaces: Unpacking Production, Resharpening, and Hammer Type. In *Lithic Technology: Measures of Production, Use, and Curation*, edited by William Andrefsky, pp. 86–105. Cambridge University Press, Cambridge.

Wing, Elizabeth S.

1978   Use of Dogs for Food: An Adaptation to the Coastal Environment. In *Prehistoric Coastal Adaptations: The Economy and Ecology of Maritime Middle America*, edited by Barbara L. Stark and Barbara Voorhies, pp. 29–41. Academic Press, New York.

Winterhalder, Bruce, and Eric Alden Smith

2000   Analyzing Adaptive Strategies: Human Behavioral Ecology at Twenty-Five. *Evolutionary Anthropology* 9(2):51–72.

Wise, John, M. G. Harasewych, and Robert T. Dillon, Jr.

2004   Population Divergence in the Sinistral Whelks of North America, with Special Reference to the East Florida Ecotone. *Marine Biology* 145(6):1167–1179.

Wobst, H. Martin

1977   Stylistic Behavior and Information Exchange. In *For the Director: Research Essays in Honor of James B. Griffin*, edited by Charles E. Cleland, pp. 317–342. Anthropological Papers 61. Museum of Anthropology, University of Michigan, Ann Arbor.

Wolfram, Stephen

1984   Universality and Complexity in Cellular Automata. *Physica* 10:1–35.

Wood, David, Jerome S. Bruner, and Gail Ross

1976   The Role of Tutoring in Problem Solving. *Journal of Child Psychology and Psychiatry and Allied Disciplines* 17(2):89–100.

Woods, Betty

1953   Zuñi Salt Lake. *New Mexico* 31(6):6.

Worrle, Bernard

1997   Salt within the Traditional Medicine of Latin America: A "Hot" Remedy against "Cold" Illnesses. *Curare* 20(2):295–309.

Worth, John E.

2000   The Lower Creeks: Origins and Early History. In *Indians of the Greater Southeast: Historical Archaeology and Ethnohistory*, edited by Bonnie G. McEwan, pp. 265–298. University Press of Florida, Gainesville.

2002   Spanish Missions and the Persistence of Chiefly Power. In *The Transformation of the Southeastern Indians, 1540–1760*, edited by Robbie Ethridge and Charles Hudson, pp. 39–64. University Press of Mississippi, Jackson.

2007   *The Struggle for the Georgia Coast*. University of Alabama Press, Tuscaloosa.

Wright, Alice P., and Edward R. Henry

2013   Introduction: Emerging Approaches to the Landscapes of the Early and Middle Woodland Southeast. In *Early and Middle Woodland Landscapes of the Southeast*, edited by Alice P. Wright and Edward R. Henry, pp. 1–16. University Press of Florida, Gainesville.

Wright, Alice P., and Erika Loveland

2015   Ritualised Craft Production at the Hopewell Periphery: New Evidence from the Appalachian Summit. *Antiquity* 89:137–153.

Yaeger, Jason, and Marcello A. Canuto

2000   Introducing an Archaeology of Communities. In *The Archaeology of Communities*, edited by Marcello A. Canuto and Jason Yaeger, pp. 1–15. Routledge, London.

Yerkes, Richard W.

2003   Using Lithic Artifacts to Study Craft Specialization in Ancient Societies: The Hopewell Case. In *Written in Stone: The Multiple Dimensions of Lithic Analysis*, edited by P. Nick Kardulias and Richard W. Yerkes, pp. 17–34. Lexington Books, Lanham, Maryland.

Yoffee, Norman, Susan K. Fish, and George R. Milner

1999   Comunidades, Ritualities, Chiefdoms: Social Evolution in the American Southwest and Southeast. In *Great Towns and Regional Polities in the Prehistoric Southwest and Southeast*, edited by Jill A. Neitzel, pp. 261–271. University of New Mexico Press, Albuquerque.

Zeanah, David W.

2000   Transport Costs, Central Place Foraging, and Hunter-Gatherer Alpine Land Use Strategies. In *Intermountain Archaeology*, edited by David B. Madsen and Michael D. Metcalf, pp. 1–14. University of Utah Anthropological Papers 122. University of Utah Press, Salt Lake City.

Zucker, Paul

1959   *Town and Square: From the Agora to the Village Green.* Columbia University Press, New York.

Contributors

Casey R. Barrier is assistant professor of anthropology at Bryn Mawr College. He is an anthropological archaeologist. His research is broadly concerned with the development and histories of complex societies through time, with a focus on the political-economic organization of preindustrial food-producing and agricultural groups.

Andrew P. Bradbury is principal investigator and lithic specialist for Cultural Resource Analysts, Inc. He has conducted archaeological fieldwork since 1981, primarily in Tennessee and Kentucky but also in West Virginia, Pennsylvania, Delaware, New Jersey, Indiana, Illinois, and Missouri. He has supervised and authored reports for over 100 archaeological projects ranging from archaeological reconnaissance to large phase III data recovery.

Stephen B. Carmody is postdoctoral fellow in archaeology and visiting assistant professor at Sewanee: The University of the South. He is a paleoethnobotanist specializing in the origins of agriculture and works in the southeastern United States

Philip J. Carr is professor of anthropology and Chief Calvin McGhee Endowed Professor of Native American Studies at the University of South Alabama. He has edited or coedited several volumes, including *Contemporary Lithic Analysis in the Southeast: Problems, Solutions, and Interpretations.*

Beth A. Conklin is associate professor of anthropology at Vanderbilt University. She is a cultural and medical anthropologist, specializing in the ethnography of indigenous peoples of lowland South America (Amazonia). Her research focuses on the anthropology of the body, religion and ritual, health and healing, death and mourning, the politics of indigenous rights, and ecology, environmentalism, and cultural and religious responses to climate change.

Ashley A. Dumas is assistant professor of anthropology at the University of West Alabama, Livingston. Her current research projects include the eighteenth-century Fort Tombecbe site and salt manufacturing in southwest Alabama. She is assistant director of the Black Belt Museum and teaches all of the anthropology courses. Dumas holds a Ph.D. from the University of Alabama.

Zackary I. Gilmore is a postdoctoral researcher in anthropology at the University of Florida. He is the author of *Gathering Places: Hunter-Gatherer History and Community at Florida's Late Archaic Shell Mounds.*

Lance Greene is assistant professor of anthropology at Wright State University. His research interests focus on marginalized groups (American Indians, women, minorities, the poor, and the institutionalized) in the United States during the eighteenth and nineteenth centuries.

Bryan S. Haley is project archaeologist and remote sensing specialist. He specializes in prehistoric, historic Native American, and historic American archaeology of the southeastern United States and archaeological applications of geospatial technologies such as geophysics, airborne and satellite remote sensing, GIS, and Global Positioning System (GPS).

Kandace D. Hollenbach is assistant professor of anthropology at the University of Tennessee Knoxville. Her research interests include paleoethnobotany; prehistoric foodways among hunting-gathering and agricultural peoples of the southeastern United States; gender and identity among hunting-gathering peoples; and use and meaning of landscape among hunting-gathering peoples.

Richard W. Jefferies is professor of anthropology and director of undergraduate studies at the University of Kentucky.

Megan C. Kassabaum is assistant professor of anthropology at the University of Pennsylvania. Her research interests include archaeology of southeastern North America, prehistoric archaeology of the Woodland Period, the Native American South, monument construction and communal ritual, food and feasting, and ceramic technology.

Tristam R. Kidder is Edward S. and Tedi Macias Professor of Anthropology and professor of environmental studies at Washington University in St. Louis. Much of his work is focused in the realm of geoarchaeology and landscape archaeology, emphasizing geomorphology in large river systems and the relationships of climate change, river responses, landscape change, and human cultures.

Jayur Madhusudan Mehta is research affiliate for the Center of Archaeology at Tulane University. His varied professional interests include the environmental history and archaeology of the New World.

Martin Menz is a doctoral student in anthropology at the University of Michigan.

D. Shane Miller is assistant professor of anthropology at Mississippi State University. He is a prehistoric archaeologist whose primary research interests are the Ice Age colonization of the Americas, the origins of agriculture in eastern North America, and how we can use lithic technology, GIS, and geoarchaeology to make inferences about past human behavior.

Christopher R. Moore is assistant professor of anthropology at the University of Indianapolis.

Lori O'Neal is a master's degree student in anthropology at the University of South Florida.

Thomas J. Pluckhahn is associate professor of anthropology at the University of South Florida. His research interests include eastern United States prehistory, Mesoamerican prehistory, Cultural Resource Management, settlement pattern studies, household archaeology, environmental anthropology, ceramic analysis, and GIS applications for anthropology.

Sarah E. Price is a senior archaeologist with Wiregrass Archaeological Consulting. Her primary research interests are prehistoric lithic technology, Geographic Information Systems (GIS), and landscape archaeology.

Asa R. Randall is assistant professor of anthropology at the University of Oklahoma.

Christopher B. Rodning is Paul and Debra Gibbons Associate Professor of Anthropology at Tulane University. Professor Rodning received his A.B. in anthropology from Harvard University in 1994 and his Ph.D. in anthropology from the University of North Carolina at Chapel Hill in 2004.

Sarah C. Sherwood is associate professor of anthropology at Sewanee: The University of the South. She is an anthropological archaeologist with a specialty in geoarchaeology. She is specifically interested in prehistoric land use change over time and site formation processes of sandstone rockshelters on the Southern Cumberland Plateau.

Jesse Tune is assistant professor of anthropology at Fort Lewis College. His professional interests include hunter-gatherer behavioral adaptations during the Pleistocene/Holocene transition, lithic technological organization, environmental archaeology, geoarchaeology, human/environment interaction, and public archaeology.

Renee B. Walker is professor of archaeology at State University of New York, Oneonta. Her primary research and teaching interests are zooarchaeology, eastern North American archaeology, Paleoindian and Archaic period subsistence patterns, prehistoric North American dog domestication, and the archaeology of hunter-gatherers. She has fieldwork experience in North America and Europe and has conducted much of her research at the Dust Cave site in Alabama.

David J. Watt received his B.S. in anthropology and history with a minor in Native American studies from Illinois State University in 2013. He received his M.A. in 2016 from Tulane University, where he is currently a Ph.D. student. His research interests include social and environmental histories of cultural landscapes and colonial experiences. His dissertation focuses on crisis, social memory, and community response in the material record among Mississippian Native American communities in Louisiana and Mississippi.

Index

Ripley P. Bullen Series

Florida Museum of Natural History
Edited by Neill J. Wallis, Charles R. Cobb, and Kitty F. Emery

The Timucuan Chiefdoms of Spanish Florida, by John E. Worth: vol. 1, *Assimilation*; vol. 2, *Resistance and Destruction* (1998; first paperback edition, 2020)

Ancient Earthen Enclosures of the Eastern Woodlands, edited by Robert C. Mainfort Jr. and Lynne P. Sullivan (1998)

An Environmental History of Northeast Florida, by James J. Miller (1998)

Precolumbian Architecture in Eastern North America, by William N. Morgan (1999)

Archaeology of Colonial Pensacola, edited by Judith A. Bense (1999)

Grit-Tempered: Early Women Archaeologists in the Southeastern United States, edited by Nancy Marie White, Lynne P. Sullivan, and Rochelle A. Marrinan (1999; first paperback edition, 2001)

Coosa: The Rise and Fall of a Southeastern Mississippian Chiefdom, by Marvin T. Smith (2000)

Religion, Power, and Politics in Colonial St. Augustine, by Robert L. Kapitzke (2001)

Bioarchaeology of Spanish Florida: The Impact of Colonialism, edited by Clark Spencer Larsen (2001)

Archaeological Studies of Gender in the Southeastern United States, edited by Jane M. Eastman and Christopher B. Rodning (2001)

The Archaeology of Traditions: Agency and History Before and After Columbus, edited by Timothy R. Pauketat (2001)

Foraging, Farming, and Coastal Biocultural Adaptation in Late Prehistoric North Carolina, by Dale L. Hutchinson (2002)

Windover: Multidisciplinary Investigations of an Early Archaic Florida Cemetery, edited by Glen H. Doran (2002)

Archaeology of the Everglades, by John W. Griffin (2002; first paperback edition, 2017)

Pioneer in Space and Time: John Mann Goggin and the Development of Florida Archaeology, by Brent Richards Weisman (2002)

Indians of Central and South Florida, 1513–1763, by John H. Hann (2003)

Presidio Santa María de Galve: A Struggle for Survival in Colonial Spanish Pensacola, edited by Judith A. Bense (2003)

Bioarchaeology of the Florida Gulf Coast: Adaptation, Conflict, and Change, by Dale L. Hutchinson (2004; first paperback edition, 2020)

The Myth of Syphilis: The Natural History of Treponematosis in North America, edited by Mary Lucas Powell and Della Collins Cook (2005)

The Florida Journals of Frank Hamilton Cushing, edited by Phyllis E. Kolianos and Brent R. Weisman (2005)

The Lost Florida Manuscript of Frank Hamilton Cushing, edited by Phyllis E. Kolianos and Brent R. Weisman (2005)

The Native American World Beyond Apalachee: West Florida and the Chattahoochee Valley, by John H. Hann (2006)

Tatham Mound and the Bioarchaeology of European Contact: Disease and Depopulation in Central Gulf Coast Florida, by Dale L. Hutchinson (2007)

Taíno Indian Myth and Practice: The Arrival of the Stranger King, by William F. Keegan (2007; first paperback edition, 2022)

An Archaeology of Black Markets: Local Ceramics and Economies in Eighteenth-Century Jamaica, by Mark W. Hauser (2008; first paperback edition, 2013)

Mississippian Mortuary Practices: Beyond Hierarchy and the Representationist Perspective, edited by Lynne P. Sullivan and Robert C. Mainfort Jr. (2010; first paperback edition, 2012)

Bioarchaeology of Ethnogenesis in the Colonial Southeast, by Christopher M. Stojanowski (2010; first paperback edition, 2013)

French Colonial Archaeology in the Southeast and Caribbean, edited by Kenneth G. Kelly and Meredith D. Hardy (2011; first paperback edition, 2015)

Late Prehistoric Florida: Archaeology at the Edge of the Mississippian World, edited by Keith Ashley and Nancy Marie White (2012; first paperback edition, 2015)

Early and Middle Woodland Landscapes of the Southeast, edited by Alice P. Wright and Edward R. Henry (2013; first paperback edition, 2019)

Trends and Traditions in Southeastern Zooarchaeology, edited by Tanya M. Peres (2014)

New Histories of Pre-Columbian Florida, edited by Neill J. Wallis and Asa R. Randall (2014; first paperback edition, 2016)

Discovering Florida: First-Contact Narratives from Spanish Expeditions along the Lower Gulf Coast, edited and translated by John E. Worth (2014; first paperback edition, 2016)

Constructing Histories: Archaic Freshwater Shell Mounds and Social Landscapes of the St. Johns River, Florida, by Asa R. Randall (2015)

Archaeology of Early Colonial Interaction at El Chorro de Maíta, Cuba, by Roberto Valcárcel Rojas (2016)

Fort San Juan and the Limits of Empire: Colonialism and Household Practice at the Berry Site, edited by Robin A. Beck, Christopher B. Rodning, and David G. Moore (2016)

Rethinking Moundville and Its Hinterland, edited by Vincas P. Steponaitis and C. Margaret Scarry (2016; first paperback edition, 2019)

Gathering at Silver Glen: Community and History in Late Archaic Florida, by Zackary I. Gilmore (2016)

Paleoindian Societies of the Coastal Southeast, by James S. Dunbar (2016; first paperback edition, 2019)

Cuban Archaeology in the Caribbean, edited by Ivan Roksandic (2016)

Handbook of Ceramic Animal Symbols in the Ancient Lesser Antilles, by Lawrence Waldron (2016)

Archaeologies of Slavery and Freedom in the Caribbean: Exploring the Spaces in Between, edited by Lynsey A. Bates, John M. Chenoweth, and James A. Delle (2016; first paperback edition, 2018)

Setting the Table: Ceramics, Dining, and Cultural Exchange in Andalucía and La Florida, by Kathryn L. Ness (2017)

Simplicity, Equality, and Slavery: An Archaeology of Quakerism in the British Virgin Islands, 1740–1780, by John M. Chenoweth (2017)

Fit for War: Sustenance and Order in the Mid-Eighteenth-Century Catawba Nation, by Mary Elizabeth Fitts (2017)

Water from Stone: Archaeology and Conservation at Florida's Springs, by Jason O'Donoughue (2017)

Mississippian Beginnings, edited by Gregory D. Wilson (2017; first paperback edition, 2019)

Harney Flats: A Florida Paleoindian Site, by I. Randolph Daniel Jr. and Michael Wisenbaker (2017)

Honoring Ancestors in Sacred Space: The Archaeology of an Eighteenth-Century African-Bahamian Cemetery, by Grace Turner (2017; first paperback edition, 2023)

Investigating the Ordinary: Everyday Matters in Southeast Archaeology, edited by Sarah E. Price and Philip J. Carr (2018; first paperback edition, 2024)

New Histories of Village Life at Crystal River, by Thomas J. Pluckhahn and Victor D. Thompson (2018)

Early Human Life on the Southeastern Coastal Plain, edited by Albert C. Goodyear and Christopher R. Moore (2018; first paperback edition, 2021)

The Archaeology of Villages in Eastern North America, edited by Jennifer Birch and Victor D. Thompson (2018)

The Cumberland River Archaic of Middle Tennessee, edited by Tanya M. Peres and Aaron Deter-Wolf (2019)

Pre-Columbian Art of the Caribbean, by Lawrence Waldron (2019)

Iconography and Wetsite Archaeology of Florida's Watery Realms, edited by Ryan Wheeler and Joanna Ostapkowicz (2019)

New Directions in the Search for the First Floridians, edited by David K. Thulman and Ervan G. Garrison (2019)

Archaeology of Domestic Landscapes of the Enslaved in the Caribbean, edited by James A. Delle and Elizabeth C. Clay (2019; first paperback edition, 2022)

Authority, Autonomy, and the Archaeology of a Mississippian Community, by Erin S. Nelson (2019; first paperback edition, 2024)

Cahokia in Context: Hegemony and Diaspora, edited by Charles H. McNutt and Ryan M. Parish (2020)

Bears: Archaeological and Ethnohistorical Perspectives in Native Eastern North America, edited by Heather A. Lapham and Gregory A. Waselkov (2020; first paperback edition, 2024)

Contact, Colonialism, and Native Communities in the Southeastern United States, edited by Edmond A. Boudreaux III, Maureen Meyers, and Jay K. Johnson (2020)

An Archaeology and History of a Caribbean Sugar Plantation on Antigua, edited by Georgia L. Fox (2020)

Modeling Entradas: Sixteenth-Century Assemblages in North America, edited by Clay Mathers (2020)

Archaeology in Dominica: Everyday Ecologies and Economies at Morne Patate, edited by Mark W. Hauser and Diane Wallman (2020)

The Making of Mississippian Tradition, by Christina M. Friberg (2020)

The Historical Turn in Southeastern Archaeology, edited by Robbie Ethridge and Eric E. Bowne (2020)

Falls of the Ohio Archaeology: Archaeology of Native American Settlement, edited by David Pollack, Anne Tobbe Bader, and Justin N. Carlson (2021)

A History of Platform Mound Ceremonialism: Finding Meaning in Elevated Ground, by Megan C. Kassabaum (2021)

www.ingramcontent.com/pod-product-compliance
Lightning Source LLC
Chambersburg PA
CBHW050338270326
41926CB00016B/3515